# The International
# Labor Movement

# The International Labor Movement

## HISTORY, POLICIES, OUTLOOK

by
Lewis L. Lorwin

GREENWOOD PRESS, PUBLISHERS
WESTPORT, CONNECTICUT

**Library of Congress Cataloging in Publication Data**

Lorwin, Lewis Levitzki, 1883-1970.
    The international labor movement.

    Reprint of the 1st ed. published by Harper,
New York.
    Bibliography:  p.
    1.  International labor activities—History.
I.  Title.
[HD6475.A1L66  1973]        331.88'091        73-13404
ISBN 0-8371-7060-5

Originally published in 1953 by Harper & Brothers,
New York

Reprinted with the permission of Harper & Row, Publishers,
Inc.

Reprinted by Greenwood Press, Inc.

First Greenwood reprinting        1973
Second Greenwood reprinting      1977

Library of Congress catalog card number  73-13404

ISBN  0-8371-7060-5

Printed in the United States of America

# CONTENTS

PREFACE      vii

INTRODUCTION      xi

### Part One. THE TRADITION, *1830-1876*

I. ANTICIPATIONS, 1830-1848      3

II. THE FIRST INTERNATIONAL, 1864-1876      7

### Part Two. PEACE AND PROGRESS, *1880-1914*

III. THE SECOND INTERNATIONAL, 1889-1914      19

IV. INTERNATIONAL LABOR SECRETARIATS      30

V. AMERICAN-EUROPEAN LABOR RELATIONS, 1881-1914      37

### Part Three. WAR AND REVOLUTION, *1914-1924*

VI. ORIGIN OF THE THIRD INTERNATIONAL, 1914-1919      45

VII. INTERNATIONAL FEDERATION OF TRADE UNIONS, 1914-1919      53

VIII. WORLD UPHEAVAL, 1919-1920      61

IX. CONFUSION AND RETREAT, 1921-1923      68

X. THE AF OF L AND IFTU, 1919-1924      78

XI. PAN-AMERICAN LABOR, 1918-1924      85

### Part Four. STABILIZATION AND REORGANIZATION, *1924-1929*

XII. THE MOVEMENT FOR UNITY, 1924-1926      97

XIII. REVISIONS AND REALIGNMENTS, 1926-1928      107

XIV. PROGRAMS AND POLICIES IN 1929      118

XV. PROGRAMS AND POLICIES IN 1929 (Continued)      138

vi                    *Contents*

Part Five.  DEPRESSION AND WORLD TENSIONS,
                    *1929-1939*

XVI.    Unemployment and Fascism, 1929-1934          165
XVII.   United Action and Unity, 1935-1938           175
XVIII.  Campaign Against Aggression and War, 1935-
        1939                                         185

Part Six.  THE SECOND WORLD WAR AND AFTER,
                    *1939-1951*

XIX.    Formation of World Federation of Trade
        Unions, 1939-1945                            197
XX.     Promise and Performance, 1945-1947           219
XXI.    The AF of L Versus the WFTU, 1945-1947       233
XXII.   Conflicts and Rift, 1947-1949                238
XXIII.  International Confederation of Free Trade
        Unions, 1949-1951                            262

Part Seven.  CURRENT TRENDS AND OUTLOOK

XXIV.   The Free Trade Union International in
        Action                                       285
XXV.    The International Trade Secretariats         310
XXVI.   The World Federation of Trade Unions         316
XXVII.  The Christian Trade Unions                   325
XXVIII. Interpretation and Outlook                   332
Glossary of Abbreviations                            345
Table of ICFTU Membership in 1953                    348
Bibliography                                         353
Index of Names                                       358
Index of Subjects                                    361

ON THE tenth of January 1953, The *New York Times* carried a story which gave readers a glimpse into a little-known sphere—labor's new role in international affairs. In Northeast Africa, in the Sudan, which is administered jointly by the British and the Egyptians, in the city of Khartum, where Lord Kitchener once held sway, a conference was held by an organization known as the Sudanese Federation of Labor. Some of the trade unions represented at this conference threatened to withdraw from it because the Sudanese Federation had become a member of an international organization, known as the World Federation of Trade Unions, which was under Communist influence. They favored affiliation with the International Confederation of Free Trade Unions, which is strongly anti-Communist and hostile to the World Federation of Trade Unions.

In an editorial, headed "Far-Flung Labor Front," The *New York Times* described the background of this incident. After the Second World War, the British Labour Government and the British trade unions set up in the Sudan a labor code and a system of collective bargaining, and helped to establish trade unions to carry on relations with employers. The plan was to have the Sudanese workers run their own trade union movement and to create a new liberal spirit in industrial relations as an antidote to the attitudes and practices of the old colonialism. But the federation fell under the control of Communists who were interested in the unions as centers for "propagandizing class strife" and for promoting political agitation. The above meeting of the Federation of Labor at Khartum reflected the struggle between the two opposing forces.

The significance of the Khartum incident is that it is one of many similar developments occurring in other parts of colonial Africa. Its meaning is that the "cold war" has now been carried to Africa, as it has been carried to Asia and other areas outside Europe and the

United States, and that the labor movements in these areas are one of its important arenas.

The Khartum labor incident raises a number of questions. Why should American and European organized labor be interested in the labor movements of Africa? What are the objectives of the International Confederation of Free Trade Unions and of the World Federation of Trade Unions around which the struggle centers? What bearing has this struggle on international relations?

These questions arise also in connection with other situations in which organized labor appears on the international stage. An illustration of this may be given by reference to the United Nations. A visitor to the meetings of the Economic and Social Council, one of the five principal organs of the United Nations, can observe there evidence of the new international position of organized labor. Facing the delegates from the eighteen members of the United Nations who form the Council are two rows of seats arranged in semicircles. The first row is reserved for representatives of the specialized agencies, which are official international organizations established by intergovernmental agreement for specific purposes as indicated by their names. Among these are the International Labor Organization, the Food and Agriculture Organization, the World Health Organization, the United Nations Educational, Scientific and Cultural Organization, the International Bank for Reconstruction and Development, and the International Monetary Fund. The specialized agencies are part of the United Nations system, and have large rights and privileges in the Economic and Social Council.

In the second row, behind those of the specialized agencies, are seats for representatives of six voluntary nongovernmental organizations, known as NGO's. Three of these are the International Confederation of Free Trade Unions, the World Federation of Trade Unions, and the International Confederation of Christian Trade Unions. These international labor organizations have a less privileged position in the Council than the specialized agencies, but they enjoy a consultative status which entitles them to take part in its discussions in certain specified ways.

What this arrangement signifies is that the governments of the world have recognized organized labor as a factor to be considered in official deliberations on international economic and social problems. This is certainly a big change from the days when workers even in Western Europe and the United States were fined and jailed for trying to form trade unions and when the voice of labor was but seldom heard in any land.

Why do the organized workers of different countries demand representation in the United Nations? Why do the governments feel that they have to grant such representation to international labor organizations? What use does labor make of these rights? What are the effects of labor's participation in the work of the United Nations?

These and other related questions are examined in this book. Why do trade unions of different countries find it necessary or desirable to band themselves together for international cooperation? Why are they divided into several international organizations? What are their aims and programs? How do they try to put them into effect? What is the source of power of these organizations and what influence have they on world events?

Such questions are becoming more important because the international activities of organized labor are assuming increasing significance. Growing general awareness of this fact is shown by the greater attention to international labor developments in the daily press and in weekly and monthly publications, by the new books on foreign labor movements, and by the number of colleges and universities which have added courses on foreign labor relations.

The purpose of this book is to help answer the questions raised above by providing the needed historical background. In 1929, the present writer made a study of international labor organizations for the Brookings Institution, on whose staff he then was. The book was published by the Brookings Institution under the title *Labor and Internationalism*. In his preface to the book, Dr. Harold G. Moulton, the then president of the Brookings Institution, pointed out that it filled a gap in economic and social literature. "There never has been," he wrote, "in any language, a systematic and comprehensive account of the international labor movement as a whole—of its subdivisions, its internal struggles, and its meaning to world relations as a whole." The book was favorably reviewed in the United States and abroad and was translated into French, Spanish, German, and Japanese.

During the two decades following the publication of *Labor and Internationalism,* the international labor movement underwent many changes. Repeatedly, the present writer was asked by students and teachers of labor problems, by newspapermen, by persons in the foreign service, and by others to bring the book up to date. The present study is a response to such requests and an attempt to give a new comprehensive account of the subject.

In planning this book, the writer wished to place emphasis on recent events and current issues. But he also felt that the pre-1929 story was essential for an understanding of current developments. He therefore rewrote and condensed that story as told in *Labor and Internationalism.* The first fifteen chapters of the present book are the result of such rewriting and condensation. In their present form, these chapters are free of details which are no longer of interest, and the pre-1929 events are related in the light of subsequent developments. The remaining thirteen chapters are entirely new and cover the history of the movement since 1929 and its current trends. The present volume is thus a new book.

The writer is under deep obligation to the Brookings Institution for permission to use *Labor and Internationalism* for purposes of revision. He also wishes to express his appreciation to members of the International Confederation of Free Trade Unions, particularly to Mr. Arnold Beichman, its New York representative, to Professor John Philip Windmuller for the opportunity to read his interesting doctoral thesis on *American Labor's Role in the International Labor Movement, 1945 to 1950,* to officials of the American Federation of Labor and of the Congress of Industrial Organizations (CIO), to the Bureau of Labor Statistics of the US Department of Labor, and to all others who have assisted him with documentary material and with other information.

Lewis L. Lorwin

June 16, 1953

FOR nearly a hundred years, trade unions and other labor organizations of different countries have formed international associations for mutual aid and cooperation. In the course of these years, some of the organizations came to an end, but they were succeeded by others which repeated the main features of those that preceded them. Obviously, there are forces in modern industrial and political life which impel national labor organizations to combine internationally.

To some extent, the growth of international labor organizations during the nineteenth century reflected a general condition of the times. From 1830 on, many social groups, inspired by humanitarian and religious ideals, formed numerous associations for international cooperation in political, economic, and cultural matters. These were also years when international organizations for the promotion of permanent peace grew and flourished. Toward the end of the century, they began to have some influence on the policies of governments, and later they played a role in developing, and in making possible the realization of, the idea of a League of Nations.

More important, however, in stimulating international labor contacts were the economic and political conditions affecting the national labor organizations themselves. Workers in some countries found that they often lost strikes because workers from other countries were imported as strikebreakers. They became interested in preventing such occurrences not only by law but also by intercountry labor agreement. When industrial conflicts became prolonged and costly, the strikers in such cases sought financial and other aid from workers in other countries. As industries grew in size and developed national and international combinations and cartels, labor unions in different countries came to regard such "concentration of capital" as a threat which had to be counteracted by international organization of labor. As international trade expanded and world markets became more competitive, organized workers in advanced industrial countries became

xi

apprehensive of the competition of "low standard" and "sweatshop" labor in underdeveloped countries, and sought a remedy for the situation in proposals to establish minimum labor standards by international agreement.

Large groups of workers in Western countries became interested also in international political issues. Their sympathy was aroused by movements for political freedom and national independence in Central and Eastern Europe, and later by the struggles against foreign domination in the countries of Asia and Latin America. They were also stirred by questions of war and peace, and lent their support to proposals for the peaceful arbitration of international disputes, reduction of armaments, and the establishment of a world court of justice.

The idea which had perhaps the greatest earliest influence in bringing together workers of different countries was that of a "final emancipation of labor," which was developed in part by socialist intellectuals but in large measure also by workers who played a leading part in the trade union movements of their countries. In general terms, the idea was that the workers had a historic mission to "emancipate" themselves from the "evils of capitalism" by establishing a new society in which the means of production would be owned by all the people in common and would be used to foster greater economic and social equality and democracy. It was claimed that such a socialist reorganization would be in the interest not only of the workers but of all mankind and would inaugurate a higher form of civilization. The workers of all lands were urged to unite to achieve this end.

Under these various influences, national labor organizations of different countries became concerned not only with international aspects of industrial and labor problems but with all questions of international life. Their leaders developed a concept of "labor internationalism" which rested on two premises. The first was that the workers, as a distinct social-economic group, had common interests and common goals and were the standard-bearers of economic and social progress not only in each country but also in international relations. The second was that, because of the first premise, the workers could not entrust the solution of international problems to other social groups or to official diplomacy. They had to build their own international organizations in order to be able to act as an independent force internationally.

The international labor movement is the result of these general ideas and practical considerations. It may be defined as the system of mutual relations which organized workers of different countries develop and of the activities which they carry on through international organizations for the purpose of improving working and living conditions, of shaping general international policies, and of raising their economic and social status ultimately. It is a movement in the sense that the international activities involved and the international organizations through which they are carried on have developed from simple beginnings to more complex forms and are still in process of change.

Owing to the nature of the aims and methods of the international labor movement, three types of organization have come into being. One comprises international associations of labor unions in a given industry in different countries, e.g., international associations of miners, transport workers, printers, textile workers, and so on. These associations are known as international trade secretariats. They now exist in practically all industries and among many groups of salaried employees. A second type is the general international associations which combine national labor federations (also designated as national trade union centers) of different countries for the promotion of general economic and social programs. Several such internationals have existed in the past; today there are three—the International Confederation of Free Trade Unions, the World Federation of Trade Unions, and the International Confederation of Christian Trade Unions—which differ in general ideas and methods of action. The third type is that of international political associations which unite political labor parties and groups of different countries.

It has been the aim of the international labor movement from its beginning to unify the labor forces of all countries on a common program. The idea of unity epitomized the premises, hopes, and idealistic aims of the movement. But experience soon showed that it was difficult to achieve such unity or, when achieved, to maintain it, owing to differences of interests and traditions in the national labor movements. Before the First World War, three main tendencies emerged in the international labor movement, based on such national differences. The labor movements of Great Britain and the United States represented a pragmatic and functional approach to international problems. Their interest was in measures for dealing with migration, mutual aid in strikes, and similar practical issues. The labor movement of France and various minorities in the labor movements of other countries, though differing on many points, bespoke a social-revolutionary tendency. They advocated radical theories and methods of class struggle and prepared for the "abolition of capitalism" by means of a more or less violent social revolution in the not too distant future. In between were the trade unions of Germany, Austria, Belgium, Switzerland, the Scandinavian and other West European countries whose outlook was social-reformist. They were concerned primarily with immediate improvements in labor conditions, but also professed faith in socialism as a more or less distant goal to be achieved gradually, cooperated with socialist parties, and aimed to imbue the international labor organizations with these aims.

Before 1914, a relative degree of unity in international labor relations was achieved, despite these national differences. There were then in existence a general international trade union organization, a number of international trade secretariats, and a political international, which worked in fairly close cooperation. The international organizations tried to hold all national labor movements together by making *ad hoc* adjustments and compromises in the formulation of programs and policies.

The First World War and the Bolshevik revolution of November 1917 changed the situation radically. Aroused by the experience of the war and repelled by the violent and dictatorial methods of the Russian Bolsheviks, British labor swung over to the social-reformist side. So did the majority of the French labor movement. Their action helped to strengthen the social-reformist labor movements of other West European countries. The social-reformist elements in the international labor movement became a moderating and reconstructive force in the postwar reorganization of Europe.

But the Bolsheviks in Russia established themselves as a ruling dictatorship and began developing a theory of "world revolution" which would justify them in imposing a socialist program on an industrially backward country. In accordance with this theory and under the pressure of their domestic difficulties, the Russian Bolsheviks tried to "capture" the international labor organizations and to use them for their own political purposes and in the interest of the Soviet state. Their disruptive tactics, their dictatorial theories and methods, their subjection of the trade unions to the control of the state, and their attempts to stir up revolutions in other countries aroused strong opposition and deep resentment among the social-reformist labor groups of Western Europe, which became more determined than ever to protect the political independence and strengthen the peaceful and democratic character of their national and international organizations.

The international labor movement was thus split into opposing camps: West European organized labor, with a few exceptions, aligned itself against the Soviet trade unions and the Communists; American organized labor pursued an independent course in fighting communism and in trying to rally to its banner the labor organizations of Latin America.

During the Second World War and for a short while afterward, an effort was made to unify the international labor movement on the assumption that the experience of the war had made such unity possible. The effort proved futile because of the refusal of the Soviet government to cooperate with the West in the Marshall Plan, because of the resulting pressures of the Communists to make the new international labor organization serve the foreign policies of the Soviet Union, and because of the opposition of American and West European labor to the Soviet trade unions and to communism. Since 1949, the conflict between international labor organizations has mirrored the general East-West struggle.

The main fact in the evolution of the international labor movement is the growing strength and influence of the pragmatic and social-reformist tendencies. While they are still distinct in some ways, they have come closer together in their opposition to communism. They have also modified their earlier premises and programs. They still proceed on the assumption that the workers of different countries have common interests and problems and must act in concert across national frontiers, but they also stress the idea of cooperation with other social groups and with governments for the solution of international as well as national problems.

The chief strength of the social-reformist tendency today is in Great Britain and in most countries of Western and Northern Europe. The labor movements of these countries have gained greatly in economic and political power; they have reached a position which makes them responsible in large measure for the peaceful development of their respective countries. Their interest in international labor relations is strengthened by the new position of Europe, which makes it more dependent than ever on the policies of the United States and on international cooperation generally.

The West European labor movements are now reinforced by American organized labor, which is becoming an increasingly influential factor in the international labor movement. A dynamic industrialism and national traditions make organized labor in the United States impatient with "ultimate goals." The general guiding ideas of American labor are to enlarge its share of the national income, to enhance the social responsibilities of industry, to develop democratic industrial relations, and to play a larger role in national life generally. While not in accord on all issues, American and West European labor movements share the desire to make international labor organizations an independent and effective force for practical and peaceful international cooperation.

The reformist labor organizations face a new problem as a result of the entrance on the international scene of the labor movements of Asia, Latin America, and Africa. These movements differ in a number of ways, but they have one feature in common: they are influenced in varying degrees by nationalistic and revolutionary ideas and attitudes which are reactions to agrarian and industrial backwardness, extremely low levels of living, conditions of colonialism, and memories of previous dependence on foreign powers. As a result, these movements swing back and forth between cooperation with and opposition to the pragmatic-reformist international labor organizations of the Western world.

On the basis of past experience, it is expected that as the underdeveloped countries modernize their agrarian systems and become more industrialized and as living conditions and industrial relations are improved, the labor movements of these countries will follow the patterns of development of organized labor in Western Europe and the United States. The reformist international labor organizations are trying to accelerate this process by supporting Point Four programs and international investment plans for economic development, as well as by direct assistance in building solid trade unions and developing methods of collective bargaining in these countries. This work has the aim of giving the working populations of underdeveloped countries greater faith in cooperation with the West as a way of solving their economic and political problems by constructive methods. To the extent to which this work is effective, it will strengthen not only the international labor organizations but also the foundations of the free world. Therein lies the potential world significance of the social-reformist international labor movement.

The central theme of this volume is the growth of the pragmatic-reformist international labor organizations and their present-day activities. To bring out clearly the conditions and processes of this growth, it was necessary to describe in some detail the socialist organizations before 1914 and Communist activities after 1919. For it was in the struggle against the latter that the reformist international labor movement forged its independent outlook and developed the ideas and methods by which it is guided today.

The reformist labor Internationals have influenced economic and political developments in varying degree at different times. They have financed and aided the growth of trade unions in many countries. Their demand for international regulation of working standards made its impress on the Versailles Peace Treaty and resulted in the establishment of the International Labor Organization under the League of Nations. Their activities influenced the policies of governments toward Soviet Russia during 1919-1920 and afterward. Their pressures in recent years have affected the position of governments with regard to Spain and other countries, the treatment of colonies, policies of reconstruction in Germany, resettlement of refugees, and other international issues. Their support helped in carrying out the measures of the Marshall Plan, and is now a factor in promoting the policies of the Council of the North Atlantic Treaty Organization (NATO). They are playing a role in the building of the European Coal and Steel

Community and in promoting the economic integration of Western Europe. Their participation has effects on the structure and policies of the Economic and Social Council of the United Nations and of some of the specialized agencies. They are a factor in shaping democratic industrial and political attitudes in the underdeveloped countries of the world.

The international labor movement thus raises questions of general interest. How should the democratic and free international labor organizations be regarded from the point of view of society as a whole? Should they be given wider or less scope in the United Nations and other official international bodies? What part can they play in Point Four programs and in promoting economic development? In general terms, what may be their impact on international relations in the near future

The purpose of this volume is to present a historic survey which may help to answer the above and related questions. The past may not be an entirely adequate guide to the future, but against its background the perspectives ahead take on clearer and sharper outlines. It is certainly impossible to understand fully the international labor organizations now in existence, their programs and activities and the forces which may shape them in the years immediately ahead, without keeping in mind the experience that lies behind them.

A few final remarks seem called for with regard to theoretical aspects of the theme dealt with here. In view of the historical character of this study, no attempt has been made to examine critically the theoretical validity of the economic and social assumptions on which international labor organizations and their activities are based. On the other hand, the writer has tried to draw from the historic survey an interpretation of the dynamics of these organizations, of the forces which have determined, and continue to determine, their activities and course of development. He has presented a general analysis of these forces in the concluding chapter.

# PART ONE

## The Tradition

### 1830-1876

# Anticipations
## 1830-1848

A VAGUE idea of a common bond between the laboring people of different countries emerged in Western Europe during the decade from 1830 to 1840. Groups of skilled artisans and workers began during these years to think of themselves as members of a "social class" who were "oppressed" in all countries by the "power of capital" and who had to make common cause to free themselves from such oppression and to attain "true independence and equality."

These workers were influenced in their thinking by the democratic ideas of the French and American revolutions and by the new doctrines of socialism propagated by Robert Owen in England and by Saint-Simon and Fourier in France. Some of these workers also came in contact with the movements for universal suffrage in England, for a republican form of government in France, and for national unity in Italy, Germany, and Poland, which called for concerted international action to achieve their aims.

### I. LOVETT AND BLANQUI

The first suggestion to form an international labor organization was made in 1838 by William Lovett, secretary of the London Working Men's Association. As a journeyman cabinetmaker, Lovett had had a part in the fight against the Anti-Combination Laws and for the right to organize trade unions. From Robert Owen he had received his faith in the coming of a "new moral order" and of a cooperative

3

economic system. As a leader of the London Working Men's Association, formed in 1836, which helped to draw up the "People's Charter" with its six points demanding universal suffrage and other measures for democratizing the political system of England, he accepted the idea that political reform and organization were necessary for the workers to obtain their economic and social demands. As a result of his experience with middle-class reformers, he became convinced that the workers should develop leaders from their own ranks. As a result of his various activities, he came to know political exiles from Italy, France, Germany, Poland, and other countries and to espouse their cause for national independence and international cooperation.

In response to a number of "International Addresses," which were the fashion of the day, Lovett published in 1838 an *Address to the Working Classes of Europe* in which he wrote: "Fellow producers of wealth! Seeing that our oppressors are united . . . why should not we unite in holy zeal to show the injustice of war, the cruelty of despotism, and the misery it entails upon our species?"

While Lovett was developing these ideas in England, the first contacts between workers of different countries were made by the secret societies of France, which aimed to establish a socialist republic. The dominating figure in these societies was Auguste Blanqui, who carried on the tradition of the extremists of the French Revolution and particularly of Baboeuf, who in his "Manifesto of the Equals" had made the prophecy that "the French Revolution is but the precursor of another revolution far greater, far more solemn, which will be the last." Blanqui believed that it was "the mission of the nineteenth century to emancipate *la belle classe des prolétaires*," and that such emancipation could be accomplished only by means of an uprising which would establish a "revolutionary dictatorship."

By the end of the decade of the 1830's, there were in England and France small groups of trade unionists, socialists, Chartists (advocates of the "People's Charter" referred to above), and "revolutionary democrats" who harbored the project of "an international association for the emancipation of the working classes." They planned a conference for 1839 in London. But the Chartist agitation in England, which led to the arrest of Lovett, and the unsuccessful uprising of Blanqui in Paris in May, 1839, made such a conference impossible.

## II. FROM FLORA TRISTAN TO KARL MARX

After 1840, in Western countries men's minds were perturbed by the widespread distress which followed the panic of 1837 and which continued with short intervals throughout the "hungry 1840's." Many men and women began to question whether an industrial system marked by great contrasts of wealth and poverty and subject to frequent panics and crises could survive. In the hopeful and rationalistic spirit of the day, reformers and "philanthropists" put forth plans and Utopias for the "reorganization of society" and prescriptions for immediate reforms. Daniel Le Grand, an Alsatian manufacturer, aroused by the misery of the French textile workers, revived an idea, first expressed by Robert Owen in 1818, that the governments should cooperate in carrying out an international program of labor legislation. Richard Cobden and John Bright began their agitation for free trade, which in their opinion was to bring prosperity and lasting peace to the entire world. The American Peace Society, stimulated by William Ladd's pamphlet on a *Congress of Nations*, published in 1840, sponsored the first international peace congress in London in 1843. In Paris and London, groups of socialists, democrats, and nationalists met and planned for a general reorganization of society, in the conviction that they were "living during the last days of a dying civilization."

In this environment of ideas and movements, the advocacy of an international labor organization became more definite. In 1843, there appeared in France a booklet entitled *L'Union Ouvrière* in which the first concrete plan for an international labor association was presented. The author, Flora Tristan, urged the workers of France to form themselves into a class, as the bourgeoisie had done in 1789 and 1830, and to unite with workers of other countries to obtain a share in political and economic power. "The Worker's Union," she wrote, "should establish . . . in all the capitals of Europe committees of correspondence." Flora Tristan's booklet went through three editions and sold over 20,000 copies.

Between 1845 and 1847, some workers and political exiles from Germany, Scandinavia, Holland, and Hungary living in London organized a "Group for Communist Education" and carried on negotiations with Karl Marx and Friedrich Engels for the formation of a Communist federation. A conference held in London in the summer of 1847 attracted only a few Germans, who organized themselves into a "Communist League." This League held a conference in London in November, 1847, which turned out to be another gathering of German political refugees from Paris, Brussels, and London. The gathering assumed interest from the fact that Marx and Engels presented to it a declaration and a program which became known as the "Communist Manifesto."

In the Communist Manifesto Marx and Engels, both young men under thirty, brought together in a closely knit synthesis the dialectical method of Hegel, the speculations of the French socialists, the theories of the English classical economists, the political ideas of Chartism, and the insurrectionary tactics of Blanqui. Most of the ideas in the Manifesto had been common currency in the socialist circles of France for nearly a decade. It was commonly held that the development of "capitalism" was condemning the workers to increasing misery, that the concentration of industry was eliminating the middle class and bringing capitalists and workers into sharper conflict, and that the capitalist economy was subject to periodic crises which would end in a social cataclysm, ushering in a socialist society. The synthesis of Marx and Engels consisted in presenting these trends as manifestations of a single process of the struggle of classes, whose driving power lay in technological changes and whose ultimate result—the abolition of private property and the establishment of a socialist society—could be brought about only by the workers themselves, organized as a political party and establishing a "dictatorship of the proletariat."

Marx and Engels claimed that the struggle of the workers for these ultimate aims, though national in form, was international in essence. The combined action of the workers in "at least the civilized countries," they declared, was necessary for a successful revolution. They wound up their pamphlet with the appeal "Workers of all lands, unite!"

Marx and Engels thought that a "bourgeois revolution" was impending in Germany and that it would be the "prelude to a proletarian revolution." They wanted to bring about a union between the English Chartists, the French republicans, and their own Communist League, and urged the calling of a "congress of workingmen to establish liberty all over the world."

This congress was planned for September, 1848, in Brussels, but was not held. Before the date set for it, waves of revolution swept Central and Eastern Europe, set into motion the Chartist uprising in England, and caused disturbances as far as the United States in the West and Russia in the East. The course of events did not conform to Marx's prediction. The revolutionary movements of 1848 overthrew Metternich and the Holy Alliance and extended constitutional government in Europe, but they did not assume a "proletarian" character. After some temporary successes, they were suppressed in all countries. They dramatized the fact that the idea of "international labor action" was at the time only a wishful anticipation of small groups of political radicals and social theorists.

C  H  A  P  T  E  R    I  I

# The First International
## 1864-1876

AS THE waves of revolution receded in 1849-1850, an era of economic expansion set in which brought unexampled opportunities for the making of individual fortunes and for improving the condition of the people. Economic prosperity was accompanied by a general intellectual reaction. In contrast to the turbulent and "hot air" forties, the decade of the fifties was marked by a spirit of political and social realism.

## I. British Realism and French Idealism

Among the workers this was a period of building "tough and unromantic" organizations for the purpose of gaining a larger share in prosperity. This new development was especially important in England. Here there grew up in the course of the fifties not only numerous trade clubs and craft unions in different towns and districts but also the first national trade unions, such as the Amalgamated Society of Engineers, the Society of Carpenters, and the Society of Ironfounders, which by means of high dues, out-of-work, sickness, and other benefits laid the foundations of a stable trade unionism that was to serve for a long time as a model not only in England but in other countries as well.

It was among the leaders of the British trade unions that the idea of an international labor organization now appeared. It was suggested to them by their experience during the strikes in the building trades which broke out after the collapse of the building boom in the depression of 1857. The building contractors tried to break the strikes by importing strikebreakers from France, Germany, and Belgium. To promote their common defense, the trade unions of London in the summer of 1860 organized the London Trades' Council. The leaders of the Council, especially W. R. Cremer and George Odger, declared that it was necessary for the British workers, in their own interests, to establish ties with the workers of the Continent.

Three events during 1862-1863 helped to bring the British trade unionists into contact with workers from other countries. In the summer of 1862, some 300 workers from France and about a dozen from Germany were sent by their respective governments to visit the International Exhibition of London. They were entertained by the officials of the London Trades' Council, who discussed with them the idea of an international labor association. In the course of the year, further communications were established between committees of workers in London and Paris which were organized to help the workers in the cotton mills of both countries who had been thrown out of work as a result of the Civil War in America.

The third event was the Polish insurrection in the summer of 1863. Committees of workers were organized in London and Paris to help the Polish insurgents. On July 22, 1863, these committees arranged an "international meeting" in London at which Odger and Cremer, in the name of the English workers, and Henri Tolain, for the workers of France, demanded the restoration of Polish independence. The following day, the British and French workers held a private gathering, at which they decided to sponsor an international labor organization.

In accordance with the decision taken at this meeting, the British labor leaders prepared an "address" to the French workers in which they stated that in order to raise wages, shorten hours and improve the "social condition" of the workers, the "industrial classes" of all countries must maintain "regular and systematic communication" for purposes of mutual aid and cooperation. The labor leaders of Paris prepared a reply, the keynote of which was that "capital was being concentrated in mighty financial and industrial combinations" and that the workers of the world must seek "salvation through solidarity." The French workers sent a delegation of three, headed by Tolain, to London to present their reply.

## II. THE INAUGURAL ADDRESS

To receive the French delegation, a meeting was arranged at St. Martin's Hall on September 28, 1864. The meeting was attended by leaders of the London Trades' Council, worker-delegates from Paris, and by political refugees living in London. Among the latter were Italian followers of Mazzini, French Blanquists, and some German members of the former Communist League, including Karl Marx, who had been living in London since 1849 pursuing his studies in the British Museum.

The meeting voted in favor of the project submitted by the French workers, which provided for an international association with headquarters in London and with branches in all the capitals of Europe. A general committee of twenty-one British workers, ten Germans, nine Frenchmen, six Italians, two Poles, and two Swiss was elected to prepare a program and a constitution for the new organization, which was given the name "International Working Men's Association."

After considering several proposals, the General Committee on November 8, 1864, approved the draft of a program prepared by

Karl Marx. It was in the form of an "Address to the Working Classes," and became known as the "Inaugural Address." In preparing it, Marx aimed at a compromise which could unite the diverse groups of workers in the different countries. He avoided all reference to socialism or communism. He pointed to the gains made by the workers of England since 1848, such as the Ten Hour Law, and complimented the workers on their efforts to organize cooperative societies. He quoted statistics to show the great advance in material wealth between 1845 and 1864. He claimed, however, that the improvements in machinery, the growth of transportation, and the opening of new markets, emigration, and free trade could not singly or jointly do away with the misery of the "productive classes," and that the cooperative societies were inadequate to curb monopoly. Marx concluded that the workers had to use the agencies of the state to promote their common interests and that the conquest of political power was the "first duty of the working class." He urged the workers of different countries to maintain "fraternal ties" not only for economic reasons but also in order to "watch the diplomatic acts of their respective governments." The Inaugural Address wound up with the appeal: "Workmen of all countries, unite!"

Marx also wrote the preamble and the rules of the International. Membership in the Association was to be open to local and national workers' societies, known as "sections." Each section could organize in its own way and was allowed one delegate to the annual congress. A General Council, elected by the annual congress and having its seat in London, was to make studies of labor conditions in all countries, collect labor statistics, publish a bulletin, help its members in search of work in foreign countries, and promote the national consolidation of labor organizations in each country. The work of the General Council was to be financed by dues paid by the local and national councils.

### III. Growth of the International

During the first two years of its existence, the growth of the International was slow. It had small sections of skilled workers and intellectuals in France, Belgium, Switzerland, and Germany. Its largest membership was in England, where some seventeen trade unions with an estimated membership of 25,000 "adhered" to it. The sections and trade unions paid dues irregularly; the total income of the International for 1865-1866 was about $285. The General Council had its headquarters in a small room in a working-class district in London, and its work was carried on by unpaid officers.

The first congress of the International was held in Geneva in September, 1866. It was the first international labor congress ever held. Of the sixty delegates who attended, the majority came from Switzerland. The congress dealt with the aims and organization of the International, the role of trade unions, female and child labor, shortening of the working day, and with such political questions as standing armies and the necessity of destroying the power of Russia and re-establishing an independent Poland.

The discussions revealed a great diversity of ideas in the labor movements of the different countries. The British trade unionists accepted in general the prevailing British doctrines of economic individualism and political liberalism. The Swiss workers were followers of a Dr. Coullery, a "neo-Christian humanitarian." The Belgians were followers of J. G. C. A. H. Colins, who advocated a philosophy of spiritualism, collective ownership of land, and private ownership of capital. The few German delegates present were disciples of Marx. The latter did not attend the congress but sent a detailed report for the guidance of his adherents.

As against these groups, the French workers were disciples of Proudhon, or "mutualists," and believed that mutuality or reciprocity of service was the essence of social justice. The product of labor, according to their doctrine, should belong to the producer, who should exchange it for products which had cost an equal amount of labor. The French delegates were opposed to state intervention in human relations, to strikes and trade unions, and urged the workers to "emancipate" themselves by organizing cooperative societies for production, mutual insurance, consumption, and credit. They had special hopes in "People's Banks" and advocated an organization for international credit.

Owing to these disagreements, the Geneva Congress was diffuse and incoherent. However, it approved the rules drafted by Marx, and adopted a number of resolutions, the most important of which were those in favor of a maximum eight-hour day, international protective legislation for women and children, and the abolition of night work for women.

The International grew slowly during 1867, but in the summer of 1868 it took a sudden leap forward. It profited by the strike movements which followed the industrial upswing of 1868 and which led to the formation of trade unions in many countries. The International collected funds for strikers in London, Paris, Belgium, and Switzerland, and was helpful in preventing the importation of strikebreakers. As a result, it gained in numbers and influence. In France, its membership was estimated at 200,000 in 1869 and was composed of the new trade unions, which had a mushroom growth in that year. In Belgium, it had a national section composed of the newly formed national labor federation, with some sixty branches. In Italy, Spain, and Portugal the trade unions which began to be formed during these years became sections of the International. In the United States, the National Labor Union, under the leadership of William H. Sylvis, declared at its convention in 1870 its "adherence to the principles of the Working Men's Association" and its expectation to "join the Association in a short time."

In addition to trade union affiliations, mixed sections of workers and intellectuals were formed during these years in the United States, England, Denmark, Holland, and Austria-Hungary. By 1871, there were some 8,000 members in the mixed sections of England; the Danish Federal Council had 2,000 members in Copenhagen; in the United States some twenty-seven sections composed of American, German, French, Irish, Czech, and other immigrant workers paid dues for several hundred members.

Despite this growth, the finances of the International remained in a low state, as the membership was of a fluctuating character and paid dues irregularly. Rent for the offices of the General Council was in arrears, and so was the salary of four dollars a week of the general secretary. But the International had during these years considerable strength. The General Council promoted its influence by carrying on a regular correspondence with the national and local sections, by making reports on the international situation, and by its appeal for financial help during strikes.

## IV. Marx and Bakunin

The expansion of the International was accompanied by a growing influence of Marxian ideas. The French workers who had been the chief opponents of Marx were losing faith in mutualism and becoming "collectivists." The third congress of the International, held in Brussels in September, 1868, passed a resolution in favor of the nationalization of land. The fourth congress, held at Basel in 1869, voted in favor of the collective ownership of the means of transportation. It also recommended the formation of national and international trade unions, not only for the defense of the immediate interests of the workers but also because they were said to be the "cells" of the future socialist society.

Marx became during these years the dominating spirit of the General Council. British trade unionists continued to form the majority of the Council but they were no longer much interested in its proceedings. On the other hand, Marx, who was relaxing from his labors on *Das Kapital*, published in 1867, threw himself into the affairs of the International with great energy and zeal.

Marx's triumph, however, was short-lived. From a growing organization in 1869-1870, the International became a moribund body in 1871-1872. This rapid decline was the result in part of the situation created by the Franco-Prussian War and by the Paris Commune of March, 1871.[1] The Commune was not the work of the International, as has been often asserted, though members of the French sections took an important part in it. But the International approved both the purpose and the methods of the Commune. Marx wrote a pamphlet which was published as an official document of the International under the title *The Civil War in France*, and which hailed the Commune as the first true "proletarian revolution" in which the workers showed their capacity to reorganize society and the state. This pam-

---

[1] The Paris Commune is the term applied to the insurrectionary government which took possession of Paris in March, 1871, after the withdrawal of the Prussian troops.

phlet alienated the British trade unionists, who with one exception resigned from the General Council. In France, all labor organizations were destroyed with the suppression of the Commune. In other countries of Europe, the governments prohibited trade unions from joining international labor organizations.

While weakened by external events, the International was plunged into an internal struggle between Marx and the Russian Michael Bakunin. Marx tried to impose on the International his doctrine of a social revolution carried out by a politically organized working class seizing political power and using the state to carry out measures of socialization. Bakunin denounced this concept as "autocratic communism." According to Bakunin, freedom and equality could be brought about only through a revolution which would abolish not only private property but also the state, and which would transform society into a federated system of voluntary cooperative associations. The struggle between the two men and their followers was carried on in violent and abusive language and by means fair and unfair. Bakunin accused Marx and Engels of falsifying the constitution of the International, and demanded the abolition of the General Council. Marx reviled Bakunin as a conspirator and as a questionable character, and called for his expulsion from the International.

The fight came to a climax at the congress held at the Hague in September, 1872, at which Marx was present. Though his followers were in a minority, Marx managed to manipulate the proceedings. Bakunin and several of his friends were expelled. A resolution in favor of political action was adopted. Finally, to take the International out of reach of Bakuninists, its headquarters were transferred to New York.

## V. DECLINE AND DISSOLUTION

With the transfer of the General Council to New York, the International practically ceased to exist. It held meetings for a few years longer, but its time was consumed in internal squabbles. It was formally dissolved at a meeting of the General Council in Philadelphia in 1876. The followers of Bakunin maintained sections of the International in Switzerland, Belgium, Italy, and Spain, but they too were of little importance. They held their last meeting in Switzerland in 1878, after which their sections disintegrated.

For some years after its decline, the First International was pictured as a secret society with a large treasury and armies of followers ready to promote disorder and revolution. The truth was that the First International never had money enough to carry out its objectives, such as publishing a bulletin or collecting statistics. Its General Council was a "brilliant staff without an army."

Nevertheless, the First International had an important influence on the labor and social movements of the nineteenth century. It established the first regular contacts between labor leaders of different countries. It helped to formulate some of the economic and social ideas which were to become in later years the common demands of organized labor in many countries, such as the eight-hour day, bureaus of labor statistics, the need for international labor unions, and international labor legislation. It gave an impulse to trade union organization in a number of European countries. It clarified the current doctrines of social reform and socialism and their bearing on trade union and political labor movements.

For these reasons, the First International came to be regarded in later years, particularly by Socialists, as the "great tradition" of the international labor movement.

# PART TWO

## Peace and Progress

### 1880-1914

# The Second International
## 1889-1914

DESPITE diplomatic crises, local wars, and revolutions, the three and a half decades after 1880 were on the whole years of peace and social progress. In the history of international labor relations this was a period of growth and clarification. Several international organizations of, by, or for labor came into being, namely, the Second International, the International Labor Secretariat, the International Trade Secretariats, and the International Secretariat of Christian Trade Unions. Of these, the Second International became the outstanding organization of the period.

## I. THE PARIS CONGRESS OF 1889

The Second or Socialist International had its origin at a congress in Paris in 1889. That such a congress could be held was due to the growth of socialist parties in various countries after 1880. In Germany, the Social Democratic Party had grown in numbers and power, despite the antisocialist laws of Bismarck. In France, Jules Guesde, an ardent disciple of Marx, had organized a socialist party which gained influence in the French trade unions. In rivalry with the Guesdists, four other socialist groups, known as Possibilists, Allemanists, Blanquists, and Independents, were making headway in the trade unions and among French voters. In England, the Social Democratic Federation had been formed in 1880 by H. M. Hyndman, William Morris, and Tom Mann for the study of Marxian ideas, while in 1883 the Fabian Society had been founded by Sidney and Beatrice Webb and George Bernard Shaw. A new group of trade union leaders—John Burns, Keir Hardie, and Ben Tillet—had come forward to win the British trade unions to socialist ideas and had begun the work which led to the formation a few years later of the Independent Labour Party. In Denmark, the socialists won their first two seats in Parliament in 1884. In Sweden, Hjalmar Branting brought about the foundation of the Swedish Social Democratic Party in 1887. The year 1885 marked the birth of the Belgian Labor Party; in 1888, the Swiss Socialist Party was formed, while steps were taken toward the formation of socialist parties in Austria and Italy. In Russia and Finland, socialist groups started underground party organizations. In the United States, the Socialist Labor Party, organized in 1877, was taking its first steps in national politics.

Though representing a common cause, these socialist parties were far from agreement on many points. The socialists of Germany, Austria, Belgium, and Italy, the Guesdists in France, the Social Democratic Federation in England, and the Socialist Labor Party in America were Marxists. They expected the "social revolution" in the not too distant future—in fact, before the end of the century—and they wanted to prepare the workers for it economically and politically. The Fabians, Possibilists, and other socialist groups mentioned above were non-Marxian; they were interested in immediate improvements in the condition of the workers and stressed the need of gaining influence in legislative bodies.

Owing to these disagreements, two rival socialist congresses met in Paris in July, 1889. One was called by British trade unionists, the other by German socialists. The centenary of the French Revolution was being celebrated, and the French government had arranged an international exhibition which attracted large numbers of people from all corners of the globe. Both socialist congresses were well attended. The one called by the German socialists came to be regarded as the first congress of the Socialist or Second International.

Two decisions taken by this congress were of importance. One dealt with international labor legislation. The question was just becoming a matter of practical politics as a result of the invitation by the federal government of Switzerland to the governments of Europe to attend an official international conference in Bern to consider measures for the international regulation of labor conditions. Under the influence of the German socialists, the Paris Congress called upon all socialist parties and trade unions to support the action of the Swiss government.

The other decision was to support the movement for an eight-hour day which the American Federation of Labor had launched in 1886 and hoped to resume on May 1, 1890. The congress voted to arrange an "international manifestation" on May 1, 1890, in support of the American movement, thus inaugurating what became a cherished socialist tradition—International May Day.

## II. Exclusion of Antiparliamentarians

At the Paris Congress, the socialists took the first step to demarcate themselves from the elements which they regarded as the "lunatic fringe" of the labor and socialist movement. These elements were followers of Peter Kropotkin, Elie Reclus, and others, who combined the ideas of Bakunin, Proudhon, and Marx into a doctrine which they designated as communism-anarchism. In 1881, they had organized in London the International Working People's Association, known as the "Black International," which became active in France, Italy, and Spain. The followers of the Black International were convinced that the "social revolution" was impending and called upon "workers and revolutionists" to speed it by opposing both parliamentary politics and "capitalistic" trade unions and by recourse to "armed resistance" and to "propaganda of the deed."

The socialists were determined to keep the followers of these anti-parliamentarian doctrines out of international labor and socialist congresses. They carried this task forward at their congresses in Brussels in 1891 and in Zurich in 1893, and completed it at the London Congress of 1896. Much excitement prevailed at the latter gathering. Pleas for tolerance and for a spirit of cooperation were in vain. The socialists shared the general indignation aroused by terroristic acts which French and Italian anarchists had committed between 1890 and 1896, and they were tired of discussions on the subject of parliamentary politics. The London Congress definitely and finally excluded anarchists and antiparliamentarians from its meetings, and adopted a rule that only socialist parties and trade unions favoring parliamentary action should be admitted to future international socialist congresses.

### III. Marxists and Revisionists

But the socialists were confronted before long with conflicting tendencies in their own ranks. Two issues in particular divided the socialist world in the decade after 1896. One was the question of revolution and reform; the other was the issue of the relations of the political socialist parties to the trade unions.

The first question arose out of the fact that most socialist parties during these years took up Marxism as their official doctrine. This was owing to the work of a group of writers, especially Karl Kautsky, who became the leading theorist of the socialist world. In 1891, Kautsky drafted the program of the Social Democratic Party of Germany, known as the Erfurt Program, which became the model for socialists of other countries. In this program and in the commentary which he wrote for it, Kautsky presented what became during the two decades before the First World War the classic exposition of the Marxian doctrines of the concentration of capital, the increasing misery of the proletariat, the disappearance of the middle class, an inevitable social revolution, and the necessity to organize the workers into an independent political party for the conquest of political power.

The socialists were confronted in most countries of Europe, however, by conditions which were far removed from the picture drawn by Marx writing in England. Popular grievances centered around feudal survivals and inequalities in the political system. The first task which the socialists undertook was to democratize the instruments of government: to establish universal suffrage, the rights of free speech and assembly, pay for members of Parliament, and free public and secular education. In addition, they were called upon to help the workers in their demands for higher wages, shorter hours, social insurance, and other protective labor laws. The German Social Democratic Party met this situation by attaching to the general part of its Erfurt Program a list of "immediate demands" which were supposed to be attainable under "capitalism" without removing the need for a "social revolution" in the future. Their example was followed by socialist parties of other countries.

A double conflict developed out of this situation. On the one hand, the "revolutionists" began to fear that parliamentary tactics and the effort to win votes would destroy the "militancy" of the socialist parties. On the other hand, the "opportunists" began to question the value of "revolutionary ends" and urged that the socialist parties concentrate on measures of reform in the expectation that such reforms would gradually bring about a socialist society. Holding a middle ground between revolutionists and opportunists the leading Marxists insisted that parliamentary tactics and social-economic reforms strengthened the position of the workers; that the socialist parties must work within the legal framework of the democratic system to obtain a majority in the national parliaments; and that having obtained such a majority they would be able to use the powers of the state to carry out, with relatively little violence if not peacefully, a revolutionary transformation of "capitalism" into "socialism."

This conflict of ideas became a practical issue first in France as a result of the Millerand case. In 1899, Alexander Millerand, a member of the Independent Socialist Party, accepted the post of Minister of Industry in the cabinet of Waldeck-Rousseau. The Dreyfus affair was then at its most critical stage, the French Republic was endangered by monarchist elements, and Millerand entered a "bourgeois" government to save the cause of French democracy. He had the support of several socialist groups under the leadership of Jean Jaurès. His action was violently attacked by the Marxist Jules Guesde and by the Blanquist Vaillant as a "betrayal" of the principle of "class struggle."

In Germany, the question was raised by the writings of Edouard Bernstein, whose book, *Die Vorausetzungen des Sozialismus,* created a sensation. In this book, Bernstein called for a "revision" of the basic Marxian theories of surplus-value, capitalist concentration, and the progressive pauperization of the proletariat. He made light of social revolution as a "final end," and advocated political alliances with nonsocialist parties for the promotion of democratic and social reforms. For a while, it looked as though the compact and unified socialist party of Germany would be split. But at the congress of the German Social Democratic Party in Dresden in 1903, the Marxists August Bebel and Karl Kautsky succeeded in defeating the "revisionists," as the followers of Bernstein were called, and yet maintained the unity of the party. The Dresden Congress passed a resolution condemning socialist participation in "bourgeois" governments.

Between 1899 and 1904, the battle raged between Marxists and Revisionists not only in France and Germany but in most countries where socialists had an organization.

## IV. SOCIALISM AND TRADE UNIONISM

The second question which brought division into the socialist ranks was that of the relation of the socialist parties to trade unionism. By 1896, the socialists had made clear that they regarded the trade unions as necessary to better the condition of the workers. At the same time, they took the position that trade union action was secondary as compared with political and parliamentary action, and urged the trade unions to accept the leadership of the political socialist movement.

In this effort to guide the trade unions, the socialists were successful in Germany, Austria-Hungary, Belgium, Holland, Italy, Switzerland, and the Scandinavian countries. Though not without some struggle, the trade unions in these countries established a working alliance with the socialist parties. The unions carried on wage negotiations and developed methods of collective bargaining, leaving to the socialist parties the task of fighting the battles of organized labor for larger political and social rights.

In other countries, the relationships were different. The British trade unions, though turning to independent political action after 1900, held aloof from the socialist Independent Labour Party. In 1906, they formed the British Labour Party, which was to represent them in Parliament but which was to be nonsocialist in its program. In the United States, the American Federation of Labor advocated "pure and simple" trade unionism, which meant "no politics" in the unions and opposition to socialism. The American Socialist Labor Party, led by Daniel De Leon, organized in 1896 the Socialist Trade and Labor Alliance to fight the American Federation of Labor. This caused a large group of socialists, under the leadership of Eugene Debs and Morris Hillquit, to break away and to form in 1901 the Socialist Party of America, which gave its support to the AF of L. But in 1904, some elements in both socialist parties joined forces with the leaders of radical labor unions which had grown up in the West, notably the Western Federation of Miners, to form the Industrial

Workers of the World (IWW), with a revolutionary socialist program similar to that of French syndicalism (described below). The American socialists thus became involved in dual unionism, which alienated the American Federation of Labor.

A cleavage between socialists and trade unionists occurred also in France. The French trade unions, which began to grow rapidly after 1890, became tired of the continuous squabbles of the several socialist parties and fell under the influence of antipolitical and anarchistic followers of Proudhon and Bakunin. In 1895, they organized the *Confédération Générale du Travail* (General Federation of Labor) on a nonpolitical basis. By 1904, the leaders of the unions, in cooperation with a group of intellectuals led by Georges Sorel, developed the doctrine of syndicalism in opposition to both socialism and "pure and simple" trade unionism. The syndicalists rejected not only parliamentary politics, but also the traditional methods of trade unionism, such as high dues, sick and other benefits, and collective agreements. Instead, they advocated "direct action" and the "general strike," not only to obtain immediate improvements but as the means to abolish "capitalism" and the state and to carry out the "social revolution." The syndicalists gained influence not only in France but also in Italy and Spain and in a few countries outside Europe.

## V. German Leadership

Between 1899 and 1904, the labor and social movements of Europe and America thus became split into four groups following the doctrines of Marxism, revisionism, syndicalism, and trade unionism. By steering a clear course amidst these various currents, the German socialists, at two successive international congresses, held in Paris in 1900 and in Amsterdam in 1904, succeeded in forming a permanent international organization. The Paris Congress of 1900 laid down the rule that only such political parties and groups were to be admitted to the future congresses as believed in the "fundamental principles of socialism," that is, in the socialization of the means of production and distribution, in the international organization and action of the workers, and in the conquest of power by the "proletariat" organized as a political party on a class basis. The door was left open to trade unions which recognized "the necessity of political action through legislation and parliamentarism." The international congresses were henceforth to be known as "international socialist congresses." A permanent International Socialist Bureau was established with headquarters in Brussels, an annual budget of 10,000 francs, and a paid secretary.

To the delegates assembled at Paris in 1900 these steps were an indication that at last a Second International had been founded which could claim to be the heir to the First International. This feeling was expressed in a statement that the international socialist congresses were to become "the Parliament of the Proletariat" whose deliberations and decisions would "guide the proletariat in the struggle for deliverance."

The Amsterdam Congress of 1904 definitely established the leadership of the German Social Democracy in the Second International. Proud of the three million votes which they had polled in the national elections of 1903, the German socialists demanded and obtained approval of the "Dresden resolution" as the platform of the international socialist movement. Syndicalist ideas on trade unions and the general strike, favored by the French and other socialist groups, were condemned and rejected.

## VI. The "Parliament of the Proletariat"

After 1904,. the Second International assumed the character of a world movement of undisputed importance. It arranged impressive international congresses at Stuttgart in 1907 and at Copenhagen in 1910. Among the 886 delegates from 26 nationalities who attended the Stuttgart Congress and among the 896 delegates from 23 nations at Copenhagen were many men and women of growing influence in the political and social life of their respective countries. They attested the increasing hold which socialism was acquiring on the minds of the middle classes as well as of the workers of Europe.

The work of the International Socialist Bureau in Brussels also gained steadily in scope. As the Second International was a federation of autonomous national socialist parties and trade unions, the executive board had only limited and strictly defined powers. But within these limits, the Bureau steered the socialists into lines of common policy.

## VII. COHESION AND CONFLICTS

Even during these years, however, the Second International could not achieve complete inner unity. It was kept in a state of turmoil by concrete issues in which nationalism and internationalism were in conflict. It endorsed the "right of each nation to self-determination" and threw its doors open to such national groups as the Poles, the Finns, the Czechs. At the same time, the socialists favored the large states, and did not succeed in reconciling the claims of the small nationalities with those of the great nations. The International showed a similar dualism in its position on questions of migration and colonial policies.

The issue which epitomized the conflicts within the International was that of the socialist attitude in case of war. By 1900, the Second International had made clear its position that war was caused by the workings of the capitalist system and could not be done away with except by the abolition of "capitalism" and the establishment of a "cooperative commonwealth"; but that it was possible to minimize the danger of war by limitation of armaments, by substituting national militias for standing armies, by international arbitration, and by making the declaration of war subject to a referendum vote of the people. It was held to be the duty of socialists in all countries to promote these measures and to refuse to vote appropriations for war and military purposes.

In this position there were two weaknesses. It was generally agreed that the socialists were not bound to oppose a defensive war. Yet the difficulty of distinguishing between an offensive and defensive war was not met squarely. Second, the methods for preventing war could not be successfully carried out as long as the socialists were in a minority in the various parliaments. The Second International rejected the method proposed by the French socialists Jean Jaurès and Edouard Vaillant and by the British Labourite Keir Hardie, and which did not require a parliamentary majority, namely, the general strike. The German socialists, in particular, argued that the general strike was not feasible and would only expose the socialist parties to persecution by their governments. The International did approve, however, the proposal made at the Stuttgart Congress of 1907 by

Nicholas Lenin and Rosa Luxembourg that in case war broke out, the socialists should cooperate to bring it promptly to a close and use the occasion to "precipitate the downfall of capitalist domination."

For several years after the Copenhagen Congress of 1910, the Second International continued to grow in numbers and influence. By 1914, its affiliations included 27 socialist and labor parties in 22 countries with about 12,000,000 members.[1] This growth was the result of the industrial and social unrest which shook the principal countries of the world between 1910 and 1914. Large strikes for higher wages and union recognition broke out among various groups of workers—miners, railroad men, building trades operatives, textile workers, dockers—in England, France, and the United States. There was a renewal of revolutionary democratic movements in Russia, Latin America, the Near East, and China. In all countries, there were manifestations of a striving on the part of the working populations to raise their economic and social status. The social unrest stimulated new philosophies of social reform, such as the Neo-Liberalism of Lloyd George, the Progressivism of Theodore Roosevelt, and the "New Freedom" of Woodrow Wilson; but it also resulted in the spread of socialist ideas.

## VIII. Test and Failure

The socialists were soon to be tested by the problem of war and peace. After 1910, one international crisis followed another and the air was filled with rumors of an impending general war. The Agadir incident of 1911, the Tripoli War between Italy and Turkey the same year, and the first Balkan War of 1912 forced the Second International to come to grips with the issue of war. In 1912, the International

[1] The Social Democratic Party of Germany had 1,085,000 members and polled 4,250,000 votes in the elections of 1912; the Austrian Socialist Party had 145,000 members and polled 1,041,000 votes in the elections of 1907; the socialist membership of Czechoslovakia was 144,000, and in Hungary 61,000; the Unified Socialist Party of France had 80,300 members and polled 1,400,000 votes in the elections of 1914; the Italian Socialist Party had 50,000 members and polled 960,000 votes in the elections of 1913; the Socialist Party of the United States had 93,500 members and polled 901,000 votes in the elections of 1912. Large votes were cast during these years for the Socialist Parties of Belgium, Sweden, and Argentina and for the Labour Parties of Australia and New Zealand.

Socialist Bureau hurriedly called a conference at Basel which urged the socialists in the Balkan countries to take action on the basis of the Stuttgart resolution of 1907 to stop the Balkan War, but its effort proved futile.

The test came in 1914, with the Austro-Hungarian ultimatum to Serbia. On July 29, 1914, while Austrian troops were advancing toward Belgrade, the International Socialist Bureau held an emergency session in Brussels to protest against the threatening war. The German Social Democratic Party issued a manifesto urging the German government not to enter the "horrible war" and arranged huge peace meetings throughout Germany in which millions of workers took part. Similar demonstrations were held by socialists and trade unions in Belgium, Austria, Italy, and France.

However, on August 1, Germany declared war against Russia. The same day, the German socialists sent Hermann Mueller to Paris to try to agree with the French socialists on a common policy to abstain from voting war appropriations. The French socialists, deprived at this critical moment of the leadership of Jaurès, who had been assassinated on July 31 by a Frenchman unbalanced by the war hysteria, and convinced that their government was doing its best to avert a general war, would not give such a pledge. A few days later, the socialist members of the Reichstag, meeting with prominent members of the party, decided by 111 votes to 14 to vote in favor of war credits. Among those who opposed this vote were Karl Kautsky, Karl Liebknecht, and Rosa Luxembourg. On August 4, Germany declared war against France. At the Reichstag session that day, Hugo Haase read the unanimous declaration of the party, which disclaimed responsibility for the war, condemned a war of conquest but at the same time accepted the "grim fact of war," and refused "to leave the fatherland in a lurch" in the face of "the Russian peril and of the horrors of a hostile invasion." The declaration did not mention the German invasion of Belgium.

In other countries, developments varied. In Belgium, the socialists and trade unions rallied to the support of the government of King Albert, and Emile Vandervelde, chairman of the International Socialist Bureau, became a member of the Belgian cabinet. In France, not only the socialists but also the syndicalists joined in the *union sacrée* of all political parties in defense of the country. In England, huge "stop the war" meetings were arranged by the socialists and the Labour Party on August 1 and 2. But after August 4, the Trades Union Congress and the Labour Party gave their support to the government. The Independent Labour party and small socialist groups continued their opposition to the war. Ramsay MacDonald, known as a pacifist, resigned the chairmanship of the British Labour Party and was succeeded by Arthur Henderson. In Serbia, two social democrats voted against war credits in parliament. In Russia, fourteen social democrats, of the Bolshevik faction, denounced the war and walked out of the Duma, but all other socialist groups gave their support to the Russian government.

With the exception of a few small groups, the socialists in the warring countries thus rallied to the support of their respective governments. The resolutions and methods which they had approved for averting or stopping a general war proved inapplicable or inadequate when the test came. The Second International failed in the main objective which had brought it into being.

CHAPTER    IV

## International Labor Secretariats

BESIDES the Second International, there came into being during the two decades before the First World War a number of more modest organizations whose object was international cooperation of, by, and for trade unions. These organizations were the International Trade Secretariats and the International Secretariat of National Trade Union

Centers. Though obscured by the Second International, they were significant as first steps in a movement which was to assume a larger role later.

## I. TRADE SECRETARIATS

The first impetus to the idea of combining workers of the same craft or industry in different countries was given in 1889-1890 by the printers and miners. In July, 1889, seventeen delegates from printers' unions in France, Spain, Italy, Germany, England, Belgium, the United States, and six other countries held the first international conference of typographical workers in Paris. In May, 1890, over one hundred delegates from the national miners' unions of England, France, Germany, and Austria met in London and formed the International Miners' Federation.

After 1890, the formation of Trade Secretariats was stimulated by the example of the printers and miners, by the growth of national unions in many countries, by strikes which attracted international interest, and by the congresses of the Second International. The trade unionists of different countries at that time knew little of each other's activities, were suspicious of one another, and were slow in getting together. Because of this, the international socialist congresses of Zurich in 1893 and of London in 1896, did much to accelerate the process of bringing workers of different countries together by urging upon them the need for international organization.

By 1900, there were already seventeen Trade Secretariats in existence. Between 1900 and 1914, their number increased to twenty-seven, covering all branches of industry. Most of the Secretariats had their headquarters in Germany; the miners and textile workers had theirs in London, while the commercial employees and the stonecutters were located in Holland and Switzerland respectively. The secretary of the national union of the country in which the headquarters were located acted, as a rule, as international secretary, and did the work of the Secretariat in his spare time.

The main effort of these Secretariats was to keep their members informed about trade conditions in different countries and about strikes in their trades, to make appeals for financial aid in case of large strikes, to prevent workers of one country from acting as strikebreakers in another, and to promote trade unions in the less organized countries. Taken as a whole, the work of the Secretariats was narrow in scope and modest in results.

## II. SECRETARIAT OF TRADE UNION CENTERS

Wider in scope was the International Secretariat of National Trade Union Centers, whose purpose was to bring together the national trade union centers of different countries for the consideration of common problems. The first to propose such an organization in 1900, were French and British trade union leaders who resented the domination of the socialists in the Second International. They failed to get the support of the German and other Continental trade union leaders, who held that the Second International was the proper forum for the discussion of the larger problems of labor and that international trade union congresses were unnecessary. The Germans favored periodic meetings of the secretaries of the national trade union centers for limited purposes only. However, after two secretaries' conferences were held in 1901 and 1902, the Continental trade union leaders were won over to the idea of setting up an international organization.

As a result, a formal organization was set up in 1903 at a conference in Dublin under the name of International Secretariat of National Trade Union Centers. Its headquarters were to be in Berlin; Carl Legien, the secretary of the German national unions, was designated as international secretary. The new organization was to hold biennial trade union conferences, and its expenses were to be paid by the national unions of the affiliated countries at the rate of about twelve cents per thousand members per year.

### TYPES OF TRADE UNIONISM

From 1904 to 1908, the chief problem before the International Secretariat was to reconcile the different types of unionism on a common program of action. Three such types confronted each other. There was the socialist-reformist trade unionism of the German-Austrian model, composed of highly centralized, financially strong industrial trade unions which had large benefit features, practiced peaceful methods of collective bargaining, and maintained a close alliance with the political socialist parties. A second type, represented by most of the trade unions of England and the United States, was decentralized in organization, craft rather than industrial in structure, interested primarily in collective bargaining, and nonsocialist, if not antisocialist, in outlook. The third type, represented chiefly by French syndicalism, was revolutionary in aim and method.

Concretely, the clash between these different types of unionism first took the form of a demand by the French Confederation of Labor that the questions of antimilitarism and the general strike be placed on the agenda of the conference which was to be held in 1905 in Amsterdam. When this demand was rejected, the French stayed away from the conference. The American Federation of Labor also declined to attend the conference. The reason given by Samuel Gompers, president of the AF of L, was that the conference was composed of officials and not of elected delegates. Gompers also wanted the date of the conferences changed from June to September so that the fraternal delegates of the AF of L to the British Trades Union Congress could attend without too much cost in time and money. The French and Americans were also absent from the conference of 1907 held in Christiania (Oslo).

In their absence, Carl Legien and the other delegates from the Continental unions had no difficulty in committing the International Secretariat to German socialist-reformist ideas. The Amsterdam conference decided that the International Secretariat should exclude all theoretical questions from its agenda and limit its deliberations to practical questions such as the collection of trade union statistics and mutual aid in strikes. The Christiania conference censured the French syndicalists for their antisocialist tactics and gave its pledge of support to the Second International.

The French and American trade union leaders changed their attitude in 1909 and attended the sixth conference of the International Secretariat, held that year in Paris. The internal struggle continued, however. The French delegates demanded the holding of general international trade union congresses which would discuss not only trade union but general political and social questions. The American delegates criticised the name Secretariat as having no meaning for American workers and proposed that the International Secretariat be reorganized into an International Federation of Trade Unions.

These two demands occupied much of the time of the three conferences held in Paris in 1909, in Budapest in 1911, and in Zurich in 1913. The French demand was consistently voted down by a majority of the delegates as an attempt to drive a wedge between the trade unions and the socialist parties. The American proposal met with greater consideration and was finally adopted at Zurich in 1913. The change in name did not signify, however, a change in character. The International Federation of Trade Unions, like the International Secretariat, was not to be governed by a formal constitution but by resolutions passed as the occasion arose. Its scope of action was to remain as defined in 1905 and 1907. The chief rules of organization were that only one trade union center was to be admitted from each country, that each national center was to be represented by no more than two delegates, and that "every country was to be free to determine its own tendency and tactics." •

Regardless of this friction, the International Secretariat showed growth. The number of affiliated countries rose from eight in 1901 to nineteen in 1913, and the membership from 2,168,000 in 1904 to 7,394,000 in 1913. Dues were raised several times and in 1913 were about a dollar per thousand members per year. The annual budget increased from about $260 in 1903-1904 to $1,720 in 1912-1913. In 1909, a paid assistant secretary was engaged, and by 1914 the Secretariat had a staff of twelve persons: four Englishmen, four Swiss, one American, one Danish citizen, and two Germans.

*Statistics and Strike Aid*

The main work of the International Secretariat was the collection and distribution of information on the trade union movements of different countries. In 1903, it began the publication of *International Reports on the Trade Union Movement,* which became a valuable source of information on the numerical strength of trade unions, their activities, strikes, labor legislation, and other aspects of the labor movement. On January 1, 1913, the Secretariat began the publication of a bimonthly newsletter in English, French, and German.

Another task of the International Secretariat was rendering strike aid. Between 1909 and 1913, the Secretariat was instrumental in collecting about $700,000 in aid of strikers in Sweden and other countries. In 1911, a proposal was made to establish an international strike fund, but it was rejected as premature. The Secretariat also considered ways and means of preventing international strikebreaking. The Christiania conference resolved to request the representatives of labor in the parliaments of different countries to strive for laws prohibiting the importation and exportation of "scab" labor. The American delegates at the Budapest conference of 1911 proposed that immigration be suspended during strikes and industrial depressions.

The International Secretariat concerned itself with a number of other questions which affected labor internationally. Thus the Christiania conference of 1907 considered the question of an international campaign in favor of the so-called Bern conventions prohibiting the use of industrial poisons and regulating night and home work. The same conference also considered complaints made against the British trade unions, which refused to accept immigrant workers who had been members of unions in their home country, treating them as unorganized workers. This was contrary to the practice of the unions on the Continent, where members of unions of one country had the privilege of transfer to unions of another country free of charge. The conference recommended that this practice be followed by all countries.

## German Leadership

The International Secretariat, like the Trade Secretariats, was under German influence. The Germans did most to promote international trade unionism and had most to gain from it. As a rapidly developing industrial country, Germany during this period attracted labor from many countries. Craftsmen from Scandinavia, France, Switzerland, and Holland streamed into Germany in search of training and jobs, while unskilled laborers came from South and East Europe for seasonal work. The German trade unionists tried to cope with this competitive migration in various ways: where the immigrant workers were organized at home, they regulated the transfer of members into their own unions; where the workers were unorganized, the Germans undertook to promote organization by sending organizers and money into the countries of emigration. But as this was not always possible or convenient, they took the initiative in creating the International

Secretariats described above. In this work, they had the support of the countries of Central and Northern Europe, which felt the need of international cooperation because of the limitation of their own trade union resources.

On the other hand, the British trade unions during these years were little interested in international relations. Foreign workers were not important in the industrial life of England, British migration went overseas, and international competition to British goods was not yet a strong factor in the minds of the British workers. The Germans often criticised the British workers for their alleged insularity and failure to contribute to international aid in proportion to their strength. Neither was German leadership seriously disputed by the French syndicalists or by the American Federation of Labor.

*Summary*

To sum up, from 1904 to 1914 the International Secretariat was slowly feeling its way toward a larger field of activity. From a meeting of a few trade union officials, it became a permanent organization with regular conferences of duly elected delegates and with a bureau staffed by trained employees. It changed its name to International Federation of Trade Unions to indicate the larger basis to which it was moving. It built up the first body of international trade union statistics and brought about regular contacts between labor leaders of the principal countries. In the year before the First World War, it was getting into contact with the trade unions of Argentina, South Africa, and Australia, and took the first steps toward regular relations with the Trade Secretariats.

### III. THE CHRISTIAN INTERNATIONAL

The impulse to organize trade unions on a religious basis was given by Pope Leo XIII in 1891 by his Encyclical *De Rerum Novarum*. Christian trade unions, composed almost entirely of Catholic workers, were organized after 1891 in Germany, Austria, Belgium, Holland, Switzerland, and Italy. After 1900, some of these unions in the textile, boot and shoe, and woodworking trades in several countries arranged to visit each other's congresses and to maintain contacts with each other's work.

In 1908, an international conference of Christian trade unions was held at Zurich and formed an International Secretariat of Christian Trade Unions. Germany, Italy, Holland, Belgium, Austria, Switzerland, and Sweden were represented; the unions from Germany were the most numerous. Dispute arose over the question of confining membership to Catholic unions, but the attempt of certain Dutch bishops to effect such limitation was resented, and the Secretariat was declared to be interdenominational. A. Stegerwald of Germany was designated international secretary and the headquarters were placed in Cologne, Germany.

On the eve of the First World War, the Christian International had affiliated organizations in Germany, Austria, Belgium, Holland, Switzerland, and Italy with a membership of 542,213. Two thirds of this membership was in Germany. The Secretariat carried on few activities.

C  H  A  P  T  E  R   V

## American-European Labor Relations
### 1881-1914

AMERICAN participation in the international labor movement has been touched upon in preceding chapters. A clearer picture of it is necessary for an understanding of what was to come after 1914.

### I. GOMPERS' EARLY PLANS

When the American Federation of Labor was organized in 1881, it associated itself with the tradition established by the National Labor

Union of maintaining contacts with the trade unions of Europe. Between 1881 and 1889, the AF of L exchanged "fraternal greetings" with the British Trades Union Congress, corresponded with some French trade unions with regard to holding a workingmen's international exposition, and requested the international socialist congresses held in Paris in 1889 to support its movement for an eight-hour day.

Spurred on by the international congresses which were being held in Europe, Samuel Gompers, president of the AF of L, put forth a plan to call an international congress of trade unions in Chicago in 1893, in connection with the World's Fair. With the approval of the AF of L conventions of 1889 and 1890, he issued invitations to "the organized wage workers of the world." Only the British Trades Union Congress accepted the invitation. The international socialist congress held at Brussels in 1891 pointedly declined. The plan was dropped.

Gompers attributed the negative attitude of European labor to distance, lack of personal advocacy, but especially to the "malicious" misrepresentation of the AF of L by the Socialist Labor Party of America. From that time on, Gompers began to draw a sharp line between the trade unions and the socialist parties, and became eager to establish a purely trade union international organization, distinct from, if not in opposition to, the Second International. In 1894, the AF of L inaugurated an exchange of "fraternal delegates" with the British Trades Union Congress. The American fraternal delegates to the British Trades Union Congress of 1896 again suggested to the British that a "bona fide trade union congress" be convened, but failed to obtain support.

Despite these disappointments, Gompers continued to take an interest in projects of international trade union organization, and tried to develop more regular contacts between the labor unions of Europe and America. He kept up a large, and often intimate, correspondence with leading trade unionists abroad. In 1894, he began the publication of the *American Federationist*, which became a means of contact between the AF of L and the trade unions of Europe. On several occasions he issued appeals for funds to help strikers in Germany and England. In 1897-1898, about $11,150 were collected by the AF of L for the striking members of the Amalgamated Society of Engineers in England.

## II. The AF of L Joins the Secretariat

From 1899 to 1904, the AF of L was absorbed in big strikes and in domestic problems arising from its rapid growth, and showed little interest in international labor relations. After 1904, however, it began to be drawn into more regular relations with the labor movements of Europe. This was because of increasing immigration into the United States, the growth of the Trade Secretariats, and the intensified interest everywhere in the problem of maintaining world peace. Gompers brought the subject of peace repeatedly before the conventions of the AF of L, developing the theme that peace would come sooner and would be more lasting as a result of the growth of the international labor movement.

Between 1904 and 1908, the AF of L took several steps which showed its renewed interest in international labor relations. At its 1905 convention, it commended the American unions for accepting as members, without initiation fees, workers coming from other countries, and instructed the Executive Council to enter into communication with unions at home and abroad for the purpose of encouraging this practice, so as to make "the principle general and reciprocal." Second, the Executive Council, and Gompers in particular, urged the American unions to attend international conferences of their respective trades and to join the Trade Secretariats. These efforts were largely responsible for the fact that during these years the American unions of miners, molders, painters, shoemakers, lithographers, bakers, and brewers became members of their respective International Trade Secretariats. Finally, at its Denver convention of 1908, the AF of L decided to accept the invitation of the International Secretariat of National Trade Union Centers to attend its congress in Paris in 1909, and elected Gompers as its delegate.

Gompers had two aims in attending the Paris conference. He wanted to counteract the unfavorable reports about the American labor movement which were current in Europe, especially in socialist circles. He was also eager to promote the idea of an International Federation of Labor, provided that the AF of L, on joining such an organization, would still be free to pursue an independent course. The Executive Council of the AF of L voted in June, 1909, in favor of submitting to the Paris conference the proposal to establish an International Federation of Trade Unions.

Gompers' reception at the Paris conference of 1909 was not entirely friendly. His speech in which he told the conference that he had come not as a delegate but as an observer, and that the AF of L would not join unless allowed to pursue its own ways, aroused much irritation. In his turn, Gompers was far from pleased with the composition and methods of the conference. The French Confederation of Labor was represented by two "anarchists," Georges Yvetot and Leon Jouhaux. The Austrian and Dutch delegates were "wholly socialistic." Far too much time was spent in general discussion and too little in practical work.

Gompers decided to overlook all this because the Paris conference met his wishes on the main points. It declared that labor must be free in all countries to decide its own policy and methods. It adopted a provision that decisions of the international conference would be binding only if adopted unanimously. In view of this, Gompers on his return, urged the AF of L to affiliate with the International Secretariat, in the "best interests of the workers of America." The 1909 convention of the AF of L approved Gompers' recommendation, and in 1910 the American Federation of Labor became a member of the International Secretariat.

### III. The Part of American Labor

At the conference of the International Secretariat in Budapest in 1911, the AF of L successfully defended its claim to represent the American labor movement against the Industrial Workers of the World. The latter, through William Z. Foster, had brought in a demand to expel the AF of L in favor of themselves on the ground that the AF of L was connected with the National Civic Federation and was therefore unfit to conduct a true working-class struggle. The case of the AF of L was presented by its delegate, Vice-President James Duncan. The IWW were supported by the French delegates, Yvetot and Jouhaux. After a long and heated debate, the AF of L won, and the IWW were not admitted to the conference.

The AF of L made its influence felt at Budapest in several ways. It opposed the proposals of the French Confederation of Labor to discuss antimilitarism and the general strike. It helped to defeat the proposal to hold the conferences of the International Secretariat every three years, at the same time as the congresses of the Second International. It carried a proposal that all means should be taken to prevent the exportation of strikebreakers and to stop immigration in times of industrial disputes. It also introduced a resolution for the establishment of an International Federation of Labor which was referred to the national trade union centers for consideration.

At the Zurich conference of the International Secretariat in 1913, the AF of L was represented by George W. Perkins, president of the cigarmakers' union. The main achievement of the AF of L at this conference was the adoption of its proposal to change the name of the International Secretariat to that of International Federation of Trade Unions. In general, the Zurich conference showed that the trade unionists of Europe were anxious to cement relations with America. The delegates accepted the invitation to hold their 1915 conference in San Francisco, in connection with the exposition which was to celebrate the opening of the Panama Canal. As the expense was beyond the means of some of the affiliated organizations, it was arranged to share expenses. The AF of L agreed to contribute $2,000 toward the costs.

From 1910 to 1914, the AF of L and the International Secretariat carried on a lively correspondence. The Secretariat sent to the AF of L general communications, special reports, and appeals for aid to strikers in different countries. In its turn, the AF of L used the offices of the Secretariat to obtain information on wages and conditions of labor in Europe, especially in cases where American firms operating in Europe were involved. The AF of L paid its dues regularly: $600 for 1910-1911, $635 for 1911-1912, and $1,947 for 1913-1914.

On the eve of the First World War, American organized workers were thus becoming interested in the international labor movement. A number of important American trade unions belonged to the International Trade Secretariats. The AF of L was taking an increasing interest in its relations with European labor and in world affairs generally. Though the ties were rather tenuous, they prepared the ground for the part which the AF of L was to play in international affairs during and immediately after the First World War.

## PART THREE

War and Revolution

1914-1924

# Origin of the Third International
## 1914-1919

THE collapse of the Second International and of the trade union Internationals in August, 1914, did not signify the end of the international labor and socialist movements. On the contrary, the experience of the war and of the revolutions which followed stimulated efforts to reconstruct the prewar Internationals and brought into being a new International—The Third International. As the latter was closely connected with the events of the war and was the first to emerge in 1919, the story of its origin may serve as a link to connect the developments of these years.

## I. RIGHT, CENTER, AND LEFT SOCIALISTS

For awhile after the outbreak of the war, the socialists of neutral countries continued their efforts to bring the International Socialist Bureau into action. The Italian socialists made the first attempt. The Italian Socialist Party had a large membership, a strong group in the Italian parliament, and close relations with the trade unions. It had an antiwar tradition, having opposed the Tripolitan War in 1912. In August, 1914, it published a manifesto against all wars and declared in favor of Italian neutrality. It thus felt called upon to try to reunite the socialists of all countries in a move to end the war. In September, 1914, after the first battle of the Marne, it called a joint conference with the Swiss socialists at Lugano. This conference declared that the war was "imperialist," that there were no "innocent governments," and

45

demanded that the International Socialist Bureau be convened at once. Similar efforts were made soon afterward by the American Socialist Party and by the socialists of the Scandinavian countries and Holland.

These efforts had no practical results. They only helped to accentuate the divisions within the ranks of the socialists in the warring countries. By the spring of 1915, the socialists became divided into three groups: the "Majority" or "Right" socialists, the "Minority" or "Center," and the "Left." The leaders of the Majority, such as Philip Scheidemann, Gustav Noske and Friedrich Ebert in Germany, Albert Thomas in France, Emil Vandervelde in Belgium, and H. M. Hyndman in England, identified themselves completely with their respective governments. The leaders of the Center, such as Karl Kautsky and Eduard Bernstein in Germany, Jean Longuet in France, and Ramsay MacDonald in England, admitted that the workers in each country had acted as was inevitable, but claimed that it was necessary to maintain the idea of socialist internationalism above the din of battle and that war budgets should not be voted by the socialists unconditionally. They called upon their governments for statements of peace terms which would hasten the end of the war. The leaders of the Left groups, such as Karl Liebknecht, Clara Zetkin, and Rosa Luxembourg in Germany, Friedrich Adler in Austria, A. Merrheim in France, members of the Independent Labour Party in England, and Nicholas Lenin and Leon Trotsky in Russia, demanded vigorous antiwar action by the International Socialist Bureau.

## II. ZIMMERWALD

The initiative in bringing members of the Minority and Left groups together was taken by the Italian Socialist Party in May, 1915. Some Italian socialists and syndicalists, notably Benito Mussolini, had by this time become converted to the war, but the party continued to oppose the war even after Italy joined the Allies on May 23, 1915. The Italian Socialist Party was aided in its efforts by Swiss socialists, especially Robert Grimm, who became the center of socialist antiwar negotiations.[1]

In response to the call issued by the Italian Socialist Party, forty-

[1] Grimm and other socialists active in these negotiations were accused of being "pro-German agents."

two socialists and syndicalists from France, Germany, Italy, Switzerland, Holland, Sweden, Norway, Poland, Rumania, Bulgaria, and Russia gathered secretly in a peasant house in the village of Zimmerwald, near Bern, on September 5, 1915. After meeting for a week, the Zimmerwald conference issued a manifesto which placed the responsibility for the war on the governments, secret diplomacy, and the capitalist press; rebuked the socialists of all countries for straying from their principles; and wound up with the slogan: "No annexations, no indemnities. Across frontiers, battlefields, devastated cities and countries—Workers, Unite." Lenin, who was present at the conference, wanted to start a new International at once, to "carry the revolution" into the warring countries. But the majority of those present were primarily interested in bringing the war to an end. They set up an International Socialist Commission, which became known as the Zimmerwald Commission, to cooperate with the International Socialist Bureau, whose seat had been transferred from Brussels to The Hague, on behalf of a speedy peace.

During the winter of 1915-1916, the antiwar Minority socialists carried on an active propaganda in favor of the Zimmerwald resolutions. In Germany, the Minority socialists on December 15, 1915, declared that Germany was in a position to offer peace and cast twenty votes against the war budget in the Reichstag. In France, Jean Longuet gained the support of a considerable element of the French Socialist Party and demanded the calling of an international socialist congress to discuss terms of peace. In April, 1916, the Zimmerwald Commission arranged a meeting in Kienthal, Switzerland, which was attended by forty-four "delegates." The Kienthal meeting denounced the Majority socialists as "social chauvinists," condemned the International Socialist Bureau for its failure to act, declared a durable peace to be impossible without the complete "triumph of the proletariat," and urged the socialists of all countries to make a concerted move for an immediate armistice.

### III. "ON TO STOCKHOLM!"

As a feeling of war-weariness spread during the latter part of 1916 and the early months of 1917, the antiwar elements in the socialist and labor movements of the warring countries made headway. In

Austria, there were official and unofficial moves for peace. In Germany, the Minority socialists broke completely with the Social-Democratic Party and formed the Independent Socialist Party, which agitated for a speedy peace. The extreme Left groups in Germany organized themselves under the name of the *Spartacus Bund,* which called for "peace and revolution." In France, there were strikes in the war industries and discontent in the army, and the antiwar socialists and syndicalists urged the Socialist Party of France to join with the Independent Socialist Party of Germany to bring about peace. In England, there were strikes among munition workers, shipbuilders, and miners, and the Independent Labour Party intensified its pacifist activities.

In the early spring of 1917 came two events which precipitated these several trends into a general movement. On March 8, 1917, the war-starved population of Petrograd started a bread riot which quickly turned into a revolution. Within a few weeks, the Czar was forced to abdicate, a Russian Republic was declared, and a new democratic government was formed which included some socialists. On April 7, 1917, President Wilson brought the United States into the war on the side of the Allies, expressly to make the world "safe for democracy" and to achieve peace on the basis of his Fourteen Points. The Russian Revolution and America's entry into the war gave a tremendous impetus to the hope for an early and democratic peace which developed into a "peace offensive" on both sides of the trenches.

Under these conditions, the idea of an international socialist conference to hasten peace loomed up with new force. After some negotiations, an invitation to such a conference to be held in Stockholm on August 15, 1917, was issued jointly by the International Socialist Bureau, the Petrograd Council of Workers' and Soldiers' Deputies, and a Dutch-Scandinavian Committee which had been organized by Hjalmar Branting, leader of the Swedish Socialist Party.

During the summer of 1917, the proposed conference in the capital of Sweden became a big issue of world politics and shook the socialist parties of the warring countries. The German Majority socialists suddenly decided to vote against further war budgets and to "go to Stockholm." So did the Independent Socialist Party of Germany. In France, two prominent leaders of the Majority socialists, Marcel Cachin and Frossard, after a visit to Petrograd, advised a special national convention of the French Socialist Party to "go to Stockholm." The most astonishing change took place in England. Here Arthur Henderson, a member of the British war cabinet, after a visit to Petrograd, came out in favor of attending the Stockholm conference, and the British Labour Party at a special conference approved his recommendation by an overwhelming vote. Decisions to attend the conference were also taken by the Italian Socialist Party, the American Socialist Party, and by most of the groups affiliated with the Zimmerwald Commission. Lenin urged the "Zimmerwaldians" to "boycott Stockholm" because it was called by the "social patriots," but he was overruled by other members of the Zimmerwald Commission.

The Stockholm conference, however, was not allowed to be held. The American Government refused passports to the American socialist delegates, and that encouraged the governments of Great Britain, France, and Italy to do the same. The hands of the governments were strengthened by the energetic action of the "anti-Stockholm men" in all Allied countries. Only delegates from the Central Powers, Russia, and the neutral countries arrived in Stockholm for the conference, and its purpose was defeated.

With the fiasco of Stockholm, the hope of a negotiated peace faded out. On both sides of the trenches, governments reorganized for a fight to the finish, which ended in the victory of the Allies on November 11, 1918.

## IV. ENTER THE BOLSHEVIKS

While the war was being fought to its end, a new factor was ushered in by events in Russia. On November 7, 1917, the Bolsheviks, under the leadership of Lenin, Trotsky, Stalin, Zinoviev, Kamenev and others, after a few days of street fighting in the principal cities of Russia, captured the government and established themselves in power. In January, 1918, they dissolved the Constituent Assembly and organized a government of Soviets. Early in March, they signed a separate peace with Germany at Brest-Litovsk. A constitution was promulgated which declared Russia a Socialist Soviet Republic, based on the principle of the "dictatorship of the proletariat." On the last day of June, 1918, a sweeping decree was issued nationalizing the land and the main industries of Russia. A Red Army was created, and a system of terror was instituted, to be enforced by a special commission known as the Cheka. Thus, in less than a year, the Bolsheviks had carried out the program advocated by Lenin at Zimmerwald: they had withdrawn Russia from the war and had inaugurated a "social revolution" based on "proletarian dictatorship."

The repercussions of the Bolshevik Revolution in the socialist and labor movements of Europe were twofold. On the one hand, it revived the agitation for peace and for social-economic reforms. In the countries of the Central Powers, there were numerous strikes and political demonstrations all through 1918. By October 1918, this rising tide swelled up in revolutions which swept through Bulgaria, Hungary, and Austria and which culminated in the revolution in Germany on November 9, 1918. In the Allied countries, the "new temper" manifested itself in the growing influence of the Minority socialists, and in the spread of socialistic ideas. In France, the Minority led by Jean Longuet assumed the leadership of the French Socialist Party. In England, the British Labour Party adopted a program of a "New Social Order," socialist in character, while the trade unions came out for "workers' control." The Italian Socialist Party expressed its sympathy with the Bolshevik "experiment" in Russia.

On the other hand, Bolshevism caused a wide rift in the socialist and labor movements. The Majority socialists, the Minority, and even some of the Left groups repudiated the Bolshevik methods in Russia —the forced nationalization of industry and the system of political dictatorship supported by terrorism—and proclaimed that political democracy was an inseparable part of socialism. The issue of "democracy versus dictatorship" became the subject of violent debates which aroused in members of the different factions a mutual hatred unparalleled in the history of social movements.

## V. The Bern Conference

Despite this state of mind, the socialist and labor leaders of the Allied countries hoped to effect a reconciliation and to unite the socialists of all countries on a common program of peace. With that in view, they issued a call to the trade unions and to the socialist parties of all countries to meet in a general conference at the same time and place as the official peace conference. As Georges Clemenceau, then Premier of France, refused to allow delegates from enemy countries to come to Paris, the meeting was held at Bern from February 2 to February 9, 1919. The Belgian Labor Party refused to meet with the Germans, and the socialist parties of Italy, Switzerland, Serbia, and Bulgaria would not come because the meeting was called by those who had played a "reactionary" part in the war. However about one hundred delegates from twenty-six countries attended the conference.

It proved a tense meeting surcharged with the animosities of four years of war. The German Majority socialists were reluctant to commit themselves to a direct admission of Germany's war guilt, and a compromise formula was devised which made such admission indirect. Most of the delegates were in favor of a strong declaration for the principles of democracy and against class dictatorship. A strong minority opposed it on the ground that it implied a condemnation of the Soviet regime which they would not support, on the ground that the available information about conditions in Russia was inadequate.

The Bern conference endorsed President Wilson's Fourteen Points, demanded the creation of a League of Nations which would include all nations, and voted for the reannexation of Alsace-Lorraine to France. The conference set up three committees. One was to go to Paris to exercise pressure on the official peacemakers. A second was to visit Russia and report on conditions there. The third was to reconstruct the Second International.

## VI. THE "INTERNATIONAL OF ACTION"

To the Bolsheviks, the possible revival of the Second International, begun at Bern, presaged no good. In their opinion, it meant that the socialists who opposed them would consolidate their power in Western Europe. The Bolsheviks were at the time in a desperate situation. They were surrounded by the "sanitary cordon" of the Allies in the West. British and Japanese troops were at Vladivostok; British and American troops were at Archangel; the Ukraine was in revolt; the self-proclaimed "dictator of Russia," Admiral Kolchak, was entrenched in Siberia, while in the areas under Bolshevist control there was discontent in the villages and great privation and suffering in the cities. Under these conditions, the Bolsheviks hoped that a new International, by stimulating revolutionary movements in Central Europe and then spreading them to the Allied countries, would hasten the "social revolution" which they considered inevitable and bring them political and economic aid.

To anticipate the Bern conference, the Bolsheviks hurriedly wirelessed from Moscow on January 24, 1919, a call for a meeting to form a new Communist International. The invitation was sent to a long list of groups and organizations which the Bolsheviks hoped to attract to their camp. The meeting assembled in Moscow on March 2, 1919, but was poorly attended. The conference claimed that those present were delegates from "left wing" and revolutionary organizations in thirty-four countries. Most of these "delegates" had no definite credentials and represented small and uncertain groups. The sessions were held in a small room in the Kremlin which was draped with banners in many languages bearing the motto: "Long live the Third International."

The Moscow conference regarded itself as the continuation of the "Zimmerwald movement." It dissolved the Zimmerwald Commission and proclaimed the establishment of the Third or Communist International. The ideas which were to guide the new organization were formulated in a "Manifesto to the Proletariat of all Countries." According to this Manifesto, the "imperialist war" was changing in all countries into a civil war. The "bourgeoisie" which had allegedly brought on the war was said to be paying the price for the devastation it had wrought. It was declared to be bankrupt, unable to organize production, and to be making vain efforts to reestablish international life by means of a League of Nations. It was said to be helpless in the face of the very forces which it had called into being—a socialized war economy, a revolutionary working class, rebellious colonies, and militant small nationalities—which were presumably breaking down the framework of "capitalist imperialism."

A return to the past was declared to be impossible. The workers were urged to rise at once, disarm the bourgeoisie, form councils of workers and peasants, socialize industry and credit, and establish a "dictatorship of the proletariat" on the Russian model. The Manifesto called upon the workers to fight both the Right and the Center socialists and to follow only those Left groups which were willing to join the new Communist International for the immediate overthrow of capitalism.

The Moscow conference adopted provisional statutes and appointed a provisional executive committee. Gregory Zinoviev became chairman of the committee, and Angelica Balabanoff its secretary. They were entrusted with the task of cementing the hastily produced new organization.

The founders of the new International declared that they were the "followers and fulfillers of the program" announced seventy-two years before by Karl Marx in his *Communist Manifesto*. In their perspective, the First International had been "the prophet of the future," and the Second International the "organizer of millions." The task of the Third International, they said, was to become the "International of Action."

C H A P T E R     V I I

# International Federation of Trade Unions
## 1914-1919

IN THE political sphere, the war and the Russian Revolution resulted in socialist divisions and in the formation of the Third International. In the trade union movement, their effects were evidenced in the reestablishment of the International Federation of Trade Unions (IFTU) on a larger basis and with a new program. The story of this reestablishment is the second link in the chain of pre-1914 and postwar developments.

## I. Trade Unions and the War

During the first months of the war, trade union leaders of warring and neutral countries continued to exchange letters. Legien, the German secretary of the International Federation of Trade Unions, took the position that since the workers were not responsible for the war, and since it would not last long, it was necessary to maintain international labor contacts during that time. He requested the national trade union centers to continue to send him reports and information. Appleton of Great Britain and Gompers responded in a friendly spirit, but Jouhaux of France and Mertens of Belgium were irritated by such requests and informed Legien that the time was not opportune for such communications.

As the military conflict became more intense, Legien's activities became suspect to the trade union leaders of the Allied countries. Legien tried to meet the difficulty by designating the national trade union center of Holland as a branch office of the International Federation, under the direction of Jan Oudegeest, to deal with the Allied countries. His office in Berlin continued to deal directly with the neutral countries. The British and French trade unionists would not accept this arrangement, and requested that the headquarters of the Federation be transferred to Bern. Legien was hurt by this request, but he instructed Oudegeest to call an international trade union conference to consider the proposal. The majority of trade union centers declared against holding such a conference and against making any changes in the IFTU during the war. Jouhaux was displeased with this decision and set up an International Correspondence Bureau in Paris for communications between the trade unions of the Allied and neutral countries. Thus, by May, 1915, there were three international trade union offices—in Berlin, Amsterdam, and Paris.

During 1915, the trade union ranks were further split by the appearance of small antiwar groups in Germany, England, and France. In the first two countries, these antiwar trade unionists followed the lead of the antiwar socialists. In France, however, they took the lead in the antiwar campaign. A. Merrheim, secretary of the Metal Workers' Federation, and Bourderon, a member of the executive committee of the General Confederation of Labor, attended the Zimmerwald conference. In the course of 1916, these two labor leaders and their associates, such as Pierre Monatte, gained influence and cooperated with the antiwar socialists to bring about a speedy end of the war. On the other hand, the officials and most of the leaders of the national trade unions in France worked in close cooperation with the prowar Majority socialists.

## II. Leeds and Bern

From 1916 on, trade union leaders in all countries began to formulate demands which labor should make in the coming treaty of peace. The first to show this concern were the labor leaders of England, France, Belgium, and Italy, who met in an Inter-Allied Trade Union Conference at Leeds on July 5, 1916. The resolution adopted by the Leeds conference called for the inclusion in the peace treaty of special labor clauses which would guarantee to the workers the right to organize, shorter hours of work, social insurance, and other protective laws; it also demanded the establishment of an international labor office to collect statistics. Jouhaux sent this resolution to the trade unions affiliated with the International Federation of Trade Unions for their consideration.

Legien was aroused by the Leeds proceedings and by Jouhaux's activities and tried to counteract them by arranging an international trade union conference in Stockholm in June, 1917. But the invitations sent out by Oudegeest from Amsterdam were ignored by the British and French trade unionists and declined by the trade unions of Switzerland, Belgium, and the United States. Only trade union delegates from the Central Powers and from neutral countries gathered at Stockholm on the appointed day. All the Stockholm conference did was to request the Swiss Federation of Labor to try to arrange a representative international conference in Bern on October 1, 1917.

The Bern conference also was attended by trade unionists only from the Central Powers and some neutral countries. It received a telegram from Jouhaux urging the transfer of the headquarters of the IFTU to a neutral country. Legien opposed this on the ground that it would mean "a vote of censure on Germany." The proposal was dropped, but the branch office of the IFTU at Amsterdam was authorized to act henceforth as the intermediary in international labor relations.

The delegates at Bern adopted a program which incorporated most of the demands of the Inter-Allied Leeds conference, with several additions. Of these the most important were the demands that the governments at war should allow trade union representatives to take part in formulating the economic and social sections of the peace treaty, and that the IFTU should be recognized as the official spokesman of labor in official diplomatic proceedings dealing with international labor legislation.

### III. Role of Gompers

As the war neared its end, the labor leaders of different countries became anxious to unite their forces in order to play a role in the making of the peace. Intense rivalry developed as to who should take the lead and how the task should be carried out. In October, 1918, Oudegeest wired a request to the trade union centers of the IFTU to appoint delegates to an international conference to meet at the same time and place as the official peace conference. Oudegeest explained that he was acting in accordance with the wishes expressed at Leeds in 1916 and at Bern in October, 1917, and by Gompers on various occasions. After consulting labor leaders in the Allied countries, Oudegeest decided that it would be impossible to hold an international meeting in Paris and changed the place of the meeting to Amsterdam.

Gompers was unpleasantly affected by Oudegeest's initiative. In the course of 1917-1918, he had come to feel strongly that American labor should play the leading part in renewing international relations and in formulating the labor clauses of the peace treaty. As a member of the National Defense Council of the United States, Gompers had played an important part in promoting war activities; during 1917-1918 he had received many invitations to visit the Allied countries to strengthen the war morale of the workers, and he came to believe that he was to play a vital part also in the making of the peace. Under Gompers' influence, the Executive Council of the AF of L notified Oudegeest that it would itself issue invitations for an international labor conference to help in the peace discussions and to establish a new international trade union federation.

Gompers also resented the call issued by Arthur Henderson for the international labor and socialist conference in Bern, as related in the preceding chapter. Gompers' prewar animosity toward socialism and the socialists had been accentuated by the antiwar attitude of the American Socialist Party. He informed Henderson that American trade unionists would not sit in conference with delegates from enemy countries "for the present at least," or in a conference in which the aims of labor would be "subordinated to those of any partisan political movement."

Gompers objected to holding a general conference in a neutral country, as that might facilitate a "Bolshevist stampede" and enable the Germans to assert for themselves a "position of equality." Instead, he suggested an inter-Allied conference in Paris. The French and Belgian trade union leaders agreed with him. Jouhaux, in the name of the International Correspondence Bureau, issued a call for a preliminary labor conference to be held in Paris. Thus, after the armistice was proclaimed on November 11, 1918, three labor conferences were projected—to take place in Paris on January 30, 1919; in Bern on February 5, 1919; and in Amsterdam on March 8, 1919.

## IV. The Bern Conference of 1919

Of the three labor conferences planned, that which convened at Bern on February 5 and 6, 1919, was the first after 1914 at which trade unionists from the Allied and neutral countries and the Central Powers were present. The fifty-three delegates from sixteen countries included representatives from the British Trades Union Congress, the French Confederation of Labor, and the Belgian unions. The AF of L stayed away.

The Bern conference drew up an International Labor Charter which combined the programs of Leeds and the 1917 Bern meeting. The Charter demanded compulsory free primary and higher education, an eight-hour working day, a weekly rest period of thirty-six hours, the abolition of night work for women, social insurance, labor exchanges, and an international labor code for seamen. It also called for an International Labor Parliament, to consist of an equal number of trade union and government representatives, which would meet regularly and enact laws affecting labor and having the same validity as national legislation. A committee was appointed to present this Charter to the Peace Conference at Versailles.

The Bern conference also commissioned Oudegeest to call a general international conference, in cooperation with the International Correspondence Bureau of Paris, for the purpose of reconstituting the International Federation of Trade Unions.

## V. The Versailles Labor Charter

While the Bern conference was assembling, the first effects of the postwar upheaval, which is described in the next chapter, made themselves felt at Versailles. Aroused by the threat of revolutionary movements, the Versailles Peace Conference on January 25, 1919, appointed a Commission on International Labor Legislation to formulate labor clauses for the treaty of peace. Gompers was elected chairman of the Commission. He did his utmost to model the report of the Commission on the principles formulated at the 1917 convention of the AF of L, which he regarded as a specific American contribution. However, the final draft of the Commission's report fell short of the demands of the AF of L and of the Bern Charter. It provided for a weekly rest of twenty-four hours instead of thirty-six; it said nothing about night work for women or a seamen's code or social insurance. It rejected the proposal for an International Labor Parliament and set up instead an International Labor Organization with limited powers.

The report of the Commission was adopted by the Versailles Peace Conference. It became Part XIII of the Versailles Peace Treaty, signed on June 28, 1919, generally referred to as the Labor Convention.

## VI. The Amsterdam Congress

Within a month after the signing of the Versailles Peace Treaty, an international trade union congress was convened at Amsterdam. This time Gompers, who had become deeply interested in the success of President Wilson's peace program, accepted the invitation to attend and led a delegation composed of himself, Daniel Tobin of the

Teamsters' Union, and John J. Hines of the Amalgamated Sheet Metal Workers.

Some preliminary meetings were held to allow the Belgians to "square accounts" with the Germans and to wind up the affairs of the prewar organization. These meetings were marked by bitter indictments of the German delegation by Mertens of Belgium and by Gompers, and by a demand that the Germans admit their war guilt. The German delegates accepted, then retracted, and then reaffirmed their acceptance of a resolution introduced by a German delegate, John Sassenbach, to the effect that Germany had been the aggressor in the war. With the settling of the war guilt in this manner, the prewar international organization was liquidated, and the first constituent congress of the new International Federation of Trade Unions (IFTU) was declared open.

The congress, which lasted from July 28 to August 2, 1919, was a new departure in the history of international trade unionism. It was attended by ninety-one delegates duly elected by the national trade unions of fourteen countries with a membership of 17,740,000 workers. The countries represented were the United States, Great Britain, France, Belgium, Holland, Luxembourg, Switzerland, Sweden, Norway, Denmark, Germany, Austria, Czechoslovakia, and Spain. The discussion ranged over the whole field of economics and politics.

Hardly a session passed without stormy discussions and collisions on the questions of the Versailles Labor Convention, the League of Nations, and socialism. Gompers and the British delegates felt that the Versailles Labor Convention was the achievement of Allied labor, and asked for its endorsement. Gompers admitted that the Versailles Peace Treaty was not perfect, but claimed that "for the first time in history the rights, interests and welfare of the workers" had received "specific recognition in an international peace treaty." The congress, however, led by Legien, adopted a resolution censuring the Labor Convention. The congress consented nevertheless to take part in the first International Labor Conference under the League of Nations, scheduled to meet in Washington in October, 1919, on condition that Germany and Austria be invited and that only representatives of trade unions affiliated with the International Federation of Trade Unions be admitted.

The Amsterdam Congress, in opposition to Gompers, also passed a resolution criticizing the League of Nations as constituted. It further declared that "capitalism" was unable to "reorganize" production so as to ensure the well-being of the people, and called for "complete trade union organization as the necessary basis for the realization of the socialization of the means of production."

There were further clashes on questions of organization and dues. The per capita tax agreed on was one half of 1 cent per member per year. The American and British delegates thought this too high; the dues of the AF of L for 1919 under this tax would have been $20,000. The American delegates objected in particular to the rule which was adopted that all decisions should be made binding by majority vote instead of by unanimity, which had been the rule before the war.

Despite these difficulties, a constitution and by-laws were finally adopted which launched the International Federation of Trade Unions on its new career. A system of proportional voting was adopted. The headquarters were transferred from Berlin to Amsterdam. A bureau consisting of a president, two vice-presidents, and two secretaries was to direct the affairs of the Federation, subject to the review of a Management Committee of Ten which was to meet semiannually. W. A. Appleton, of the British Federation of Trade Unions, was elected president. The Germans wanted Legien to be first vice-president; when he was not offered that position, he refused to take the second vice-presidency. Jouhaux, of the French Confederation of Labor, and Mertens, of the Belgian trade unions, were elected vice-presidents; Jan Oudegeest and Edo Fimmen, both of Holland, were elected secretaries. Gompers was not eligible for office since the American delegates did not commit themselves to joining the Federation, pending a decision by the AF of L convention.

When the Amsterdam Congress adjourned, its principal participants felt that they had taken the first step toward a "new international unity" of labor. What had been broken up by the war had presumably not only been repaired but improved. In place of the prewar International Secretariat with its limited program there was now an International Federation of Trade Unions designed for concerted trade union action on a large scale.

# World Upheaval
## 1919-1920

THE First World War was followed by one of the greatest social upheavals of modern times, which assumed worldwide scope in 1919-1920.

There were many elements in this upheaval which influenced its manifestations in different countries. There was an unloosening of discipline due to war-weariness and demobilization. There was the bitterness of defeat in the countries of the Central Powers. There were the high hopes in the Allied countries, aroused by the winged phrases of President Wilson, and subsequent disappointment with the Versailles Treaty. There was the enthusiasm of building a new national life in the newly created states such as Czechoslovakia, Poland, Yugoslavia, and Finland, and the outburst of nationalistic conflicts in connection with the fixing of boundaries. There were the difficulties of repairing the devastations of the war. There was the hovering fear of renewed war on account of reparations, relations with Soviet Russia, and the rising nationalistic temper in Europe, the Near East, and Asia. And permeating all was the industrial unrest fed by the inflation of the postwar boom.

## I. LABOR AND POSTWAR UNREST

Labor's part in this upheaval took several forms. There was a great expansion of labor organization in most countries. The trade union membership of the world increased from some 15,000,000 in 1913 to 45,000,000 in 1920. Conscious of the power which they had gained during the war and stirred by the vision of a "new social order" which had been promised them, the workers reached out in most countries for new rights and wider powers. New laws were enacted to give the trade unions a more recognized place in the economic and legal system. Plans for social insurance were formulated to replace older more limited provisions. Collective bargaining was extended on a scale unknown before the war. New demands were added to labor's list, such as family allowances, paid annual vacations, larger educational opportunities, consultative functions in management, nationalization of key industries, and more democracy in political life. In pursuance of these aims, labor in many countries vented its postwar temper in strike movements which for scope and intensity had not been equaled before.

Merging in various ways, the currents of labor, agrarian, and social unrest gave rise to large movements over wide areas. In Eastern and Southeastern Europe, these movements were directed at the redistribution of land among the peasantry and at obtaining more political power for the industrial workers. In Central Europe, they had as their aim the establishment of workers' republics and the socialization of industry. In Italy, they followed lines leading to a possible revolution. In Western and Northern Europe, and in the United States, they assumed the form of large strikes for higher wages and for basic improvements in economic and social conditions. In several countries of Latin America, they exploded in mass strikes, some of which assumed the character of uprisings without any clear objectives. In Japan, they expressed themselves in food riots, in demands for democratic reform, and in the formation of labor unions. In the Near East, in India and in China, they burst forth in demands for national independence and internal political and economic reforms.

## II. Amsterdam's Leadership

The question which loomed up in Europe was who would assume leadership. The workers were torn in most countries between the factions and groups which had arisen since 1914—Right, Center, and Left—and were fighting among themselves over the issue as to whether the upheaval should be guided into channels of "reconstruction" or "revolution." The reconstructive forces in Europe were represented by the Second Socialist International revived at Bern in February, 1919, and by the International Federation of Trade Unions (IFTU) set up at Amsterdam in July of that year. The forces of revolution gathered around the Third International formed in Moscow in March, 1919. These three Internationals were called, after their places of origin, the Bern International, the Amsterdam International, and the Moscow International; in current discussions, they were referred to as "Bern," "Amsterdam," and "Moscow."

Of the three Internationals, the IFTU or Amsterdam, loomed up as the leading organization. Within a few months after its foundation it emerged as the spokesman of over 23,000,000 organized workers in twenty-two countries. Its budget was in tens of thousands of dollars. It had well-appointed headquarters and a regular staff. Its leadership was eager to act in the spirit of its rules, which called for "wide activities of general interest to trade unions."

Amsterdam scored its first success at the first annual conference of the International Labor Organization of the League of Nations which convened in Washington in October, 1919. The conference was attended by workers', employers' and government delegates from forty-one countries. Though fourteen countries sent only government delegates, though the AF of L was not represented because of the failure of the U. S. Senate to ratify the Versailles Treaty, and though German and Austrian labor delegates were absent owing to passport and other obstacles, the workers' group, consisting of delegates from trade unions affiliated with Amsterdam, was treated as the spokesman of labor in all countries. Thanks to the discipline and solidarity which they achieved under the leadership of Amsterdam, the workers succeeded in getting through the Washington conference several draft conventions relating to child and female labor, to the prohibition of white phosphorus in the manufacture of matches, and to unemployment. The most important draft convention adopted by the Washington conference, to which the leaders of Amsterdam pointed with special pride, was that on the eight-hour day. It was hailed as a victory for an idea for which organized labor had battled for half a century.

Encouraged by this success, the Amsterdam leaders threw themselves into a number of varied campaigns. In the fall of 1919, they issued an appeal to all trade unions for "mass action" to "raise the blockade" of Russia. They shipped carloads of food donated by British, French, Belgian, Dutch, and Scandinavian workers to the starving people of Vienna. They dispatched special commissions to investigate economic and political conditions in the Sarre, in Austria, and in Upper Silesia. In the summer of 1920, they carried on a boycott against Hungary, in protest against the dictatorial regime of the regent Horthy and for the "restoration of civil rights." The boycott lasted seven weeks and cut off communications between Budapest and the outside world, though it failed to achieve its objective. In the midst of the Russo-Polish War in the summer of 1920, the Amsterdam leaders undertook to coordinate the efforts of labor and socialist organizations in a number of European countries to enforce an embargo on munitions destined for Poland. The effect of this embargo on the course of the war was small, if any, but it was hailed by Amsterdam as the first significant antiwar action by an international labor body.

The high-water mark of Amsterdam's activities during these years was the special congress which it convened in London in November, 1920, to draft a program for the rebuilding of Europe. The program formulated by the London Congress called for the cancellation of all war debts, the stabilization of the international exchanges, an international loan by the League of Nations for purposes of reconstruction, international control and distribution of raw materials under the supervision of the International Labor Office, the socialization of mines and transport, and the elimination of tariffs. The congress instructed the Amsterdam Bureau to present this program to the Committee of Experts of the League of Nations who were to meet in Brussels in December, 1920, and to carry on a campaign for its adoption by the League.

### III. THE SOCIALIST INTERNATIONAL

While Amsterdam was developing these activities, the Bern International was trying to establish itself on a firm foundation. The hopes of Bern were based on the fact that socialism was lifted by the war and the postwar upheaval to a new position of power in European politics. For the first time in history, there were socialist or partly socialist governments in Germany, Austria, Czechoslovakia, Sweden, and several other countries. Organized labor in most countries of Europe gave its support to the more moderate socialist parties and groups. It seemed possible to effect an international union of these parties and groups on a program of peaceful reconstruction.

After several attempts, the Bern leaders arranged an international socialist congress in Geneva on July 31, 1920. It brought together seventeen national parties, but its strength derived from the fact that it was attended by the British Labour Party, the British Trades Union Congress, and the Fabian Society of Great Britain; by the Majority socialists of Germany; and by the representatives of the Belgian, Dutch, Danish, and Swedish socialist parties. The Geneva Congress reaffirmed the faith of the socialists in universal suffrage and democratic parliamentary action, declared that socialization should proceed step by step from one industry to another, and warned the workers not to destroy private enterprise in any industry until they were in a position to replace it with a more efficient form of organization. It condemned attempts to suppress "bourgeois" governments by force and to establish the "dictatorship of the proletariat," reminding the workers that it was the mission of socialism not to suppress democracy but to carry it to completion.

The Geneva Congress of the Bern International appointed an executive committee of three members to direct its work, and designated London as its headquarters. The Bern International, however, remained inactive.

## IV. BOLSHEVIST PLANS

In contrast to Bern and in opposition to the reconstructive activities of Amsterdam, the Third International was determined to harness the tides of unrest for an immediate "world revolution." Despite the suppression of the Spartacist uprising in Berlin in January, 1919, the overthrow of the Bavarian Soviet Republic soon afterward, the collapse of the Soviet government in Hungary, and other reversals the leaders of the Third International claimed that the world was "hurrying towards proletarian revolution at break-neck speed." The situation seemed to them to become more revolutionary during 1920.

General strikes in the Balkans in February of that year, the Communist uprising in the Ruhr in March, mass strikes and the seizure of factories in Italy in the spring of the year, and the general strike in France in May for the nationalization of the railroads kept Europe in a state of turmoil, and were interpreted by the Communists as signs of the imminence of a general "social revolution." Communist hopes rose especially during the last stages of the Russo-Polish War, in July and August of 1920. The Russian Red Armies, which between December, 1919, and the spring of 1920 had destroyed Kolchak, scattered the forces of Yudenich, beaten back Denikin, and cleared Russia of foreign troops, were marching westward. Their aim was to take Warsaw, march on Berlin, and join with the revolutionary groups of the West to establish a Soviet Europe.

It was amidst such expectations, from July 19 to August 7, 1920, that the Third International held its second congress in Moscow. Several hundred delegates from thirty-seven countries crowded the halls of the Kremlin where the congress was held. It was a motley gathering. There were present members of the newly formed Communist parties in several countries, ready to follow in the footsteps of the Russian Bolsheviks. There were the "repentant sinners," such as Cachin and Frossard of the French Socialist Party, who had been ardent supporters of the war but who were now swinging to the other extreme. There were delegates from the socialist parties of Italy and Switzerland, which had pursued an antiwar policy during 1914-1918 and which were for revolutionary action now. There were various "left wing" socialist groups, such as the Independent Socialists of Germany and the Independent Labour Party of Great Britain, which had broken with the Bern International. There were radical trade union groups, such as the British Shop Stewards' Committees, American IWW, French, Spanish, and Italian syndicalists, and German Laborites, who did not agree with the tenets of the Russian Communists but who were willing to make arrangements with them for the sake of immediate revolution. And there were men and women from Turkey, Egypt, Persia, India, China, Korea, Japan, who saw in the Third International an instrument of anticolonialism and "antiimperialism."

On the basis of their diagnosis of the international situation, the

Russian Communists summoned the assembled delegates to begin the work of "world revolution" at once. "We are living in an epoch of civil war," proclaimed the congress; "the critical hour has struck." The congress adopted elaborate "theses" which explained the meaning of proletarian dictatorship; pointed out the ways in which Communists should utilize parliaments, trade unions, and other social-economic institutions for their purposes; laid down the conditions under which Soviets should be formed; and defined the Communist attitude toward the peasantry and toward the nationalist movements of the colonial countries.

The Moscow Congress urged all those in agreement with its views to break away from the socialists and to form independent communist parties. It adopted 21 Points which were conditions of admission to the Third International. According to these points, all groups wishing to join the Third International had to accept fully the Communist program, engage in illegal work, carry on propaganda in the army, submit to "iron discipline," and form "nuclei" in all proletarian and "semi-proletarian" organizations. The purpose of these points was to keep out of the Third International not only members of the Majority socialist parties but also the Center socialists, to break up the socialist parties and to destroy their influence among the workers.

The 21 Points were also aimed at Amsterdam. Point Ten demanded that all parties and groups belonging to the Third International should carry on "a stubborn struggle against the Amsterdam International of the yellow labor unions" and against the International Labor Organization of the League of Nations. To promote this "struggle," the trade unionists attending the congress held a meeting and set up a Provisional International Council of Red Trade Unions.

Soon after the second congress of the Third International, it became clear that the force of the world upheaval was spending itself. The Red Armies were repulsed from Warsaw and had to retreat. In August and September of 1920, the big lockout and strike of the metal workers in Italy, during which the workers seized the factories, was settled by a compromise between the workers and the employers. In other countries general strikes and attempted uprisings collapsed. Then toward the end of the year came an economic recession which, beginning in Japan and spreading to England and the United States, developed into a worldwide industrial depression. The leaders of the Third International claimed at the time that Amsterdam and the socialist parties prevented the workers in 1919-1920 from establishing themselves in power in Europe and from inaugurating a socialist reorganization. There is no question that Amsterdam and the socialists were determined to keep the unrest within bounds and to prevent it from overflowing Europe in Bolshevist fashion. They had behind them the solid industrial and political organizations of labor, while the Third International was a loose conglomeration of heterogeneous fragments manipulated by the Russian Communists. But the efforts of Amsterdam and of the socialists would not have been successful had they not been in harmony with the desire of the European workers for a return to peaceful ways of living.

CHAPTER    NINE

# Confusion and Retreat
## 1921-1923

CONSIDERING the world economy as a whole, the industrial depression which began toward the end of 1920 lasted till the end of 1923. It was marked by a sharp fall in world trade, much unemployment, and serious financial dislocations. In world political life, these years witnessed a recession from the hopeful expectations aroused by the war. Europe was "Balkanized," the reparations issue became acute, while democratic governments gave way to dictatorships in Italy, Spain, the Balkans and elsewhere.

As a result of these developments, organized labor was forced to retreat from the positions won during 1919-1920. In most Western countries, employers resorted to wage cutting and actively opposed labor organizations and collective bargaining. Trade unions lost heavily in membership; in Germany, they were reduced to a mere paper existence by inflation. The sense of power felt by organized labor in 1919-1920 gave way to a feeling of disillusionment and uncertainty.

In view of changing conditions, the Amsterdam and Socialist Internationals moderated their activities and tried mainly to consolidate their organizations so as to stem the "tide of reaction." But the Communists, after first sounding a note of retreat, embarked on new adventures which resulted in strife and bloodshed. The confusion in international labor relations caused by their activities was dispelled only as events reached a climax toward the end of the period.

## I. THE VIENNA UNION

The first to show a change of mood were the Center and Left socialists, who turned against the Third International. The delegates of the British Independent Labour Party who had attended the second congress of the Third International in July-August, 1920, upon their return home painted a dark picture of conditions in Russia, which dealt Soviet communism a serious blow. The leaders of the German Independent Socialist Party, irritated by the dictatorial manner of the Russians and fearful that the Russian Communists in their own interests were trying "to precipitate an untimely revolution" in Germany, refused to join the Third International. In Italy, Sweden, the United States, and other countries, with the exception of France, the Communists also failed to win over the Center and Left socialist parties, and could only gain the support of small groups which formed splinter Communist parties.

To formalize their break with the Communists, eighty delegates from Center and Left socialist parties in thirteen countries, with an alleged following of about 10,000,000 members, met in Vienna in February, 1921, and formed the International Working Union of Socialist Parties. It became known as the "Two-and-a-Half International" because of its intermediate position between the Second and the Third International. The Vienna Union was willing to use other than parliamentary methods, but it disapproved "mechanical imitation" of the methods of the Russian Bolshevik Revolution.

## II. NEP in Russia and the German "Putsch"

While losing the support of Left groups, the Communists were threatened by internal developments in Russia and Germany. In March, 1921, the sailors of Kronstadt, the "bulwark of the Bolshevik Revolution," rose in revolt against the Soviet government, demanding democratic reforms and "freedom of trading." The revolt was ruthlessly suppressed but it had the effect of forcing a drastic change in Soviet economic policy. The requisitioning of grain was abolished and superseded by an agricultural tax, and private trade was made legal. Lenin justified this New Economic Policy—the so-called NEP —as a temporary retreat, necessary to restore the Russian economy exhausted by war and revolution.

In Germany, the United Communist Party, the largest and strongest Communist party outside Russia, fell victim to its adventurous policies. Taking advantage of a strike situation caused by inflation and economic conditions, the German Communists tried to make the strike general and seized factories in a number of towns in the Ruhr. Banking on the excitement produced by the French occupation of several industrial centers in the Rhineland, the Communists on March 21, 1921, issued a call for a general uprising. The general strike as well as the *Putsch* (uprising) were a failure, as the masses of German workers, following the leadership of the trade unions and the socialist parties, did not respond to the Communist call. The *Putsch* resulted in bloodshed, and had the effect of further aggravating existing dissensions in the Communist Party and causing some of its best-known leaders to break away.

## III. The RILU

It was with these developments in the background, and with the spector of famine on the horizon in Russia, that the third congress of the Third International met in Moscow in June, 1921. Lenin struck the keynote of the congress with an admission that "revolutionary developments had slowed down" and that the Communists had been mistaken in 1919-1920 to believe that they could win with the help of a minority of organized workers. Taking its cue from Lenin, the congress approved the NEP in Russia and adopted a new slogan for the Communists in all lands: "To the Masses." In politics, this meant that the Communists were to continue to split and break up the socialist parties and to consolidate the Communist parties. But in all other spheres, the Communists were to remain within existing organizations and try to control them through "cells" or "nuclei." They were to make special efforts to gain control of the trade unions and other labor organizations, from "works councils to sport clubs and musical circles."

Immediately after the Communist congress, a "world congress" of trade unionists was held in Moscow with 220 delegates from 42 countries. Prominent among the delegates were Tom Mann of England, William D. Haywood and William Z. Foster of the United States, and Pierre Monatte of France. The guiding spirits were the Russians A. Lozovsky and M. Tomski.

There was much acrimonious debate at the congress, especially on two points. The American IWW and German Laborites were for breaking up the existing unions and forming new ones under their own control. This was rejected, and the congress pronounced itself in favor of remaining within existing labor unions and "boring from within" with a view to "capturing them." The other point was raised by the French syndicalists, who opposed the policy of combining trade unions and political parties into a single International. To placate them, the congress set up the Red International of Labor Unions (RILU), with the proviso, however, that the RILU and the Third International should have an "organic connection." For this purpose, each of the two Internationals was to have representatives on the executive committee of the other.

The program adopted by this first congress of the RILU was in complete agreement with the program of the Third International. According to this program, the Communists were to form "nuclei" in all labor organizations, to "capture the masses," and to overthrow the non-Communist leadership of the unions. Internationally, the RILU was to conduct a continuous attack on Amsterdam.

### IV. Amsterdam Versus the RILU

At first, Amsterdam was inclined to take the trade union activities of the Third International lightly. It branded the RILU as "bluff and humbug" and continued to invite the Soviet trade unions into its own ranks. But when the RILU attracted a few trade union centers, namely those of Finland, Yugoslavia, and Bulgaria, Amsterdam adopted a rule to expel any organization which affiliated with the RILU.

Amsterdam tried also to counteract general Communist agitation by proposing measures for improving political and economic conditions in Germany. It demanded that Germany be admitted to the League of Nations, and that an International Reconstruction Office be set up to raise international loans guaranteed by the League to be used for the rebuilding of German industry; the interest and principal of the loans were to be paid by Germany.

### V. The Berlin Meeting for United Action

All through 1921, the attitude of Amsterdam and the socialists became more embittered against the Communists, owing to the splitting and disrupting tactics of the latter. But before the year drew to an end, the Russian Communists became interested in obtaining the support of the socialists and of the "reformist" trade unions for the program, which they proposed to submit to the Genoa Conference called by the Allied Prime Ministers for April 10, 1922. The Genoa Conference was to consider reparations, war debt settlement, and European and Russian rehabilitation as interrelated aspects of the general problem of world reconstruction.

After some preliminary negotiations, about fifty delegates, representing the executive committees of the Bern or Second International, the Two-and-a-Half or Vienna International, and the Third International, met in Berlin on April 5, 1922, to consider a common program of action, in view of the approaching Genoa Conference. A committee of nine, three from each International, was formed to carry on negotiations.

There were mutual recriminations and much wrangling at the Berlin meeting. The socialists demanded three things: that the Third International should stop its "cell-building" tactics; that the Soviet

Government should free its socialist prisoners and give a fair trial to a group of Russian Social-Revolutionists who were imprisoned in Moscow on accusations of treason; and that a commission should be appointed to investigate the *coup d'état* which the Bolsheviks had carried out against the socialist government of Georgia in the Caucasus. The delegates of the Third International accepted the two last demands. The socialists then agreed to call a general international conference as soon as possible. The Berlin meeting issued an appeal to the workers in all countries to arrange mass demonstrations during the Genoa Conference for the eight-hour day, for the resumption of political and economic relations with Soviet Russia, and for the "establishment of a proletarian United Front."

However, as soon as the Genoa Conference ended on May 10, having blasted the hopes it had raised, socialist-Communist negotiations broke down. On May 23, the committee of nine met again but took no action. In June, the trial of the thirty-four Social-Revolutionists accused of plotting against the Soviet government opened in Moscow, but Vandervelde and other socialists who were to act as counsel for the defendants objected to the legal proceedings and withdrew. The trial ended on August 8; fourteen of the accused were condemned to death, but the sentence was stayed on condition that the Social Revolutionist Party cease its terroristic and insurrectional tactics. The trial drove the wedge between socialists and Communists still deeper. Shortly afterward, the negotiations between the three Internationals were called off formally.

## V. COMMUNIST SPLITS

While failing in its purpose at the Berlin meeting, the policy of the "United Front" also caused the Third International much internal trouble. In some countries, the Communists interpreted it broadly and made electoral alliances with the socialists. In other countries, the Communists defied the policy and would have nothing to do with the "reformist" trade unions and the socialist "traitors." The chief difficulties of the Third International in 1922 were with the French Communist Party. Not only were the French Communists quarreling among themselves, but their leaders were ignoring the instructions of the Third International and accusing the Executive Committee of the

Third International of rash judgment and hasty action. Similar issues were disrupting the Communist parties in Italy, Norway, Czechoslovakia, and the United States. The Russian Communist Party itself was being rent by a "Workers' Opposition" under the leadership of Alexandra Kollontai and others, who protested against the NEP, the United Front, and bureaucratic methods and who demanded a "democratic" reform of the party organization.

These internal difficulties were the main topic of the fourth congress of the Third International held in Moscow in November, 1922. The malcontents of various countries lost the battle. The congress asserted the right of the executive committee of the Third International to intervene in the internal affairs of the separate parties and to make binding rules and decisions. It approved once more the NEP, the United Front, and the policy of building "cells" in the trade unions.

The decisions of the congress caused further splits in Communist ranks. In France, Frossard, who had played a large part in organizing the French Communist Party, broke away and with his followers formed a new group known as the Unitarian Party. Similar defections took place in other countries. The syndicalists would not accept the subordination of the trade unions to a political party. On December 25, 1922, syndicalist groups from France, Germany, Holland, and Sweden left the RILU and formed a separate organization under the name of International Working Men's Association with headquarters in Berlin.

### VII. Amsterdam and Socialist Unity

On the other hand, the activities of the Third International stimulated the socialists and the Amsterdam trade unions to greater cooperation among themselves. In September, 1922, the Majority and the Independent Socialists of Germany decided to forget the past and to join forces in a new party, which they formed under the name of United Social Democratic Party of Germany. In December, Amsterdam arranged at The Hague a large "international peace congress," which was attended by some 700 representatives of trade unions, cooperatives, and socialist parties. Finally, aroused by the spread of Fascism in Italy, by the beginnings of Hitlerism, and by the French occupation of the Ruhr, the Bern and Vienna Internationals convened a "unity congress" in Hamburg in May, 1923. Over 400 delegates, representing 43 parties in 30 countries and claiming a following of 6,700,000, were present and merged the two Internationals into a new organization—the Labor and Socialist International—which was to represent a unified socialist movement. Oudegeest, as secretary of the IFTU, attended the congress and declared that Amsterdam would cooperate with the new organization, while "strictly preserving its equality and independence."

### VIII. OCCUPATION OF THE RUHR

The question which agitated European labor organizations during 1923 was the French occupation of the Ruhr. One of the secretaries of the IFTU, Edo Fimmen, urged the calling of a general strike in the Ruhr. The other secretary, Oudegeest, and the majority of the Amsterdam Bureau felt that such a strike could not be carried out successfully in view of widespread unemployment, internal strife in the ranks of labor, and prevailing public opinion that Germany had not carried out her obligations with regard to reparations. Instead of a strike, Amsterdam urged mediation by the League of Nations. In September, 1923, Amsterdam presented to the Fourth Assembly of the League a memorandum on the reparations problem setting forth the program it had advocated since 1920. It had no immediate results. Besides attempting to influence public opinion, Amsterdam collected $190,000 for the German trade unions, whose financial structure went to pieces with the Ruhr occupation and inflation.

In opposition to Amsterdam and to the socialists, the German, French, Dutch, Czechoslovak, and Italian Communists decided to embark on "militant action." On May 24, 1923, the German Communist Party started strikes in the Ruhr and seized the towns of Gelsenkirchen and Bochum, which they held for a few days. On August 11, 1923, the German Works Council, under Communist influence, called a general strike. For several days there were riots throughout Germany, which forced the fall of the government. The new government formed by Gustav Stresemann suppressed the strike but the Communists continued their aggressive tactics, organizing "food control committees" and armed "factory guards."

### IX. "SECOND WAVE OF REVOLUTION"

The Russian leaders of the Third International then decided that the struggle in Germany was not local but a phase of a general situation. In the phrase of Zinoviev, Europe was heaving with "a second wave of revolution." Large strikes were taking place among the dockers of England, the metal workers of France, and various groups of workers in Czechoslovakia and Poland. The Balkans were in an acute political situation as a result of the assassination of the Bulgarian Premier, A. Stambolisky, who had maintained for several years a personal dictatorship with the support of the Peasant Party. The Zankov government, which came to power through a *coup d'état* in June, 1923, and which had the support of the industrial and financial interests, allied itself with the socialists to consolidate its power. On September 12, 1923, the Zankov government arrested many Communists on the accusation that they were plotting against it. An uprising followed on September 21, in which the Communists and the Peasant Party joined forces. Though it was suppressed within a week, the situation remained tense.

Viewing these developments as signs of a revolutionary revival, the leaders of the Third International approved a plan for an armed uprising in Germany. Karl Radek was sent to Germany by the Third International as adviser to the German Communists. A successful outbreak in Germany, according to the plan, would have thrown Central and Eastern Europe into upheaval again, resulting in a general crisis, for which Soviet Russia was to hold itself in readiness.

On October 23, 1923, the Communists of Hamburg gave the signal by declaring a general strike, starting food riots, and attempting to seize the city government. The undertaking proved an immediate failure. The Hamburg Communists were quickly suppressed, while the rest of Germany refused to take its cue from Hamburg. Again, as in 1921, the mass of the German workers followed not the Communists but their trade union and socialist leaders. And, as in 1921, the Communists were weakened by internal dissensions. The "October uprising" was sponsored by the left wing of the German Communist Party. The right wing advised against it and won Radek over to its side. Thus, at the decisive moment, the Communist leadership was divided.

A few days later, on October 29, government troops marched into Dresden and deposed the "workers' government" of Saxony, composed of Communists and Left socialists. Thousands of Communists were arrested throughout Germany and Communist papers were suppressed. On December 8, the Reichstag conferred dictatorial powers on President Ebert to deal with the situation.

Zinoviev and other leaders of the Third International blamed Radek and the right-wing German Communists for the failure of the "October uprising." But they had to admit that the October event marked a retreat for the Third International on all fronts.

On the other hand, Amsterdam and the Socialist International felt strengthened in their position. All through 1923, socialists and trade unions pursued a vigorous policy of separating themselves from the Communists. The British Labour Party rejected the application of the British Communist Party for affiliation; the Italian Socialist Party expelled one of its prominent leaders, Serrati, for advocating affiliation with the Third International; a Communist, William F. Dunne, was refused admission to the Portland convention of the American Federation of Labor. Several times during the year, Amsterdam rejected offers of the RILU and of the All-Russian Council of Trade Unions for common action and "unity," except on condition that the Soviet trade unions become free and independent of the Soviet government and that the Communists cease their cell-building activities.

In brief, the "October uprising" revealed both the adventurous character of the Third International and the waning of Communist influence in Western Europe. Amsterdam and the socialists interpreted the defeat of the Communists as a victory for their own ideas and programs, and as a vindication of their activities.

# The AF of L and the IFTU
## 1919-1924

BETWEEN 1914 and 1919, the American Federation of Labor, represented by Gompers and others, played an important part in creating the International Labor Organization of the League of Nations and in reestablishing the International Federation of Trade Unions. After 1919, the AF of L found itself drifting away from European labor, but building up closer relations with the labor organizations of Latin America. In both ways, by its attitude toward Europe and by its activities in Latin America, the AF of L exercised an influence on the course of the international labor movement from 1919 to 1924. For a better understanding of the events of these years, it is necessary to sketch the story of the relations of the AF of L first with the IFTU and then with Pan-American labor.

### I. AMERICAN MISGIVINGS

When Gompers and the two other American delegates to the Amsterdam Congress of the IFTU in July, 1919, left for home, they felt that it was important for American labor to form part of the new International. They had made a vague promise to that effect. They were worried, however, by the per capita tax, which they thought too high, by the socialistic bias of the Amsterdam leaders, and by the by-laws which provided that a simple majority vote was sufficient to make a decision binding. This rule, in their opinion, abrogated in practice the autonomy of the national trade union centers.

## II. Labor Unrest and Foreign Policy

The decision on affiliation with the IFTU rested with the convention of the AF of L which was to meet in Montreal in June, 1920. During the intervening months, American labor displayed a restless mood which, in a milder form, resembled the labor upheaval in Europe. The AF of L was proclaiming to the nation a "reconstruction program" which, in addition to prewar slogans, emphasized "human rights versus property rights" and demanded a larger place for labor in the "industrial democracy" said to be coming. The United Mine Workers were advocating the nationalization of the mines. The Railroad Brotherhoods were supporting the "Plumb Plan"[1] for nationalizing the railroads. In the iron and steel and other industries, large bodies of hitherto unorganized workers were striking for higher wages and shorter hours. Political labor parties were springing up in many cities and states, and an American Labor Party was in process of formation on a national scale, in opposition to the wishes of the leaders of the AF of L.

This unrest, as well as the events of the day, stimulated labor's interest in international problems. The AF of L was deeply concerned in President Wilson's campaign for the League of Nations. The holding of the first annual conference of the ILO in Washington brought international labor problems nearer home to American workers. The likelihood of increased immigration from the war-wrecked countries of Europe caused much apprehension. The discussion of the Versailles Peace Treaty agitated large groups of workers, interested in the destinies of the countries from which they or their families had come. The demand for the independence of Ireland found a loud and officially approved echo in American trade unions, while some groups expressed sympathy for Russia. Some of the trade unions which had been in close contact with the socialist movement were aroused by the issues of the Third versus the Second International, which split the American Socialist Party and threatened to disrupt several labor organizations.

The officials of the AF of L, under the leadership of Gompers,

[1] The plan was named after Glenn E. Plumb, counsel of some of the Railroad Brotherhoods, who developed it.

were anxious to hold the labor unrest within the bounds of traditional American trade unionism. They fought for the maintenance of the policy of no partisan politics in the unions and against the formation of a labor party. They followed craft and trade lines in organizing the workers in the steel and other industries. They tried to restrain the Railroad Brotherhoods in their agitation for the Plumb Plan. They counteracted radical demands by conducting a campaign for collective bargaining and against the inimical labor laws which were being adopted in many states.

### III. The Montreal Convention

Owing to their position at home, Gompers and the Executive Council of the AF of L were greatly disturbed by the activities of Amsterdam during 1919-1920, which they regarded as encouraging the radical elements in the labor movement. The Amsterdam leaders made no effort to conciliate the Americans and to establish better personal relations. Some of the European labor leaders, on their return home from the Washington conference of the ILO, made statements to the effect that they were unfavorably impressed by much of what they saw of the American labor movement. To make matters worse, the Management Committee of the IFTU, meeting in April, 1920, refused the request of the AF of L for a reduction of the per capita tax on the grounds that it had no authority to do so and that the question would have to be considered by the next regular congress of the IFTU.

All these matters were placed before the Montreal convention by the Executive Council of the AF of L. The convention was in some ways "the most remarkable" in the history of American labor: it was the high-water mark of the expansive movement which had begun in 1917. The membership represented was over four million; the general spirit was one of militancy, which found its most striking expression in the approval of the Plumb Plan. There was a tendency in the convention, largely as a result of the influx of new elements, to carry decisions against the wishes of the older leadership.

This did not apply, however, to international affairs. The Committee on International Relations, of which Matthew Woll was secretary and guiding spirit, approved the "courageous, dignified manner" in which the American delegates to the Amsterdam Congress of July,

1919, had "upheld the honor of our country and the soundness of our trade union movement and its policies." It agreed that before affiliating with Amsterdam, American labor should receive satisfaction on the points it had raised with regard to a reduction of per capita taxes and autonomy in internal affairs. On the recommendation of the committee, the convention by an overwhelming majority referred the question of affiliation with Amsterdam to the Executive Council.

While reserving decision on Amsterdam, the Montreal convention endorsed the Versailles Peace Treaty and the League of Nations, and declared that it was of the "utmost importance" for American labor to be represented in the International Labor Organization. It also resolved that no action should be taken which could be "construed as an assistance to, or approval of, the Soviet Government of Russia."

## IV. THE BREACH

Negotiations between the AF of L and Amsterdam during 1920-1921 tended to widen the breach. On June 29, 1920, Oudegeest invited the AF of L to attend the special congress which the IFTU was arranging in London in November. The AF of L replied that it might consider sending a delegate if the congress would refrain from political discussions and would consider the question of the per capita tax. Oudegeest wrote to Gompers that in view of the resolution of the Montreal convention in favor of an Irish Republic, it was rather inconsistent on the part of the AF of L to protest against the inclusion of political questions in the program of the IFTU. He further informed Gompers that the question of per capita tax could not be considered at London since it was to be a special congress.

As a result of this correspondence, the AF of L did not send a delegate to London and ceased further payment of dues. Leaders of the British Trades Union Congress tried to bring about a reconciliation, but without success. On March 5, 1921, the Executive Council of the AF of L wrote Oudegeest, stating definitely that the AF of L was not affiliated with the IFTU. The Council objected specifically to Amsterdam's appeals for general strikes against war and in aid of Soviet Russia, and to its placing on the agenda of the London Congress a discussion of the "socialization of the means of production."

The Executive Council of the AF of L stated that it was "most anxious" to be part of the international labor movement, but that it could not be part of a movement which undertook the destruction of the American labor movement or the overthrow of the democratic government of the United States. The Executive Council concluded that if the IFTU would guarantee the autonomy and independence of the AF of L, "we shall join it regardless of the policies and theories for which the various national movements may declare in their own countries."

To this letter Oudegeest replied in a petulant vein. Article Three of the IFTU constitution, he asserted, did guarantee national autonomy. The various manifestoes issued by the Amsterdam Bureau, he claimed, were not regarded as revolutionary in Europe and had been approved even in many "bourgeois" circles. Moreover, he asked, how could the AF of L object to a discussion of "socialization" when Gompers was honorary president of the Plumb Plan League which favored the nationalization of the railroads? Oudegeest accused Gompers of having failed to live up to his pledge of cooperation given in Amsterdam in 1919. Oudegeest sent a copy of this letter to the international unions belonging to the AF of L. The Executive Council replied to this letter in a resentful and caustic tone, characterizing the letter as an "insult" and protesting against Oudegeest's attempt to go over the heads of the officials of the Executive Council and to address the American unions direct.

Such was the situation when the Denver convention of the AF of L met in June, 1921. There all the discontent which had been accumulating in the labor movement since 1919, came to a head. It revealed the radical ideas which had been spreading among American workers as a result of the industrial depression, widespread unemployment, the "open shop" movement of employers, writs of injunction, and consequent loss of strikes and cuts in wages. In a number of constituent unions of the AF of L, internal divisions had arisen similar to those in Europe in the form of such organizations as "shop stewards' leagues," shop councils, "One Big Union" committees, "Friends of Russia," and various "propaganda leagues." The state of mind of the delegates was reflected in the passage of radical resolutions, and, more dramatically, in the fact that for the first time in fifteen years Gompers had a rival for the presidency of the AF of L in John L. Lewis of the United Mine Workers, who, though defeated, polled about half the votes cast by the convention.

The spirit of the convention was also shown in the more heated discussion of the "Russian question" and of reaffiliation with Amsterdam. With regard to Russia, the convention upheld the Executive Council and approved Secretary of State Charles E. Hughes' policy of not extending credit to, or promoting trade with, Russia as long as its political and economic system remained unchanged. The convention also approved, with only a few dissenting votes, the attack of the Executive Council on the Third International and on the Red International of Labor Unions. But with regard to Amsterdam, the convention recommended that negotiations be continued with a view to eventual affiliation.

Relations between the AF of L and the IFTU were soon further strained as a result of the Washington Conference on the Limitation of Armaments called by President Harding in the fall of 1921. In accordance with a resolution passed at the Denver convention to support the Conference, the Executive Council wrote to the Amsterdam Bureau for assistance. It received no satisfactory response. Gompers then addressed the trade union centers of England, France, and Italy, urging them to request their governments to appoint labor delegates on the technical commissions of the Conference. The Management Committee of Amsterdam resented this, and an unfriendly correspondence ensued. When the regular congress of the IFTU held at Rome in April, 1922, endorsed all the policies to which the AF of L had objected, the Executive Council of the AF of L decided that the Rome Congress had made it more difficult to arrive at an agreement. It was upheld in its decision by the 1922 convention of the AF of L in Cincinnati.

## V. NOTE OF RECONCILIATION

Nevertheless, during 1923-24 the attitude of the AF of L toward Amsterdam began to change. In part, this was due to the efforts of Johann Sassenbach, the German-speaking secretary of the IFTU who replaced Oudegeest in 1923 in conducting correspondence with the AF of L, and who adopted a friendly and conciliatory tone. A more important factor was the increasing activity of the Communists in the American labor movement. From 1919 to 1922, the American Communists had been absorbed in political issues, quarreling among themselves and with the socialists as to the exact meaning of "proletarian dictatorship" and as to the tactics for establishing such a dictatorship. As a result of these quarrels and personal animosities, the Communists split up into groups which had little contact with, and still less influence on, the trade unions.

But beginning in 1922, the American Communists changed their tactics. They organized themselves into a legal party—the Workers' Party of America—and started to apply the policy of the United Front in the trade unions. William Z. Foster formed the Trade Union Educational League, which began a systematic work of "boring from within" and of building cells and nuclei in factories and in the labor unions, in accordance with the decisions and instructions of the Moscow Internationals. Between 1922 and 1924, the Trade Union Educational League made some headway in the unions in the clothing and textile industries, in mining, in the machine trades, and in some of the railroad shop crafts. In the latter, feeling ran high as a result of wage cutting, injunctions, and the 1922 strike, which was disastrous for the union. In several other industries, the trade unions, which had brought about many improvements in working conditions during the preceding decade, were finding it hard to hold their own because of the postwar depression, overdevelopment, and excessive competition. By concentrating on the weak spots in these unions and by indiscriminate attacks on the leaders, the Trade Union Educational League was able to mobilize some of the discontented elements under its banner.

The fight against this "radical menace" broke the ice between the AF of L and the IFTU. The leaders of the AF of L saw that their fight was but a phase of the general international conflict against communism which Amsterdam and the Socialist International were conducting in Europe. They also became less apprehensive of the socialists as they realized that the American Socialist Party, which was reduced to a shadow of its former self as a result of Communist tactics during 1919-1923, was ready to help the labor unions in their fight against the Communists and the Trade Union Educational League.

The more friendly attitude of the AF of L toward the Amsterdam International was shown at the El Paso convention in October, 1924. For the first time since 1920, the hope was expressed that reaffiliation of the AF of L with the IFTU would take place in the not distant future.

C H A P T E R    X I

# Pan-American Labor
## 1918-1924

IN ITS relations with Amsterdam, the American Federation of Labor was much influenced by developments in Latin America. Impelled at first to turn its attention in that direction by political more than by economic considerations, the AF of L soon discovered there what it came to regard as its special opportunity. Here was a continent with new and growing labor movements which had many interests in common with the labor movement of the United States. If coordinated, these labor movements seemed capable of counteracting the preponderance of Europe in international labor relations. Slowly but steadily, the AF of L became interested in accomplishing this end by developing a Pan-American labor organization.

### I. PAVING THE WAY

The beginnings of inter-American labor relations may be traced to the late eighties and early nineties of the past century. It was during those years that Samuel Gompers, working as a cigarmaker in New York, came in contact with Cuban revolutionists who sought refuge and work in the United States, and became interested in their struggle for political independence. Under his influence, the AF of L at its 1896 convention endorsed the demands of the Cuban revolutionists. After the Spanish-American War, the AF of L demanded "freedom and independence" for Cuba, and protested against "forcing our system of government upon an unwilling people," whether in Cuba, Puerto Rico, or the Philippines.

*Puerto Rico and Mexico*

At the AF of L convention in 1900, Santiago Iglesias, a Spanish syndicalist who had emigrated to Puerto Rico and started organizing labor unions there, presented a report on labor conditions on the island, which he described as oppressive. The convention voted $3,000 for a campaign on behalf of free speech, freedom of assembly, fair trials, and civil government. In 1901, the Puerto Rican unions became affiliated with the AF of L; in 1902 they sent delegates to the AF of L convention. Iglesias was appointed organizer on the AF of L payroll to promote trade union organization in Puerto Rico. By this time, the AF of L had recognized that Puerto Rico would become a possession of the United States and wanted to encourage the "complete fraternization" of the Puerto Rican workers with the American labor movement.

Between 1908 and 1914, the AF of L also became interested in Mexico. A number of American trade unions were concerned about the immigration of low-paid and semiservile Mexican laborers into the border states of the Southwest. Convinced that the condition of Mexican labor was the result of the Diaz dictatorship, they lent support to the political parties or "juntas" which were fighting against Diaz. John Murray, a member of the International Typographical Union, took up the cause of the Liberal Party of Mexico with zeal and aroused Gompers' enthusiasm for it.

As a result of the teamwork of these two men, the AF of L was won over to the Mexican revolutionary movement. In 1910, when the revolution against Diaz was begun by Madero under the banner of "Land and Liberty," the AF of L used its influence against intervention by the United States. When Madero was assassinated in 1913, the AF of L "helped in sustaining the attitude of the American Government in its refusal to recognize Huerta." In 1914, it supported Carranza.

Regardless of this friendly attitude, the AF of L could not establish close relations with the Mexican labor organizations at this time. As in other countries of Latin America, labor in Mexico received its baptism in trade unionism from men who thought in syndicalist and socialist terms. The first Mexican unions, which were formed between 1904 and 1910 among cigarmakers, carpenters, boilermakers, blacksmiths, textile and railroad workers, were led by Spanish syndicalists and socialists or by Mexicans who had been influenced by them and by the IWW. These men loomed up as leaders in the new unions which began to be formed rapidly after the revolution. They also became predominant in the federation of trade unions which was brought into being in July, 1912, under the name of the *Casa del Obrero Mundial* (House of the Workers of the World). The program of this federation embodied the doctrines of syndicalism as developed in France and Spain and as modified by the IWW in the United States. They advocated direct action, sabotage, the general strike, and ultimate social revolution. For men and women of such views and antecedents, and in the midst of revolution, the AF of L held no attraction.

## South America

The same may be said of the labor movements in the South American republics. The relations of the United States with South America before 1914 were slight. The cultural affinities of the countries were with Spain and France; their financial and commercial relations were chiefly with England and Germany. Accordingly, the labor movements of these countries followed the patterns either of German socialism or French-Spanish syndicalism, introduced by native intellectuals educated abroad or by immigrants from Germany, Spain, and Italy. A socialist party was organized in Argentina as early as 1896 and it joined the Second International in 1904. The *Federacion Obrera Regional Argentina* (Argentine Regional Workers' Federation) was organized in 1901 under syndicalist influence, but it split into two separate trade unions—socialist and syndicalist—in 1905. In Brazil, a federation of labor was formed among German and Sicilian immigrants in 1906, while some native Portuguese formed socialist groups. Small socialist parties were organized in Chile in 1912 and in Uruguay in 1913. These trade union and political groups were not friendly to the AF of L in view of the latter's opposition to socialism.

## II. Mexican Civil War and World War

With the outbreak of the First World War, the AF of L, urged by Gompers, began to take a wider interest in Pan-American affairs. The war forced South America into closer business connections with the United States, which were further stimulated by the opening of the Panama Canal in 1915. When Gompers failed to obtain labor representation at the Pan-American Financial Conference held in Washington in May, 1915, he put forth the proposal for a Pan-American organization of labor. At the San Francisco convention of the AF of L in 1915, the Executive Council was instructed to enter into correspondence with Latin American labor unions and to invite them to a "great Pan-American convention" in Washington to consider the economic problems confronting Latin America as a result of "the fraternization and combinations between Wall Street and South American capitalists."

### Carranza and the "Casa del Obrero"

A favorable condition for carrying out the plan was created at this time by events in Mexico. During the civil war in which Carranza, Huerta, Villa, and Zapata were engaged between 1913 and 1915, the labor leaders threw their support to Carranza at a critical moment when his fate was in the balance. In return for this support, Carranza made a pact with the leaders of the *Casa del Obrero* promising them progressive labor legislation. The labor leaders then raised six "red battalions" composed of workers who fought under the banners of their trade unions—as tailors' battalions, stonemasons' battalions, and so on—and who helped to decide the issue in favor of Carranza.

Anxious to strengthen the Carranza government, the Mexican labor leaders turned to the AF of L for aid and support. Gompers, in his turn, was willing to overlook the radicalism of the Mexican labor movement in order to promote his Pan-American labor plans, and responded favorably.

Action was precipitated by the sudden crisis in Mexican-American relations in the spring of 1916, when some American soldiers who had crossed the Mexican border were arrested by Carranza's troops. The leaders of Mexican labor, the most influential of whom was Luis N. Morones, asked the AF of L to use influence with President Wilson to secure the withdrawal of the American expedition. Gompers on his own initiative wired Carranza on June 28, 1916, asking for the release of the American soldiers. Carranza acceded to this request the very next day, and the crisis was brought to an end. Following this successful collaboration, the leaders of the AF of L and of Mexican labor met on July 3 and agreed to cooperate in working out a plan for maintaining relations between the labor unions of the two countries.

For a while, the Mexican labor leaders were slow in living up to this agreement. They became absorbed during 1916-1917 in a struggle against Carranza, who after his triumph over Villa turned against labor because of the numerous strikes which swept Mexico, largely as a result of inflation caused by the revolution. Carranza dispersed the "red battalions," prohibited strikes, and tried to suppress the *Casa del Obrero*. He failed in this, as the labor unions consolidated their forces against him. Profiting by the struggle of political factions in the Queretaro constitutional convention of 1917, they obtained the inclusion in the Mexican Constitution of Article 123—the Magna Charta of Mexican Labor—which contained some of the most advanced protective labor provisions in the world.

## The AF of L and the CROM

Gompers, however, pursued his Pan-American plans, especially after the United States entered the First World War. On a smaller scale, the war produced in the labor and socialist organizations of Latin America divisions similar to those in Europe. In Argentina, Chile, and Peru there were antiwar groups, while in Mexico there was a strong current of opinion favorable to Germany. A Pan-American labor organization, as Gompers saw it, could counteract these antiwar and Germanophile tendencies and create favorable opinion for the cause of the Allies.

With this in mind, Gompers urged the Mexican labor leaders to push the plan for a Pan-American meeting. Mexican labor at this time was taking an important step toward reorganization. In May, 1918, delegates from unions in eighteen states of Mexico met in Saltillo, the capital of Coahuila, and laid the foundations of a new labor federation, the *Confederacion Regional Obrera Mexicana,* which became known as the CROM. The program adopted by this new federation was less radical than that of the *Casa del Obrero.* Though advocating the ultimate ownership and management of industry by the workers, it laid stress on immediate economic and social improvements such as land distribution and the enforcement of the newly adopted labor laws.

With the organization of the CROM under the leadership of Morones and Trevino, a more solid basis was created in Mexico for Gompers' plans. He sent a labor mission to Mexico for further discussions. He also persuaded President Wilson that Pan-American labor unity would help the war effort, and the President allotted several thousand dollars from his special funds to finance the publication near the Mexican border of a newspaper in Spanish and English, which was shipped in thousands of copies to Mexico and which advocated inter-American labor cooperation in the cause of the Allies.

### III. Foundation at Laredo

As a result of these efforts and activities, there was brought together at Laredo, Texas, on November 13, 1918, the first Pan-American labor conference. It was attended by forty-six delegates of AF of L unions, twenty-one delegates from Mexico, and one delegate each from Guatemala, Costa Rica, San Salvador, and Colombia. The delegates from the latter countries were mostly political refugees living in the United States and played little part in the proceedings.

The conference opened with expressions of cordiality, an "international celebration" on the plaza of Laredo, and official speeches by representatives of the American and Mexican governments. It then settled down to business, which brought out the points at issue. The Mexicans presented eight demands, the most important of which were for (1) the appointment by the AF of L and the CROM of resident representatives in border cities who would try to secure proper treatment for Mexican immigrants, (2) the extension to Mexicans of facilities for joining American unions with full privileges, (3) an agreement to secure justice for workers imprisoned in the United States, and (4) the exclusion from the conference of questions bearing on Mexican neutrality in the war and on the internal policies of either country.

In connection with the first two points, the Mexicans recounted the bad treatment which, they said, Mexican immigrants were receiving from U. S. immigration authorities, and the discrimination practiced against them by the American trade unions. These complaints were referred to the Executive Council of the AF of L for investigation and action. Point 3 developed into a debate on the IWW, many of whom were then in prison. Gompers denounced the IWW as "American Bolsheviks." Morones urged greater tolerance on the part of the AF of L but did not press for definite action.

Despite point 4, Gompers introduced a resolution endorsing the Treaty of Versailles, the League of Nations, and the International Labor Organization. The Mexicans objected strenuously, but finally voted for the resolution on the understanding that it would be subject to ratification by the Mexican labor organizations.

Composing their differences, the delegates adopted the report which formally organized the Pan-American Federation of Labor. Its main objectives were to be the betterment of conditions for workers migrating from one country to another, and the establishment of friendly relations between the labor movements and peoples of the Americas. Gompers was elected chairman of the Federation, John Murray its English-speaking secretary, and Canuto Vargas its Spanish-speaking secretary. Dues were to be paid by the affiliated organizations in proportion to membership. The labor organizations of each country were to send two delegates to the annual congresses.

## IV. Migration and Politics

From its foundation to its third congress in 1921, the Pan-American Federation of Labor was faced with the condition of labor unrest in Latin America which was part of the world upheaval described in preceding chapters. The older unions, whose membership increased, and the newer unions formed in many industries carried on strikes for higher wages and the eight-hour day. Some of these strikes assumed a violent character. On several occasions, Buenos Aires in Argentina, Callas and Lima in Peru, and the mining districts of Chile were paralyzed by general strikes and were in the hands of the labor organizations led by syndicalists, anarchists, IWW, Communists, and left-wing socialists. The governments used troops to put down these strikes and jailed many of the leaders.

In Mexico, the upheaval took the form of the so-called "revindicating revolution" of 1920. Its aim was to "revindicate the principles of 1917," which Carranza was accused of trying to violate by attempting to impose on the country as his successor a man chosen by himself. The revolution ended successfully with the election of General Alvaro Obregon to the Presidency. Mexican labor played a leading part in this revolution through the CROM and through the Partido Laborista Mexicano (Mexican Labor Party).

As in Europe, so in Latin America, the upheaval and reaction of 1919-1921 resulted in splitting the labor unions between various doctrinal groups. In Mexico, at the second congress of the CROM in 1920, groups of syndicalists and Communists, displeased with the political tendencies of the CROM, seceded and formed the *Confederacion General de Trabajadores* (General Confederation of Workers), which became known as the Mexican CGT. At first the CGT joined the Red International of Labor Unions, but late in 1921 it canceled its affiliation and made contacts with the Syndicalist International in Berlin. The CGT staged several large unsuccessful strikes, which weakened it. The chief effect of its activities was to help the CROM to clarify its position. The CROM emerged from the turmoil of 1919-1921 stronger economically and politically, bitterly opposed to the Communists and the syndicalists, and more definitely committed to methods and policies similar to those of the AF of L.

Despite the unrest of 1919-1921, the AF of L steered the Pan-American Federation of Labor upon a moderate course. It had, however, to work against an undercurrent of anti-American feeling, which came to the surface at the third congress of the Federation in 1921 in Mexico City. Aside from the immigration issue, the delegates from

Mexico, Peru, Ecuador, San Salvador, Nicaragua, and Santo Domingo voiced the belief that the AF of L had not sufficiently protested against President Wilson's interventionist policies in Santo Domingo and Nicaragua. Despite Gompers' reassurances, the congress protested against these policies and demanded the immediate evacuation of American marines from Santo Domingo. A telegram to this effect was sent to President Wilson, much to the latter's displeasure.

The Latin American delegates also wanted more recognition for their own brand of unionism, but on this issue they had little success. The platform which was adopted, while couched here and there in radical terms, emphasized only three definite ideas: the need of political freedom, the importance of collective bargaining, and the value of education to the workers of Latin America. The Mexico City Congress was significant as a demonstration of the friendly attitude of the AF of L toward the regime of President Obregon. He and his supporters were praised by Gompers and other American speakers as "men who have the best interests of the Mexican people at heart."

## V. A "Labor Monroe Doctrine"

During the four years from its third to its fourth congress in El Paso, Texas, in 1924, the Pan-American Federation of Labor made little headway. Owing to lack of funds, it failed to place organizers in the field, and owing to inadequate means of communication, it was incapable of establishing close connections with the labor movements of South America. In Central America, it was hampered by the fact that American policy in Nicaragua had contributed toward an Anti-American feeling among organized workers.

Against this background, the relations of the AF of L and the CROM stood out in their friendliness. The CROM during these years became the representative labor organization of Mexico. Its membership increased from 300,000 in 1920 to 1,200,000 in 1924; it included not only industrial workers but also agricultural laborers; it was the main support of the new Mexican state and of the Obregon government.

The CROM continued to place great value on friendly relations with the AF of L. During 1923-1924, the chief interest of the CROM was to assure the good will of the United States for General Plutarco Calles as successor to President Obregon. On the other hand, the leaders of the AF of L were worried not only by the inroads which the Red International of Labor Unions and the Syndicalist International of Berlin were making in Latin America, but also by Amsterdam's plan to seek direct affiliation of Latin American trade unions.

Representatives of the AF of L and of the CROM met at El Paso in the fall of 1923 and reached an agreement on these matters. The Mexican labor leaders reassured the AF of L that they would not affiliate with Amsterdam or any other International without first consulting with it. Under Gompers' inspiration, the American and Mexican delegations jointly announced what they termed a "Monroe Doctrine of Labor," that they would oppose efforts on the part of European labor to encroach upon the "sovereignty" of labor in the Western Hemisphere.

In their turn, the officers of the AF of L expressed their sympathy with President Obregon, who was then engaged in quelling the revolt of Adolpho de la Huerta. Gompers wrote to Secretary of State Hughes asking that the law against shipping arms into Mexico be strictly enforced. American trade unionists, especially the International Association of Machinists and the Seamen's Union, became active in blocking the activities of de la Huerta agents in the border cities and in preventing shipments of arms to them. American organized labor thus played an important part in the crushing of the revolt and in the victory of the Obregon government. In November, 1924, a delegation from the AF of L attended the inauguration of President Calles in Mexico City, which was made the occasion for "fraternal celebrations."

The success of the cooperation between the CROM and the AF of L was the main topic of discussion at the fourth congress of the Pan-American Federation of Labor at El Paso in December, 1924. The congress demonstrated that, if not entirely successful in his larger plans, Gompers had succeeded in cementing a Mexican-American labor alliance and in making it a factor in American-Mexican relations. The affirmation of this alliance at the El Paso Congress was Gompers' last public act. He died on his way back from El Paso to Washington.

## PART FOUR

# Stabilization and Reorganization

## 1924-1929

# The Movement for Unity
## 1924-1926

AFTER five years of turmoil, the year 1924 brought signs of a turn toward industrial recovery and social stability. The German reparations problem seemed to be in process of solution through the Dawes Plan;[1] the German mark was stabilized; international loans for the rebuilding and rationalizing of German industry were floated; most countries of Europe gave evidence of economic improvement. In international politics, peaceful trends came to the fore, as shown by the growing influence of the League of Nations and the negotiations for the Locarno treaties.[2] In the world of labor, the feeling that a new era of stability was setting in gained ground.

However, in some countries, particularly in England, the trade unions feared that monetary stabilization would involve them in difficult problems of readjusting wages and labor standards. The British trade unionists thus became eager to bring about a unification of international labor organizations in the hope that it would help them meet their problems. They began a movement for labor unity which continued during 1924-1926 and was one of the factors in the trade union reorganizations of these years.

---

[1] The Dawes Plan provided for annual reparation payments by Germany of one billion marks, increasing gradually to two and a half billion at the end of five years; Germany was to get a foreign loan of eight hundred million gold marks.

[2] The Locarno treaties provided for mutual guarantee of frontiers and for arbitration treaties between various European countries.

97

## I. THE BRITISH PROPOSAL

The British made their first move at the fourth congress of the IFTU[3] which opened in Vienna on June 2, 1924, demanding that the Management Committee of the IFTU open negotiations with the Soviet trade unions for unification. Because of their attitude on the "Russian question," the British labor leaders—A. Purcell, George Hicks, and J. W. Brown—came to be regarded as a "left wing" within Amsterdam. Their influence was considerable, since the British Trades Union Congress was the strongest member of the IFTU; the German trade unions had not yet recovered from the debacle of 1923, and the AF of L was not affiliated. After heated debates, the Vienna Congress passed a resolution regretting the absence of the Russians and directing the Amsterdam Bureau to continue consultations with them insofar as that was compatible with the dignity of the IFTU. It was stipulated that the Soviet trade unions would be admitted to the IFTU if they accepted its rules and conditions of membership.

To placate the British further, A. Purcell was elected president of the IFTU. J. W. Brown was appointed English-speaking secretary, in addition to the two other secretaries—Jan Oudegeest of Holland and Johann Sassenbach of Germany.

## II. RESPONSE OF MOSCOW

Soon after the Amsterdam Congress at Vienna, the Third International held its fifth congress in Moscow. The leaders of the Third International still hoped for "violent struggles" in the immediate future, but they were no longer certain whether these struggles would end in the "downfall of capitalism" or in its stabilization. The Third International was also rocked by internal dissensions. The Communist parties in the different countries of Europe were split into Right and Left wings which either opposed or misapplied the policy of the United Front and which defied the authority of the Executive Committee of the Third International and its Russian leadership.

Under these conditions, the Moscow Congress was mainly con-

[3] In this and the following chapters, IFTU, which are the initials standing for the International Federation of Trade Unions, is used interchangeably with "Amsterdam."

cerned with reasserting the control of the Russian Communist Party. The congress condemned all "deviations" to the Right and to the Left. The program adopted was declared to be an application of Marxism-Leninism, thus coupling for the first time the names of Marx and Lenin as exponents of Communist doctrine. The statutes of the Third International were revised so as to make it a more centralized "world party"—a "monolith hewn out of a single block." The policy of the United Front was reaffirmed.

In accordance with these decisions, the Red International of Labor Unions, which held its third congress immediately afterward, launched the slogan of "international unity" in the trade union movement. The leaders of the RILU proposed that a "world unity" congress be held at which Amsterdam and the RILU would be proportionately represented and a new international labor organization would be formed.

It was on the heels of these developments that the Executive Bureau of the IFTU in July, 1924, invited the All-Soviet Council of Trade Unions to affiliate with it. The Russians replied by requesting a conference between the IFTU and the RILU on the basis of "equality and mutual attention." The IFTU Executive Bureau asked for "something in writing" as a basis for discussion. Tomski, as chairman of the All-Soviet Council of Trade Unions, replied that the Russians would cooperate in a trade union international whose guiding principle was "class war to the knife." He requested a preliminary meeting between the IFTU and the Russian unions to talk matters over. On December 5, 1924, Oudegeest informed Tomski that the Executive Bureau of the IFTU had no competence to pass on such a proposal, and that it would be submitted to the next meeting of the General Council of the IFTU.

### III. THE ANGLO-RUSSIAN COMMITTEE

When the General Council met on February 5, 1925, the British delegates urged that a conference without conditions be called by the IFTU with the Russian trade unions. This was rejected by a vote of 13 to 6. A resolution was adopted to the effect that the IFTU would convene a conference with the All-Soviet Council of Trade Unions only after the latter indicated a desire to affiliate.

Displeased with this resolution, the leaders of the British Trades Union Congress held a meeting with representatives of the Soviet trade unions in April, 1925, and signed an agreement of cooperation. The Russians were to notify Amsterdam that they were willing to join a trade union international not essentially different from the IFTU. The British were to induce Amsterdam to call an unconditional conference with the Russians. If Amsterdam persisted in its refusal, the British themselves were to convene a trade union conference "to promote international unity." A joint Anglo-Russian Advisory Committee was formed to carry out the agreement.

### IV. Divergent Policies

Developments during 1925 and the early part of 1926 continued to stimulate the interest of the labor movements of Europe in the question of unity. In England, Germany, Sweden, and several other countries, labor and liberal governments gave way during 1925 to conservative governments unfriendly to organized labor. Though world economic conditions continued to improve, there was much unemployment in England and Germany, while France and Belgium were in the throes of inflation. Big strikes against wage cuts, counteracted by lockouts, took place in Sweden and Denmark, among seamen in England, and in the textile industries of Germany and Austria. An Asian labor movement emerged with the strikes of cotton mill operatives in Shanghai and 135,000 textile workers in Bombay, while a wave of nationalist unrest swept the colonial countries from Morocco to Egypt, Syria, and India.

In trying to cope with these developments, Amsterdam and the Socialist International, on the one hand, and the Moscow Internationals, on the other, followed divergent lines. Amsterdam and the socialists accepted the Dawes Plan as "the only possible solution," though criticizing what they regarded as its defects. They greeted the Locarno agreements as the "first step towards the pacification of Europe." They hailed the "awakening of the great working masses of the Chinese, Indian, and Mohammedan world," called for the abolition of extraterritorial rights in China and for modern labor legislation for Chinese workers, and condemned the French Socialist Party for supporting the Painlevé and Herriot governments in the Riffian and

Syrian wars. Amsterdam sent some $13,000 to the strikers of Bombay, and collected about a million dollars for the locked-out workers of Scandinavia, which helped the Danish workers to win their demands and the workers of Sweden to make a more favorable settlement. In general, while criticizing official government policies, Amsterdam and the socialists promoted the trends toward peace and stability.

On the other hand, the Third International and the RILU steered a zigzag course. Zinoviev and his associates admitted now that the "bourgeois world" was becoming stabilized owing to the Dawes Plan. But they denounced the Dawes Plan *in toto* and called upon their followers to obstruct its operations.

The Third International at this time was losing ground in Europe. The Communist parties were losing members in most countries. They were being destroyed or driven underground in Italy, Spain, the Balkans, and the Baltic countries. The German Communists, under Left leadership, were in rebellion against the Executive Committee of the Third International and were denouncing the Russian Communist leaders for "bureaucracy" and "opportunism." The reason for this quarrel was the fact that the Third International had censured the German Communists for defying the policy of the United Front and for refusing to support for the presidency of the German Republic the former Chancellor, Wilhelm Marx, who was the coalition candidate of the Socialist and Republican Parties. The Communists had put up a candidate of their own, thus splitting the labor vote and assuring the election of Marshal Hindenburg. In France, the Communist Party had lost much of its following as a result of the action of the Right-wing elements who in the elections of 1924 had made deals with other political parties. The Executive Committee of the Third International had stepped in to "purify" the French party, but had created more dissensions in the process. The French Communist Party alienated some of its members also by its unsuccessful attempt to obstruct French military operations in Morocco in 1925.

Discouraged by events in Europe, the leaders of the Third International turned their attention to the rising nationalist movements in Asia. Communists were urged everywhere to pursue an aggressive "anti-imperialist" policy. They staged demonstrations in England,

France, the United States, and elsewhere with the slogan "Hands off China." The RILU sent about $15,000 to the strikers in Shanghai.

## V. Amsterdam and the Anglo-Russian Committee

Despite these divergent policies, agitation for labor unification continued. On May 10, 1925, Tomski sent a letter to Amsterdam so worded as to fulfill formally the agreement of the Anglo-Russian Committee and yet maintain the original Russian demands. The British labor leaders at the same time called for a reconsideration of Amsterdam's decision of February 5, 1925. The impression was created that the British were not averse to breaking up Amsterdam in order to organize a new trade union international.

In view of this, the Continental leaders of Amsterdam went to London on December 1, 1925, to sound out the British trade union leaders. The British explained that they were opposed to Communist principles and that they had no intention of breaking away from Amsterdam. But they wanted to give the Russian unions all the consideration possible in order to heal the split in the trade union movement.

Thus reassured, the Amsterdam General Council, on December 4, 1925, reaffirmed its decision of February 5, against the votes of the British members of the Council. In February, 1926, the British requested that the matter be reconsidered, but their request was declined by Amsterdam's Executive Bureau. The Continental leaders of Amsterdam argued that the British were being duped by the Russians, who were trying to gain admission to the IFTU in order to disrupt it from within.

## VI. Failure of Socialist-Communist Unity

Concurrently with the negotiations for trade union unity, the British Independent Labour Party tried to bring the Socialist and Third Internationals together for the purpose of forming an "all-inclusive" political International to fight "capitalist and imperialist reaction and the menace of fascism." But as soon as the proposal was made public, in March, 1926, Zinoviev declared that the Communist answer was "No. A thousand times no!" and that unity could be based only on "communism, on Leninism." In its turn, the Executive Committee of the Socialist International at its session in Zurich on April 13, 1926, rejected the proposal by a vote of 247 to 3, the British Labour Party also voting against it.

## VII. THE BRITISH STRIKES OF 1926

Though efforts for unity failed, the year 1926 witnessed the greatest manifestation of labor solidarity in the history of the international labor movement. It was evoked by the strike of the British coal miners in April, 1926, against wage reductions owing to the decline of the industry. The International Miners' Federation at first considered calling an international strike of coal miners, but then decided in favor of an embargo on imports and exports of coal into and from Great Britain. On May 3, the International Federation of Transport Workers, in response to the request of the British miners, wired its affiliated unions in most countries of Europe to stop all movements of coal to England and to prevent the bunkering of coal and the recruitment of crews for British ships.

On May 4, the General Council of the British Trades Union Congress declared a general strike in support of the miners. The same day, the Amsterdam Bureau wired its affiliated centers, as well as non-affiliated trade unions in the United States, Mexico, South Africa, Australia, India, and Japan, asking for aid in enforcing the embargo and for funds.

The response to these requests was extraordinary. Railwaymen, dockers, and other transport workers in Denmark, Sweden, Norway, Holland, and France enforced the embargo with vigilance. In Germany, the transport workers' union refused to handle coal or strikebreakers for England. The Christian trade unions of the Ruhr joined with those affiliated to Amsterdam to prevent German coal from going to England. The Polish unions at Danzig forbade all coal exports. In Czechoslovakia, the miners' and railwaymen's unions placed "Trade Union Control Commissions" at the frontiers to stop increased exports of coal. Measures intended for the same purpose, though less radical in character, were taken by the trade unions of Canada, Mexico, India, and Australia. Soviet transport workers and dockers held up all British ships in Russian ports, and Russian ships on their way to England were instructed by wireless to join the strike on their arrival in British ports.

The financial aid extended was large. Besides giving varying amounts from their general funds, the trade unions of many countries made collections in the shops and the streets and imposed special "solidarity assessments" on their members. The collections for the British miners, during the six and a half months of the strike, totaled $9,375,000. Of this sum, about $3,000,000 were contributed by the workers and people of England, about $5,750,000 by the Russian trade unions, and about $650,000 by the trade unions of other countries. The contributions of the Amsterdam unions were relatively small, as many of them were in a weakened financial condition as a result of inflation and recent costly strikes.

A few days after the general strike began, the British Trades Union Council asked that the embargo be extended to all goods destined for England and that a complete embargo be placed on the discharge of all British ships in European ports. On May 8, representatives of the International Miners' Federation, the International Federation of Transport Workers, and the IFTU met at Ostend to consider the British request. Both measures involved great difficulties; a complete embargo threatened in some countries to stop the national industries from receiving necessary raw materials. In view of this, the three Federations decided to request the trade unions in different countries to extend the embargo only "if possible."

The activities on behalf of the British miners were having only partial effects. Exports of coal to England were seriously interfered with, and the bunkering of British ships in most European ports was reduced to a minimum. But the extension of the embargo to all merchandise going to England was not making much headway. With every day of the general strike, the difficulties of international labor action increased. The British trade union leaders, facing the determined opposition of the British government and the general public, were too absorbed in their problems to keep Amsterdam fully informed. The Amsterdam Bureau and Edo Fimmen, the secretary of the International Federation of Transport Workers, who carried the brunt of the international campaign, found themselves hampered by lack of information. Many trade unions on the Continent were unwilling to do anything which would be in violation of their agreements with their employers.

On May 12, a joint meeting of the Executive Committees of Amsterdam and of the Socialist International was held to consider further support for the British strikers. None of the British members arrived to report on the situation. The members of the Socialist International then decided that the strike was industrial in character, and that whatever international aid it needed should be given by Amsterdam.

While these meetings were in session, the British Trades Union Congress called off the general strike. That changed the situation. Under its rules, the IFTU could not collect funds for a strike in a single industry, as that was the function of the International Trade Secretariats.

The International Federation of Transport Workers not only had to drop its plans for the extension of the embargo to all merchandise, but found itself in an embarrassing position with regard to the embargo on coal. Though Ernest Bevin, Secretary of the British Transport Workers, requested that the international embargo on coal be continued, British transport workers were resuming work and handling all goods, including British and foreign coal. In view of that, Fimmen rescinded previous instructions to non-British transport workers and authorized them to handle British vessels in Continental ports.

With the collapse of the embargo, A. J. Cook, secretary of the British Miners' Federation, again suggested that an international miners' strike be called. He was opposed by Frank Hodges, secretary of the International Miners' Federation, who felt that the coal miners of Germany and other countries could not be expected to make the sacrifice. The International Miners' Federation discussed the question for several months, but kept putting off a decision until the strike came to an end.

Soon after the general strike was called off, the British Trades Union Congress turned to Amsterdam for help in rebuilding its financial structure. The largest and strongest trade unions of England had depleted their funds during the general strike, and the General Council of the Trades Union Congress was in financial straits. A special conference was called with the Amsterdam organizations on May 31, at which it was agreed to make a loan to the British Trades Union Congress in the amount of $380,000. The loan was consummated in July, 1926.

## VIII. End of the Anglo-Russian Committee

As soon as the general strike was called off, the Third International and the RILU let loose a torrent of abuse against British labor leaders, as well as against the International Miners' Federation and the IFTU, for "sabotaging" and "betraying" the British workers. Regardless of such abuse, the Soviet trade union leaders demanded that the Anglo-Russian Committee be convened to consider further aid to the British miners. The British acceded to this request and met with the Russians in Paris in July and in Berlin in August. At the Paris meeting, the British told the Russians in no uncertain terms that they would not "grant any one the right to interfere in the internal affairs of the British trade union movement." At the Berlin meeting, the British rejected the Russian proposals for another embargo and for a condemnation of Amsterdam.

A compromise was reached, however, at the Berlin meeting on "international unity." The British again promised to try to arrange a preliminary conference "without any restrictive conditions" between the IFTU and the Russian trade unions. Despite this agreement, the Berlin meeting marked a breach in the Anglo-Russian Committee. The breach was widened when Tomski, in September, 1926, sent a telegram to the Bournemouth conference of the British Trades Union Congress heaping abuse and criticism on the British trade unions and offering them unsolicited advice. The reply of the British Trades Union Congress was a sharp protest against such "ill-instructed and presumptuous criticism."

The movement toward unity between Amsterdam and the All-Soviet Council of Trade Unions, and between the latter and the British Trades Union Congress, thus came to an end, though the fact was not formally acknowledged until a year later.

# Revisions and Realignments
## 1926-1928

THE events of 1926 left in their trail much bad feeling between the labor leaders of different countries and of the different organizations. During 1927, problems of policy and tactics and personal animosities caused internal strains in the Amsterdam as well as in the Moscow Internationals so that they seemed to be on the verge of breaking up. However, the internal crises ended in a revision of programs and strategy, and in a realignment of forces which established a new balance of power within the several internationals and between them. The course of these developments is described below, first in Amsterdam, then in the Moscow internationals, and lastly in the Pan-American labor movement.

## I. Reorganization of Amsterdam

Soon after the strike of the British coal miners, the moderate elements of Amsterdam (its so-called "right wing")—led by Oudegeest, Jouhaux, Sassenbach, Leipart, and Mertens—decided to face the two main problems which were causing internal friction. The first was the "Russian question," which the British brought up again at a session of the Executive Bureau of the IFTU in February, 1927. The majority of the Bureau put an end to this question by ruling that no change could be made in the position taken by the General Council in 1926. That ended formally for the time being further efforts for the admission of the Soviet trade unions to the IFTU.

The second problem was that of relations with the British "left wing." This problem took much of the time of the fourth congress of the Amsterdam International held in Paris in August, 1927. J. W. Brown, the English-speaking secretary, accused Oudegeest and the Amsterdam Bureau of hypocrisy and unfairness in their negotiations with the Russians. He was supported by Walter Citrine, head of the British delegation. A special committee was appointed to investigate the matter. It upheld Oudegeest, and its findings were endorsed by the congress over the objections of the British.

Conflict broke out again in connection with the election of officers. The British insisted on having A. Purcell reelected president of Amsterdam. Theodore Leipart, secretary of the German Federation of Trade Unions, supported by the Dutch, Swedish, and Danish delegates, refused to accept Purcell and proposed another British delegate, George Hicks, instead. The British delegation would not agree to this and left the hall of the congress, followed by the delegates from Palestine, South Africa, and India. These proceedings were taken as a setback for the British left wing and as a comeback for the Germans who led the fight against Purcell.

The Paris Congress of 1927 made a thorough change in the Amsterdam organization. Both Oudegeest and Brown resigned as secretaries and their offices were abolished. Henceforth, the IFTU was to have only one general secretary. The General Council was enlarged, and the headquarters were to be removed from Amsterdam to another place.

The manner in which the British delegates walked out of the Paris Congress heartened the Communists, but their comfort was not to last long. On September 8, 1927, the British Trades Union Congress, meeting at Edinburgh, decided by a vote of 2,551,000 to 620,000 to break off relations with the All-Soviet Council of Trade Unions, thus ending formally the career of the Anglo-Russian Committee. At the same time, the British labor leaders made clear that their behavior in Paris was merely a protest against what they regarded as wrong procedure, but that it did not mean a break with Amsterdam.

On September 25-26, 1927, the General Council of the IFTU held a special meeting in which the British members took part.

Walter Citrine, secretary of the British Trades Union Congress, was elected president of the IFTU and Johann Sassenbach was appointed general secretary. Amsterdam was retained as headquarters until further action by the IFTU congress in 1930. Thus, the Amsterdam International came into 1928 with a reorganized structure, revised program, and new leadership.

## II. TRIUMPH OF STALIN

Of far greater intensity and scope was the internal crisis in the Third International. By the summer of 1926, it had become honeycombed with "factions" of Rights and "ultra-Rights," Lefts and "ultra-Lefts," who disputed with one another the leadership of the Communist parties in different countries. The greatest schism developed in Russia, where various dissident groups—led by Trotsky, Zinoviev, Kamenev, Radek, and others—formed an "opposition bloc" against Stalin and his followers for the purpose of gaining control over the Central Committee of the Communist Party. This meant also a struggle for control both of the Soviet government and of the Third International.

The issues around which this struggle centered covered the whole range of Communist Party organization and policy. The "opposition" accused Stalin and his supporters of having formed an inner clique which was ruling the Communist Party high-handedly and suppressing free discussion within the party. They demanded more "democracy" within the party and larger powers and functions for the trade unions.

In matters of Soviet domestic policy, the opposition directed its attacks against the NEP (the New Economic Policy introduced by Lenin in 1921). There was no question that, thanks to the NEP and several good harvests, Russian agriculture and industry had increased their output, and improved their position. It was also clear that the NEP was reviving prerevolutionary social patterns. Though the national ownership of land remained, the peasants under the NEP were allowed to cultivate their land as they saw fit, to employ hired labor, to sell their produce to cooperatives and private individuals, and to make profits. Under the circumstances, the Russian village was again experiencing a differentiation into the three traditional classes of rich peasants (kulaks), so-called "middle peasants," and poor peasants.

In the cities, the NEP mushroomed the growth of small private industrial enterprises which produced for the local and peasant markets. Privately owned shops and stores sprang up everywhere, and a growing number of merchants, commission men, and private "capitalists" were operating as middlemen between the city and the village. Though the large-scale industries such as mining, iron and steel, textiles, oil, and transportation remained nationalized and were managed by government "trusts" and syndicates, the "private sector" of the economy was growing and playing an increasing role.

The overwhelming majority of the workers were in the large-scale nationalized industries. Their wages, hours of work, and conditions of employment were fixed by collective agreements between the trade unions and the managers of the trusts and syndicates. As the managers were expected to make profits, they tried to increase productivity by introducing methods of scientific management, piecework, and other schemes of "rationalization." The workers too became differentiated into various groups depending on their skill and earnings.

Between these groups and classes there developed between 1923 and 1927 an economic struggle, which centered around prices and taxes. As Russian industry was unable to supply the market with manufactured goods, industrial prices rose out of proportion to agricultural prices, which were fixed by the government. The richer and middle peasants withheld grain from the market, upsetting the government's export plans. Private traders made capital out of the government's predicament, while the workers suffered from low and irregular wage payments and from unemployment. The Soviet government tried to placate the peasants by shifting prices and taxes in their favor and by other concessions.

It was these developments that the opposition viewed with alarm. In the opinion of the opposition groups, Russia was drifting toward capitalism and the future of the Russian Revolution was in jeopardy. As the capitalistic elements were growing rapidly, they claimed, the Soviet state and the government industries were becoming more and more dependent on them for food, raw materials, and export surpluses. If the trends of the NEP were allowed to continue, the opposition argued, the kulaks in the villages, the private traders in the towns, and the "intellectuals" holding high positions in industry and government were bound to become conscious of their power, and, backed by the capitalists of the rest of the world, threaten the existence of the Soviet system and the "proletarian dictatorship."

The opposition blamed the Soviet government and the Russian Communist Party for these developments. It argued that by their tax and price policies, they had prevented a sufficient rise in wages, had enriched the peasants, and had made impossible a rapid industrialization of the country. Even more serious than that, according to the opposition, was the effort of the Russian Communist Party to sacrifice the cause of the "world revolution" to the alleged interests of Russian reconstruction. According to the opposition, Stalin and his "henchmen" were doing violence to Marxist and Leninist principles in order to maintain themselves in power, and were spinning a false theory that it was possible to "build socialism in one country" while the rest of the world remained capitalistic.

In reply to the opposition, Stalin and Bukharin maintained that their policy was winning the good will of the middle peasants—the mainstay of Russian agricultural life—and stimulating the managers of industry to improve production methods and to lower costs, which meant higher real wages for the workers. Private capital, they claimed further, was playing a subordinate part in the Soviet economy, while the socialistic elements were growing rapidly. They quoted from Marx, Engels, and Lenin to prove that it was possible to "build socialism in one country," especially in a country like Russia which had a large internal market and abundant resources. Finally, they argued that the building of socialism in Russia would help the international revolutionary movement because it gave assurance that when another revolutionary outbreak came, Russia would be in a position to help it with the economic and military strength which it would have built up. The Stalinists denied that there was a lack of "democracy" within the party, but insisted that no "factions" could be allowed as they weakened party discipline and obstructed the work of reconstruction.

The opposition in Russia encouraged the dissident Communist

groups in other countries. Rights and ultra-Rights, Lefts and ultra-Lefts, made fun of the "peasant king Stalin," denounced the "kulak-ized" regime in Soviet Russia and the "bureaucracy" of the Russian Communist Party, and called for a "revolution" against its Central Committee and its dominating influence in the Third International. The phrase "Thermidorean reaction," coined by Trotsky to indicate an alleged parallel between the turn in the French Revolution (when Robespierre was overthrown in 1794) and events in Russia, became the rallying cry of the oppositional forces in the Third International, and Trotsky became their spokesman.

In the fall of 1926, it seemed for a while as if a compromise was about to be reached. The leaders of the opposition signed a statement promising to carry on their agitation within the limits of party regulations. As they ignored their promise almost at once, disciplinary measures were taken against them. Trotsky was excluded from the Politbureau of the Russian Communist Party and Zinoviev was forced to resign as president of the Third International. The most vociferous Rights and Lefts in various countries were expelled from their respective Communist parties.

The final phase of the battle was fought in 1927. With regard to Soviet domestic policy, the opposition attacked the draft of the first Five-Year Plan as soon as it was made known by the Gosplan (State Planning Commission). According to the leaders of the opposition, the funds allotted in the Plan for the development of large-scale nationalized industries were inadequate; not enough was allowed for improvements in wages, housing conditions, and social insurance; a greater burden of taxes was imposed on the industrial workers than on the peasants. The opposition groups put forth their own program, which called for a compulsory loan on the rich peasants, for an excess-profits tax on private enterprise, and for a reduction in prices of consumer goods. In Communist terms, the opposition called for pursuing a sharper "class struggle" and for accentuating the "proletarian dictatorship."

In the international field, the opposition of 1927 shifted the center of its attacks to the Far East. In the early phase of the Nationalist successes in China, the Russian Communists and the Third International had taken the position that the Chinese Revolution was similar to the Russian Revolution of 1905, that is, agrarian-industrial-democratic in character. Even after Generalissimo Chiang Kai-shek in the fall of 1927 expelled the Chinese Communist Party from the Kuomintang, the Executive Committee of the Third International, following Stalin and Bukharin, advised the Chinese Communists to stay in the Hankow government, but to promote trade unions and stir up agrarian discontent. The Third International blamed the troubles of the Chinese Communists on the Chinese Left, which it censured for disobeying instructions and for making extravagant claims as to the character and goals of the Chinese revolution.

The policy of the Third International in China was criticized by the opposition as opportunist and dictated entirely by the interests of Russia. The opposition was in sympathy with the Chinese Left Communists and demanded that the Third International give them active support.

As the discussion grew warmer, the opposition in Russia grew bolder. It organized local and central committees and set up illegal printing presses to print its literature. Outside of Russia, the Left groups formed an International Left Communist Federation. The plan of the opposition was to build up an organization which could overthrow the leadership of Stalin in the Russian Communist Party and in the Third International and step into his place of power.

The official party administration now accused the opposition of trying to form a "second party" in Russia, which was a high crime against party discipline. After several warnings, the Central Control Committee of the Russian Communist Party held a meeting in August, 1927, to consider the expulsion of Trotsky and Zinoviev from the Executive Committee of the Party. Impressed by this move, the several leaders of the opposition issued a declaration that they were devoted to the defense of the "socialist fatherland" and did not intend to form a second party, but that they would continue to defend their ideas. In fact, the opposition continued its agitation. During the celebrations of the tenth anniversary of the Bolshevik Revolution, they staged anti-Stalinist demonstrations in Moscow and Leningrad.

The Russian Communist Party and the Third International then took the final steps. In October, 1927, Trotsky was excluded from the

Executive Committee of the Third International. In November, he and Zinoviev were both expelled from the Russian Communist Party, and Trotsky was exiled to a small town in Turkestan. In December, the congress of the Party expelled over one hundred leaders of the various opposition groups, among whom were the oldest members of the party who had been its original founders and builders. Soon thereafter, the Enlarged Executive Committee of the Third International expelled Communist leaders in various countries who were in sympathy with the Trotskyist opposition.

These measures had their effect. In the course of 1928, there was a steady stream of retractions on the part of expelled leaders of the Russian opposition who asked for readmission to the Party. Trotsky, from his place of exile in Turkestan, tried to mobilize his followers in and outside Russia for the purpose of capturing control of the Russian Communist Party and of the Third International, but his plans failed. He was soon exiled from Russia to Turkey. The Left Communists outside Russia organized themselves into independent parties, which were unable, however, to rise above the position of small dissident groups.

The victory of Stalin, Bukharin, Rykov, and their followers was acknowledged officially and sanctioned by the sixth congress of the Third International held in Moscow in 1928. However, the agitation of the opposition had some results. This was shown by the congress in the abandonment of the policy of the United Front. In politics, this meant that the Communists were henceforth to put up their own candidates in local and national elections and not to support socialist or labor party candidates. With regard to the trade unions, this spelled a policy of building separate and dual unions wherever possible, of abandoning the slogan of "international unity." The Russian trade unions, as a result, dropped their efforts to affiliate with Amsterdam or with the International Trade Secretariats or to reestablish the Anglo-Russian Committee. The RILU began a new campaign against Amsterdam, and redoubled its efforts to set up rival labor organizations in different regions, such as a Latin-American and a Pan-Pacific Secretariat of Trade Unions.

By 1928 the Third International thus emerged more centralized under the control of the Russian Communist Party under Stalin's leadership. It entered upon its Stalinist period.

### III. THE AF OF L AND THE "NEW ERA"

Compared with the stormy developments in the Amsterdam and Moscow Internationals during 1926-1928, the course of the American Federation of Labor and of the Pan-American Federation of Labor was relatively calm. But they too had their internal problems which affected their relations to each other and to the European Internationals.

In a general way, conditions after 1924 tended to weaken the interest of the AF of L in European affairs. With the passage of the immigration laws of 1921 and 1924, American labor felt secure against competition from foreign workers. The failure of the United States to join the League of Nations made the AF of L less interested in the International Labor Organization. The AF of L became absorbed during these years in the new domestic problems ushered in by the "New Era." The American labor movement was confronted during these years with a "new industrialism" characterized by the extension of mass-production methods; the growth of the automotive and electrical industries, in which unionism was practically unknown; by the migration of older industries to the South, which weakened some of the oldest trade unions; by the standardization of technical processes, which gave rise to "technological unemployment"; and by new employers' labor policies as expressed in "employee representation plans" and "company unions," which threatened to undermine the structure of American trade unionism.

To meet this "new capitalism," individual unions and the AF of L as a whole came forward with new ideas and weapons. To hold and strengthen the interest of their members and to prove to them the larger social capacities of trade unionism, they opened labor banks and began developing group insurance, old-age homes, sanatoria, summer camps, workers' education, and cooperative housing. To maintain and raise wages in the face of falling real prices, they proclaimed a "new wage policy" based on the idea that labor was entitled to a share in the larger national income due to increased productivity. To win employers away from the "company union," they emphasized their willingness to cooperate with employers in maintaining economic stability and peace in industry.

A number of individual unions had some success in putting these

ideas and policies into practice. The total effect was far from satisfactory to the unions. The AF of L during these years suffered a loss
of membership and a decline in income, in economic power, and in
social influence.

Absorbed by these domestic problems, the AF of L pursued only
mildly, though in a friendly manner, its negotiations with Amsterdam.
The Los Angeles convention of the AF of L in 1927 again instructed
the Executive Council to try to reach "satisfactory arrangements"
with the IFTU on the basis of a reduction in per capita tax and a
change in its constitution. In 1928, the New Orleans convention upheld the position of the Executive Council that the question of
"strict autonomy" was the real "stumbling block" to active affiliation
with the IFTU. As no agreement was reached on this issue, the
AF of L did not become a member of the IFTU at this time, and
remained unaffiliated for a decade longer.

### IV. Decline of Pan-American Federation of Labor

While facing new and complex internal problems, the AF of L
was beset by increasing difficulties in the Pan-American Federation
of Labor. The strain was caused by two issues. At the Detroit convention of the AF of L in 1926, an attack was made on the CROM,
on the grounds that it was not a real trade union but part of the
machinery of the Mexican government, and was lending its support to President Calles in his conflict with the Catholic Church. The
demand was made by some delegates that the AF of L clear "its skirt
of the slime which has attached to it through the deception practiced"
on its Executive Council by "the paid propagandists of Bolshevik
Mexico."

The other issue was the growing immigration of Mexican workers
into the United States under the Immigration Act of 1924, which
exempted Mexico from the quota provisions of the law. In August,
1925, representatives of the AF of L and the CROM tried to meet
the problem by adopting a declaration in favor of the "principle of
self-restraint" in order to avoid restrictive legislation. This principle
was formulated into an agreement between the two labor federations
in August, 1927, according to which the AF of L promised to continue to support the policy of keeping Mexican immigration on a non-

quota basis; in return the CROM was to discourage Mexican workers from going to the United States or Canada. The CROM was also to urge those Mexicans who did seek work in the United States to join the American trade unions. The latter were to admit Mexicans on a footing of equality.

Despite attacks by delegates from the Southwest and the Pacific Coast, the agreement was ratified by the AF of L convention of Los Angeles in 1927. The convention was also presented with a memorandum of the Executive Council of the AF of L on the CROM which emphasized the latter's independence from the Calles government. This memorandum was accepted by the delegates to the convention, determined to keep religious issues out of the American labor movement.

The Pan-American Federation suffered a setback, however, in 1928. The AF of L convention of that year in New Orleans reversed the decision of 1927 and voted to abandon the policy of "self-restraint" and to bring Mexico under the quota provisions of the immigration law. Furthermore, the convention did not protest against several instances of United States intervention in the internal affairs of some of the Latin American countries, to the latter's disappointment.

As a result of these developments, the AF of L lost much of the good will which Gompers had built up in Latin America. The fifth congress of the Pan-American Federation of Labor, scheduled for 1928, had to be postponed. The leading trade union organization of Argentina, for instance, the *Confederacion Obrero Argentina,* refused to attend the congress, expressing apprehension that the Pan-American Federation was being used by the State Department to extend American influence. A number of trade unions joined the Latin American Secretariat organized and supported by the RILU. Syndicalist unions began new efforts to form a Latin American Syndicalist Federation. The anti-Communist unions of Argentina, Uruguay, Cuba, and Venezuela entered into negotiations with Amsterdam to establish a Latin American Federation under its auspices—a *Federacion Obrero Ibero Americana*—with headquarters in Buenos Aires.

By the end of 1928, the Pan-American Federation of Labor was thus beginning to disintegrate. Though it lingered on for some years, it ceased to be a factor in the international labor movement.

# CHAPTER XIV

# Programs and Policies in 1929

AFTER ten years of postwar history, the international labor movement in 1929 presented a complex picture. It was divided into five systems—socialistic, nonpartisan, Communist, syndicalist, and Christian—which together included some seventy international organizations competing for the support of the workers. The several Internationals looked forward to a period of development on the basis of their respective programs and policies. In order to follow more clearly the course of events after 1929, these programs and policies are described in this and the following chapter.

## I. THE AMSTERDAM INTERNATIONAL

Despite setbacks after 1921, the International Federation of Trade Unions (IFTU), or "Amsterdam," was still in 1929 the largest and strongest labor International, with a membership of over 13 million. It was allied with the Trade Secretariats and the Socialist International, and played an important part in the International Labor Organization of the League of Nations.

### Outlook and Policies

Amsterdam regarded socialism as the ultimate goal of social evolution. Its ideal was a world society composed of independent socialist nations cooperating for the general improvement of the conditions of mankind. It regarded the coming of socialism as a gradual and peaceful process, for the success of which a violent revolution was neither necessary nor desirable. Capitalism, in its view, would be modified in a socialist direction through the extension of "workers' control" and "industrial democracy," that is, through the growth of institutions such as shop committees, factory councils, and national economic councils, by means of which the workers would acquire a greater share in management and an increasing influence in the making of national economic policy.

For the calculable future, Amsterdam stressed policies of economic cooperation, political democracy, and world peace. It favored the "rationalization" of industry, that is, scientific management, provided it was carried out with due regard for the protection of wages and for the human dignity of the worker. It advocated freedom of migration, free trade, exchange stability, international agreements for the distribution of raw materials, and an International Cartel Office under the League of Nations to curb and control monopolies. It supported the League of Nations as the embryo of a democratic world federation, favored a United States of Europe, and was strongly pacifist.

*Tactics and Methods*

In its tactics, Amsterdam proceeded on the theory that economic and political developments were shaped largely by the struggle of classes. That implied that there was a basic solidarity between the workers of all countries, especially in the preservation of peace. The theory was not interpreted too rigidly. The class struggle was considered compatible with cooperation with employers for specific economic and social ends. All liberal and progressive groups were urged to cooperate with organized labor in the maintenance of peace. In brief, the tactics of Amsterdam were those of bargaining with employers, governments and official international organizations.

As an industrial organization, Amsterdam supported and promoted the formation of trade unions where they were weak, as in the Balkans. It collected funds to aid strikes in which workers of several industries were involved. It aimed to prevent international strikebreaking by various means, including embargoes against countries in which big or general strikes were taking place.

Amsterdam was also political in character. It took a stand on all big issues of the day, such as reparations, world debt settlements, the occupation of the Ruhr, and disarmament. It demanded and obtained representation at official international conferences and on commissions dealing with these problems. It addressed memorials and demands to the Assembly and Council of the League of Nations on these issues, and called on its affiliated trade union centers to bolster them up by pressure on their national governments.

For educational purposes, Amsterdam maintained a bureau of information, issued a weekly newsletter and a monthly journal, and published books on trade unionism and on current international problems.

The program and policies of Amsterdam were formulated at its congresses, held once every three years. Under its rules, only one national trade union center from each country could be affiliated with it. Each national center sent delegates in proportion to its membership; voting was by countries, each country having a number of votes in proportion to its trade union membership.

The application of policies was entrusted to a General Council, an Executive Bureau, and the general secretary. Each country had representatives on the Council. The Executive Bureau consisted of a president, five vice-presidents, and the general secretary. It met every two months to review the work of the organization.

As the national centers had autonomy in their internal affairs, the powers of Amsterdam were limited. Its effectiveness lay in its capacity to mobilize the trade union leaders of different countries for common action when necessary. Communication by mail, telegraph, and long-distance telephone enabled the labor leaders to keep in close touch between meetings of the executive bodies. The officers and staff of the Amsterdam secretariat visited the meetings of affiliated trade unions as fraternal delegates. Most of the leaders of Amsterdam and of its affiliates had influence with their governments or with the opposition parties, and were familiar figures in the assemblies of the League of Nations and at international conferences.

*Scope and Leadership*

Amsterdam in 1929 was essentially a European organization. Of the 28 national trade union centers with 13,000,000 members affiliated with it, 23 centers with 12,500,000 members were in Europe. The five non-European centers were in Canada, Argentina, Palestine, the Union of South Africa, and Southwest Africa.

Even in Europe, Amsterdam had difficulty in extending its membership. In Italy, Hungary, Lithuania, and elsewhere, the free trade unions were suppressed or hindered by dictatorial governments. In France, Czechoslovakia, and the Balkans, the Communists had set up rival trade union federations. The trade union centers of Norway and Finland belonged to the RILU.

In Asia and in the Middle East, e.g., Egypt, labor organizations were just beginning and tended to come under Communist influence. The Australian labor unions were opposed to Amsterdam's immigration policies and were influenced by radical elements. In Latin America, Amsterdam could make little progress owing to syndicalist and Communist opposition and to the aloofness of the American Federation of Labor.

By 1929, the Germans had again come forward as the chief claimants for Amsterdam's leadership. As before 1914, the German trade unions were leading the other trade union centers in numbers, finances, cohesion, and in their interest in international affairs. They justified their claim to leadership also on the ground that Germany was again becoming the most dynamic country of Europe industrially, and that, after her admission to the League of Nations in 1926, she was gaining in importance politically. The Germans had a real interest in Amsterdam in view of its potential influence in shaping public opinion on such issues as reparations, international trade, and disarmament.

German preponderance was held in check by the fear of "Germanization" on the part of the British, French, and Belgian trade unions. A more or less stable equilibrium was achieved by 1929 by the election of a British trade unionist as president, the appointment of a German general secretary, and the allotment of the five vice-presidencies to France, Belgium, Germany, Czechoslovakia, and Denmark. These arrangements did not entirely eliminate personal and national friction, but they gave Amsterdam sufficient unity to carry on its activities in accordance with its program.

## II. THE TRADE SECRETARIATS

Amsterdam was closely allied with twenty-seven International Trade Secretariats, which were international associations of workers in a single trade or in several related trades and industries. By 1929, a division of functions had been agreed on. The Secretariats were to protect the international interests of their respective trades and industries. The IFTU was to act as the spokesman of the general international interests of labor. The Secretariats were autonomous in their internal affairs, but they were under obligation to consult with Amsterdam on general questions. For purposes of coordination, the General Council of Amsterdam and officials of the Secretariats met in annual conference. Officiáls of the Secretariats had the right to attend the congresses of Amsterdam and the sessions of its Executive Bureau in a consultative capacity.

### Membership and Structure

The twenty-seven Secretariats had in 1929 over 13 million members in thirty-five countries. Some of the Secretariats were organized on a craft or trade basis and had small memberships, e.g., those of the painters, stone workers, diamond workers, and lithographers. The largest Secretariats were the International Federation of Transport Workers with about 2,250,000 members, the International Miners' Federation with about 1,900,000 members, the International Union of Woodworkers with about a million members, and the International Federation of Textile Workers with about 950,000 members.

In organization and structure, the Secretariats differed only in detail. They all held international congresses once every two or three years or at call. In the intervals between congresses, they were managed by an executive committee and a secretary. The headquarters of the Secretariats were located in twelve different cities in seven countries: the Miners' Federation had its offices in London; the Transport Workers, Woodworkers, and several other Secretariats had their headquarters in Amsterdam; the Metal Workers in Bern; the others were located in Berlin, Paris, Brussels, Zurich, and several other cities of Switzerland and Germany.

A large part of the tasks of the international secretaries were of a routine character, such as collecting dues, keeping accounts, arranging congresses, publishing journals, and maintaining contacts with affiliated organizations. The budgets of the Secretariats ranged from a few thousand to about $50,000 a year. Only six of the Secretariats employed full-time secretaries who were assisted by one or more clerks. The largest organization was the International Federation of Transport Workers, whose annual budget was about $45,000. It had its own four-story building in Amsterdam and employed a staff of fourteen. Its general secretary, Edo Fimmen, had two full-time assistants.

*Theories and Assumptions*

Most Secretariats approved the general program of Amsterdam with regard to industrial democracy and the socialization of industry, economic reconstruction, and the maintenance of peace. But as their primary purpose was to improve working and living conditions in the immediate future, they developed a specific theory of international trade unionism on which their activities were based. The essence of the theory was that both international competition in world markets and international combinations to control these markets, when left to themselves, had injurious effects on the workers. The effects of international competition were felt in two ways. First, as the greater ease of travel increased the international mobility of labor, the workers of different countries came into direct personal competition for jobs. Second, as the products of different countries with different labor standards were sold in world markets at different prices, the workers of one country were pitted against those of another indirectly. In either case, the competitive battle was most often decided in favor of employers who paid the lowest wages and lengthened working hours.

International competition, it was claimed, tended in many industries also to affect adversely profits through price cutting, dumping, and in other ways. Large corporations were therefore combining to form international cartels in order to control the supply of raw materials and to regulate world production and prices. Owing to their ability to close down plants at will, these international combines and monopolies were said to be in a position to pit the workers of one country against those of another for the purpose of depressing wages and labor standards.

It was the task of the Secretariats, according to their theory, to counteract the injurious effects on labor of both international competition and international combination. For this purpose, it was necessary to protect the higher labor standards achieved in the advanced industrial countries and to equalize competitive conditions by raising standards in the less developed countries. This was possible, in the view of the Secretariats, insofar as higher living standards for labor meant a larger world trade and thus greater purchasing power and prosperity for all countries.

*Devices and Methods*

To carry out their tasks, the Secretariats applied on an international scale the trade union methods of mutual insurance, collective bargaining, legal enactment, and education. The method of mutual insurance included devices to reduce the competition of workers moving from country to country. Such were the arrangements for free transfer of union members and for the mutual exchange of union benefits. It was a rule common to all the Secretariats that a member of an affiliated trade union who emigrated to another country should be admitted to the appropriate trade union of that country without paying an initiation fee. Some Secretariats, e.g., the printers, hatters, and diamond workers, maintained special funds for the payment of traveling benefits to their members. An immigrant worker who could not find work on union terms was given money to proceed to another city or country where he might have better luck. Some of the Secretariats also entered into "reciprocity agreements" under which a worker who transferred from the trade union of his home country to a trade union of another country received the sick, out-of-work, and other benefits provided by the trade unions for their own members.

The method of mutual insurance also included provision for aid in organizing. Many of the Secretariats sent funds to the Balkan countries, Italy, and Switzerland for local organizing campaigns. Several Secretariats employed special organizers among immigrant workers in the frontier districts of Europe, such as Northern France and Belgium.

Efforts to promote international action in collective bargaining took several forms and were unequally developed. The rule to which the Secretariats held their affiliated organizations most strictly was that of keeping workers and professional strikebreakers away from a country in which a strike was on. This was in substance a form of international picketing which was regarded as the most elementary duty of international labor solidarity. In contrast, provisions for international strikes and boycotts were exceptional. The International Federation of Transport Workers pledged itself to support "sympathetic strikes, passive resistance and boycotts." The International Union of Workers in the Food and Drink Trades carried on international boycotts on several occasions.

All the Secretariats were pledged to render financial aid to their members in case of strikes or lockouts. Some of the Secretariats e.g., the printers, metal workers, boot and shoe workers, provided for special strike assessments. The textile workers maintained an international strike fund. These differences were of little importance. In practice, most of the strike aid rendered by the Secretariats between 1919 and 1929 came from collections obtained through appeals for voluntary contributions.

Several Secretariats tried to promote greater uniformity in methods of wage payment. The Hotel Workers' Secretariat, for instance, urged its members to demand the abolition of the "tipping system." The Diamond Workers' Secretariat called for a general system of piece rates. A few Secretariats discussed the idea of an international minimum rate of wages, but it did not advance beyond the discussion stage.

Most of the Secretariats advocated international agreements for the regulation of working conditions. The painters, for instance, demanded that the use of white lead in industrial processes be prohibited by international treaties; the bakers agitated for the abolition of night and Sunday work; the transport workers urged that no person be allowed to carry loads of over 150 pounds; the seamen called for international agreements as to legislation on behalf of greater personal freedom and more decent accommodations on board ships. National legislation on these matters was obstructed by the claim of employers in some countries that it would place them at a disadvantage in their competition with employers of other countries. To meet this objection, the Secretariats demanded international agreements between governments to set up minimum standards. As the International Labor Organization was set up in 1919 for that purpose, the Secretariats became active supporters of the ILO.

All the Secretariats had provisions for keeping their members informed on developments in their respective trades. Most of them published journals which contained valuable material on technical improvements, on the growth of trade unions in the different countries, on strikes, on comparative wage rates and wage movements, and on international economic developments generally.

### The Secretariats as Going Concerns

As going concerns, the Secretariats differed widely in importance. Some of the Secretariats, such as those of stone cutters, hatters, land workers, and hairdressers, were little more than paper organizations and annexes to the German trade unions in these trades. A second group, those of the printers, lithographers, and building trades workers, who were seriously affected by intra-European migration, had the best developed provisions for mutual insurance and mutual aid in strikes, but showed little interest in carrying their activities beyond this point.

A third group of Secretariats in industries working for world markets, such as textiles, clothing, metals, glass, and coal mining, had large memberships but were weak in action. They had low dues, small offices, and only part-time secretaries. Most of them did little more than serve as information centers. There was, however, much agitation in these Secretariats on the need for larger international action in view of the effects upon these industries of the spread of industrialization to new countries.

The transport workers—seamen, dockers, railwaymen, and others —were a group by themselves. They showed considerable capacity for prompt and cohesive action which had potential serious international repercussions. The International Federation of Transport Workers stood out as the largest and strongest Secretariat, with a wide range of interests and activities.

The Secretariats had a wider distribution of membership than the International Federation of Trade Unions. Fourteen of the twenty-seven Secretariats had in 1929 about 1,500,000 affiliated members in the United States, Cuba, Brazil, India, the Dutch East Indies, and Australia. The trade unions in the United States which belonged to their respective Secretariats were the United Mine Workers, the International Association of Machinists, the United Brotherhood of Carpenters and Joiners, the United Brotherhood of Painters, the International Ladies' Garment Workers' Union, the Bakery and Confectionery Workers of America, the Boot and Shoe Workers' Union, the National Federation of Post Office Clerks, the International Longshoremen's Association, and a few others. Still, most of the Secretariats were essentially European organizations.

The Secretariats were much concerned in 1929 about their relations with Amsterdam. A few officials, notably Edo Fimmen of the Transport Workers, proposed that the Secretariats should be made the basis of a new labor International which would be industrial in character. They argued that under the new conditions of competition and combinations, the national trade union centers were incapable of effective worldwide action. The Secretariats, in their opinion, could in a few years assume "practical and theoretical leadership in industrial struggles."

Most of the leaders of the Secretariats, however, held that the "internationalization of capital" was proceeding slowly, that the workers were animated by craft and national motives, and that "industrial struggles" must therefore remain for a long time national in scope. In view of that, they argued that the Secretariats could play only an auxiliary part in the international labor movement, and that Amsterdam must continue to be an international association of national trade union centers.

The arrangements linking Amsterdam and the Secretariats described above were in accord with this second view. Still, there was considerable sentiment in 1929 for combining the Secretariats and the IFTU into one international labor organization on a coordinate and equal basis.

### III. AMSTERDAM AND THE ILO

The activities of Amsterdam and the Trade Secretariats called for their cooperation with the League of Nations and especially with the International Labor Organization (ILO).

*Structure and Functions of ILO*

The nature of this cooperation was determined by the structure and functions of the ILO. As set up under the Versailles Peace Treaty, the ILO was composed of, and functioned through, three organs—the Annual Conference, the Governing Body, and the International Labor Office (ILO). It was the business of the Annual Conference to discuss and prepare draft conventions and recommendations. The conventions were legal texts of international treaties on labor and social matters; the recommendations were merely statements of general principles to guide legislation on particular labor and social questions. If approved by a two-thirds vote of the Conference, a draft convention had to be submitted by the member states of the ILO to their respective legislatures for consideration within twelve or, in exceptional cases, eighteen months. The legislature of a country was free to ratify or reject any draft convention; but if it ratified, it was under obligation to adopt national legislation embodying the provisions of the draft convention. Recommendations also had to be approved by a two-thirds vote of the Conference and if approved, had to be submitted by the member states to their legislatures for information. A recommendation did not require ratification.

Amsterdam and the Secretariats could exercise influence on the preparation and adoption of draft conventions owing to the part they played in the Annual Conference. Under the Versailles Treaty, members of the League were *ipso facto* members of the ILO. The latter could also admit states which were not members of the League. In 1929, the League had fifty-four member states, while the ILO had fifty-five. Each member state could send to the Annual Conference four delegates. Two of these were government representatives; the other two represented employers and workers and were appointed by the governments on the nomination of the most representative employers' and workers' organizations. In the Annual Conference, the delegates acted as three distinct groups—the Government Group, the Employers' Group, and the Workers' Group. The Employers' and the Workers' Groups held separate caucuses to determine their stand on matters under discussion. Under the rules of the ILO, each delegate voted as an individual, but the Employers' and Workers' Groups usually cast their votes in accordance with the decisions taken at their caucuses; most often, they cast opposing votes. The decision in such cases lay with the government delegates, who generally divided their votes, some voting with the employers and some with the workers. By obtaining the support of a sufficient number of worker and government delegates, Amsterdam could shape decisions of the Annual Conference.

*Amsterdam and the Workers' Group*

As a matter of fact, such was the situation in the years from 1924 to 1929. Though some governments, e.g., that of Italy, sent officials of its Fascist unions as delegates to the ILO Conference and some governments appointed as delegates representatives of the Christian trade unions, Amsterdam exercised a controlling influence in the Workers' Group. At the Annual Conference of 1928, for instance, of the ninety workers' delegates and advisers, fifty-four were from organizations affiliated with Amsterdam; seven were from Christian trade unions and five from the Fascist unions of Italy; of the remainder about twenty were in sympathy with the views and policies of Amsterdam. Besides, the Christian trade unions usually supported Amsterdam on important practical issues. The general secretary of Amsterdam acted as secretary of the Workers' Group.

Amsterdam also played an important part in the Governing Body of the ILO. Like the Annual Conference, the Governing Body had a tripartite membership of government, employer, and worker representatives: of the twenty-four members of the Governing Body, the governments elected twelve, the employers six, and the workers six. Elections were held once every three years at the Annual Conference. Eight of the government representatives were nominated by the eight states considered of chief industrial importance; in 1929 these states were Great Britain, France, Germany, Belgium, Italy, India, Japan, and Canada. The other four government representatives were elected by the Government Group. The employers' and the workers' representatives were elected by the Employers' and Workers' Groups respectively. The workers' representatives on the Governing Body were leaders of national trade union centers affiliated with Amsterdam, except for one who represented the International Federation of Christian Trade Unions.

The Governing Body considered the items to be placed on the agenda of the Annual Conference, the subjects for draft conventions, and the questions on which reports and studies were to be made. It appointed the director of the Labor Office, issued general instructions for his guidance, and reviewed periodically the work of the Labor Office. Through the Governing Body, Amsterdam could help to determine the draft conventions to be discussed, the studies on labor and social matters to be made, and the general work of the International Labor Office.

*Importance of ILO*

Amsterdam attached great importance to the work of the Labor Office and kept in close touch with its director, Albert Thomas, its deputy director, Harold B. Butler, and other officials. To Amsterdam, the five-story building on the shores of Lake Geneva in which the ILO was housed symbolized the great advance made by labor in international prestige and recognition. Within this building, ornamented with panels and murals on labor themes and donated by governments and labor organizations, was the largest international staff ever assembled for the study of labor and social problems. In 1929, nearly 400 persons of 34 different nationalities were employed by the International Labor Office, whose budget was over a million and a half dollars. The main functions of the office were useful to Amsterdam in its work. The extensive research by the ILO on problems of social insurance, unemployment, industrial hygiene, hours of labor, and other labor subjects helped Amsterdam to promote international action by governments through the adoption of draft conventions. The Trade Secretariats also came to regard the office as a technical research staff which could supply them with reports and studies which they themselves were not equipped to make.

The Amsterdam unions valued their participation in the ILO for other reasons also. Owing to such participation, Amsterdam appeared as the recognized spokesman of the international interests of labor. Its position in the ILO helped it to play a part in the League of Nations and to secure representation on the League's committees and commissions. Last but not least, the Annual Conferences of the ILO gave the leaders of Amsterdam an opportunity to make contacts with labor men from Latin America, Asia, and Africa with whom they otherwise could have but meager communications.

Despite these advantages, Amsterdam in 1929 was far from satisfied with the results of its cooperation with the ILO. After ten years' experience, the processes of making and ratifying draft conventions began to appear as slow and uncertain. The 26 draft conventions adopted between 1919 and 1929 had obtained only 304 ratifications, or only about one third of the 1,200 ratifications which were possible. Twenty-five countries belonging to the ILO had not ratified a single convention. Amsterdam was particularly displeased with its experience with the eight-hour-day convention. The latter had been hailed as the great achievement of the ILO. Yet in ten years, it had been ratified unconditionally by only seven countries (Belgium, Bulgaria, Chile, Czechoslovakia, Greece, Rumania, and India), while France, Italy, Latvia, and Austria had ratified it only on condition that it be ratified by all other countries. Despite this meager success, the British government was demanding a revision of the convention which would make it less favorable to labor.

As a result, some of the trade unions of Amsterdam in 1929 were suggesting that organized labor place less reliance on the ILO and accentuate its own industrial activities. On the other hand, there were some, especially among employer and government officials, who were of the opinion that the ILO should give up making draft conventions and devote itself entirely to industrial and social research. As matters stood in 1929, however, the forces making for cooperation between Amsterdam and the ILO were strongest. The ILO looked to the trade unions for support against employers and governments who were inimical to or sceptical of its work. On the other hand, the organizations affiliated with Amsterdam valued it as the only official international institution in which they had a big part and which could be useful to them in various ways.

## IV. AMSTERDAM AND THE SOCIALISTS

As related earlier, the various socialist parties and groups adjusted their differences in 1923 and formed the Labor and Socialist International as successor to the pre-1914 Second International. By 1929, this new International had the affiliation of 36 socialist parties and groups, with a membership of over 6,500,000; it had established a working organization with headquarters in Zurich, with an annual budget of about $25,000. Under the direction of its secretary, Friedrich Adler, who was assisted by a small staff, it published a regular bulletin and occasional "documents and discussions" dealing with questions of socialist policy and tactics. The Executive Committee of forty members, representing the affiliated parties in proportion to membership, met regularly four times a year to consider current problems on which a common socialist policy was to be formulated.

The Socialist International could not claim in 1929 that it had achieved a unity of views and program. In fact, the three main divisions of Right, Center, and Left socialists which developed during 1917-1921 continued to divide the international socialist movement.

### Right Socialists

The Right socialists were numerically and politically the most important. They were dominant in the Social-Democratic Party of Germany, in the British Labour Party, and in the socialist parties of France, Belgium, Holland, Sweden, Denmark, Czechoslovakia, Hungary, Poland, Spain, the Balkan states, and the United States. With some exceptions, the Right socialists, while paying homage to the memory of Karl Marx, seriously modified his doctrines. With the experience of Soviet Russia and Fascist Italy in mind, they vigorously defended political freedom, parliamentary government, and majority rule as "working class ideas" and as inseparable elements of socialism.

A peaceful meaning was now given by the Right socialists to the ideas of class struggle, the conquest of power, and the socialization of industry. As the state was becoming more democratic, they argued, the workers could exercise an increasing influence on the government by gaining the support of the farmers and the middle class. To do so more effectively, it was necessary for the workers to sublimate the class struggle by relying on intellectual and moral strength, and to build up industrial, political, and cultural institutions which would give them economic and social leadership in the community.

By acquiring greater political power, the Right socialists maintained, the workers could use the powers of state regulation to give industry a public character and to guide it gradually in a socialist direction. Insofar as capitalism was becoming a "planned capitalism," they argued, it was itself preparing the way for a change to a socialist society, and the process was proceeding so rapidly that it might be completed within a generation.

The socialists were sure that they would in the course of time win a parliamentary majority in most countries and assume the powers and responsibilities of government. When such a peaceful "conquest of power" was achieved, the socialists would begin the systematic socialization of economic life. But even then, the Right socialists said, it would be necessary to nationalize industries gradually, and to make the process as painless as possible by compensating the owners either *in toto* or in part.

For the time being, the socialists, according to the Right, should in all countries where they were the largest single or a major party form the government or enter into coalition governments with liberal parties. Such coalition tactics were desirable to carry out immediate reforms, to promote the nationalization of basic industries, and to habituate the people to the idea of being under a socialist government.

### Center Socialists

The Center socialists regarded themselves as followers of Marx as interpreted by the Austrians Karl Kautsky and Otto Bauer. They were the dominant element in the Socialist Party of Austria, in the socialist parties of Switzerland and Norway, in the United Socialist Party of Italy, in the Independent Socialist Party of Poland, and in the Russian Social-Democratic Party known as Mensheviks.

According to the Center socialists, the Marxian analysis of the historical process had proved correct and there was no need to revise the theoretical foundations of socialism. They accepted the Marxian doctrines of the growing concentration of capital, the increasing poverty and insecurity of the workers under capitalism, and the class struggle which would become more acute with time and lead to a final social revolution.

The Center socialists were convinced that capitalism was incapable of utilizing fully the productive powers of society or of raising living standards for all the people. Because of that, capitalism would have to give way to a socialist society within the calculable future. That is why the "conquest of power" was in their opinion the central socialist question. The Center socialists claimed that the Right socialists were, owing to their tactics, in danger of succumbing spiritually to capitalism and thus being unprepared for a revolutionary social change when the time came. Though not rejecting entirely the policy of forming coalition governments, the Center socialists urged caution in applying such policy.

The Center agreed with the Right socialists in stressing the need of peaceful and legal methods, and in condemning attempts to gain control of the government by force. Such attempts, they said, could only lead to civil war and to terroristic dictatorships which would hurt the cause of the workers. As long as democratic institutions were maintained, they believed, the socialists had a chance to win over the majority of the people and to gain power by peaceful methods. They argued, however, that capitalism could not pass into socialism directly, but that there must be a "transition period." During this period, it would be the task of the socialist government to nationalize the banks, transport, mining, large manufacturing enterprises, insurance companies, and large land holdings; whether the owners would be compensated or not would depend on circumstances. The property of the small traders, small businessmen, and farmers would be respected.

Politically, the transition period, according to the Center socialists, meant the rule of the working class, but this was not to be interpreted in the sense in which the Bolsheviks applied the "dictatorship of the proletariat" in Russia. On the contrary, the Austro-Marxists claimed that the transition period would be marked by an extension of political and human rights, by a greater freedom of the press, and by wider cultural opportunities for all.

### Left Socialists

The strongest single party of the Left was the Independent Labour Party of Great Britain. In other countries there were Left groups which together with the Center formed the opposition within the socialist parties. Some of the Left socialists, e.g., the Labor Party of Norway and the Maximalists of Italy, refused to join the Socialist International because of their opposition to the Right socialists.

According to the Left, a new type of capitalism was developing, that of finance-capitalism, under which combination was taking the place of competition and the "captains of industry" were becoming the "puppets of the bankers." According to their analysis, fianance-capitalism was unable to direct industry in the interests of the people, to control the business cycle, to stabilize prices, and to raise standards of living; it was destroying political freedom and using the powers of the state for the benefit of small groups of large capitalists and bankers.

The Left groups demanded that the socialists in all countries where they had influence make decisive moves to bring about "socialism in our time." Like the Center socialists, the Left visualized a transition period during which the foundations of a socialist society would be laid. Concretely, the Left demanded that wherever labor governments came into power in Europe, they should make a "frontal attack" on poverty, establish a "living wage" for the workers, encourage consumption by a credit policy which would do away with excessive savings, and nationalize and rationalize the basic industries and banking.

The Left groups, especially in England, claimed that their program could be carried out by peaceful and parliamentary means. They opposed violent revolution, which they said was a doctrine of the middle nineteenth century no longer justified by the new conditions of political life. Even if the first socialist steps of a labor government should arouse violent opposition from the propertied classes, the labor government, according to the Left, should rely on parliamentary methods to enforce the will of the majority; in an extreme case, it might have to call upon the workers to use a general strike in its support.

The Left socialists differed from the Center and the Right particularly in their attitude toward Soviet Russia. While the Right socialists were bitter in their opposition to the Russian Communists and to the Soviet government, and while the Center did not believe in the possibility of immediate reconciliation with the Soviets, the Left groups thought that a compromise between socialists and communists was possible. The Left groups were thus responsive to Communist offers of "united action."

*The Labor and Socialist International*

In view of the differences between and within the socialist parties, the Labor and Socialist International made no attempt to formulate a general international socialist doctrine. All it demanded of its affiliated parties was that they advocate the establishment at some time of a socialist commonwealth, accept the principle of the class struggle as expressed in the formation of independent political parties by the workers, support democratic institutions and immediate economic and social reforms, and promote peace and cooperation in international relations.

In this spirit, the Labor and Socialist International took its stand on the issues of the day. On the reparations issue, it was for limiting the total amount to the actual material damage done. It advocated autonomy and equal cultural rights for the national minorities of Europe, and the right of self-determination for the nations of Asia and Africa. It called for the limitation of armaments and for compulsory arbitration of international disputes. For the pacification of Europe, it urged the demilitarization and neutralization of certain frontier areas and the revision of frontiers by arbitration and plebiscites.

The Labor and Socialist International believed that the best way to promote its policies was by supporting and cooperating with the League of Nations and the International Labor Organization. Despite its defects, the League, in the opinion of the socialists, was an instrument for transforming the international "bourgeois" system into an international socialist society. With this in view, the Socialist International advocated the gradual reform of the League, namely, that the Assembly of the League be made independent of the Council and given wider powers, that representation in the League be made proportional to population, and that representatives to the Assembly be chosen by parliaments and not by governments. They also called for the establishment under the League of an International Economic Council, with the participation of officials from trade unions and cooperative societies, to deal with problems of production and consumption, distribution of raw materials, monetary policy, and the liberalization of commercial policy.

By 1929, the Labor and Socialist International had become established enough to exercise an influence on international politics and economics. Socialist leaders of France, Belgium, Sweden, Germany, England, and other countries were active in the Assembly of the League of Nations, were from time to time members of the Council of the League, and were influential in the various commissions of the League. These and other socialist leaders were brought together by the Socialist International for periodic discussions and for the elaboration of common policies.

The Labor and Socialist International was in 1929 a European organization. It had only a few small affiliated groups in China, Turkey, and Armenia, while the socialist parties of the United States and Argentina, with 15,000 and 10,000 members respectively, were not of much significance nationally or internationally. As a European organization, the Socialist International found itself involved in contradictions with regard to developments in China, India, and North Africa. The Socialist International hailed the popular movements in these countries for political independence and economic advancement, but was unable to give them much support because of disagreements of the different socialist parties on the issues raised. The socialists of the Scandinavian countries, Austria, Czechoslovakia, and some other countries urged a strong "anti-imperialist" policy. On the other hand, the socialist and labor parties of countries with colonial possessions often opposed action which was likely to disturb the relations of the home countries with their colonial dependencies.

## The Amsterdam-Socialist Alliance

When the Labor and Socialist International was formed in 1923, Amsterdam agreed to cooperate with it. By 1929, their cooperation had become regular and systematic. Both Internationals found such cooperation useful. Amsterdam brought the support of the trade unions to the Socialist International, while the latter gave help to Amsterdam in national parliaments and in the League of Nations.

Cooperation was effected in several ways. The executive committees of the two Internationals held joint meetings to consider current economic and political issues. When agreement was reached, statements and manifestoes were issued jointly. From time to time, the two Internationals held joint conferences. The secretaries and bureaus of the two organizations acted jointly to put into effect decisions taken.

For several years after 1923, Amsterdam played the leading part in this cooperative relationship. By 1929, the socialist parties had regained sufficient standing in a number of countries to reassert their pre-1914 claim to superiority over the trade unions in national affairs. Internationally, however, Amsterdam remained the stronger of the two allies.

CHAPTER     XV

# Programs and Policies in 1929 (Continued)

THE Amsterdam International and its allied Trade Secretariats and Socialist International were opposed in 1929 by the other Internationals which tried to win the support of the workers—namely, the Third International, the Red International of Labor Unions, the Syndicalist International, and the International Federation of Christian Trade Unions. The programs and policies of these internationals are considered in the present chapter.

## I. THE THIRD INTERNATIONAL

The Third or Communist International, also referred to as the Comintern, was in 1929 the center of a closely knit system of international bodies which aimed to gain control of the political, industrial, and cultural organizations of labor in all countries.

## Membership and Organization

In 1929, the Third International claimed the affiliation of Communist parties and groups in over fifty countries, with a membership of about 1,800,000. Nearly three fourths of this membership was in Soviet Russia. Outside the USSR, the largest following of the Comintern was in Czechoslovakia (150,000 members), Germany (about 125,000 members), and France (over 52,000 members). In these countries, the Communist parties had legal status, took part in electoral campaigns, and were represented in parliament, but they also carried on illegal and secret propaganda and activities in the army and navy. They had large offices in buildings which they owned; published daily and weekly papers, magazines, and books; and maintained hundreds of employees.

In other countries, the Third International presented a spotty picture. In Italy, Spain, the Balkans, Poland, and the Baltic states, the Communist parties were illegal or semilegal, and, excepting Poland, were not of much importance. In Austria, Switzerland, Belgium, Holland, and the Scandinavian countries, the Communist parties were small and weak as compared to the socialist and labor parties. The same was true of England, where the membership of the Communist Party was about 9,000. In the United States, the Workers' Party, which was the largest Communist political organization, claimed about 12,000 members. In Asia, Africa, and Latin America, Communist parties and groups were small but took an active part in, and aimed to lead, the nationalist, agrarian, and "anti-imperialist" movements.

In most countries, the Communist parties were organized on a similar basis. Members working in the same factory, mine, store, or office formed "industrial cells," while persons living in the same neighborhood formed "street cells." The cells were combined into local and district organizations which together constituted the national party. Each Communist Party was governed by a central executive committee elected at a national conference. The committee met a few times a year, but power was vested in a body of five or seven members known as the Political Bureau, or Politburo for short.

Each national Communist Party was a section of the Third International conceived as a "world party." The supreme organ of the Comintern was a world congress which was supposed to meet every two years but which actually met at call. The number of votes allowed each party was fixed by the congress itself, on the basis of membership and political importance. The congresses were held behind closed doors, and their debates were reported in the Communist press in expurgated form.

Between congresses, the Third International was governed by an Executive Committee. The Communist parties of the different countries were arranged in groups, and each group was allowed one or more members on the committee. The sixth congress of the Third International elected 58 members and 42 "candidates" to the Executive Committee. The Executive Committee of the Third International had large powers: it could issue "imperative instructions" to the sections, annul or amend decisions of the national parties, and expel individuals, groups, or entire parties for alleged violation of its directives.

The Executive Committee met at least once every six months. In addition, there was held twice a year an "enlarged plenum" of the Executive Committee, which varied in size from 100 to 200 members. The executive committee elected a "praesidium" of thirty members and nine candidates who held meetings in Moscow every two weeks. The praesidium elected a "political secretariat" of eleven members and three candidates, who resided in Moscow and directed the work of the International. The Secretariat of the Third International had its offices in Moscow in a large building assigned to it by the Soviet government. It maintained a large staff in its various departments concerned with propaganda, organizing, work among women, Oriental affairs, and so on. It published journals and bulletins in many languages, giving accounts of party affairs and surveys of world economic and social developments. It promoted personal contacts between Communist leaders of different countries who came or were called to Moscow to attend committee meetings, to report on conditions at home, or to receive instructions.

The Third International held its sections together also by financial means. In 1927, it spent, according to its published reports, about $345,000, or over half of its total receipts, in subsidies to seventeen of its sections to assist them in publishing newspapers, in organizing, in "cultural" work, and in other ways.

## Ultimate Aims

The activities of the Third International in 1929 were guided by the doctrines described as Marxism-Leninism, which were regarded by the Communists as a new synthesis concerned with the aims and methods of the "world social revolution." Lenin was said to have completed Marx's original theories by his analysis of imperialism and of the relations between revolutionary movements in industrial countries and nationalist movements in colonial and dependent countries.

The ultimate aim of the social revolution, according to this doctrine of Marxism-Leninism, was the establishment of a Communist society. Marx and Lenin never described a future Communist society, but merely indicated in general terms its principles of organization. In their terms, the future Communist society would do away with social inequalities, eliminate the opposition between brain and manual workers, and abolish exploitation of man by man; the state would cease to be an instrument of force and "wither away"; an abundant and steady flow of goods would be secured through a planned system of socialized production, and all goods would be distributed in accordance with the principle: "from each according to his ability, to each according to his needs"; freed from social conflicts, mankind would develop a common culture based on science and reason.

## Dictatorship of the Proletariat

Before entering this final state, society had to pass, according to the Communists, through a "lower phase of communism," or socialism. As productivity under socialism would not be high enough, control of work and output would be necessary and inequalities of distribution would remain. Also, due to the survival of old habits and attitudes, the state would have to exercise coercive powers.

Even this socialist society, according to Communist doctrine, would have to be built consciously, and the process would extend over a prolonged period. A transition period from capitalism to socialism would thus be necessary: it would be characterized by the forcible nationalization of industry and credit, and by the construction of socialist institutions under a regime of the "dictatorship of the proletariat," the prototype of which was Soviet Russia.

The Communists laid special stress on the concept of "proletarian dictatorship" as it epitomized their theories of the state, class struggle, and party leadership. Following Marx, the Communists described the state as an organ of class domination. To realize their socialist aims, the workers could not, according to the Communists, use the capitalist state, even in the form of a democratic republic, but had to set up a state of their own, a "proletarian democracy." The essential features of the workers' state were that the electorate would include only the "toiling masses"; that the electoral system would be based on place of work instead of residence; that there would be no separation of legislative, executive, and judiciary powers; and that the "bourgeoisie" would be disarmed while the workers would be fully armed and constitute the ruling class.

The industrial workers, the Communists said, could not by themselves carry out the above program, because they were a minority of the population in most countries. It was the task of the workers to win the support of the middle and poor farmers and peasants by appropriate promises to improve their position. Moreover, the workers and peasants could exercise their class dictatorship only through the Communist Party, which had a clear program and strict discipline and which, they said, was therefore the "vanguard of the proletariat." The dictatorship of the proletariat thus meant in practice the political dictatorship of the Communist Party and of its executive committees and leaders.

The Communists emphasized their belief that a violent revolution would be necessary in most countries to seize the powers of government. During the transition period, they warned, they might have to use force even against workers who opposed the Communist program. Violence would diminish gradually, they held out a hope, as resistance to the building of a socialist society was eliminated.

### "General Crisis" of Capitalism

In Marxian tradition, the Third International viewed the social revolution which it advocated as an inevitable outcome of capitalist evolution. After 1900, the Communists maintained, capitalism entered its last stage, which was that of finance capitalism or imperialism and in which monopolies and "financial oligarchies" ruled the world. Between 1900 and 1914, finance capitalism carried the world to unprecedented heights of production, but it also presumably brought on the First World War and the Russian Revolution. The former, in the Communist view, marked the "general crisis of capitalism," while the latter was the beginning of the international revolution which presaged capitalism's final downfall.

The general crisis of capitalism, so ran the Communist theory, would become aggravated because finance-capitalism was continually widening and sharpening its inherent contradictions. Finance-capitalism, said the Communists, stimulated the development of productive forces, but it also hampered them by high prices and limitation of markets; it raised efficiency, but it also increased the exploitation of the workers and thereby intensified their discontent; it exported capital to develop the newer areas of the world, but it also "plundered" the colonial peoples and oppressed them politically; it brought the world closer together, but it also placed its destinies in the hands of "millionaires" and "billionaires" and promoted militarism and war.

The contradictions of finance-capitalism, according to the Third International, found concrete expression in five major conflicts. First and foremost, in its view, was the division between Soviet Russia and the rest of the world, due to the rift between the capitalist and socialist systems of economy. Second in importance was the antagonism between the United States and Europe, which was allegedly the result of rivalry between American and British monopolies and imperialisms. Third was the remergence of Germany as a competitor of France and England. Fourth were the antagonisms in the Pacific, which were primarily a struggle between the United States and Japan. As fifth it counted the growing revolt of the colonial and semicolonial peoples in Asia, Africa, and Latin America against the "imperialist" powers.

The capitalistic world, as the Third International saw it, was making frantic efforts to find a new equilibrium. It was trying to bolster the League of Nations as a means of world cooperation. It was spinning utopian plans to organize the industries of the world on a unified and trustified basis. But these efforts were bound to fail, and what was to come was another world war, more furious and destructive than that of 1914-1918. Preparations for such a war, the Communists said, were but poorly screened behind the "phrases and gestures" of the League of Nations and could not be stopped by what they called the "mendacious babble" of the socialists and Amsterdam about peace and disarmament.

### World Revolution

The Communists were sure that the world revolution was maturing as a result of the general crisis of capitalism. They regarded the stabilization which had taken place during 1924-1928 as partial and temporary in character. They described the conditions of these years as a "revolutionary lull" which would give way in the not distant future to new revolutionary upheavals.

The theory which the leaders of the Third International developed at this time was that capitalism was subject to a "law of uneven development." That meant that industrialization was growing at a different rate in different countries and gave rise to different types of capitalism and to differences in its "stages of ripeness." Because of this, the social revolution also had to follow an uneven line. It could break out at one time in a country of mature capitalism; at another time it might flare up in an industrially undeveloped country or in the colonies. While workers' uprisings in the industrial countries were to be regarded as the main nucleus of the world revolution, national wars for independence and colonial insurrections were of special importance since they undermined the structure of world imperialism.

This meant, according to the theory, that the world revolution would be a prolonged process. For an indefinite period of time, the world would present the spectacle of conflicting economic and social systems existing side by side. But after a while, the workers will presumably gain the upper hand in the "decisive centers of capitalist power"; they would then combine their forces, establish a "world dictatorship" in the form of a World Union of Soviet Socialist Republics, and begin a systematic reconstruction of the world on a socialist basis. That will mark the "completion of the world revolution."

### The "Socialist Fatherland"

The Soviet Union, according to the Third International, was the center of the world revolution: it stimulated the workers of other countries to try to gain political power; it encouraged revolutionary movements in the colonies; it held out to the "oppressed" classes everywhere the promise of a new life based on the value of labor. For these reasons, the Soviet Union was to be regarded as the "only fatherland of the international proletariat."

There was constant danger, according to the Third International, that the "imperialist powers" would combine and make war on the USSR. It was the duty of the workers in all countries to prevent that by undermining the armed strength of the capitalist countries by propaganda, desertions from the army, fraternization, and general strikes. In case of war, the workers were to do everything in their power to assure the triumph of the "socialist fatherland."

### Communist Tactics

Since it regarded the world revolution as a prolonged process, the Third International called upon its members to be flexible in their strategy and tactics. In the advanced industrial countries, the Communists were told to carry on a "theoretical and practical" struggle for the conquest of political power. In the colonial and semicolonial countries, they were to join in the struggle for national independence and for the abolition of feudal conditions. In all countries where the "tides of revolution were not flowing," they were to concern themselves with immediate improvements in economic and social conditions, provided they used methods which would foster a revolutionary spirit among the workers.

The Third International urged its members to penetrate and infiltrate all organizations which had a mass membership or which could influence public opinion. In addition to the Red International of Labor Unions (considered separately below), the Third International promoted and maintained a number of auxiliary organizations such as the International Peasants' Council, the Communist Youth International, and the International Workers' Relief. Through these organizations, the Communists aimed to win adherents or sympathizers through a variety of activities such as collecting funds for the relief of strikers, arranging "children's days" and sports days, supporting farmers' demands, and so on. Some of these organizations were openly under Communist control and leadership; in others, the Communists operated behind the scenes through "cells" and through appeals to the humanitarian sentiments of workers, intellectuals, and middle-class people generally.

### Position of the Russians

The Third International continued to be rent in 1929 by internal divisions. In part, that was due to the fact that some members of the Communist parties revolted every now and then against the iron discipline and dictatorial methods of thinking and policy making imposed by the Politburos. As the Communist parties were composed of heterogeneous elements with different economic and educational backgrounds, it was inevitable that disagreements should arise every now and then, especially whenever the Comintern made a shift in policy.

In part, the internal dissensions were the result of national strains caused by the dominance of the Russian Communists in the Third International. This dominance expressed itself in various ways. In matters of theory, the Third International, while sanctifying Marx, put Lenin more and more into the foreground. At the congresses of the Third International, the Russians headed the important committees, presented the leading reports, spun the "theses," and coined the slogans. They had their hands on the wheels of the Executive Committee of the Third International. They financed its international activities.

There was resentment in various countries against this predominance of the Russians and against "orders from Moscow." Repeatedly, the Russian Communists were accused by Communists of other countries of using the Third International as a means of furthering the foreign policy of the Soviet Union. The Third International fought such national resentments ruthlessly, but was unable to suppress them entirely.

The internal strains brought the Third International to the breaking point in 1923 and again in 1926-1927. By 1929, however, Stalin and his supporters had gained the upper hand in the Russian Communist Party and in the Third International. But following this victory of Stalin, and in consequence of it, the attitude of the Russians toward the Comintern became increasingly dual. Insofar as the Russian Communists then thought that world economic conditions would remain relatively stable for some time and that such stability was helpful to the Soviet government in dealing with its own agrarian and industrial problems, they were inclined to slow down the operations of the Third International and to keep it in the background. On the other hand, the Comintern was regarded as a weapon of diplomacy to support the international demands of the Soviet government, particularly in case of a threat of war, since it could stir up mass movements to divide and weaken the non-Soviet world. Because of this dualism in the Russian attitude, the Third International was in a state of uncertainty in 1929 as to the role, aggressive or otherwise, which it was to play in the years immediately ahead.

## II. THE RILU

The Third International urged all Communists to pay their utmost attention to the trade unions as the most important mass organizations. The Communists were told to try by all means "to be at the head of trade unions, to direct them, to make them a field of Communist activity, an instrument of class struggle, in order that the millions of workers who have not as yet come to an understanding of Communism may come to it."

With this end in view, the leaders of the Third International helped to set up in 1921 the Red International of Labor Unions, known also as the Profintern. According to their original plan, the Communists were to penetrate the existing trade unions and become the elected officials. Trade unions and national labor federations thus "captured" were to affiliate with the RILU.

Between 1921 and 1928, this plan proved anything but successful. In country after country, the trade unions expelled the active Communists. The International Trade Secretariats refused to admit Communist unions to membership. Amsterdam did not accept the Soviet trade unions. The syndicalists rebelled against Communist control. Still, the Third International and the RILU continued during these years to warn their members against breaking up the existing trade unions, but to form "cells" in them and to "bore from within."

In 1928, the Third International and the RILU abandoned the policy of the "united front" and of "international trade union unity." The Communists were now told to fight the existing trade unions and to form dual unions under their own control wherever possible.

As a result, the RILU in 1929 had a varying and fluctuating membership, consisting of a few leading national trade union centers (Finland and Norway), dual national labor federations (France and Czechoslovakia), some independent industrial unions, and such organizations as the National Minority Movement in England and the Trade Union Educational League in the United States. The total membership claimed was 17,000,000 in fifty countries. This figure included over 10,000,000 members in Soviet Russia, over 2,000,000 in China, over 500,000 in the Unitary Confederation of Labor in France, and about 200,000 in Czechoslovakia. The remainder were said to be members of "revolutionary minorities" in thirty countries and of organizations which could not affiliate openly because of political conditions. In addition, the RILU had fifteen international "propaganda committees" for agitation in the International Trade Secretariats and such bodies as the Pan-Pacific and the Latin American Trade Union Secretariats.

The prop of the RILU was the Soviet trade unions. The financial support of the RILU came from them. The headquarters of the organization were in Moscow in the Palace of Labor, an immense building housing the administrative agencies of the Soviet trade unions. The general secretary of the RILU was Arnold Lozovsky, a Russian Communist and a member of the Executive Committee of the Third International. He was assisted by a large staff engaged in organizational work, collecting information, and publishing the monthly journal in many languages. The Executive Bureau of the RILU consisted of twenty-one members elected by the central council of over one hundred members, who were elected by the congresses of the organization. These congresses were held in connection with or following the congresses of the Third International.

In accordance with Communist doctrine and tactics, the followers of the RILU were exhorted to connect the day-to-day activities of the trade unions with Communist aims. They were to oppose long-term collective agreements and to treat them as temporary armistices. They were to oppose all plans for industrial peace as "class collaboration" and to stress instead "class struggle." In trying to gain control of the unions, they were not to take "too much into account formalities or the right of the bureaucrats." They were to advance more radical demands than the "reformist" leaders in order to win the support of the workers. In case of strikes, they were to call for the election of special strike committees or of "unity committees" in which they could play a leading role.

In general, the RILU was a loose-jointed organization. Its relations with its affiliated organizations which had a recognized trade union character, as in Finland, Norway, Czechoslovakia, and France, were not always harmonious. Its contacts with the "cells" in the trade unions of other countries were not close. It had little influence with Communists outside Russia, who looked to the Third International for guidance in trade union matters. Its secretariat was materially and otherwise dependent on the Third International and the government-controlled Soviet trade unions. In practice, the RILU was thus an agitational center which served the interests of the Third International.

### III. The Syndicalist International

When the Communists launched the RILU in 1921, they made every effort to win over the leaders of syndicalist unions and groups which had a following in France, Spain, Portugal, Italy, Germany, Sweden, the United States (the IWW), and Latin America. They were successful in a measure. Some well-known labor leaders—Tom Mann of England, Rosmer and Monmousseau of France, and William D. Haywood of the United States—brought many of their followers into the fold of the RILU.

Many syndicalists, however, did not like the "proletarian dictatorship" in Soviet Russia or the centralized methods of the Third International. A number of these syndicalists met in Berlin from December 25, 1922, to January 2, 1923, and formed a new organization under the name of the International Workingmen's Association (IWMA). They claimed to be the real heirs of the "revolutionary tradition of labor," which they traced not to the German socialist Karl Marx but to the French and Russian anarchists, Pierre Proudhon and Michael Bakunin, and to their disciples in the First International.

Syndicalism in 1929 remained in essence what it had been before 1914, namely, a doctrine which advocated the reorganization of society by the means of and on the basis of trade unions. However, it had undergone some changes, as a result of the experience of 1919 and because leadership had passed to German, Swedish, and Dutch labor men and intellectuals.

### Monopoly and Authority

The emphasis in the syndicalist program in 1929 was against monopoly—the monopoly of possession as expressed in private property and the monopoly of authority as embodied in the state. Private property in land and other means of production, according to the syndicalists, enabled small groups of owners to run industry for private profit and not for the needs of the people, and to appropriate the fruits of scientific progress, thus reducing the mass of the workers to economic insecurity and social misery. Between nations, private property pitted the monopolists of different countries against each other, making for depressions and war.

The state, according to the syndicalists, came into being as a result of private property and class divisions. Whatever its form—whether monarchy or republic, autocracy or democracy—the state always had the same function: to keep the people in economic and social subjection to the privileged minority. By its very nature, the state tended to promote centralization and to reduce the individual to the position of a cog in a machine.

Capitalism, the syndicalists claimed, tended more and more to abandon free competition and to become "collective capitalism." It organized international cartels and used the powers of governments with a view to exploiting the resources of the world according to a uniform plan. This development was bound to lead to state capitalism and to industrial slavery for the workers. It could not lead to socialism, the syndicalists said, because it was guided by motives of "economic dictatorship." Socialism, on the contrary, meant economic freedom, decentralization, social justice, and personal liberty.

*The Future Syndicalist Society*

The syndicalists pictured their ideal of "free socialism" as a society in which all resources would be owned by the people, work would be carried on by autonomous associations of workers on the land and in industry, everyone would work according to his capacity and be rewarded according to his needs, and there would be no state and the "government of men" would be replaced by the "administration of things."

In the society which the syndicalists projected, economic and social life would be regulated by two parallel systems of organization. On the one hand, the workers in any branch of industry would belong to an industrial union which would control the means of production and the raw materials pertaining to that branch of industry. Each such industrial union would administer its industry through works councils formed in separate plants and through local associations combining all plants in a district. The industrial unions of all industries would form a national federation for purposes of general administration. On the other hand, the workers in all the industries of a city or region would form a "labor exchange" which would administer consumption and social affairs. The local labor exchanges would form a national federation to administer the consumption of the entire country. The federation of industrial unions and the federation of the labor exchanges together would direct all economic and social activities, by means of contracts freely entered into by the various units of the system.

The syndicalists visualized the industrial unions and labor exchanges of the different countries linked into a world federation. They decried nationalism as the "religion of the modern state"—a screen for the selfish interests of the possessing classes. In their future federation, they said, every nation and regional or ethnic group would have the right to manage its own affairs and to develop its own cultural values in solidarity with all other groups.

*Role of Trade Unions*

Since the syndicalists aimed to abolish the state, they were opposed to legislative institutions and to participation in elections and political campaigns. They condemned all political parties—the socialist and Communist included—as groups seeking power for themselves. The "dictatorship of the proletariat" was, in their opinion, the worst kind of state and an excuse for a political clique to exercise its iron rule over the people for selfish ends. They urged the workers to boycott the League of Nations and the International Labor Organization.

The workers could achieve their ultimate aims, the syndicalists said, only through the trade unions. When, as a result of a depression or a war, conditions would appear favorable, the workers would declare a "social general strike"; the trade unions would then proceed to expropriate the means of production and exchange and declare them public property. They would set up industrial unions and labor exchanges and assume the tasks of reorganizing production and consumption.

To be successful, the social general strike would have to be extended into a world general strike. If the possessing and ruling classes resisted, violence would have to be used. It would not be necessary for the workers, the syndicalists said, to entrust the "protection of the revolution" to a political or military organization: the trade unions could do that themselves by arming the workers.

To improve conditions immediately, the workers were urged by the syndicalists to form trade unions on an industrial basis and to use methods of "direct action." Among such methods were strikes, boycotts, and "small" and "big" sabotage. The former consisted in doing inferior work on the job or in otherwise obstructing production and was to be used to win strikes; the latter consisted in damage to machinery and plants and was to be applied only in emergencies such as war or a *coup d'état* which might threaten the lives and freedom of the workers.

Regarding the trade unions as the "cells of the future society," the syndicalists advocated educational activities to train workers in the technical and managerial problems of industry. To develop a sense of common interests among workers of different countries, they urged the trade unions to carry on international strikes and boycotts against international cartels and combinations, and to strengthen their international labor organizations for the purpose.

*Membership and Activities*

The International Workingmen's Association in 1929 claimed 162,000 members distributed in Germany, France, Holland, Denmark, Norway, Sweden, Mexico, Argentina, and Uruguay. Its total dues from affiliated organizations from May 1, 1926, to April 30, 1928, were about $9,235; of this total about 60 per cent was paid by the Swedish unions and about one third by the German members. On such a budget the Secretariat of the IWMA, which had its headquarters in Berlin, published a mimeographed bulletin once every two weeks, issued manifestoes on such occasions as May Day or "Anti-Militarist Week," and made periodic appeals on behalf of political prisoners in Russia, Bulgaria, Hungary, Italy, and other countries.

The membership of the IWMA in 1929 was on the decrease. In Spain, Portugal, and Italy, the syndicalist unions, which had at one time played an important part in the labor movement were now persecuted by the governments and driven underground. In France and Germany, the syndicalist unions suffered from the inroads of the Communists. In Sweden and the United States, the syndicalists confined their activities to groups of workers who were neglected by other trade unions and who did not form stable organizations, such as lumberjacks and migratory agricultural laborers.

In the international labor movement, the syndicalists in 1929 played chiefly the part of critics. They denounced Amsterdam for its "reformism" and "spirit of national imperialism." Their main shafts were directed against the Third International and the RILU. Few lashed as mercilessly as they did the "Bolshevik capitalism" of Soviet Russia, the "cruel barbarism" of the Soviet dictatorship, the "wrecking tactics" of the Communists in the trade unions, the "lies of Moscow," and the "fraud and swindle" of the RILU. The IWMA in 1929 was thus mainly a thorn in the flesh of the Third International.

## IV. THE VOICE OF THE CHRISTIANS

In the world of organized labor in 1929, a distinct place was held by the trade unions which condemned in about the same degree socialist, Communist, and syndicalist ideas and which aimed to apply Christian doctrines to modern industrial and social conditions. As related in an earlier chapter, Christian trade unions had been formed in a number of countries before 1914. They were reconstituted after the First World War with increased membership. Anxious to play a part in the shaping of postwar labor policies, especially in the ILO, the leaders of the Christian trade unions of Holland took the initiative in arranging an international conference at The Hague; it was attended by ninety-eight delegates representing over three million workers organized in Christian trade unions in ten countries. On June 19, 1920, they organized the International Federation of Christian Trade Unions (IFCTU).

Between 1920 and 1922, the IFCTU helped to establish fifteen international Christian trade secretariats, which became affiliated with it. In 1922, at its second congress, the Christian International adopted a "world economic program." By 1929, the Christian Trade Union International had revised and consolidated its organization and program.

Protestant workers formed a minority in the Christian International in 1929; Catholics played a leading part in it as organizers, officials, and spokesmen. The sources of their inspiration were the encyclicals of Pope Leo XIII and his successors and the writings of Catholic bishops and recognized Catholic philosophers.

### Man's Destiny

The starting point of the doctrine of the Christian trade unions was the idea of man as a rational being called to a personal and super-natural destiny. As man could not live without society, it was the duty of society to enable every individual to obtain an adequate share of material welfare and to achieve his ultimate destiny. For over a century, they claimed, these ends had been thwarted by modern capitalism. For the capitalist regime was built not on the idea of man but on that of wealth. To ensure riches for the fortunate few, modern capitalism had turned the workers into mere tools of production, and man, "king of creation," was forced to subordinate his "human majesty" to the productive process.

### Individualism and Socialism

Modern capitalism, according to this doctrine, was anti-Christian in its nature and purpose. The theories of economic liberalism, with which capitalism was bound up, were false in their premises and wrong in their conclusions. As man was a composite of contradictory tendencies, he not only had to exercise self-control but also had to be guided by authority in his economic as well as his personal conduct.

The Christian trade unionists saw no hope for the worker in socialism, communism, or syndicalism. All these varieties of the labor movement were based on materialist ideas which ignored the spiritual needs of mankind, and held out the promise of a millennium on earth which was unattainable. These movements were hostile to religion and to the Church, which was evidence of their lack of understanding of the highest destiny of man. They advocated the abolition of private property—the essential condition of economic progress, freedom, and peace. They wanted to suppress all competition, though that would result in negligence and irresponsibility. They stirred up class struggle, thus undermining the bonds of unity between the different elements of society. They practised coercion, which was a violation of the deepest sentiments of human personality.

## Trade, Class, Nation, and State

The Christian trade unionists rejected the view that the social problem was a question of intergroup struggles. In their view, the social problem was the "eternally bleeding wound of mankind in search for the true meaning of brotherhood on earth." Its solution could be found only in drawing inspiration from the great act of self-sacrifice of the Saviour on the Cross. To achieve that end, it was necessary to build a "Christian house on earth" on the Christian principles of justice, charity, and the common good.

To embody Christian principles in the life of the individual and of society, it was not necessary to destroy but to purify existing economic and social institutions and to organize their interrelations on a correct basis. The individual should be enabled to find his proper place in society through the institutions of the family, private property, his trade, his class, his nation, the state, and the Church. The family should be recognized as the cell of society and as the source of all social sentiments and moral habits. Private property should be regarded as the necessary foundation of the well-being and independence of the individual and the family, but it should not be an absolute right and should be made subordinate to the interests of the community. The individual should regard his trade as the "worldly task given to man by God," as a source of joy and as a moral obligation, and he should have a sense of attachment to the enterprise or business with which he was connected.

The Christian trade unionists recognized that the workers formed a distinct social class. That did not, in their opinion, imply a recognition of "class struggle." Social classes, according to their analysis, were rooted in individual and economic differences inevitable in any society. The task was not to fan the flames of class conflicts, but to harmonize differences and make possible the peaceful cooperation of all classes for the common good.

Neither did the Christian trade unionists see any contradiction between class and nation. It was natural for Christian workers to be national in outlook, to love their country and fatherland and to be patriotic, but to oppose chauvinism and strife between nations.

The Christian trade unions regarded the state as also rooted in the material and moral needs of society. The state was to protect the weak, moderate the strong, and correct the balance of power between different groups and classes. But the state must not become all-inclusive. It should avoid excessive centralization so as not to hinder voluntary organizations through which groups and classes could set forth their special views and interests.

It was the function of the Church to minister to man's need for salvation. The state and other social organizations must give the Church freedom and opportunities to transmit with authority the Divine Revelation and to create the spiritual environment in which economic and social activities could bear fruit.

*Industrial Councils*

In accordance with their general principles, the Christian trade unions advocated a system of industrial relations based on harmonious cooperation between capital and labor. Under private property, they said, the owners of capital and the entrepreneurs should carry the pecuniary risks of enterprise and should receive a reasonable reward for this as well as for their managerial efforts. Capital should also have freedom to exercise the rightful functions of organizing and directing production. But capital must keep in view that it was not superior to labor and that labor was the lifegiving factor of production. Capital should not claim an exclusive right to control production and distribution, but should recognize the right of labor to share in such control.

In its turn, labor should do its best to make industry fulfill its economic and social ends. In return for his efforts, the worker was entitled to compensation which would enable him to live the life of a civilized human being. Labor was not to be treated as a commodity subject to the laws of supply and demand, but as the embodiment of human personality. The worker should be protected against everything which might impair his health, stunt his personal development, or injure his moral life.

The ideal of the Christian trade unions was an economic system based on industrial councils. Under this system, each industry would be guided by a council, composed of an equal number of employers and workers, which would study the problems of the industry, fix conditions of employment, and make general rules legally binding. A central council composed of representatives of all the industrial councils would protect the consumers against unjust demands of particular industrial groups. The central council would serve as an "economic parliament," regulating and directing economic life as a whole. It would have the aid of the state in exercising its functions of guidance and direction, but the role of the state would be limited as much as possible. This program was to be realized through a series of gradual steps and reforms.

*Immediate Program*

For the immediate future, the Christian trade unions advocated specific measures similar to those which formed the program of the Amsterdam unions, namely freedom of combination, union recognition, collective bargaining, adequate factory inspection, protective legislation for women and minors, the eight-hour day, social insurance, vocational guidance, universal technical training, and facilities for young workers to receive higher education. They wanted a "just wage," that is, a minimum wage which would be sufficient to maintain a family, including special allowances for workers with large families, calculated on a cost-of-living basis.

The Christian trade unions laid special emphasis on the need for peaceful negotiations and collective bargaining between employers and workers. They were wary of strikes and justified them only as measures of last resort. Instead, they favored mediation, conciliation and arbitration, industrial courts for the hearing of disputes, shop committees for the settlement of grievances, and similar schemes of industrial peace.

The Christian trade unions assigned an important role to the state in improving industrial relations. The governments, according to their program, were to establish trade boards to fix minimum wages in sweated industries, collect statistics on the cost of living, make provisions for family allowances, aid the workers in building low-cost homes, enforce factory inspection, and liberalize the social insurance laws. In all these activities, the governments were to enlist the cooperation of the trade unions so that the latter could gradually become an integral part of the industrial system.

### Membership and Organization

In 1929, there were Christian trade unions in about fifteen countries in Europe, Canada, and a few South American countries, with a total membership of about three million. About half of this membership was in Germany, and about 25 per cent in Belgium and Holland. France, Czechoslovakia, and Poland had substantial memberships. In all these countries, the Christian trade unions were organized along the usual lines of local unions, national unions, district councils, and national federations or trade union centers. In several countries, the Christian unions were interconfessional, having both Catholic and Protestant members. In Holland and Switzerland there were separate Catholic and Protestant organizations.

In industrial make-up, the Christian trade unions differed from country to country. The French Confederation of Christian Workers, for instance, consisted of fifty-three local and regional unions and seven national trade unions, but its strongest support came from unions of office and government workers. The Federation of Christian Trade Unions of Germany was composed of eighteen national trade unions covering as many industries, but the bulk of its membership were miners, metal workers, and textile workers in the Rhineland and in

Westphalia. The Belgian Federation of Christian Trade Unions had its greatest strength in the mining regions and among the textile workers of Flanders. In the other countries of Europe, the Christian trade unions had their largest following among textile and railroad workers and among post-office employees and clerks.

All Christian trade unions stressed the need of building up strong benefit funds. They paid sickness, death, invalid, and out-of-work benefits to their members. All of them also, except the civil servants, maintained strike funds and paid strike benefits.

*Relations with Other Unions*

By 1929, the Christian trade unions had won a recognized place for themselves in the countries of Europe. They took part in elections to shop committees and industrial councils, were represented in hearings before mediation and arbitration boards, and cooperated with the unions of the Amsterdam type in negotiations with employers and in signing collective agreements.

The relations between the Christian trade unions and the trade unions of the Amsterdam type were generally strained. The leaders of the free unions argued that there was no reason for the existence of Christian unions and that their reluctance to strike weakened the general labor movement. On the other hand, the Christian trade unions justified their separate existence on the ground that the free trade unions were in fact antireligious and socialistic, and that even neutrality in matters of religion was harmful to the mind and soul of the worker.

The Christian trade unions, therefore, stressed the religious aspect of their work. Union meetings began and ended with prayer. In some of the houses where the Christian trade unions had their offices, there were chapels and daily services. In the educational work of the Christian trade unions, much time was devoted to discussion of Christian doctrine in relation to industrial life. The Christian trade unions also kept in close contact with religious organizations and with political parties which professed religious aims. They supported the Center Party in Germany, the Social Christian Party in Austria, the Christian Democrats in Belgium, the People's Party in Italy, and the Catholic and Protestant political parties in Holland.

*Relations with the Church*

Insofar as their relations with the Church were concerned, the Christian trade unions fell into three groups. In the Catholic unions of Holland, priests acted as advisers to the trade union leaders, and special priests were assigned by the episcopal authority to supervise the work of the trade unions. In Belgium, a committee of six ecclesiastic directors acted as delegates of the bishops in their relations with the trade unions.

Germany represented the other extreme. Owing to their interconfessional character and to the fact that they had to deal with employers who were more often Protestant than Catholic, the German Christian unions steered an independent course in relation to the Church. In other countries, the Christian trade unions kept in close contact with the Church authorities but were not supervised by them.

*The International Federation*

The Christian trade unions of Germany, Austria, Switzerland, Luxembourg, Holland, Belgium, France, Spain, Italy, Czechoslovakia, Hungary, and Yugoslavia were affiliated with the International Federation of Christian Trade Unions. The membership of the latter in 1929 was about 1,500,000. It maintained offices in Utrecht, Holland. Its secretary-general was P. J. S. Serrarens, a former Dutch school teacher, who was assisted by a staff of three in carrying on the routine business of correspondence and in publishing a monthly journal. The affairs of the International Federation were managed by an Executive Committee of five appointed by the International Council elected at triennial congresses. Each affiliated national center was free to send as many delegates as it wished to these congresses, but the voting was on the basis of proportional representation in accordance with membership. The budget of the Federation was about $10,000 a year.

The main task of the secretary-general and of the International Council was to make the voice of "Christian labor" heard on issues of international policy. The Christian International advocated the cancellation of inter-Allied debts, a gradual approach to free trade, and the reduction of nonproductive expenditures; it censured Fascism and social repression; it demanded that the Soviet government recognize the pre-1914 Russian foreign debts and the rights of private property as a condition of its recognition; it supported the program of the International Labor Organization.

The International Federation of Christian Trade Unions did not think that labor could obtain its international demands by means of strikes, boycotts, or embargoes. It ridiculed the "loud cries" and "small results" of the Amsterdam International. Neither was it very optimistic about the possibilities of international governmental action. It found that even the ILO, which it hailed at first as "an institution of the greatest importance to the working class of the whole world," did not show brilliant results because governments failed to live up to the draft conventions which they ratified. In view of this, the Christian International confined itself to the more modest role of creating public opinion in favor of international labor legislation.

Nevertheless, the Christian International demanded that it be given recognition in official international bodies dealing with labor and social matters. It was represented at the Annual Conferences of the ILO and in the Workers' Group. It had a place also on the Governing Body of the ILO. It was represented in the Advisory Economic Commission set up by the Council of the League of Nations in 1927. It insisted on official recognition in these and other bodies as a means of breaking "the monopoly of the socialists to represent the workers in the international field."

The Christian International was supported in its activities by fifteen international trade secretariats (of miners, textile workers, and so on) which it had helped to organize. These secretariats were part of the Federation, whose council they consulted on important matters. In organization, these secretariats did not differ from those affiliated with Amsterdam. Most of them in 1929 were little more than bureaus of information on trade questions.

In seeking avenues of expansion, the Christian International did not look toward England or the United States. It regarded the British and American unions as Christian in spirit if not in name. Neither did the Christian trade unionists look with much hope to the newly developing labor movements of Asia and Africa. Their interest lay in Continental Europe and in South America, where conditions appeared to them favorable to the spread of their principles and program.

The Christian International in 1929 formed a minority in the international labor movement. It could neither inaugurate important action in the trade union world nor exercise independent influence on international labor and social policy. In practical economic and social matters, and especially in the work of the ILO, it tended to support and reinforce the position of Amsterdam.

## PART FIVE

# Depression and World Tensions

## 1929-1939

# Unemployment and Fascism
## 1929-1934

IN mid-1929, the several labor Internationals looked ahead to a period of relative stability and peace. These expectations were shattered by events. For ten years, from the crash on the New York Stock Exchange in October, 1929, to the outbreak of the Second World War in September, 1939, the problems of world labor were determined by economic depression and political tensions.

The story of the international labor movement during these years centers in the International Federation of Trade Unions (IFTU) and in its relations with the other international organizations. The IFTU represented the main current of organized labor in the Western world and was a standard-bearer of Western ideas of democracy, social justice, and peace. It was the recognized spokesman of labor in the League of Nations and in the International Labor Organization. To the extent to which organized workers could deal officially with the international problems of these years, they could do so primarily through the IFTU.

The activities of the IFTU are thus the main thread of the narrative in this and the following two chapters. In this chapter, covering the years from 1929 to 1934, the main themes are the efforts of the IFTU to meet the problems of economic depression and to help protect the democratic unions of Western Europe against the spread of Fascism. During the following four years, from 1935 to 1938, the dominant question before the IFTU was that of "unity" with the Soviet trade unions for "united action" against Fascism and war. During 1938-1939, the overshadowing problem of the international labor movement was whether, and by what means, it could help prevent the impending war.

## I. Internal Changes in the IFTU

During 1929-1930, the IFTU continued to maintain its headquarters in Amsterdam. It devoted much of its time to the work of the ILO and, in particular, to the ratification of the eight-hour-day convention. This was still regarded as the greatest achievement of organized labor and as the symbol of labor's advance since 1900. The IFTU kept hammering at members of the ILO, especially the British Government, to ratify the convention. The leaders of the IFTU also showed increasing concern about growing unemployment in England and Germany, and the rise of dictatorships in Poland and several Baltic and Balkan states. It also had to deal with the problem of internal reorganization, in view of the decision of its Paris Congress in 1927 to remove the headquarters from Amsterdam and the determination of its elderly general secretary, Johann Sassenbach, to retire.

These problems were considered by the IFTU at its triennial congress in Stockholm in July, 1930. The congress expressed its "indignation" that the eight-hour convention had not yet been fully ratified. It decided to initiate a world campaign for the forty-four-hour week. It approved a resolution for closer economic relations between European states, adopted as its slogan "war against war," and declared its determination to wage a struggle against "international reaction and all forms of dictatorship."

The Stockholm Congress settled the question of the location of the headquarters, which had been a source of friction since 1927. The British and Germans had agreed between themselves in 1928 to move the headquarters to Berlin and to appoint a non-German as general secretary. The French, Belgian, Dutch, and other trade unions opposed this arrangement. They argued that Amsterdam had become the symbol of the free international labor movement and that it was best to keep the IFTU there. In any case, they objected to Berlin on the ground that the IFTU would be dominated by the powerful German unions. After much discussion, the congress decided by 55 to 30 votes to move the seat of the IFTU to Berlin. Sassenbach's resignation was accepted, and the Executive Committee was instructed to appoint a non-German secretary.

On September 30, 1930, the Executive Committee appointed Walter Schevenels, a Belgian metal worker, as general secretary. He took office on January 1, 1931. Shortly afterward, G. Stolz, a Czechoslovakian civil servant, was appointed assistant secretary. On July 1, 1931, the offices of the IFTU were installed in Berlin. The newly elected Executive Committee consisted of Walter Citrine of the British Trades Union Congress as president, and Leon Jouhaux of France, Corneille Mertens of Belgium, Jacobson of Denmark, Schorsch of Austria, Tayerle of Czechoslovakia, and Theodore Leipart of Germany as vice-presidents. Subject to the decisions of the General Council, these men were to lead the IFTU during the difficult four years which followed.

## II. Planning Against Depression

The leaders of the IFTU were slow in grasping the gravity of the economic depression which followed the financial panic of October, 1929. They proposed at first to meet it chiefly by a reduction of the working week to forty-four hours and by introducing paid workers' holidays.

However, in January, 1931, a joint committee of the IFTU and of the Socialist International took a more serious view of the "unemployment crisis" and produced an elaborate program for coping with it. According to this committee, the "basic fact of the crisis" was the "disproportion between productive capacity and consumption due to low wages." It was impossible, from this point of view, to overcome the crisis by wage reductions. The committee called for reductions of the working hours to forty and five days a week, unemployment insurance, and the greatest possible expenditures by the state for public works. The international measures advocated by the committee were lower tariffs, reduction of war debts, restoration of economic relations with Soviet Russia, a more equal distribution of gold to stabilize currencies, and the transformation of the Bank of International Settlements into "an organ of international credit policy." The committee held that while unemployment could be abolished only by the introduction of socialism, it could be reduced and the crisis shortened under capitalism by the measures which it proposed.

As the situation in Europe worsened during 1931-1932, the IFTU proposed to hold an informal international trade union conference to consider the "economic crisis." The American Federation of Labor refused to attend, and the proposal was abandoned. The IFTU concentrated its attention on cooperation with the ILO to obtain a forty-hour draft convention. It also gave its support to the project advanced by Albert Thomas, director of the International Labor Office, for a series of inter-European public works to be financed and carried out under the auspices of the League of Nations.

While stressing the forty-hour week and public works as means to combat unemployment immediately, the IFTU declared during 1932-1933 for "economic planning" as the long-run method for doing away with depressions. The idea of planning was then gaining ground in France, Belgium, Holland, and the United States and in the Secretariat of the ILO. The IFTU emphasized that it was opposed to Fascist and Communist planning and that it believed in the possibilities of democratic planning. The idea was discussed at the congress of the IFTU held at Brussels in July and August, 1933, at which time a statement on "Demands for Economic Planning" was approved.

Though economic conditions began to improve in 1933-1934, the IFTU continued its agitation for the forty-hour week and for economic planning. It helped in promoting the forty-hour draft convention which was adopted by the ILO in 1934. Its propaganda had some influence in stimulating the idea of economic planning in Western Europe. The trade unions of France, Belgium, Holland, Switzerland, and the Scandinavian countries formulated "labor plans," advocating among other things the nationalization of credit and of key industries. These ideas were to have a considerable effect on national economic policy in France and Belgium in the course of the decade.

### III. DEMOCRACY AND DISARMAMENT

During 1931-1932, the anxiety of the IFTU was aroused by the spread of Fascist movements in Poland, Germany, Austria, Yugoslavia, Lithuania, and Finland. The IFTU saw in these movements a general trend which threatened the free trade unions, and placed on its agenda the question of how to aid the "trade union movement in countries without democracy."

One form of aid which the IFTU was able to give to a limited extent was to assist trade unionists in Fascist countries to carry on underground activities. The other form was to help such trade unionists to escape and to support them in exile. In 1930, the IFTU contributed 10,000 florins (about $2,500) to the Matteoti Fund (named after the Italian socialist who had been assassinated by agents of Mussolini), which had been organized in 1926 to help the victims of Italian Fascism. During 1931-1932, the IFTU arranged jointly with the Labor and Socialist International public meetings to protest "against Fascism and Reaction" as well as against the "mass execution of intellectuals in Russia." It also organized a Balkan trade union conference to help the free trade unions of Greece and Yugoslavia by bringing the pressure of West European public opinion to bear on the governments of these countries.

The IFTU linked the issues of unemployment and Fascism with that of war, which it denounced as the greatest enemy of the workers. At its congress in Stockholm in 1930, the IFTU declared that the trade unions must remain "in the center of the peace movement." It advocated a reduction of armaments, government supervision of the private manufacture of arms, the ultimate nationalization of the armaments industries, and compulsory arbitration of international disputes. In particular, it tried to bring pressure on European governments and on the League of Nations to hasten the convening of the Disarmament Conference which had been planned since 1926.

The IFTU was aroused by the "Manchurian incident" of September 1931 and by the failure of the League of Nations to deal with it effectively. In February, 1932, the Executive Committee of the IFTU, jointly with the Executive Committee of the Socialist International, held a meeting in Geneva, to demand that the League apply sanctions to Japan and that members of the League withdraw their diplomatic representatives from Tokyo. In May of the same year, the IFTU and the Socialist International held a joint conference in Geneva and protested against the slow and unsatisfactory proceedings of the Disarmament Conference, which had been convened in the meantime by the League of Nations. The two Internationals submitted a memorandum to the League demanding the limitation of war budgets, the internationalization of civil aviation, and the rigorous control of aircraft production.

During 1933, the international situation continued to deteriorate. Between January and March of that year, Hitler carried out his Nazi revolution in Germany. In July, the London Economic Conference called by President Roosevelt collapsed. At the same time, the Disarmament Conference was clearly heading toward an inglorious end, which came officially a few months later.

Confronted with these facts, the sixth congress of the IFTU, which met in Brussels in July and August, 1933, decided that its antiwar position needed some revision. Though reaffirming its traditional pacifist demands, the IFTU called now for a struggle not only against war but also against aggression. It suggested the need of mutual aid between peaceful states against aggressor nations. This new departure was to become the basis of its peace action after 1935.

## IV. THE IFTU AND THE COMMUNISTS

In view of political and economic conditions, the IFTU showed no growth during 1929-1932. The general secretary expressed satisfaction that, despite unemployment and the spread of Fascism, the membership remained constant. It was 13,730,000 in 1929 and 13,615,-000 at the end of 1932. The composition of the IFTU also remained unchanged. It continued to be a West and Central European organization with small outposts in Canada, Palestine, South Africa, and Argentina. Its two largest affiliates were the German Federation of Labor, with over four million members, and the British Trades Union Congress, with some 3,600,000 members. Its other more solid affiliates were the trade union centers of France, Austria, Belgium, Holland, Switzerland, Sweden, Denmark, Czechoslovakia, and Spain. It had smaller and weaker affiliates in Hungary, Poland, Rumania, and Yugoslavia.

The IFTU discussed repeatedly the question of how to establish working relations with the trade unions of Latin America, Asia, and Australia, but was unequal to the task. In Latin America it had to face the opposition of the American Federation of Labor as well as the Communist and syndicalist groups. In Asia, it was hampered by its lack of means. It was unable to send missions or organizers to the countries where trade unions were beginning to take root, such as Ceylon, India, China, Japan, and the Dutch East Indies. When the first Asiatic Labor Conference was held in Colombo, Ceylon, in 1934 by the unions of Ceylon, India, and Japan, the IFTU greeted it but could give it no help. The IFTU discussed the idea of establishing a branch office for the countries of the Pacific Ocean, but could not carry out the project.

On the other hand, the Communists were in retreat during these years in the labor movements of Europe. The Third International and the RILU kept reiterating the "theses" and directives of their 1928 congresses, urging their followers to fight the socialists, to form separate unions, and to "win the mass organizations of the workers," but their activities were hampered by several conditions. In the first place, Soviet Russia was engaged between 1929 and 1933 in carrying out its first Five-Year Plan and the forcible collectivization of the land, which created great internal strains. Absorbed by these problems, the Russian Communists had less interest in, or energy for, agitation in Europe. Second, Stalin's dominance and his concentration on national problems accentuated factional dissensions in the Communist ranks of Europe and America. Third, the efforts of the Communists to break up existing unions and to form new ones under their own control alienated workers even in countries with large radical labor groups, such as Norway, Finland, France, and Czechoslovakia.

During 1931-1933, the RILU tried to organize committees of unemployed and to use them as an entering wedge into the European trade unions. The RILU advanced demands for systems of unemployment insurance which would pay the workers the full equivalent of their working wages, for reductions in rent, for free coal, and so on. The RILU had to acknowledge lack of success. The trade unions affiliated with the IFTU kept their hold on the organized workers of Europe.

The IFTU thus came through the depression with a feeling that the Communist challenge, which had been serious between 1921 and 1928, had lost its force. This feeling was clearly expressed by Walter Citrine, president of the IFTU, in a speech to the 1934 convention of the AF of L. "Communism," he said, "has ceased to be in the majority of countries of Europe at least a serious factor which might menace the strength of the working class." In accord with this feeling, the IFTU paid little attention to the Third International, the Red International of Labor Unions, or the Soviet trade unions.

## V. The Nazi-Fascist Attack

On the other hand, the IFTU was confronted with the threat of Fascism, which came to a head in Germany and Austria in the course of 1933-34.

After Hitler became Chancellor of Germany, the Executive Committee of the IFTU held a special meeting in Berlin on February 18, 1933, to consider action against the "Fascist danger." The leaders of the German trade unions said that they would defend their constitutional liberties. Despite the wave of popular indignation against all left parties aroused by the Reichstag fire of February 28, instigated by the Nazis, the situation remained indefinite for a while. In the Reichstag elections of March 5, some 7,000,000 votes were cast against the Nazis, who received 44 per cent of the popular vote. Nevertheless, on March 23 Hitler carried through the Reichstag an Enabling Act which gave his government dictatorial powers for four years. On the basis of this act, Hitler destroyed within a few months the democratic institutions of the Weimar Republic and reorganized Germany into a totalitarian state with himself as all-powerful Führer.

On April 9, 1933, the IFTU convened its General Council in Brussels to consider the situation. Theodore Leipart, president of the German Federation of Labor, and other representatives of the German unions did not attend, being unable to leave Germany. The Council decided to "fight Fascism" and to open a fund for German refugees. In view of anticipated events, the Council also decided to move the headquarters of the IFTU to Paris immediately. The Secretariat acted quickly and within less than two weeks the offices of the IFTU were established in Paris.

The leaders of the IFTU and of the German trade unions still hoped that Hitler would not follow the example of Mussolini, and would allow the trade unions to carry on their activities as usual. "Germany is not Italy, not Russia," was their view. However, on

May 2, 1933, Hitler dissolved the trade unions, seized their offices and funds, and instituted the Nazi Labor Front, which put an end to free trade unionism in Germany. The German labor leaders refused to compromise with Nazism. Many of them were jailed; others were sent to concentration camps; some went into hiding or exile. They made no attempt to mobilize their nearly five million members for resistance.

At its congress in Brussels in July, 1933, the IFTU declared an economic boycott against Germany and called upon the International Trade Secretariats to help enforce it. The trade unions of Great Britain, Belgium, Holland, Sweden, and several other countries tried to popularize the boycott among their members, urging them to refuse to buy German goods, e.g., Christmas toys. A number of unions in several countries, affiliated with the International Federation of Transport Workers, refused to load and unload ships destined for or coming from Germany. The 1933 convention of the American Federation of Labor declared its adherence to the boycott, and some of its unions were particularly active in applying it. However, it became clear before long that the boycott could have little influence on political and economic conditions in Germany.

Meanwhile, a situation dangerous to the free trade unions was developing in Austria, where Chancellor Dollfuss was intent on creating a corporative state, similar to Italian Fascism but based on Catholic principles. In October, 1933, the IFTU called a special meeting of its General Council in Vienna to consider help for the Austrian unions "in their fight against Fascism." Representatives from twenty-three national trade union centers and from twenty-one International Trade Secretariats attended. The leaders of the Austrian trade unions made it clear that they would resist Dollfuss' attempts to destroy them. With the experience of Germany in mind, the General Council of the IFTU promised to help by all practical means possible.

Within the next few months, the leaders of the IFTU tried to help the Austrian trade unions through diplomatic channels and also threatened to call general strikes. Their efforts were of no avail. On February 11, 1934, Dollfuss used the Heimwehr (National Guard) to seize the trade union buildings and property. The labor organizations and the Socialist Party put up a fierce resistance. For four days,

Vienna was the scene of sanguinary battles. The workers barricaded themselves in the model houses which had been built for them by the socialist municipality of Vienna a decade before, and were subjected to artillery fire and bombardment. When they were defeated, many of them retreated to the mountains, where they carried on guerrilla warfare for some time. Dollfuss won the day, put an end to the free trade unions, took over their funds and offices, and began forming corporations and labor syndicates similar to those organized by Mussolini.

The resistance of the Austrian workers aroused the admiration and sympathy of the organized workers of Europe. Contributions poured in to the International Solidarity Fund which the IFTU established. In the course of 1933-1934, over 6 million French francs (about $500,000) were collected for the relief of the workers' families and for aid to those who went into exile or hiding. The largest contributions came from the British Trades Union Congress, the Dutch trade Unions, and the unions of Czechoslovakia, Sweden, Denmark, and Belgium.

The Nazi-Fascist attack on the German and Austrian trade unions greatly weakened the IFTU. Its membership dropped from 13,615,-000 in 1932 to 8,211,000 in 1934. Its financial resources were much reduced. The developments in Germany and Austria had also a profound psychological effect. The leaders of the IFTU realized that they had underestimated the power of Nazism and the extent of Fascist disregard for legal procedures and constitutional rights. At the meeting of the General Council of the IFTU in August, 1934, the general secretary of the IFTU stated that "the campaign against Fascism can and must to-day be made the decisive battle for Democacy." A few months later, Walter Citrine, in his speech to the convention of the American Federation of Labor already quoted, declared that "Fascism to-day is the danger."

# United Action and Unity
## 1935-1938

THE triumph of Hitler in Germany and the suppression of the free trade unions in Austria revealed the weaknesses of organized labor in Europe in its fight against Nazism and Fascism. Some of the leaders of the IFTU suggested that the trade unions should try to strengthen their forces by cooperation with farmers' organizations and middle-class groups. The question was also raised whether, under the circumstances, it would not be desirable for the IFTU to seek joint action with the Soviet trade unions. Owing to a change in Communist tactics at this time, the question began to agitate the labor movemens of Europe and America. For the next four years it remained a central issue of the international labor movement.

## I. NEW COMMUNIST TACTICS

Though preoccupied with internal problems, the Soviet government was alarmed by the events of 1931-1933, particularly by the spread of Nazism in Central Europe. It began to seek reconciliation with the democratic countries of the West. In 1933, the Soviet Union sought and obtained recognition by the United States. During 1932-1933, it took part in the Disarmament Conference. In 1934, it joined the League of Nations, which it had vilified for over a decade. In May, 1935, the USSR concluded an alliance with France, which the latter readily accepted in fear of the threatening rebirth of a strong and aggressive Germany.

In accordance with this new policy of the Soviet government, the international Communist organizations adopted a new line of propaganda and agitation. At its seventh congress, held in Moscow in August, 1935, the Third International announced that its policy henceforth would be to organize "broad popular fronts" with socialist and liberal parties and "united action" with "reformist" trade unions. While not changing its fundamental doctrines, the Third International admitted that it had misjudged the course of historic events and had committed many "errors" of strategy and tactics. It had failed to foresee the menace of Fascism, which it now declared to be the chief enemy. The "theses" and declarations of the 1935 congress were ambiguous: they left room for the Communists to continue their disruptive tactics against "labor governments" where the latter were in power, and in the trade unions. But the new Communist slogans were "united action," "unity," and "popular fronts."

One of the results of this change in Communist tactics was the abandonment of the Red International of Labor Unions. While it was not formally dissolved, it was allowed to lapse. By this time, the RILU was little more than a shell holding the Soviet trade unions. Of its membership of 20,000,000, 19,500,000 were reported for the Soviet Trade unions. The RILU had lost most of its following in Western Europe, Latin America, the Far East, and the United States. It still had substantial organizations in France and Czechoslovakia, but their membership and influence were also declining.

In view of these facts, the IFTU felt that it could ignore the RILU. The situation was complicated, however, by developments in several countries, especially in France, where political conditions gave force to the Communist appeal for unity.

## II. United Action in France

About the time that Dollfuss began his attack on the Austrian trade unions, the threat of a Fascist *coup* convulsed France. On February 6 and 7, 1934, antidemocratic and royalist groups staged serious riots in Paris against the Third Republic. Conditions recalled the Dreyfus affair of the 1890's and aroused most Republican parties and groups to form a coalition cabinet in defense of the republic. The *Confédération Générale du Travail* (CGT)—the strongest labor organization of France affiliated with the IFTU—supported by the Socialist Party, carried out a general strike on February 12. The strike, which was joined by the Communist *Confédération Générale du Travail Unitaire* (CGTU), which had split off in 1922, was a demonstration of strength which spelled defeat of the antidemocratic forces for the time being.

The political situation in France remained uneasy, however. Under these conditions, the idea of unity among the left political parties and the trade union groups gained ground. In July, 1934, the French Communist Party proposed to the Socialist Party to form a "united front against Fascism and war." The Socialists accepted the offer. At the same time, the CGTU offered to be reunited with the CGT. Negotiations for unity dragged on, but were accelerated after the 1935 congress of the Third International. In September, 1935, the CGT and the CGTU appointed a committee to work out a basis for the readmission of the CGTU to the CGT. In November, 1935, all labor and middle-class political groups formed a Socialist and Republican Union and established close relations with the Communist Party. A "Popular Front" was thus formed against the antidemocratic forces of Colonel de la Rocque and his Fascist Croix de Feu.

In 1936, the CGT and the CGTU, after holding a "unity congress" at Toulouse, proceeded to carry out their unification. The CGTU was dissolved, and its constituent locals and city and departmental unions were instructed to amalgamate with those of the CGT. The Communists were allotted a number of positions on the central administrative council of the CGT, in proportion to their former membership. The Communists agreed not to form "fractions" or cells within the unions and to obey majority decisions. The unification was a victory for the CGT led by Jouhaux.

On June 5, 1936, the first Popular Front government of France was formed by Leon Blum, leader of the French Socialist Party. Stirred by this event and by their new trade union unity, hundreds of thousands of workers started a wave of "sit-down" strikes which led to far-reaching economic and social reforms. Within less than a month, the Blum government passed laws establishing the forty-hour week, vacations with pay, and collective bargaining. Under the pressure of the strikes and the government, the employers' organizations met with the CGT and concluded the so-called Matignon Agreement providing for collective bargaining on a nationwide scale. In December, 1936, the government passed legislation for the compulsory arbitration of industrial disputes. The Blum government also put the Bank of France under its control, nationalized the munitions industry, and suppressed the Fascist groups.

The French workers hailed these reforms as the beginning of a "new era." They joined the CGT in large numbers, bringing its membership up to over five million within less than a year. Though the Communists continued to make trouble in the trade unions and gained influence among the newly organized workers in the war-production industries, the "Toulouse program" of 1936 was carried out in the course of the year. The CGT emerged as a real force in the economic and social life of France and as one of the largest and most influential labor organizations in Europe and in the IFTU.

### III. THE 1936 CONGRESS OF THE IFTU

The expansion of the labor organizations of France during 1935-1936 was paralleled by a lesser growth of membership in other European trade unions affiliated with the IFTU, which was due primarily to economic recovery. In addition, the ranks of the IFTU were strengthened in· 1936 by the affiliation of three trade union centers —the Norwegian Federation of Trade Unions, the newly organized Mexican Confederation of Workers (CMT), and the All-India Federation of Trade Unions.

Partly as a result of this growth, the IFTU was forced to consider again the question of labor unity. The French CGT and the Spanish trade unions demanded, in view of their own experience, that a new attempt be made to achieve international labor unity. They were supported by the Norwegian and Mexican labor union leaders. The trade unions of Norway had belonged to the RILU before 1931; and though they had broken with it, they wanted to bring the Soviet trade unions into the IFTU. The Mexican CMT included a considerable Communist element which called for "united action."

On the other hand, the trade unions of Belgium, Holland, Switzerland, Czechoslovakia, Denmark, and Sweden refused to work with the Communists in their own countries and were opposed to cooperation with them internationally. The labor movements of these countries did not have to cope with serious Fascist threats to their democratic institutions, and they had no faith in Communist offers or promises. The British Trades Union Congress also rejected all offers of the Communists for cooperation in Great Britain and was no longer willing to play the role of devil's advocate for the Soviet trade unions, as it had done in 1924-1926. The British felt, however, that Fascism was a worldwide menace which the IFTU could fight more effectively if it had the support of all trade union centers whether in the United States, Soviet Russia, Australia, or Latin America.

The issue was brought before the congress of the IFTU held in London from July 8 to July 11, 1936. The congress registered the new growth of the IFTU, being attended by 132 delegates from 22 national trade union centers with 11,000,000 members and by 37 delegates from 19 International Trade Secretariats. The London Congress reaffirmed the general program of the IFTU for the forty-hour week, economic planning, international currency stabilization, international control of raw materials, the nationalization of the armaments industries, and so on. It also adopted a strong statement against Fascism as leading to "rearmament and war."

The greatest interest of the congress was aroused by the proposal of the Norwegian delegates that the IFTU start negotiations with the Soviet trade unions for common action against Fascism and war. The proposal was supported by Benoit Frachon, French Communist trade union leader, Largo Caballero of Spain, and the delegate of Mexico. It was opposed by Mertens of Belgium, Kupers of Holland, Jensen of Denmark, and others. After a three-day discussion, a compromise resolution was adopted which read as follows:

The Congress, approving the efforts made by the IFTU with the aim of international trade union unity, considers that, in view of the serious nature of the present international situation, these efforts should be continued.

With this purpose, it urges the IFTU to open negotiations with the national centers of America, Australia, New Zealand, the Far East, USSR and all other non-affiliated trade union centers, with a view to establishing a united Trade Union Movement throughout the world.

Thus, the Norwegian delegation, though defeated on its own motion, achieved its purpose of making necessary a new series of negotiations between the IFTU and the Soviet trade unions.

## IV. REAFFILIATION OF THE AF OF L

In accordance with the decision of the 1936 congress, the general secretary of the IFTU addressed letters to the national trade union centers of the United States, the USSR, and several other countries inviting them to affiliate with the IFTU. To his satisfaction, his letter struck a responsive chord in the American Federation of Labor.

The change in the attitude of the AF of L began in 1933 after the advent of the Hitler regime. Declaring that the Nazi regime was a "threat of industrial slavery," the 1933 convention of the AF of L declared an economic boycott against Germany. At the same convention, David Dubinsky, as head of the delegation from the International Ladies' Garment Workers' Union, introduced a resolution urging the AF of L to reaffiliate with the IFTU. The convention instructed the Executive Council of the AF of L to "investigate" the matter.

In 1934, the United States government accepted membership in the International Labor Organization. As the "representative labor organization" of the United States, the AF of L sent a delegate to the 1935 Annual Conference of the ILO. The leaders of the AF of L were favorably impressed by the work of the ILO, which was then discussing a forty-hour draft convention, and by the part which the IFTU played in the ILO. In its report to the 1935 convention, the Executive Council of the AF of L eulogized the IFTU as a "vital force against reaction and dictatorship" and declared that, by joining the IFTU, the AF of L would be able to "increase the voice of American labor" in the ILO. The convention decided that the time had come to reexamine the "basis of reaffiliation" with the IFTU, and authorized the Executive Council and President William Green to initiate discussions with officers of the IFTU, with power to act.

During 1936, the overshadowing question in the AF of L was the internal struggle which ended in the formation of the Congress of Industrial Organizations (CIO) as an independent labor organization.

The "conversations" with the IFTU dragged on somewhat uncertainly. The emergence of the CIO, however, spurred the leaders of the AF of L to quicker action. They felt that affiliation with the IFTU would strengthen the position of the AF of L not only abroad but at home.

Accordingly, the Executive Council of the AF of L sent Matthew Woll, one of its leading vice-presidents, to attend the meeting of the General Council of the IFTU held at Warsaw from June 30 to July 3, 1937. The meeting was attended by some sixty delegates from sixteen national trade union centers and thirteen International Trade Secretariats. Matthew Woll submitted the application of the AF of L for admission formally, without stipulating any conditions or reservations.

There was some uneasiness in the General Council of the IFTU about accepting the application in view of the split with the CIO. Under the rules of the IFTU, only one national trade union center could be admitted from any one country. By admitting the AF of L, the IFTU might have appeared as passing judgment on the dispute between the AF of L and the CIO. Many members of the General Council of the IFTU had for years deprecated the "craft unionism" of the AF of L and were rather pleased with the emergence of the CIO, with which they felt a greater kinship of ideas.

The application of the AF of L was nevertheless approved unanimously. The resolution adopted stated, however, that the action of the IFTU "should not be interpreted as approval or condemnation of the methods of action or forms of organization of any of the bodies concerned."

The reaffiliation of the AF of L with the IFTU was approved by the 1937 convention of the AF of L and hailed as a "profound and historic achievement." It was also warmly welcomed by the officers and leaders of the IFTU. To the latter it meant an addition of over three million members, a considerable increase in financial resources, and a widening of international contacts and prestige. The reaffiliation of the AF of L also brought reinforcement to those groups in the IFTU which were opposed to collaboration with the Soviet trade unions.

### V. Negotiations with the Soviet Trade Unions

The Warsaw meeting of the General Council of the IFTU also considered the question of relations with the Soviet trade unions. The general secretary, Walter Schevenels, reported that he had received no reply from the Russians to his letters of invitation to affiliate. Furthermore, the Soviet trade union leaders had again made a fierce attack on the IFTU. Walter Citrine, president of the IFTU, irritated by the abusive attacks of the Russians, declared that "trade union unity was not their earnest desire, but purely a political manoeuvre."

Nevertheless, the Council requested the general secretary to try once more and to invite the Russians in writing to open negotiations for affiliation. On July 8, 1937, another letter was dispatched to Moscow inviting the Soviet trade unions to join the IFTU. On August 13, the Soviet trade union leaders replied that they were ready to open negotiations to establish "trade union unity throughout the world," and requested the IFTU to appoint a delegation. On September 16, the Executive Board of the IFTU appointed Leon Jouhaux, Walter Schevenels, and G. Stolz as a delegation to Moscow to carry on the negotiations.

For several days, beginning November 23, 1937, this delegation held meetings in Moscow, in the Palace of Labor, with a Soviet delegation of three headed by N. Shvernik, president of the All-Union Council of Soviet Trade Unions. The meetings were far from smooth; the Russians showed themselves to be tough negotiators. The IFTU delegation was divided, Jouhaux and Schevenels pulling in opposite directions. Still, on November 26, a joint communiqué was issued, according to which the two delegations "accepted the fundamental conditions of unity of the Trade Unions of the USSR with the IFTU, on the basis of Trade Union unity to fight war and Fascism throughout the world." The conditions referred to were not published; they were to be submitted first to the Executive Board of the IFTU.

On January 12, 1938, the Executive Board of the IFTU met in Paris to receive the report of its delegation. The Russian conditions were then made known. The Russians demanded that the IFTU be reorganized so as to have three presidents, one of whom was to be from the Soviet unions. A second general secretary, a Russian, was to be appointed. Guarantees were to be given that the large dues to be paid by the Soviet trade unions would not be used for propaganda against the USSR. The IFTU was to intensify its fight against Fascism, and to organize "working class sanctions against aggressor states," such as strikes in factories producing war materials for Germany, refusing to load and unload ships, and so on. The IFTU was also to give effective aid to the Loyalists in Spain and to China. It was to support united action in the trade unions and people's fronts. An extraordinary international congress was to be called to ratify these conditions and to "strengthen trade union unity." Upon the fulfillment of these conditions, the Soviet trade unions would apply for admission to the IFTU.

The Executive Board of the IFTU was astounded by these conditions. Several members of the Board pointed out that they were disingenuous, since the Soviet workers could not strike, even though the Soviet Union was known to be supplying oil and other materials to Germany, Italy, and other Fascist states. The whole procedure of laying down conditions for affiliation irritated the members of the Board. After a heated discussion, the Board rejected the Russian proposals as "unacceptable," and decided to recommend negative action in the matter to the General Council of the IFTU.

## VI. The Oslo Decision

For several months the subject was vehemently discussed in the labor press of Europe and America. The Russians claimed that the IFTU delegation had accepted their conditions. The IFTU denied that any definite agreement had been reached in Moscow. The record seemed to indicate that the IFTU delegates had more or less agreed that the Russian proposals were a workable basis for further negotiations.

On May 17, 1938, the General Council of the IFTU met in Oslo, Norway, and dealt with the Russian question for several days. The meeting was attended by 87 delegates from 14 national trade union centers, including the United States and Mexico, and from 19 International Trade Secretariats. Jouhaux and the delegates from France, Spain, and Mexico led the fight for the acceptance of the Russian conditions. The opposition was strong and bitter. The Dutch and Belgian delegates were particularly opposed to admitting the Russians, claiming that it would strengthen the Communists. The Polish and Swiss delegates said that, since they were trying to form alliances with the farmers and middle-class groups of their respective countries to defend democratic and constitutional government, they could not work with the Russians. The delegate from Sweden declared that the idea of negotiating with the Russians had been a mistake and that the Soviet Union was more dictatorial than ever. Matthew Woll denounced the Russian proposals, saying that "it was an impossible situation to fight against the Fascist dictatorships in partnership with other dictatorships." He reaffirmed the general attitude of the AF of L that the IFTU could not admit the Soviet trade unions since they were not free and bona fide trade unions but part of the Soviet economic administration.

The resolution to accept the Russian conditions was defeated by 16 votes to 4 (Jouhaux as member of the Executive Committee, France, Spain, and Mexico) and one abstention (Norway). A joint motion was then made, sponsored by Woll and supported by the delegates from Belgium, Holland, Poland, and Switzerland, that no further negotiations be carried on with the Soviet trade unions. This motion was adopted by 14 to 7 (Jouhaux, Tayerle of Czechoslovakia, France, Norway, Czechoslovakia, Spain, and Mexico).

Thus came to an end the second attempt since 1925-1926 to establish a unified international labor organization.

## VII. Socialist-Communist Negotiations

During the period of the IFTU negotiations with the Soviet trade unions, there were negotiations for united action also between the international political organizations. In June, 1937, representatives of the Third International and of the Labor and Socialist International met at Annemasse in France, near Geneva, and reached a tentative agreement to cooperate in the struggle against Fascism and war. The main question was to determine the forms of such cooperation. On June 26, 1937, Maurice Thorez transmitted a letter from the Executive Committee of the Third International to Louis de Brouckère, chairman of the Socialist International, and to the IFTU, outlining a series of proposals. The latter included joint measures to be advocated in the parliaments of the different countries for the recall of Italian and German troops from Spain, joint action in the League of Nations to apply the covenant of the League against the Fascist states, and a joint appeal to the workers of all countries to support these demands.

De Brouckère replied that these proposals were in agreement with the action favored by the socialist parties. However, when Thorez proposed issuing a "joint manifesto," de Brouckère replied that he could not do anything which would bind the separate national parties affiliated with the Socialist International. The negotiations came to an end without achieving practical results.

Though the IFTU was not directly involved in these negotiations, it had an interest in them because of its close cooperation with the Labor and Socialist International. The failure of the Communist and Socialist Internationals to work out an agreement for united action thus sharpened the break with the Soviet trade unions in the IFTU.

CHAPTER XVIII

# Campaign Against Aggression and War
## 1935-1939

BETWEEN 1935 and 1939, The International Federation of Trade Unions increased its membership and gained a larger foothold outside Europe. By the middle of 1939, it consisted of twenty-seven national trade union centers, of which eighteen were in Europe and the other nine in the United States, Canada, Mexico, Argentina, Palestine, India, China, the Dutch East Indies, and New Zealand. Its affiliated unions in Europe had grown in strength and influence, partly owing to economic recovery stimulated by rearmament, partly as a result of political and social changes, as in France. The total membership of the IFTU, which had fallen to 8,211,000 in 1934, increased to 13,064,000 in 1936 and to 19,425,000 at the end of 1937. By the middle of 1939, it was estimated at about 20,000,000, which was close to the peak reached in 1920.

## I. The IFTU During 1935-1939

Despite this numerical growth, the IFTU did not engage during these years in any important industrial or organizational activities. There were some large strikes in a number of countries during this period, but the IFTU played little part in them, in contrast to its activities during 1921-1926. Neither did it send advisers or organizers to the struggling unions in Eastern Europe or Asia.

A large part of the work of the IFTU during these years was of an educational character. The IFTU Secretariat, which had been moved to Paris in 1933, published in its bulletin numerous articles on economic planning, monetary stabilization, tariffs and world trade, the international distribution and control of raw materials, and so on. In expectation of the "next slump," the Executive Board called several conferences of trade union experts to discuss the "labor plans" which were then being elaborated in various countries of Europe, and to harmonize them with the international objectives of the IFTU. These conferences helped to formulate proposals for international public works and other antidepression measures.

The IFTU concerned itself more specifically with "workers' education." The assistant secretary, G. Stolz, who was in charge of this work, developed a plan for establishing an International Center for Workers' Education, to discuss subjects and methods of teaching. The Center was not established, but international meetings were held which dealt with such problems as an international survey of workers' education and the development of methods for the use of radio and films in teaching workers' classes. An International Study Week and an International Summer School for Young Trade Unionists were arranged annually under IFTU auspices in one or another country, with the cooperation of the national trade union centers. The IFTU also sponsored an International Committee for Youth and Educational Questions, conferences of young unemployed workers, an International Committee of Women Workers, all of which had the purpose of discussing economic and international issues.

One of the tasks of the IFTU during these years was providing relief to victims of Nazism and Fascism. At least ten countries of Europe were under Fascist governments during these years—namely, Germany, Austria, Italy, Portugal, Latvia, Lithuania, Estonia, Poland, Greece, and Yugoslavia. In view of the persecution or suppression of free trade unions in these countries, the IFTU collected through its International Solidarity Fund considerable sums for the relief of the trade unionists affected and their families.

The Secretariat and the Executive Board of the IFTU were criticized during these years for not carrying on a more vigorous campaign for the forty-hour week, for lack of forcefulness in fighting Fascism, and for being too placid generally. Some of the critics felt that the difficulty lay in the absence of dynamic leadership. Others stressed the small financial resources of the IFTU. After the collapse of the German and Austrian unions, the IFTU lost one of its main sources of revenue. Besides, some of its affiliates were generally in arrears in the payment of dues. Even after the reaffiliation of the AF of L and the growth of union membership in Europe, the budget of the IFTU remained small.

One of the proposals made during these years to strengthen the IFTU was to reorganize it on an industrial basis. The argument was that as long as the IFTU remained a federation of national trade union centers, it would be hampered by the conflict of national interests and points of view. It was proposed that the International Trade Secretariats become the constituent units of the IFTU or that the IFTU and the Trade Secretariats be brought into closer relations in some other way.

After the London Congress in July, 1936, the IFTU and the Trade Secretariats instructed the Coordination Committee, which they had formed in 1934, to promote joint action in the campaign against Fascism and to devise a more unified organization. The results were not satisfactory. The national trade union centers insisted on the primacy of their role in the international labor movement, while the Trade Secretariats, though much weakened by the events of 1933-35, refused to give up their independent status. The Warsaw meeting of the General Council of the IFTU in July 1937 abolished the Coordination Committee.

Despite its weaknesses, the IFTU was regarded during these years, in the phrase of the American Federation of Labor, as a "progressive force in international relations." This was reflected particularly in its efforts to reinforce the League of Nations and the democratic governments of Europe in their struggle against aggression and war. The part which the IFTU played in this struggle is sketched in the rest of this chapter.

## II. Sanctions Against Italy

During 1933-1934, the IFTU kept repeating that the Fascist governments were bent on war and imperialist aggression, and that the workers must take the lead in combating them. When the Italian-Ethiopian arbitration negotiations ended without agreement in July, 1935, the Executive Committee of the IFTU, in a joint meeting with the Executive of the Socialist International, warned of the danger of war and suggested that the League of Nations apply economic sanctions against Italy. On September 6, the two Internationals held a large conference in Geneva to arouse public opinion in favor of sanctions. Public demonstrations were organized for the purpose in France, Belgium, and Holland. On October 12, after the Italian forces had invaded Abyssinia, the Joint Anti-War Committee of the IFTU and the Socialist International met in Brussels, approved the action of the Council of the League of Nations declaring Italy an aggressor, and called for specific sanctions, which the two Internationals promised to help enforce.

When the League on November 18 voted to apply economic sanctions against Italy (including an arms embargo, a financial embargo, and a prohibition against the import of Italian goods), the IFTU began propaganda to help enforce them. In March, 1936, the IFTU, jointly with the Socialist International, held protest meetings deploring the failure of the League to apply oil sanctions against Italy and denouncing Hitler's reoccupation of the Rhineland. For several months afterward, the IFTU continued to publish articles criticizing the West

European governments for their failure to make the sanctions against Italy effective. The IFTU could not stir up further action by these governments. On May 8, 1936, the Italian government proclaimed the annexation of Abyssinia. The IFTU had to acknowledge that its first attempt to help enforce international sanctions against aggression had failed.

### III. Aid for the Spanish Republic

Two months later, the Spanish Republic, which had been established by popular vote in 1931, was confronted with a revolt of army officers headed by General Francisco Franco, which soon assumed the character of a civil war. The IFTU made an appeal to its members for aid to the supporters of the Republican government, or Loyalists, as they came to be called. Contributions came in almost at once from many trade unions, including one of 4,000 pounds sterling from the British Trades Union Congress and of $5,000 from the International Ladies' Garment Workers' Union. Between July, 1936, and the end of 1938, the International Solidarity Fund of the IFTU raised 35,000,-000 French francs for food, medical supplies, and ambulances as well as for direct financial aid. The supplies were carried from time to time to Madrid by caravans of lorries, which aroused widespread sympathy for the Spanish Loyalists, especially in France. To many trade unionists, the civil war in Spain became the symbol of a life-and-death struggle between Fascism and democracy.

Throughout the entire civil war, from July 1936 to the surrender of Madrid and Valencia in March, 1939, the IFTU held numerous meetings with the Socialist International to discuss the situation in Spain. The two Internationals approved at first the nonintervention policy adopted by the French and British governments, and gave their support to the nonintervention committee in which twenty-seven nations, including Germany and Italy, took part. They denounced Germany and Italy for violating the nonintervention agreement and for sending troops, "volunteers," and war materials to General Franco. They made few, if any, references to the help given to the Loyalists by the Soviet Government. They supported the "Popular Front" government in Spain formed by Largo Caballero in September, 1936, though it included not only socialists and trade unionists but Communists and other left-wing groups.

As the insurgents under Franco made headway, with the aid of Germany and Italy, the IFTU and the Socialist International began denouncing the nonintervention policy, demanding "freedom for the Spanish Republic to procure arms." They tried to bring pressure to bear on the governments of England and France to achieve this purpose, but without success. Their efforts were defeated owing to the inclination of the British and some other governments to support Franco, and to the widespread fear that the Spanish civil war might develop into a general European war.

As the civil war in Spain went through its various stages in 1938 and approached its climax early in 1939, the IFTU could give less and less aid to the Loyalists.[1] The IFTU had to face other crises which followed one another at a fast pace—the invasion of China by Japan in 1937, the annexation of Austria by Hitler in March, 1938, the Munich crisis of September, 1938, and finally the extinction of Czechoslovakia as an independent state by Hitler in March, 1939. All these events gave point to the warnings of the IFTU about the imminent danger of war. The question before the IFTU was whether the international labor movement, in line with its oft-repeated declarations, would be able to help prevent the impending conflict.

### IV. PLAN OF ACTION FOR PEACE

Already in 1933, shocked by the "Manchurian incident" and by the failure of the Disarmament Conference, leaders of the IFTU raised the question whether the League of Nations could prevent a war. The failure of the League during 1935-1937 in the case of Ethiopia, Spain, and China strengthened the doubts of the IFTU about the League and the feeling that other methods must be found

---

[1] The role played by the Communists in the Spanish Civil War and the internal fights between Stalinists, anti-Stalinists syndicalists and anarchists can not be gone into here. It must be noted, however, that practically all groups of organized labor in Europe and America denounced the recognition of the avowedly Fascist Franco Government by Great Britain and France in February 1939 and by the United States and other governments soon afterwards. The demand for the withdrawal of recognition became one of the few points on which the IFTU, the Socialists, the AF of L, the CIO and various left-wing groups were agreed.

for the defense of peace. The method which was suggested was to build up a force outside the League capable of counteracting aggression.

At its annual meeting in the fall of 1937, the British Trades Union Congress declared that war might still be prevented if a strong group of peaceful states would pledge themselves to mutual aid against aggression. The IFTU welcomed this suggestion as being in line with its own ideas. In March, 1939 the enlarged Executive Committee of the IFTU, at a meeting in London, formulated a specific proposal. It urged the governments of Great Britain, France, Poland, and the Soviet Union to form a "common peace front" open to all nations. The four governments were to invite the United States to cooperate in calling an international conference to settle all outstanding disputes.

This "plan of action for peace" was the chief topic of discussion at the eighth congress of the IFTU, held at Zurich, Switzerland, July 5-8, 1939. The congress was a demonstration of the progress made by the IFTU since 1933-1934. The general secretary proudly reported that the IFTU now had twenty-three "large and active" affiliated national trade union centers. Though there had been some losses as a result of developments in Spain and Czechoslovakia, and though the trade unions of Greece, Danzig, Memel, South Africa, and Southwest Africa had withdrawn or been dropped for nonpayment of dues, the total membership of the IFTU was over 20,000,000. The IFTU, the secretary said, was no longer a European but a truly international organization, with affiliates in the United States, Canada, Mexico, Argentina, India, China, the East Indies, Palestine, and New Zealand. Some of its affiliates had grown greatly in numbers: the British Trades Union Congress had about five million members, the French CGT over four million, the AF of L over three and a half million, and the Scandinavian unions about 1,700,000, of whom some 900,-000 were in Sweden. The congress was attended by 106 delegates from 19 trade union centers, including the American Federation of Labor, and by 35 delegates from 21 International Trade Secretariats.

Leon Jouhaux introduced the new "plan of action for peace." Neutrality in the developing international struggle, he said, was no longer possible. There was still a chance to prevent a war by resolute action of the nations opposed to Fascism. An Anglo-Franco-

Russian Pact, Jouhaux claimed, was the only means to stop the further aggression of the Berlin-Rome Axis. He urged the congress to vote in favor of the proposed pact.

The resolution on the subject was objected to by the delegates from Sweden and the United States, who contended that the proposed pact was not the only possible way to defend peace. As amended to meet their objections, the resolution declared that an Anglo-Franco-Russian pact offered "the possibility of creating an important and immediate basis for the defense of peace and freedom" and expressed the hope that such a pact "may come into being as early as possible." The resolution welcomed the initiative of President Roosevelt to hold an international conference to solve all economic, financial, and colonial problems. It asked all governments to attend such a conference and to bring about "the disarmament which will finally liberate humanity." In this amended form, the resolution was adopted by the congress, with no opposing votes and with the abstention of Denmark, Finland, and Sweden.

## V. Peace and Unity

The action of the Zurich Congress on peace raised once again the question of unity with the Soviet trade unions. If the governments of Great Britain and France were to ally themselves with the Government of Soviet Russia, it seemed logical to the British and French labor leaders that the IFTU should resume relations with the Soviet trade unions. Shortly before the Zurich Congress, the Third International in its May Day proclamation had urged the IFTU and the Socialist International to initiate negotiations immediately for the purpose of convening "a world conference of all workers' organizations" to draw up a "concrete plan of action" and to create "a single coordinated body" for a joint campaign against war. Independently of this offer, the British Trades Union Congress had circulated on the eve of the Zurich Congress a memorandum to all affiliated members of the IFTU, proposing to extend an invitation to the Soviet trade unions to affiliate with the IFTU "on the basis of the statutes and rules of the IFTU." Soviet affiliation, the British claimed, was necessary to strengthen the IFTU and to resist Fascism.

Even before the Zurich Congress convened, the IFTU Secretariat received unfavorable comments on the British memorandum from the Belgian, Swedish, and American trade unions. William Green wrote to the IFTU on June 15, 1939, opposing the British proposal and warning that the admission of the Soviet trade unions would make it necessary for the American Federation of Labor to withdraw from the IFTU.

Despite these comments, George Hicks, the delegate from the British Trades Union Congress, introduced a resolution at the Zurich Congress to extend another invitation to the Soviet trade unions to join the IFTU. Walter Citrine, president of the IFTU, vigorously defended this resolution, emphasizing that the help of Russia was needed to defend the West against further conquests and to build peace. The delegate from Norway offered an even more strongly worded resolution to the same effect.

The British resolution was opposed by the delegates of the United States, Belgium, Holland, Sweden, Switzerland, and other countries. They argued that the admission of the Soviet unions would only weaken the IFTU and paralyze its capacity for action. Robert Watt, the delegate from the American Federation of Labor, made a strong statement in which he referred to Green's letter of June 15 and again warned that the AF of L would leave the IFTU if the Russians were admitted.

The British resolution was defeated by 46 to 37 votes. Robert Watt then introduced a resolution to reaffirm the decision of Oslo of May, 1938, that no further negotiations be carried on with the Soviet trade unions. The Oslo decision was reaffirmed by 60 votes to 5, with 18 abstentions. The voting was on a proportional basis: the five negative votes were cast by Mexico; the abstentions were by France and Norway.

At the time the Zurich Congress was in session, negotiations for a pact were proceeding between the governments of Great Britain, France, and the USSR. An Anglo-French military mission was in Moscow conducting conversations with the Russians. Six weeks after the Zurich Congress, as the Danzig-Polish crisis entered an acute stage, Soviet Russia made a trade treaty with Germany. On August 23, 1939, a German-Russian pact, better known as the Hitler-Stalin Pact, was concluded. Among other things, Soviet Russia and Germany agreed not to attack each other, and to maintain neutrality if either country were attacked by a third power. Great Britain and France at once dropped further discussions with the Russians for a "peace front." After a week of appeals and offers by President Roosevelt, Premier Daladier, and the British Government to find a peaceful solution for the Polish-German issue, Hitler began his March on Warsaw on September 1. On September 3, 1939, England and France declared war on Germany. The Second World War was on.

Few events in recent history had such a shattering effect on public opinion in democratic countries as the Stalin-Hitler Pact. The Soviet government was condemned by trade union and liberal groups as the betrayer of freedom, justice, and peace. The IFTU expressed indignation at the Soviet action. Those who had opposed negotiations with the Soviet trade unions pointed to this action as proof that the IFTU had been right in refusing to trust the Russians and to have dealings with them.

## VI. THE LAST ACT

Tense and threatening as the international situation was, the Zurich Congress of the IFTU seemed to look ahead to continued peaceful activities. It discussed such questions as the establishment of industrial councils and economic planning for the "next slump." It increased the number of vice-presidents on its Executive Committee from five to six, with a view to electing an American to the post. It approved two proposals made by the Swedish delegate. One was to add an expert on social questions to the staff; the other was to set up a committee to study the "future form of activity" of the IFTU.

The Zurich Congress proved, however, to be the last important act of the International Federation of Trade Unions. Though it continued to exist for a few years longer, events soon showed that it had run its historic course. Born of the First World War, the IFTU found its end in World War II. The story of its demise and of its successors is told in Part Six.

## PART SIX

# The Second World War and After

## 1939-1951

# Formation of World Federation of Trade Unions
## 1939-1945

WHEN the war broke out in September, 1939, the International Federation of Trade Unions and the socialists were fully united on the issue
of supporting the Allied governments. British trade union leaders
entered the cabinet of Winston Churchill and assumed an important
part in organizing war production. The British Labour Party, at its
annual congress at Bournemouth in May, 1940, adopted by an overwhelming vote a declaration of policy which read in part that "the
Labour Party unreservedly supports the Allied war of resistance to
Nazi aggression because, though loathing war, it regards this war as a
lesser evil than the slavery which finally would be the only alternative."

A similar attitude was taken by the national trade unions of other
Allied countries. In the United States, the American Federation of
Labor, at its convention at New Orleans in 1940, declared in favor of
extending all "help and assistance possible" to Great Britain on the
ground that if Great Britain were defeated, then America and democracy would be increasingly menaced.

Criticism of unconditional support of the war was voiced in Allied
countries by small left-wing socialist groups such as the Independent
Labour Party of Great Britain. These groups recognized the necessity
of fighting against Hitler, but argued that it was necessary to put an
end to both Nazism and "capitalist imperialism." They called upon the
workers to establish as soon as possible labor and socialist governments, which alone, in their opinion, could overthrow Hitler and
establish a stable system of social justice and peace.

Opposition to the war was voiced only by the Communists, who, with the conclusion of the Hitler-Stalin Pact, veered from advocacy of "anti-Fascism" to attacks on the Allies. British, French, and American Communists decried the war as a "ruthless struggle between British and German imperialists for the domination of the whole earth" and denounced the labor and socialist leaders supporting it.

## I. The IFTU During 1940-1943

For about ten months after the outbreak of the war, the IFTU maintained its headquarters in Paris. In March and May, 1940, the Executive Committee of the IFTU, under the chairmanship of Walter Citrine, held meetings in Paris, but little was accomplished at these meetings except to elect William Green a vice-president. A meeting of the General Council of the IFTU was scheduled for June, 1940, to map a course of action. Before this meeting could be held, Hitler began his rapid march into Belgium, Holland, Denmark, and France. On June 9, 1940, the headquarters of the IFTU were transferred to London. The British Trades Union Congress provided an office for Schevenels in its own building (Transport House).

As a result of the events of 1939-1940, the trade unions affiliated with the IFTU ceased to exist in the countries overrun by Hitler. The French General Confederation of Labor was dissolved by Marshal Pétain. The trade unions of the United States, Canada, Mexico, India, and Argentina continued to maintain their affiliation with the IFTU. It was clear, however, by the middle of 1940 that the IFTU could play little part in the titanic struggle which was developing on a world scale.

Still, on the ground that the IFTU should be revived at the end of the war to help shape the peace, Citrine persuaded the British Trades Union Congress (TUC) to help it carry on. In October, 1940, the IFTU resumed publication of its bulletin, which had been suspended the previous June. In January, 1941, Citrine and Schevenels came to the United States to meet with William Green and other members of the Executive Council of the AF of L. The American labor leaders agreed that the IFTU should be maintained during the war as "an expression of the workers of suppressed, oppressed and conquered nations." The IFTU was to make itself useful by aiding "underground movements in all conquered lands," by collecting information on conditions in Europe under Nazi occupation, and by extending help and encouragement to escapees from the Nazis. The AF of L showed its interest by continuing to pay affiliation dues, which amounted to $5,222 for the year ending August, 1940, and to $9,103 for 1941-1942. The trade unions of Sweden and Switzerland also continued to support the IFTU financially and morally.

Several steps were taken during 1941-1942 to enhance the prestige of the IFTU. In the summer of 1941, a joint committee of officers of the IFTU and officials of Trade Secretariats who had fled from Nazi-occupied countries to London met to consider the establishment of an Emergency International Trade Union Council (EITUC) for the duration of the war. In November, 1941, in connection with the special session of the ILO held in New York, an informal international trade union conference was arranged which was attended by representatives of twenty-two national trade union centers. William Green, as vice-president of the IFTU, presided, and Citrine and Schevenels spoke for the IFTU. The trade union officials attending the conference promised that their national labor organizations would fulfill their obligations to the IFTU.

On September 1, 1942, the Emergency International Trade Union Council held its first meeting in London. The Council was composed of six members of the executive committee of the IFTU, seven representatives of national trade union centers, and seven members from "trade union groups in exile." The meeting decided that the Emergency Council would act as the "principal representative of international organized labor" during the war. Two committees were appointed: one to prepare a plan for the reconstruction of the international trade union movement, the other to formulate the social and economic demands of labor for the postwar world. On January 1, 1943, the IFTU began publication in English and Spanish of a monthly journal—*The Trade Union World*—which discussed the problems of trade union reconstruction after the war.

## II. The Anglo-Soviet Trade Union Committee

In the meantime, events took place which were to change the international trade union situation. On June 22, 1941, Hitler launched his attack on Russia, and the Soviet Union became one of the Allied nations fighting against the Berlin-Rome Axis. In August, 1941, Winston Churchill and President Roosevelt held their dramatic meeting on the high seas and formulated the Atlantic Charter, whose eight points outlined the principles of the peace to come. On December 7, 1941, Japan made its attack on Pearl Harbor, and the United States joined the Allies in what became in fact a world war. On January 1, 1942, twenty-six nations, under the leadership of President Roosevelt, signed a joint declaration, reaffirming the principles of the Atlantic Charter as a basis for postwar reorganization and thus bringing into being the United Nations.

As a result of these events, the Soviet trade unions became interested in obtaining the good will of the trade unions in Great Britain and the United States. The Communists in all countries veered as quickly as they had in 1939, but in the opposite direction. They now declared that the war was no longer an "imperialist struggle" but a war for democracy and freedom. They threw themselves into war work and entered in large numbers the underground anti-Nazi movements of Europe. In the United States and Great Britain, they began agitating for closer relations with the Soviet trade unions.

The British labor leaders felt that closer relations between the trade unions of Great Britain, the United States, and the USSR would help the war effort, and might also prepare the ground for international labor unity after the war. Accordingly, the British Trades Union Congress, at its annual meeting in Edinburgh, in September, 1941, voted in favor of setting up an Anglo-Soviet Trade Union Committee to meet alternately in Russia and Great Britain. The declared purpose of the committee was to exchange "views and information upon the problems of both movements and for joint counsel on matters of common concern, on the definite understanding that there would be no interference on questions of internal policy, which must remain the exclusive responsibility of each body." The committee held its first meeting in Moscow in October, 1941. It agreed to cooperate on a series of "main objectives," such as strengthening industrial efforts in both countries for the maximum production of tanks, airplanes, guns, and other arms; rendering the utmost help in arms to the Soviet Union by Great Britain; support to the people of the countries occupied by Hitler in their fight for independence and the reestablishment of democratic liberties; strengthening personal contacts between the representatives of the British Trades Union Congress and the Central Council of the Trade Unions of the USSR.

The committee continued to be active during 1942-1943, arranging for the exchange of delegations to congresses, for Russian visits to British war plants, and for meetings between representatives of the trade unions of the two countries.

### III. The Anglo-American Trade Union Committee

At a meeting of the Anglo-Soviet Committee, in December, 1941, the question was raised of bringing in representatives of American labor. An invitation to join the committee was sent to the American Federation of Labor, and Walter Citrine came to the United States to give it his personal support. On May 20, 1942, he met with the executive council of the AF of L in Washington. Citrine expressed the desire that American representation "should cover all the organized workers in the USA," that is, not only the AF of L but also the CIO and the Railroad Brotherhoods.

The Executive Council of the AF of L rejected Citrine's proposal. William Green said that the AF of L was willing and ready to extend to Soviet Russia all necessary military and economic aid for the prosecution of the war. However, the AF of L regarded the Soviet trade unions not as bona fide labor organizations but as instruments of Soviet state policy dominated by the Communist party, and for that reason did not consider it possible to join with them. Green also indicated that the AF of L was opposed to sharing representation on any committee with the CIO and the Railroad Brotherhoods.

Instead, Green suggested setting up an Anglo-American Trade Union Committee. The British Trades Union Congress accepted this suggestion, and on July 23, 1942, an Anglo-American Trade Union Committee was set up. It was to consist of five American and five British trade unionists and to meet at least three times a year. One of the tasks which the AF of L wanted the committee to undertake was to formulate a program of "peace objectives" which organized labor could defend at the peace conference.

When the Anglo-American Trade Union committee held its first meeting in Washington on February 10, 1943, the British again proposed that the CIO and the Railroad Brotherhoods be included. This suggestion was again rejected by the AF of L. on the ground that the CIO was a "dual union" and that the combined membership of the CIO and the Brotherhoods was about 2,500,000 while the AF of L alone had over 5,000,000 members. The AF of L leaders cautioned the British that the American labor movement could be unified only through its own efforts and that any outside interference would defeat the objective.

The establishment of the Anglo-American Committee aroused much resentment. The Soviet unions were offended that the AF of L refused to join with them in an Anglo-Soviet-American Trade Union Council. The CIO protested against not being included in the Anglo-American Trade Union Committee. The CIO was aiming at this time to gain prestige by being given a recognized place in the international labor movement, and urged the British TUC to take steps to form a wider international labor organization.

### IV. WORLD LABOR CONFERENCE

While these labor negotiations were proceeding, the fortunes of war were turning in favor of the Allies. By the fall of 1943, the Soviet armies had for a second time taken the offensive against the Nazis. The Allies had won the campaign in North Africa and were advancing in Sicily and on the mainland of Italy. Mussolini had been overthrown. Allied hopes of victory were rising. In Great Britain, the United States, and among the Allied governments-in-exile, the new spirit of hope found expression in numerous plans for national and international reconstruction. Private and official committees were formed to discuss such plans and to prepare for the day of peace. Most of these plans, especially for the countries of Europe, projected a "new social order" in which labor would play a large role, public enterprise and nationalized industry would have a larger place, and social-economic planning by the state would assure for the workers and all the people "full employment" and social security "from the cradle to the grave."

Partly under the influence of these developments and partly as a result of discussions in the Anglo-Soviet Committee and with the

CIO, the British TUC at its meeting in Southport on October 27, 1943, decided to call a world trade union congress to consider the problems of war and peace. In November, 1943, Walter Citrine, as secretary of the British TUC, sent out invitations to seventy-one trade union organizations in thirty-one countries to meet in London on June 5, 1944. Invitations were sent to various trade unions in the same country, even when they were known to be in conflict. Thus, in the United States invitations went to the AF of L, the CIO, the Railroad Brotherhoods, and the United Mine Workers. In France, Belgium, Holland, and other countries, the Christian trade unions were invited to attend. Also invited were the IFTU, the Latin American Confederation of Labor (CTAL), and the international Trade Secretariats located in London. Each organization was invited to appoint delegates, in proportion to its membership, with a minimum of two delegates.

It was emphasized by the British TUC that the conference was to be "purely exploratory and consultative." Also, in order not to embarrass delegates from neutral countries, the conference was to be divided into two parts. During the first week, problems connected with the prosecution of the war were to be discussed; the second week was to be devoted to questions of postwar reconstruction. The trade unions of the neutral countries were invited to attend during the second week.

The provisional agenda of the conference listed four items:

1. The furtherance of the Allied war effort.

2. The attitude of the trade unions toward the anticipated peace settlement.

3. Representation of the trade unions at the peace conference, and at the preparatory commissions or conferences for relief, rehabilitation, and postwar reconstruction.

4. Problems of postwar reconstruction, including the reconstruction of the International Trade Union Movement.

In issuing the invitation for the conference, Walter Citrine raised some difficult questions. In the first place, he by-passed the IFTU, which was still in existence and which he himself had helped to maintain precisely in order that it might take the initiative in rebuilding the international labor movement. Second, he addressed his invitations to many labor organizations which were in conflict with the national trade union centers affiliated with the IFTU, despite the traditional rule that only one such center should be recognized in any one country. Third, despite British relations with the Anglo-Soviet Committee, he did not consult with the latter. Lastly, as he was aware that the AF of L wanted the IFTU to convene an international labor conference, his action seemed to suggest either a rivalry with, or a lack of confidence in, the AF of L.

The British Trades Union Congress was guided in its action by reasons which it regarded as valid. The British labor leaders were convinced that the pre-1939 divisions in the ranks of labor had been a factor in the rise of Hitlerism and in bringing on the war. They also believed that international trade union unity was essential if labor was to play an effective part in securing a durable peace and a reconstructed world order. They felt that if the IFTU were to call an international conference, it would have to leave out under its rules not only the Russians but the CIO and many other labor organizations in various countries. While having their reservations about the Soviet trade unions, the British TUC believed that an effort should be made to cooperate with them not only for the purpose of unifying the labor movement but also in order to promote concerted action between the governments of the Big Three powers. Finally, they assumed that in calling an exploratory conference they did not jeopardize the reconstitution of the IFTU or their friendly relations with the AF of L.

Under the circumstances, the AF of L refused to take part in the conference. The reasons given by the AF of L were (1) that the conference should have been called by the IFTU; (2) that the invitations had been extended to "dual unions," such as the CIO; and (3) that the AF of L was opposed to the participation of the Soviet trade unions.

In their turn, the Soviet trade union leaders criticized the British for taking unilateral action. Early in 1944, they proposed that the arrangements be changed in such a way as to make it clear that the conference was being called jointly by the British TUC, the Soviet trade unions, and the CIO.

The projected conference could not be held for reasons of war. June 5, 1944, was the date originally set for D-day, though it was later changed to June 6. On May 3, 1944, the British Trades Union Congress canceled all plans for a conference.

The AF of L reported later in the year to its convention that it considered the matter "a closed incident." In fact, the incident was only a preview of things to come. After the liberation of Italy, Belgium, and France, the British trade unionists resumed their plans for a world labor conference. On October 12, 1944, the General Council of the British TUC decided to convene the postponed conference in London on January 8, 1945. It was also agreed to hold a preliminary meeting on December 4, 1944, in London to lay down a final agenda. In deference to the Russians, the preliminary meeting was to be attended by the TUC, the Soviet trade unions, and the CIO. The conference was thus called by these three organizations jointly. In November, 1944, the date of the London conference was changed to February 6, 1945.

## V. THE AF OF L, THE CIO, AND THE CGT

The AF of L again refused to take part in the proposed conference, and called upon the IFTU to "convene a world trade union conference of the free trade unions of the world at the earliest possible time." The AF of L admitted that the IFTU was "at best only a skeleton organization with only a few national organizations paying dues." But the AF of L claimed that the IFTU had "traditions and accumulated experience which should make it the rallying force for free trade unions the world over." The Belgian and Dutch trade unions supported the AF of L and protested against any attempt to form a new labor international.

The protests of the AF of L and the other trade unions were of no avail. Though the IFTU at this time claimed 19,000,000 members in 23 countries, it was little more than a name and a memory. The Emergency International Trade Union Council set up by Schevenels in 1942 had prepared a plan for the reorganization of the IFTU which was published in 1944, but no agreement could be reached on this plan, and the General Council of the IFTU put off action on it until September, 1945. Furthermore, at the request of Citrine and Schevenels, the majority of the General Council of the IFTU decided to be represented at the London conference. So did the officials of the

International Trade Secretariats located in London who had been befriended by the British trade unions.

In contrast to the AF of L, the CIO readily accepted the British invitation to the proposed conference when it was first issued in November, 1943. When the new invitations were issued in October, 1944, the CIO announced that it would attend both the preliminary meeting of December 4 and the London conference. Philip Murray explained in a statement to the press on November 14 that the CIO was eager to establish contacts with the labor movements of other countries and that the CIO delegation to the London conference would urge the formation of a new world labor organization. Murray described the London conference as a first move toward a "labor Dumbarton Oaks" and said that it was imperative for labor to be represented at the peace table.

The movement for a new world labor organization was reinforced by the reentry upon the scene during the last months of 1944 of the French General Confederation of Labor (CGT). The latter had played an important part in the underground movement for national liberation led by the National Resistance Council. In this underground anti-Nazi and anti-Pétain movement, trade unionists, socialists, Communists, and members of the Christian trade unions had worked together. When the Allied armies in August, 1944, came close to Paris, the CGT and the French Federation of Christian Unions (CFTC) called out their followers on a general strike to speed the liberation of the capital. After the liberation, organized labor in France, and the CGT in particular, whose membership rose to nearly five million, assumed an important position in economic and political life.

The CGT soon reached out for a place of influence in the international labor movement. It reestablished the Franco-British Trade Union Committee, which had lapsed in 1940. In January, 1945, it established a Franco-Soviet Trade Union Committee. Conferences of the two committees were held in Paris, London, and Moscow. French trade union leaders felt that France was being relegated by the Allies to a secondary place in world affairs and they wanted to strengthen French prestige and influence through the international labor movement.

To achieve this end, they allied themselves with the Soviet trade unions. In January, 1945, they made an agreement with the leaders of the Soviet unions for common action in favor of a new world labor organization. The leadership of the CGT in these international activities was assumed by Louis Saillant, a young man of thirty-five who had held a rather minor post in the French trade union movement before 1940 but who had gained a reputation for his courage in the underground movement. He became a national figure when he succeeded Georges Bidault as head of the National Resistance Council after Bidault entered General de Gaulle's government as minister of foreign affairs.

## VI. The London Conference

The conference which assembled in London on February 6, 1945, brought together 204 delegates and observers from 63 local, regional, national, and international labor organizations. The Soviet trade unions sent thirty-five delegates and ten advisers and interpreters, headed by V. V. Kuznetsov and M. P. Tarasov; the British Trades Union Congress had a delegation of fifteen; the French CGT had fourteen delegates; the CIO was represented by twelve delegates, among whom were Sidney Hillman, Allan Haywood, J. B. Carey, R. J. Thomas, Joseph Curran, and Michael Ross. The delegates claimed to speak for 60,000,000 workers. This figure is of doubtful value since the membership figures reported by many delegates for their organizations could not be verified. The IFTU was represented by Schevenels.

The presence of so many delegates from Western Europe, the United States, Canada, the USSR, Mexico and other Latin American countries, India, China, Australia, New Zealand, and from mandated and dependent areas such as Palestine, Cyprus, Nigeria, Sierra Leone, the Gold Coast, Northern Rhodesia, British Guiana, and Jamaica was significant as showing the effort made to give the conference a world-wide character. The fact that the delegates could obtain passports and traveling facilities to come to London showed that the Allied governments were not only mindful of the role which organized labor was playing in the prosecution of the war, but willing to support the establishment of an international labor organization.

Officials of the British Trades Union Congress who took an active part in the conference—Sir George Isaacs, Sir Walter Citrine, and Arthur Deakin—made special efforts to win public recognition for the conference. At their suggestion, Winston Churchill was invited to address the delegates. As he was at the Yalta Conference at the time, he sent greetings and authorized his Deputy Prime Minister, Clement Attlee, to speak for him. The conference was addressed also by Ernest Bevin. The president and vice-presidents of the conference were received by their Majesties the King and Queen.

As the conference was being held at a time of some of the hardest fighting of the war, much stress was given to the first item on the agenda—the furtherance of the Allied war effort. The delegates of Great Britain, the United States, and the USSR described the contributions which organized labor had made in their respective countries to military production, while delegates from France, Belgium, Norway, and other countries gave an account of their underground anti-Nazi movements and their role in liberation. A resolution was adopted paying tribute to the workers of the United Nations, who were said to have borne the brunt of the war, and saluting the heroic armies of the United Nations. The resolution called upon the workers to increase military production needed for a speedy victory. At the same time, the resolution urged the trade unions to fight for adequate wages, better housing, proper food rationing, better social insurance laws, and equal pay for equal work without distinction of sex, race, or creed. The resolution also demanded that the liberated countries be granted freedom of speech, of assembly, of religion, and of trade union organization, and that they be supplied with food and raw materials to enable them to give employment to their workers. The resolution called upon the Allied governments to reconsider their relations with Argentina and Spain, who were said to be giving aid to the enemy. Finally, the resolution pledged the members of the conference to do everything in their power to strengthen the unity of the United Nations.

After some discussion, in the course of which delegates from the colonies gave vent to criticism of British and other "imperialisms," a resolution was adopted on the terms of peace, which on the whole was in accord with the official position of the Allied Powers. The resolution "acclaimed" the decision of the Big Three to call a conference at San Francisco for the elaboration of a United Nations Charter. It stressed, however, the demand that representatives of the trade union movement be given representation in the General Assembly of the United Nations, and also the right to take part in the work of the Economic and Social Council and the Security Council. With regard to Japan, the resolution proposed to hold the Emperor accountable for the war in the Far East, to replace the Japanese Empire by a democratic republic, and to apply strictly the Cairo Declaration.[1]

On postwar reconstruction, the conference formulated the social and economic demands current in the labor movements of Europe and the United States, such as freedom to organize and to form cooperatives; free technical education; the forty-hour week; better housing and nutrition; comprehensive social insurance, including free medical aid; special allowances for war veterans and invalids; and price control to prevent inflation. The resolution also called for international cooperation in monetary matters with a view to expand world trade, international agreements to regulate the prices of articles of mass consumption, and long-term loans to promote the economic development of colonial and underdeveloped areas.

A division of opinion developed on the issue which held the center of attention of the delegates; namely, whether the conference should form a new world labor organization at once. Sidney Hillman urged the conference to set up a new international organization immediately. The delegates, in his opinion, had proved that though they had come from many countries with different backgrounds, they were able to smooth out differences and to agree on peace aims and on a postwar social and economic program. He, therefore, saw no reason for delay. He proposed that the conference adopt a plan for a new world organization to be ratified by the national labor organizations represented; that the conference appoint a committee which would become the provisional executive of the new world organization as soon as the latter was ratified, and that this executive committee convene as soon as possible a constituent assembly at which the new world organization would be set up.

[1] Made in December, 1943, by President Roosevelt, Winston Churchill, and Generalissimo Chiang Kai-shek.

Hillman's proposal was supported by the delegates from France, the USSR, Australia, Mexico, and other countries. Louis Saillant said some harsh things about the IFTU and declared it incapable to meet the needs of the postwar period. Vincente Lombardo Toledano, president of the Latin American Confederation of Labor (CTAL), appealed to the delegates not to tinker with the IFTU but to make a new start at once without losing time.

Walter Citrine pleaded against immediate action. He pointed out that the conference had been called only for consultative purposes and that it had no mandate to make decisions. He defended the IFTU and argued that, as it was still in existence, it was preferable to reorganize it rather than start a new organization. He was supported by the delegates of most of the trade union centers of Western Europe and by the Trade Secretariats.

Citrine and his supporters hoped that by retaining the IFTU they might reconcile the AF of L to take part in an international organization with the Soviet Trade unions. They were apprehensive of the latter and wanted to counterbalance their influence through the participation of the AF of L. Citrine realized, however, that he was fighting a losing battle. Though the British had called the conference, they were unable to control it. The CIO-Franco-Soviet combination took the lead in it from the very beginning. Hillman's prestige and influence at the conference were great and he played a leading part in adjusting differences between the British and Soviet delegates. He declared that though the absence of the AF of L was to be regretted, it was necessary to go ahead without it.

In view of the situation, Citrine offered a compromise resolution. While silent on the question of setting up a new organization immediately, the resolution proposed setting up a committee to act as the provisional executive organ of the World Labor Conference. Hillman accepted the proposal, and it was approved by the conference.

### VII. THE PREPARATORY COMMITTEES

In consequence of this compromise, the London conference set up an interim committee of forty-one members to function as "the competent authority" until another World Labor Union Conference was convened. A few days after the London conference, the interim committee appointed an administrative committee of thirteen—two members each from Great Britain, France, the USSR, the United States, and Latin America. Louis Saillant was appointed secretary of this administrative committee. Its headquarters were in Paris in the offices of the CGT, which defrayed its expenses. Walter Citrine was shortly afterward elected president of the committee. A subcommittee of seven was appointed to prepare a constitution for the proposed world federation; it included Citrine, Saillant, Hillman, Tarasov, Toledano, and Schevenels.

On April 30, 1945, the subcommittee addressed to the four chairmen of the United Nations Conference at San Francisco a memorandum stating the reasons why the London World Labor Conference should be given official representation in the United Nations. The memorandum concluded with the following sentence: "We ask for such representation not only as an act of simple justice to the heroic working peoples of the United Nations, but because we are firmly convinced that the granting of our request would be of material assistance in assuring the realization of the great goal shared by all men of good will—a just and enduring peace for the peoples of the world."

Even before this memorandum was submitted, the head of the Soviet delegation to the San Francisco Conference, V. Molotov, had proposed to the Steering Committee of the UN Conference that the World Labor Conference be invited to attend in an advisory capacity. His proposal was rejected by the Steering Committee. After the memorandum was submitted, the committee of the San Francisco Conference which dealt with questions of the Economic and Social Council decided to invite the representatives of the London World Labor Conference to attend its sessions in an advisory capacity. The invitation was considered by the Steering Committee of the United Nations Conference, where it was supported by the Soviet Union, France, and China. It was opposed by Great Britain and the United States on the ground that the United Nations Conference was a conference of states and that nongovernmental organizations could not be represented. The Steering Committee overruled the decision of the committee of the Economic and Social Council, and the invitation was rescinded. .

While failing in its main effort, the Administrative Committee was successful in smoothing out its differences on matters of organization. Early in May, 1945, it approved a draft constitution for a new world labor federation. On May 23, Saillant issued from his office in Paris invitations for a second world labor conference to be held in Paris. The invitations were accompanied by copies of the draft constitution. The invited organizations were requested to study the draft, to offer amendments, and to come to Paris prepared to set up a new international organization.

## VIII. THE PARIS CONGRESS

The gathering which assembled in Paris at the Palais de Chaillot on September 25, 1945, was even more numerous than the London conference. Over 250 delegates came from 56 countries, territories, and colonial areas, representing 65 national and local labor organizations, the IFTU, and 17 International Trade Secretariats. The national trade union centers of Poland and of ex-enemy countries—Hungary, Rumania, Bulgaria, Albania, and Finland—whose right to be represented had been heatedly debated at the London conference, were represented in Paris. So were the reconstituted trade union centers of Italy, Holland, Czechoslovakia, Denmark, and Austria. The Christian trade unions of France and Switzerland sent observers. The hundreds of delegates from different races and creeds and of all shades of political opinion claimed to speak for 67,000,000 organized workers. The only important national trade union center absent was the American Federation of Labor, which refused to come to Paris for the same reasons for which it had stayed away from London earlier in the year.

Like the London conference, the Paris meeting was given much publicity and official recognition. Leon Jouhaux, the veteran French labor leader, who had but recently returned from imprisonment in Germany, extended to the delegates the greetings of Paris—the "city of revolution and freedom." As the conference coincided with the celebration of the fiftieth anniversary of the founding of the CGT, the delegates were treated to a series of festivities commemorating the event. The Soviet Embassy gave them a reception. They were also entertained at an official dinner by the head of the French Government, General de Gaulle.

It was clear from the first days of the Paris Congress that the majority of the delegates had come determined to set up a new international labor organization. Still, the British delegates made another bid for further deliberation and for connecting the new organization with the IFTU. Walter Citrine warned the delegates that they could not "create a new federation over-night by passing a resolution," and that it required time to find the necessary premises and staff. He again reminded the delegates that the IFTU was still in existence and that "the common sense thing to do" was to negotiate with it so as to use its staff and the officers. It was not the custom of trade unions, he said, to desert the officials and staff who had served them well.

The conference was not in a mood to heed Citrine's warnings and admonitions. It responded readily to Hillman, Saillant, Toledano, Tarasov, and others who called for immediate action. Hillman expressed the mood of the majority when he said, ". . . the eager eyes of the workers throughout the world are upon this all-important conference. If we do not emerge with a permanent World Trade Union organization, in my judgment, it will be disastrous to the hopes of millions who look forward to a World Federation of Labor Organizations as their sole hope for peace and a decent living."

The conference thus proceeded with the work of adopting a constitution and by-laws for a new world labor organization. The draft constitution prepared by the Administrative Committee was criticized by various delegates on five main points. It was said, in the first place, to set up a too highly centralized organization. Second, it did not provide adequate representation in the governing bodies for the smaller countries. Third, the dues were said to be too high and beyond the means of the smaller labor unions. Fourth, exception was taken to having the headquarters in Paris. Evert Kupers, of the Dutch trade unions, argued that it was more advisable to have the headquarters in a small country to avoid interference by a strong national trade union center; he proposed Zurich, Brussels, or Copenhagen. Fifth, the representatives of the Trade Secretariats opposed vigorously Article 13 of the draft constitution, which provided for the establishment of Trade Departments in the new federation to replace the existing Secretariats.

Eager to get the new organization started, the French, Soviet, CIO, Latin American, and Australian delegates agreed to amendments on the first three points. No concession was made on the question of the location of the headquarters.

The most troublesome issue proved to be Article 13 of the draft constitution, under which the International Trade Secretariats were to be replaced with Trade Departments whose activities, finances, and personnel were to be limited in various ways and made subject to the central control of the new federation. The representatives of the Secretariats refused to accept such an arrangement. J. H. Oldenbroek, secretary of the International Federation of Transport Workers, said that the Trade Secretariats were not ready to give up their independence, and that before joining the new organization they wanted to be sure that their autonomy and powers of action would be truly preserved and respected.

To prevent the conference from being deadlocked, the British, Swedish, and Dutch delegates came forward with an amendment to Article 13, which was accepted. Under this amendment, the work, duties, rights, and finances of the Trade Departments were to be governed by a "special regulation" which was to be adopted later by the executive of the new federation, in agreement with the Trade Secretariats. That left the question open for future negotiations.

## IX. FOUNDING OF THE WFTU

With these changes and amendments, the draft constitution was approved by the conference on October 3. The delegates rose to their feet and signified the adoption of the constitution by "prolonged applause." Leon Jouhaux, chairman of the session, declared that henceforth the delegates would be sitting as the first congress of the World Federation of Trade Unions.

There was one break in the ranks, however. The Christian trade unions, which had reemerged after the war with larger memberships in France, Belgium, and other countries, had expressed a desire to participate in a unified labor international. They sent observers to London and to Paris. But at both conferences, they demanded the right to maintain their separate national and international organizations. As Gaston Tessier, the delegate of the French Christian trade unions, put it: "Any organization which can point to justifiable considerations of race, ideology, or any other sort, should be able to establish, to operate freely and to affiliate."

The Paris Congress rejected this concept of "plurality of organization" as out of harmony with the traditions and needs of the labor movement. The very first article of the constitution of the new federation provided that "as a general rule, affiliation shall be confined to a single national trade union center from each country"; more than one national center and individual trade union organizations were to be granted the right of affiliation only "wherever justifiable." The delegates of the Christian trade unions were not satisfied with this provision. They took no part in the sessions of the congress which followed the adoption of its constitution.

The constitution which set up the World Federation of Trade Unions was obviously framed with a view to avoiding theoretical controversy. It stated no general theory of social development or of the labor movement. It contained no references to socialism or "class struggle" or ultimate aims. The only reference to a general goal in the Preamble was to the "establishment of a World Order in which all the resources of the world will be utilized for the benefit of all its peoples, the vast majority of whom are workers by hand and brain."

The aims of the WFTU were stated in the Preamble to its constitution as follows:

a.   To organize and unite the trade unions of the whole world, irrespective of race, nationality, religion or political opinion;

b.   To assist the workers in less developed countries in setting up their trade unions;

c.   To carry on a struggle for the extermination of all fascist forms of government and every manifestation of fascism, under whatever form it operates or by whatever name it may be known;

d.   To combat war and the causes of war and to work for a stable and enduring peace . . .

e.   To represent the interests of world labor in all international agencies, resting upon agreements and conventions concluded between the United Nations;

f.   To organize the common struggle of trade unions in all countries for democratic liberties, full employment, improvement of wages, hours and working conditions, for adequate social insurance, and for all other measures furthering the social and economic well-being of the workers; and

g.   To plan and organize the education of trade union members on the question of international labor unity.

The main body of the constitution was concerned with structure and administrative procedures. The "sovereign Authority" of the WFTU was to be a World Trade Union Congress meeting every two years. The affiliated trade union organizations were to be represented at the congress in proportion to membership but on a regressive basis: a minimum of one delegate for unions with 250,000 members or less; one delegate for every 250,000 members for unions having up to 5,000,000 members, and so on. The functions of the congress were to examine the reports of the executive organs, to amend the constitution by a two-thirds vote, to admit and expel members, and to consider all matters of policy. The congress was to elect a General Council and an Executive Committee.

The General Council was to be the governing body of the WFTU between congresses. Each affiliated trade union was to be represented on the Council in proportion to membership. The Council was to receive and act on the reports of the Executive Committee, approve the annual budget, carry out the decisions of the congress, and elect the general secretary. The Council was to meet at least once a year, each time in a different country.

The Executive Committee was to consist of twenty-six members, including the general secretary. The USSR was allotted three places on the committee; the USA and Canada, three; Great Britain, France, and Latin America, two places each; one place each was allotted to the Middle East, India and Ceylon, China, Australasia, Africa, the Scandinavian countries, Western Europe, Central Europe, and Southeast Europe. The remaining three members of the committee were to be elected from a list of candidates nominated by the Trade Departments when they were set up. The executive Committee was to act as the governing body of the WFTU between sessions of the General Council, and was to meet at least twice a year.

After each regular meeting of the congress, the Executive Committee was to elect from among its members a chairman and seven vice-chairmen. They, together with the general secretary, were to form the Executive Bureau. This body of nine members was to direct the WFTU between sessions of the Executive Committee. The Bureau was to appoint three assistant general secretaries to serve under the direction of the general secretary. The latter was to be the principal administrative officer of the WFTU, in charge of the staff and offices. He was responsible to the Executive Committee but could be removed only by the General Council.

The funds of the WFTU were to be provided from affiliation fees on the following basis: £4 per annum per 1,000 members or part thereof up to five million members, and additional fees for membership above five million. The executive committee could reduce the fees for trade unions unable to pay. Affiliation fees were to be paid quarterly. Organizations in arrears for two or more quarters were to be deprived of the right to vote at congresses.

The WFTU was to publish a monthly bulletin in several languages. The headquarters were to be in Paris.

After adopting the constitution, the Paris Congress on October 4 elected a general council of 71 members from as many organizations in 51 countries. On October 5, the council met and elected Louis Saillant general secretary. Saillant lacked some qualifications for the job, such as knowledge of languages. He was disliked by some of the British and not too popular generally. But he had the edge on the job owing to his service as secretary of the Administrative Committee. He was acceptable to the French because at this time he appeared to hold a neutral position between the socialists and the Communists, among whom the leadership of the French CGT was divided; Leon Jouhaux supported him for this reason. The Russians regarded Saillant with favor in view of his part in organizing the Franco-Soviet Trade Union Committee. The British preferred Schevenels, but his unpopularity with the French and Russians made his election impossible. The British were assured that he would be one of the three assistant secretaries.

On October 5, the General Council also elected the Executive Committee, which met the following day and elected Walter Citrine president of the WFTU. The Executive Committee also elected an Executive Bureau. The nine members of the Bureau who were to be the leaders of the WFTU were Walter Citrine, chairman; Louis Saillant, secretary; five vice-chairmen—Leon Jouhaux, Sidney Hillman, V. Kuznetsov of the USSR, Lombardo Toledano of Mexico, and H. F. Chiu of China; the other two members were Giuseppe di Vittorio of Italy and Evert Kupers of the Netherlands.

The Paris Congress adopted a number of resolutions reaffirming the social and economic demands formulated at the London conference. In addition, it greeted the adoption by the San Francisco Conference of the United Nations Charter, but protested against its refusal to allow the trade union movement to take part in its debates. It instructed the Executive Committee to take steps to ensure the participation of the WFTU in the work of the Economic and Social Council, in an advisory capacity.

The congress also approved the Yalta and Potsdam agreements with reference to Germany and Japan.[2] It directed the Executive Committee to send commissions to occupied Germany and to Japan to investigate social and economic conditions, the progress made in the "liquidation of Fascism," and the possibilities of rebuilding the trade union movement in these countries. It requested the Executive Committee to try to get representation on the Allied Control Commission of Germany and on the Occupation Authority of Japan. Finally, the congress adopted a resolution expressing its "sincere admiration for the gigantic achievements of the late President Franklin D. Roosevelt," and calling upon the leaders of the United Nations to "follow faithfully" his "noble objectives" in order to ensure "continued unity among the United Nations."

In adjourning the congress on October 8, Leon Jouhaux said: "The World Federation of Trade Unions is now established. The future is ours if we are conscious of our mission, ours if our solidarity is firm, ours if we remain firmly attached to the ideals which are ours and which must become those of all humanity."

## X. DISSOLUTION OF THE IFTU

The question remained as to what was to be done about the IFTU, which was still nominally in existence. Some of the trade union centers which had joined in forming the WFTU continued to be affiliated with the IFTU. The Swiss trade union center suggested that a special congress of the IFTU be called to take action which would indicate

---

[2] The Potsdam agreement was made in July-August, 1945, by President Truman, Clement Attlee, and Stalin; chief provisions were to demilitarize Germany, reduce its heavy industries, bring war criminals to trial, decentralize German cartels, build up democratic institutions, and to dissolve Nazi organizations.

the "continuity" of the IFTU and the WFTU. This suggestion was not practical in view of the fact that Citrine and Schevenels had gone over to the WFTU and that the American Federation of Labor was certain not to recognize any "continuity" between the two organizations. The problem was resolved more simply. On December 13, 1945, the General Council of the IFTU met and by an overwhelming vote decided to dissolve the organization. The AF of L did not attend the meeting.

Thus, after a career of 25 years, during which it had played a dominant part in the international labor movement, the IFTU came formally to an end. It succumbed to the hope of a new era of good relations with the Soviet Union, aroused by the war, and to desire for a new beginning in international labor activity through a new organization.

CHAPTER XX

# Promise and Performance
## 1945-1947

THE founding of the World Federation of Trade Unions was made possible by a coalition of the British Trades Union Congress and the CIO with the French CGT and the Soviet trade unions. Each of these organizations had special reasons for joining the combination, but they shared a common purpose—to bring their influence to bear on the making of the peace and on postwar reconstruction. They were helped by the fact that the idea of international labor unity made a strong emotional appeal to large groups of workers as a result of the war. It was in response to this appeal that the trade unions of Western Europe laid aside their traditional opposition to cooperation with the Russians and agreed to join with them. The labor groups of Latin America and Asia were under Communist influence, but they rallied around the banner of the new organization also in the hope of drawing from the trade unions of the Big Four countries strength for themselves at home and some prestige abroad.

The British labor leaders and the CIO were aware of difficulties in building the WFTU into a working body. The problem was whether, in view of its diverse elements, it would be able to act as "the spokesman for workers in all lands" or would "flounder on the rocks of political, philosophical and organizational differences." Some put the issue more pointedly, namely, whether the Soviet trade unions would try, with the aid of Communist political groups, to divert the organization from the path mapped out for it in London and Paris and to use it for political ends.

For nearly two years after the Paris Congress, the WFTU seemed to give evidence of a relative capacity to keep its different elements in working balance. Toward the end of this period, difficulties increased, but efforts to maintain internal cohesion continued. These two years may therefore be considered as a separate period during which the performance of the WFTU was influenced by its original promise and by international conditions which still reflected the hopeful expectations of the war.

## I. The Balance of Forces

Shortly after the Paris Congress, Saillant opened headquarters for the WFTU in one of the fine residential districts of Paris in a large building requisitioned for the purpose by the French government. In the organization of the secretariat a certain balance of the various national and political groups was achieved. Of the three assistant secretaries, one was a Soviet appointee; he was put in charge of the press and information department. The second was Walter Schevenels, former secretary of the IFTU and a right-wing Belgian socialist, who had been nominated for the position by the British; he was to concern himself with relations with the International Trade Secretariats. The third post of assistant secretary was allotted to the CIO. After two men designated for the position refused to stay, the

CIO appointed Elmer Cope; in the fall of 1946, he took over the department dealing with colonial and dependent countries. Saillant himself took charge of relations with the national trade union centers. The economic and social department, which was regarded as important, was placed under the direction of a French Center socialist known as a competent technician.

As to the rest of the staff, the principal assistants in the different departments included French socialists and syndicalists, a British Labour Party man, a German and a Dutch right-wing socialist, a number of Communists, and some persons without clear political affiliations. The total number of employees during these two years, including translators and clerical help, was relatively large. No information is available on the budget, but it too was relatively large, in view of the high per capita fees paid by the British, the CIO, the Soviet unions, and some of the West European trade unions. The WFTU thus started off on a much larger scale than that ever attained by the International Federation of Trade Unions before 1939.

In the opinion of those who observed it, the WFTU was not well administered during these years. It was slow in preparing and distributing its documents. The public information department functioned badly. Toward the end of the period, there was friction between Saillant and his chief assistants, some of whom, including the director of the economic department, resigned. The replacements tended to upset the balance as originally achieved.

Of greater effect on the work of the WFTU were the changes in the composition of its Executive Board. During 1945-1946, Hillman and Citrine played a leading role in the board. The prestige and influence of these two men, who together with Saillant had done most to bring the WFTU into being, helped to smooth over internal friction and to give the work of the WFTU public importance. Their conciliatory tactics were helped by the fact that the Communist parties in France and Italy were at this time taking part in coalition governments in their respective countries and cooperating in economic reconstruction.

When Hillman died in July, 1946, his place on the Executive Board was taken by Frank Rosenblum, of the Amalgamated Clothing Workers of America, who believed in a united world labor movement. In the fall of 1946, Sir Walter Citrine resigned as secretary of the British Trades Union Congress to take a post on the National Coal Board established by the Labour government of England. His place as president of the WFTU was taken by Arthur Deakin, chairman of the British Trades Union Congress. Louis Saillant remained as secretary and as a member of the Board.

As a result of these changes and also of general tension between the USSR and the West which began to manifest itself in the winter of 1946-1947, the Executive Board of the WFTU assumed more and more the character of a coalition of two blocs. On the one hand, Deakin and Kupers represented the "reformists." On the other side were Kuznetsov of the USSR, di Vittorio of Italy, Toledano of Mexico, and Chiu of the China Association of Labor, who were Communists or close to the Communists. In between were Jouhaux, who more often than not sided with the reformists, and the member of the CIO. Deakin became the spokesman of the reformists. Saillant assumed the role of defender of policies sponsored by the Communist and Soviet members. The CIO member played a conciliatory part, in accordance with the policy of the CIO which during this period took the position that the WFTU was fulfilling the purposes for which it had been founded.[1]

The members of the reformist bloc felt that Saillant was not maintaining the even balance expected of him as secretary, but they continued efforts to correct the situation, in view of the force which the "myth of labor unity" continued to have in West European labor movements. It was the influence of this myth that helped to give the activities of the WFTU during these years whatever effect they had.

## II. THE WFTU AND GERMANY

One of the first acts of the WFTU was to send in early 1946 a commission of inquiry to Germany. The commission consisted of Citrine, Hillman, Jouhaux, Tarasov, Kupers, Evan Erban of Czecho-

---

[1] While the CIO was already having its first skirmishes with the communists who had achieved influence in some of the CIO unions, the CIO leaders believed that international cooperation with the soviet unions was possible. This position was due both to the idea that international labor unity was important, and to the belief that the CIO could play a leading role in international labor affairs. The rivalry of the CIO with the AF of L for international leadership was a factor in the situation.

slovakia, Ebby Edwards of the British Miners' Federation, and Saillant. It spent three weeks in Germany in January and February, 1946, visited all four occupation zones, and held consultations with German labor leaders and with members of the occupation authorities.

The commission issued a report, the chief points of which were that denazification was proceeding too slowly and that the trade unions should be given a larger role in the machinery of denazification. The members of the commission had their reservations about German labor. The German workers, they pointed out, did not organize a resistance movement against the Nazis even after Hitler's military power began to crumble. The commission did not think, therefore, that it was wise to count on German labor alone to democratize the country and its institutions. Still, they thought that the trade unions were "one of the most reliable anti-fascist forces in Germany," and urged a larger role for them in the reeducation of German youth.

The commission found that the reviving trade unions in Germany were being organized on a democratic basis, that union officials were being elected by secret ballot, and that there were no Nazis in trade union official posts. The members of the commission were also pleased that a single trade union movement was developing in Germany, in contrast to the ideologically split unions before 1939. They expressed themselves in favor of a decentralized form of organization along Western lines, as opposed to the more centralized form of organization adopted in the Eastern Soviet zone. They called upon the British, French, and American occupation authorities to provide more meeting places for local unions, more transport facilities for union leaders, and to encourage zonewide labor organizations. The commission refused, however, to make any recommendation with regard to interzonal trade union organization. The British, in particular, were opposed to the formation of a nationwide labor federation for fear that the Communist and pro-Communist labor leaders of the Soviet zone, where trade union organization had made greater strides than in the Western zones, would take over the leadership of an all-German labor movement.

The report of the commission was discussed at a series of meetings of the Inter-Allied Control Commission in Berlin in March, 1946. Citrine and Saillant visited Berlin several times and held consultations with the Man-Power Directorate of the Inter-Allied Control Commission. The latter accepted the suggestion of the WFTU to accelerate the formation of trade unions and to give the unions a larger part in the work of denazification. On one point, however, the WFTU failed to obtain satisfaction, namely, that representatives of the WFTU be included on all consultative bodies on trade union questions which the Inter-Allied Commission might establish. The Inter-Allied Commission refused this request; it agreed to obtain the views of international labor organizations on German trade union problems only to the extent to which circumstances permitted. The Inter-Allied Control Commission did not name the WFTU in its decision, and thus gave it no special status.

The WFTU sent a second mission to Germany which stayed about a month in January and February, 1947. Its main recommendations were that the affiliation of the German unions with the WFTU should be approved "in principle," and that the WFTU should establish a "liaison bureau" in Berlin to assist the German unions in calling a general trade union congress and in organizing a national labor federation.

The proposals of the second commission of inquiry were approved by the Executive Committee of the WFTU at its session in Prague in June, 1947. The Inter-Allied Control Commission, however, refused permission to the WFTU to open a "liaison bureau" in Germany. All Saillant could do was to send a resident observer to Berlin. The proposal for the affiliation of the German trade unions was blocked by prolonged discussions in the WFTU committees and led to no action in the course of 1947. The proposal lost meaning subsequently when events led to the division of Germany into Western and Eastern spheres.

The WFTU through its commissions of inquiry thus influenced inter-Allied trade union policy in Germany to some extent. As related in the next chapter, German trade union policy was influenced in a much larger measure by the American Federation of Labor.

### III. The WFTU and the United Nations

One of the main demands of the WFTU, as related previously, was to be recognized as the only spokesman of the international labor movement and to be represented as such in official international conferences and organizations dealing with peace and postwar reconstruction. When the first General Assembly of the United Nations met in London in January, 1946, Citrine and Saillant sent a letter to Paul-Henri Spaak, president of the Assembly, in which three requests were made: (1) that the WFTU be invited to sit in the General Assembly in an advisory capacity; (2) that the WFTU be brought into regular consultative relations with the Economic and Social Council under the provisions of Article 71 of the UN Charter; and (3) that at a later date the WFTU be accorded "full participation in the work of the Economic and Social Council with the right to vote." The WFTU claimed such special status on the ground that it allegedly represented over 65,000,000 organized workers and that the support of the masses of organized labor was essential for the success of the United Nations.

When these requests were brought before the Political Committee of the General Assembly, the first and third were rejected. As at the San Francisco Conference the year before, the American and British view prevailed that the United Nations was an intergovernmental organization and that nongovernmental organizations could not be represented in its bodies. The issue thus narrowed down to the request that the WFTU be brought into consultative relations with the Economic and Social Council.

The members of the Executive Bureau of the WFTU present in London accepted the situation "in a spirit of conciliation." But at this point, the issue was complicated by the application of the American Federation of Labor requesting that it too be given consultative status in the Economic and Social Council. The leaders of the WFTU protested that this meant depriving the WFTU of the exclusive and special status which it claimed. The request of the AF of L was strongly supported by the delegations of the United States and some other countries. The WFTU then proposed a compromise, namely, that it alone have official delegates at the meetings of the Council but that these delegates be assisted by advisers, one of whom would be a member of the AF of L.

This compromise was defended in the Political Committee by the delegates of the Soviet Union, France, and Czechoslovakia, but it was voted down. On February 14, 1946, the General Assembly adopted the recommendation of the Political Committee that the Economic and Social Council make consultative arrangements not only with the WFTU but also with the AF of L, the International Cooperative Alliance, and several other nongovernmental organizations.

Meeting in Paris a week later, the Executive Bureau of the WFTU "noted with disappointment and perturbation" the discussions and decision of the General Assembly, but decided nevertheless to avail itself of the status granted to it in the Economic and Social Council. It declared at the same time that it would "insist on its rights to submit to the United Nations Organization its own proposals on subjects which it should promote in the interest of all workers."

From February, 1946, to August, 1947, the WFTU waged a persistent campaign in and outside the United Nations to achieve a larger representative status for itself in the Economic and Social Council. Owing to its persistent efforts, the WFTU was able to wring a series of concessions. At the second session of the Council in June, 1946, it was proposed to limit the role of the WFTU to that of an observer, with the right to submit written memoranda to the Secretariat which could be circulated to members of the Council only at the request of any one of them. The WFTU was also to have the right to consult with a special committee of the Council whenever it specifically requested such consultation. Such a committee was established by the Council and became known as the Committee on Non-Governmental Organizations (the NGO Committee).

This limited role was vigorously criticized by Sidney Hillman in a letter to Sir Ramaswami Mudaliar, president of the Economic and Social Council.[2]

It was also objected to by several members of the Council. To meet this criticism, the Council on June 21, 1946, established three categories of nongovernmental organizations. The most important organizations were placed in Category A, and given the right to sit in the meetings of the Council and, upon the recommendation of the NGO Committee, to present their views in the plenary sessions of the Council. The organizations placed in Category A were the WFTU, the AF of L, the International Cooperative Alliance, the International Chamber of Commerce and two others.

The WFTU found the decision of June 21 unsatisfactory. It issued

[2] This letter was Hillman's last act in the WFTU. He died a month later.

an appeal to the "workers of the world" and to "democratic organizations generally" protesting that it could not accept "a secondary part nor a subordinate position" in the United Nations. At its meeting in Washington in September, 1946, the Executive Bureau of the WFTU decided to press its claim in the General Assembly for "full representation" in the Economic and Social Council. In the meanwhile, however, it accepted the role of observer and sent representatives to sit in such capacity at the Third Session of the Council held at Lake Success in September-October, 1946. It also began negotiations with the NGO Committee for further concessions. Arthur Deakin, speaking for the WFTU, requested that it be given the right to suggest items for the agenda of the Council, to submit written memoranda direct to the Council on questions of special interest, and to defend its views in the plenary sessions of the Council.

The NGO Committee was willing to meet these demands only in part. The WFTU then took the issue to the General Assembly meeting in New York in October-November, 1946. Several members of the General Council of the WFTU, who were advisers to their national delegations at the Assembly, sent a letter to Spaak, reiterating the demands put forth by Arthur Deakin as stated above. The General Assembly granted only one of these demands: it adopted a resolution, by a vote of 22 to 12, with two abstentions, recommending that the Economic and Social Council give the WFTU the right to submit questions for inclusion in the agenda of the Council.

Having won the right to propose items for the agenda of the Council, the WFTU centered its efforts on gaining "the full right to speak" on all questions of the agenda in which it had an interest. On July 3, 1947, Saillant sent a long letter to Trygve Lie, secretary-general of the United Nations, in which he requested that the WFTU be given the right to participate in the deliberations of the Economic and Social Council as well as the right to request the convocation of the Council in special session. Saillant, in other words, was asking that the WFTU be placed on an equal footing with the specialized agencies.[3]

[3] The specialized agencies are international organizations based on intergovernmental agreements. See Preface.

At the fifth session of the Council, Elmer Cope defended the claims of the WFTU. The Council adopted a resolution which made clear that there was a basic difference between the specialized agencies and nongovernmental organizations like the WFTU, and that the latter could not have the right to request the calling of special sessions of the Council. In another resolution, however, the Council granted the WFTU the right to make statements in the plenary sessions on any item included in the agenda of a session of the Council at its request.

By the middle of 1947, the WFTU had thus obtained from the Economic and Social Council the following rights:

1. To designate representatives to sit at all public meetings of the Council in a consultative capacity.

2. To circulate direct to members of the Council written statements on matters within its competence.

3. To submit items to be included in the provisional agenda of the Council. This implied consultation with the secretary-general of the United Nations on items submitted, and the defense of such items before the Agenda Committee of the Council.

4. To take part in the deliberations of the plenary sessions of the Council by making introductory expository statements and additional statements for purposes of clarification.

The WFTU was not slow in making use of the rights gained. Its representative spoke at the very first session of the Council at which the right was granted. Saillant afterward reported with pride that "this was the first time that a representative of the WFTU had spoken at a plenary session of the Council." After that, such statements by organizations in Category A became a regular feature of the sessions of the Council.

The Executive Committee of the WFTU "welcomed with satisfaction" the 1947 decisions of the Economic and Social Council, but reaffirmed its determination to obtain for the WFTU "a status identical to that of the specialized agencies." This claim was now largely meant for propaganda purposes. In practice, the WFTU could rest content with what it had obtained since that gave it large opportunities to make itself heard at the sessions of the Economic and Social Council.

### IV. Peace and Reconstruction

In waging its campaign for larger representation in the United Nations, the WFTU was carrying out only part of its program. It also claimed the right as representative of the international labor movement to be consulted on peace settlements and questions of postwar reconstruction, which were being considered at conferences and by Inter-Allied commissions outside the United Nations.

In general, the WFTU was in accord with the official peace policies of the Allied Powers, as stated in the Atlantic Charter, the declarations of Teheran and Yalta, and in the Potsdam agreements. But it advocated certain policies and measures which were matters of controversy. Such were its proposals to place German heavy industry and other properties under United Nations control, to use German labor for the rebuilding of the devastated areas, to rebuild the trade unions and to return to them their former properties, to put an end to international cartels, to enable the Jewish people to rebuild Palestine as their National Home, to initiate schemes of international public works, and to pursue vigorous policies of "denazification and anti-fascist reeducation." Special measures and organizations were needed to put these policies into effect, and it was in this connection that the WFTU demanded a place for itself at the peace conferences.

It became clear before long that as a result of disagreements between the West and the Soviet Union, the process of peacemaking was to be more complex and difficult after the Second World War than it had been after the First. It was only after prolonged and acrimonious debates and negotiations in the Council of Foreign Ministers at their meetings in London in September, 1945, in Moscow in December of that year, and in Paris in June, 1946, that the main obstacles were cleared for the calling of an international conference to consider peace treaties with Italy, Hungary, Rumania, Bulgaria, and Finland. The Paris Peace Conference, which lasted from July 29 to October 15, 1946, was also marred by difficult and at times bitter debates, but it did result in the drafting of separate peace treaties with the five countries.

The Paris Peace Conference dealt with problems on which the WFTU had taken a stand, such as German reparations, trade policy, civil rights, and so on. The WFTU was not, however, "associated" with these phases of the peace settlements. Some labor leaders who were members of the executive bodies of the WFTU were present at the Paris Peace Conference as technical advisers to their national delegations. If they voiced views held by the WFTU, they did so informally. Officially, the WFTU was not given a place at the peace table.

In matters of reconstruction, the WFTU had some influence on trade union policy in Germany, as already described. It participated in discussions on full employment and standards of living in the commissions of the Economic and Social Council. It was invited to be represented as an observer at the meetings of the Preparatory Commission of the International Conference on Trade and Employment, held in London and Geneva during 1946-1947.

The WFTU tried to influence policies of rehabilitation and reconstruction by holding conferences of experts under its own auspices. In January, 1947, it arranged an international conference of coal experts, which was attended by representatives of the trade union centers of eight European countries and of the International Trade Secretariats of miners and transport workers. The conference made a number of recommendations for increasing the output and supply of coal by modernizing the mines, improving wages and living conditions in order to attract man power, and placing the Ruhr coal mines under the management of an international body in view of the unreliability of the German engineers.

It is hard to say whether this conference had any effect. The winter of 1946-1947 was marked by extreme cold and bad weather in Europe, and the shortage of coal not only slowed down production but caused great hardships to people in their homes. In all countries, urgent appeals were made to the coal miners to increase production. In this atmosphere, the WFTU conference was another voice in the general chorus.

In one of its resolutions, the WFTU coal conference recognized that coal exports from the United States were "an essential factor for the economic recovery of the world," and expressed the opinion that the production and distribution of coal in the United States should "take into account the pressing needs of countries whose recovery was impeded by lack of coal." This resolution, which was approved by the Executive Bureau and General Council of the WFTU, was pointed to as illustrating the spirit in which the WFTU carried on its work at that time and the recognition which it gave to American efforts on behalf of world economic recovery.

## V. OTHER ACTIVITIES

Besides those described above, characteristic activities of the WFTU during this period were its "action against Franco Spain" and its organizational efforts in Africa and Asia. All through 1946, Saillant addressed letters, telegrams, and memoranda to the Council of Foreign Ministers, to the Security Council and the General Assembly of the United Nations, protesting against conditions in Spain and the "Franco dictatorship." In the name of the WFTU and "the workers of the world," Saillant called for the severance "by Democratic governments of diplomatic relations with the Franco Government." At the urging of the WFTU, workers' demonstrations against Franco were staged during 1946 in various cities, and attempts were made by some unions to carry out a systematic sabotage of trade with Franco Spain.

On December 12, 1946, the General Assembly of the United Nations adopted a resolution barring the Franco government from membership in all international organizations connected with the United Nations. The resolution also recommended that, if within a reasonable time there was not established a government deriving its authority from the consent of the governed and committed to respect for freedom of speech, religion, and assembly and to the holding of democratic elections, the Security Council was to consider "adequate measures to remedy the situation." In the meanwhile, the General Assembly recommended that members of the United Nations recall their ambassadors and ministers accredited to Madrid.

The WFTU greeted this resolution as a "first victory,"[4] but declared that more had to be done to bring about "the inevitable overthrow of the man and the regime." The Executive Bureau of the WFTU instructed Saillant to organize a series of radio broadcasts to Spanish workers, to create a "solidarity committee in favor of the Spanish

---

[4] This claim was clearly exaggerated. The General Assembly was influenced by the unfriendly attitude towards the Franco Government of the AF of L and other labor organizations as well as of some governments.

people," and to take other measures to stimulate and support internal resistance in Spain to the Franco government.

Saillant tried to carry out these instructions during 1947, but without success. The radio broadcasts could not be arranged because of "diplomatic difficulties"; the efforts to stir up internal resistance resulted in some strikes which were suppressed; the appeal for solidarity met with response only from a few of the affiliated trade union organizations; Spain's exports to Great Britain and the United States increased; the withdrawal of ambassadors from Madrid was "only half fulfilled." The Security Council refrained from considering any further measures "to remedy the situation." Saillant admitted this lack of success, but claimed that at least the "manoeuvres of international reaction" had not succeeded in breaking entirely "the isolation of Franco."

The WFTU had only partial success in its efforts to establish its influence in Asia and Africa. In March, 1947, a WFTU mission came to Tokyo to make contacts with the Japanese trade unions. The mission was officially received by General Douglas MacArthur and was given facilities by American officials of the Far Eastern Command to visit the industrial centers of Japan and to hold meetings with Japanese trade union officials. The mission made a report in which it recommended that the Japanese unions should set up a unified national trade union center based on industrial unions, and that a general system of collective bargaining should be established. However, in June, 1947, the WFTU admitted that it was unable to maintain contacts with the trade unions in Japan, owing to the unfriendly attitude of the Far Eastern Command and to the opposition of the American Federation of Labor.

In April, 1947, the WFTU arranged a Pan-African Trade Union Information Conference at Dakar which was attended by sixty delegates from twenty-one trade union organizations of Gambia, Nigeria, the Gold Coast, Dahomey, Madagascar, the Sudan, Tunisia, Morocco, Algeria, and several other areas. Of the delegates, forty-seven were natives and thirteen Europeans. The French CGT and the British Trades Union Congress took part in the conference.

After hearing reports on industrial and trade union conditions in the different regions of Africa, the conference adopted recommendations to promote trade union organization, social legislation, the abolition of racial discrimination, and measures for raising living standards. The General Council of the WFTU, at its meeting in Prague in June, 1947, approved these recommendations and instructed the general secretary to work out a program to that effect in cooperation with the United Nations and the specialized agencies. Not much was done to carry out these recommendations. Saillant blamed this lack of success on the "lethargy" of the colonial department of the WFTU; he accused Elmer Cope, who was in charge of this department, of "deliberately paralyzing" its activities. The first Pan-African Conference was nevertheless an entering wedge into Africa which the WFTU was to try to drive deeper in its subsequent activities.

To sum up, the performance of the WFTU during 1945-1947 was relatively effective in several ways, but far from fulfilling the promise of its founders. As it was engaging more in political than industrial activities, it ran into difficulties of a political character. These led to dissensions and internal divisions which by the end of the period began to rock the organization.

CHAPTER XXI

## The AF of L Versus the WFTU
## 1945-1947

THE claim of the WFTU that it spoke for world labor was challenged by the American Federation of Labor, which had grown in numbers and influence during the war. The AF of L refused to join the WFTU and denounced it as a "caricature of a free trade union movement" conceived by the "Russian dictatorship" as a successor to the Red

International of Labor Unions. To counteract the activities of the WFTU, the AF of L developed a large international program, which became an important factor in international labor relations.

## I. Labor and Foreign Policy

In assuming this role on the international stage, the AF of L based itself on a number of general and specific premises. The time had passed, it declared, when the labor movement could safely refrain from interesting itself in foreign policy, in view of the impact of foreign affairs on domestic policies. In the phrase of the AF of L, peace and prosperity—that is, life and livelihood—were inseparable from the very heart of foreign policy. The leaders of the AF of L claimed that the mounting menace of starvation, collapse, and chaos in many parts of the world made it necessary for organized labor to play a more dynamic role than ever in formulating and promoting a genuinely democratic foreign policy by the American government. While the AF of L was ever ready, as it stated, to support the government in promoting the cause of peace and democracy, it could not be just an echo of the government and government departments. As the free trade unions were the bulwark of democracy, they had to be ever alert and active to the end that the United States pursue foreign policies free from every vestige of imperialism and aggression.

The tragedy of the international situation, according to the AF of L, was that the world was traveling with great speed toward another global conflagration, for which the heaviest responsibility lay with the Soviet government. It was clear to the AF of L that the Soviet purpose was aggression and domination of the world and that the world crisis was thus not a struggle between East and West but between freedom and Communist totalitarianism. The American people had a vital stake in this struggle, for a world engulfed by "totalitarian slavery" could not have islets of freedom. It was thus necessary to oppose in every way the "Bolshevik bureaucracy" in its drive to infect the world with its destructive doctrines, and to strengthen the democratic forces of the world.

In this struggle, the AF of L maintained, the free trade unions could play a decisive role, because they were by their very nature opposed to government domination and totalitarian ideas. They were built on voluntary action by their members, on contractual relations with employers, on freedom from state intervention in their internal affairs, and on the principle of raising living standards by peaceful action. They were thus a basic "pillar in the reconstruction" of a free democratic world.

## II. Trade Unions in Germany

In the view of the AF of L, the free trade unions were called upon to play a particularly important part in Germany, which the AF of L considered to be the key to the reconstruction of Europe and to the reestablishment of world order and peace. The essential object, therefore, was to help rebuild the free trade unions of Europe, and especially of Germany, and to help maintain them wherever they were threatened by Communist inroads and infiltration.

The free trade unions in Germany were having many difficulties, which were aggravated by the fact that they had no rallying center after the liquidation of the IFTU. To the AF of L, the WFTU was deluding the labor movements of Europe by pretending to be a bona fide international labor organization, when in fact it was dominated by the Soviets. By its activities in Eastern Europe and by its failure to criticize the Soviet Union at any time, the WFTU had proven itself to be a "camouflaged and delicately controlled instrument of Soviet imperialist interests and policy." In the interests of free trade unionism and rebuilding a free world, the false role of the WFTU and the Communist elements which controlled its "bureaucratic machine" had therefore to be exposed. The AF of L saw it as its duty to serve as a rallying center for the free trade unions of Europe and particularly of Germany.

## III. Role of the AF of L

Acting on these ideas, the AF of L took its first step against the WFTU in January, 1946, in the United Nations. As described in the preceding chapter, the AF of L protested against giving the WFTU exclusive consultative status in the Economic and Social Council, and demanded the same status for itself. With the aid of the US and other delegations, it obtained its demand. When the Council set up Category A of nongovernmental organizations, the AF of L was placed in that category, on an equal footing with the WFTU. The AF of L thus appeared at the sessions of the Economic and Social Council as a rival and antagonist of the WFTU.

The AF of L displayed its greatest energies in counteracting the WFTU in Germany. Late in 1945, it appointed Irving Brown, a member of the International Association of Machinists, to act as its European representative. Later, in 1946, Brown opened an AF of L European Bureau in Brussels, while Major Henry Rutz became the AF of L representative in Germany. Brown soon developed wide connections with European labor leaders and established close relations with the American and British occupation authorities. Owing to his energy, he became an active factor in mobilizing opposition to the WFTU. His activities were supplemented by the work of the Free Trade Union Committee, which the AF of L had set up previously to provide relief and aid to the free labor movements of all countries and to combat Communist influences in the trade unions abroad.

The aims of the AF of L in Germany were to rebuild the German trade unions and to make them the chief instrument in the democratization of the country. Accordingly, the AF of L urged the occupation authorities of the US zone to encourage the trade union leaders in their work and to assist them by providing more paper for their publications, typewriters, gasoline for their automobiles, and so on. Because of their relations with the American authorities, Brown and Rutz were able to obtain tangible results. In addition, the AF of L assisted the German trade union leaders in a material way. The AF of L supported vigorously the appeal to the American people to send grain to Europe, including Germany, to alleviate the hardships caused by the severe winter of 1946 and the drought in the summer of 1947. In the course of 1946-1947, the AF of L sent 500 food packages of 40,000 calories each a month. They were distributed to trade union officials who because of their official duties had no time to earn extra rations. It also sent 500 food packages for distribution in youth camps run by the trade unions. It helped the trade unions in their publication and organizing work. A German edition of the *International Free Trade Union News*, published by the Free Trade Union Committee, was distributed widely.

In this and other ways, the AF of L representatives in Germany gave encouragement and help to the trade union leaders who were active in preventing the unions from falling under Communist influence. They also took steps to counteract the work of the WFTU. They induced the occupation authorities to forbid officials of the WFTU to enter the US zone. They were instrumental in preventing the granting to the WFTU of permission to open a liaison bureau in Berlin. They opposed the formation of an all-German labor federation at a time when it might have fallen into Communist hands. They won over large numbers of workers in Western Germany by opposing the dismantling of plants engaged in the production of nonmilitary goods and by demanding that the occupation authorities return to the unions their pre-1933 properties. They maintained a continuous propaganda through news sheets, leaflets, and booklets which expounded the ideas and activities of the AF of L, and were distributed widely among trade union officials and members.

That these activities were effective was shown by the complaints of the WFTU against the "disruptive" and "dividing" tactics of the AF of L. Saillant ascribed his failure to achieve more in Germany to the work of the AF of L representatives.

The European Bureau of the AF of L extended help also to anti-Communist unions in France and Italy. It encouraged the International Trade Secretariats in their opposition to the WFTU. These activities assumed importance at the end of 1947, and in 1948, as described in the next chapter.

Some leaders of the AF of L were eager to take a longer step against the WFTU. At the 1947 convention of the AF of L, Daniel Tobin, president of the Teamsters' Union, proposed that the AF of L set up an Information Bureau to assist free trade unions in all countries and to promote the formation of a free trade union International. The proposal was received favorably by the convention, but the Executive Council of the AF of L took no action on it. However, the AF of L continued to play an important part in the developments of the following two years which brought about the results intended by Tobin's proposal.

# Conflicts and Rift
## 1947-1949

UNTIL the middle of 1947, the World Federation of Trade Unions, despite internal friction, was able to maintain the precarious balance of forces on which it was founded. The progress of the organization and its future work were the subject of discussion at the meetings of the Executive Bureau, Executive Committee, and General Council which were held in succession from June 2 to June 14, 1947, at Prague and which marked the high water mark of the effort to maintain internal unity.

Soon after the Prague meetings, the situation began to change. The latent strains came into the open, and friction developed into conflict. In the course of 1948, these conflicts became steadily aggravated. By the early months of 1949, the leading trade union groups found it impossible to work together any longer, and the WFTU was torn apart by the rift between them.

Developments in the WFTU reflected the general trend of international relations during these years. The outstanding feature of this trend was the growing tension between the United States and the Soviet Union which led to the division of the world into two opposing camps and to a "cold war" between them. The issue around which this tension developed was the Marshall Plan. The events which grew out of the Marshall Plan and which form the landmarks in the history of these years were the formation of the Communist Information Bureau or Cominform in October, 1947, the Communist *coup d'état* in Czechoslovakia in March, 1948, the setting up of the Organization for European Economic Cooperation (OEEC) in April, 1948, the Berlin blockade in July, 1948, the division of Germany into Western and Eastern spheres in the spring of 1949, and finally the conclusion in 1949 of the North Atlantic Pact. While these events were of different degrees of interest to organized labor, they formed the background of developments in the international labor movement.

The questions which aroused the greatest concern of organized labor in the United States and Europe were those connected with the Marshall Plan. They caused the first serious disagreements in the WFTU. As these grew deeper, other factors of internal division came into play, namely the increasing influence of the Communist elements in the Secretariat of the WFTU, the relations with the International Trade Secretariats, and general questions of organization and policy. The Marshall Plan is thus the starting point in the story of the international labor movement from 1947 to 1949.

## I. The WFTU and the Marshall Plan

The CIO and the AF of L greeted with enthusiasm the address of Secretary of State George C. Marshall at Harvard University on June 5, 1947, in which he proposed that the European governments adopt a joint program of recovery which would place Europe "on its feet economically" and which the United States could aid and support. Both the AF of L and the CIO assumed the task of presenting the purposes of the Marshall Plan to the labor movements of Europe and of enlisting their support for it.

There was little doubt at the time that the labor organizations of most countries of Europe would respond favorably to the Marshall proposal. Economic recovery in Europe, which had been making rapid headway during 1946, was slowed up by the effects of the hard winter of 1946-1947 and the drought in the spring of 1947. Shortages of food, coal, and raw materials were retarding production, and increasing unemployment and inflation were inflicting great hardships on the working population. The trade unions of Great Britain, Belgium, Scandinavia and other countries thus were eager for their governments to accept the Marshall offer. To many trade union leaders, the Marshall Plan also made an appeal because it implied a concerted effort on the part of the European countries to work out a planned program of recovery and reconstruction—something which they had advocated during the war and immediately after.

It also seemed possible at first that the Soviet Union might join in the common effort. The governments of Poland, Yugoslavia, Hungary, Rumania, and Czechoslovakia were in economic straits and desirous of American aid. Some of them expressed officially their willingness to take part in the proposed program. The situation changed, however, when Molotov walked out of the meeting with Bidault and Bevin in Paris in July, 1947, where the Marshall Plan was discussed. The Soviet government, instead of joining in the Marshall program, initiated a scheme of its own which involved a reorientation of Eastern Europe toward Moscow. On October 5, 1947, the newly organized International Communist Information Bureau (Cominform) issued a proclamation opposing the Marshall Economic Recovery Program (ERP) as a "scheme of Wall Street" and of "American monopolists" seeking to impose their domination on Europe. This meant, of course, that the Communist-controlled trade unions of France and Italy and of Eastern Europe would follow suit and oppose the Marshall program.

The issue was brought before the WFTU at the meeting of its Executive Bureau in Paris in November, 1947. The Marshall Plan was not on the agenda. The CIO member of the Bureau requested, however, that James Carey, secretary of the CIO, be permitted to present a statement on the subject.[1] The motion was opposed by di Vittorio of Italy, Sidorenko of the Soviet Union, and Saillant. Arthur Deakin, chairman, then asked the members of the Bureau to vote first whether they would hear Carey's statement, and then decide whether they would discuss it. By four votes to three, it was agreed to hear the CIO statement.

In his statement, Carey pointed out that the European Recovery Program was in accord with the declarations of the London and Paris World Labor Conferences, and was an important step to put those declarations into effect. "I am here," said Carey, "to talk to you not about ideologies, because we have no American ideologies

---

[1] Though Rosenblum remained a vice-president of the WFTU, Carey assumed the role of CIO spokesman on the Board from the middle of 1947 on.

to export, but about food and coal and fertilizers, and agricultural machinery, and power plants, and transportation, and cotton, and steel. These are the things you want, these are the things the American people want to provide, to give you an opportunity to feed and warm your people, get your industries going, enable you to raise your standard of life, and become self-supporting." Carey concluded by requesting that the Secretariat of the WFTU encourage consultations between the national trade union centers interested in the proposed program.

After hearing Carey, the Bureau decided not to discuss his statement, but to record it in the official minutes of the meeting and to report it in the WFTU bulletin. It was voted, however, to place the question of the Marshall Plan on the agenda of the next meeting of the Bureau.

The Paris meeting left in its wake bad feeling on the part of the British TUC and the CIO against Saillant. Feelings were further strained by discussions as to the date of the next meeting of the Executive Bureau. The British and the Americans requested that the meeting be held in February, 1948. The members of the Bureau opposed to the Marshall Plan wanted a later date. Saillant argued that it would save expenses if the meetings of the Executive Bureau and the Executive Committee could be held at the same time later in the year. The CIO and the British TUC claimed that the delay was part of Saillant's strategy to sabotage discussion of the ERP.

All through January and February, 1948, as governmental negotiations with regard to the ERP were making progress, Communist attacks on the Program became more continuous and vituperative. The *Bulletin* of the WFTU published a number of such attacks which were made by the trade unions of Poland, Rumania, Bulgaria, and by other Communist-controlled labor unions. These attacks referred to British and American trade union leaders as "agents of American imperialism" and as "betrayers of trade union unity." The French General Confederation of Labor (CGT) requested the Executive Bureau of the WFTU not to place the Marshall Plan on its agenda. The CGT published a series of articles in its official journal, *Le Peuple*, criticizing the Plan on the grounds that it would lead to interference in the internal affairs of the recipient countries, that it was a scheme to establish United States bases in Europe with a view to another war, and that it gave no assurance to Europe to become self-supporting. Saillant echoed the arguments of the CGT at public meetings.

## II. ERP TRADE UNION CONFERENCE

Disturbed by the delay in convening the Executive Bureau and irritated by the articles against the Marshall Plan in the *Information Bulletin* of the WFTU, the British TUC and several West European trade union centers decided to take independent action in favor of the ERP. In this, they had the support not only of the CIO but also of the AF of L. Already at the San Francisco convention of the AF of L in October, 1947, David Dubinsky had proposed that the AF of L take the initiative in calling a conference of the free trade unions of the sixteen countries cooperating in the ERP with a view to ensuring the active role of labor in the program. The convention endorsed the proposal. It was taken up by Irving Brown, who discussed it with Paul Finet of Belgium, Evert Kupers of Holland, and labor leaders of other ERP countries. One of the first to endorse it was the Belgian Federation of Labor, which on December 16, 1947, adopted a resolution to call such a conference. In January, 1948, a similar resolution was approved by the trade union center of the Netherlands.

Early in February, 1948, the British TUC again requested Saillant to convene the Executive Bureau of the WFTU in the middle of the month to discuss the Marshall Plan in view of its urgency. Sir Vincent Tewson warned that if the request were refused, the TUC would have to take independent action. Tewson defended the TUC against the accusation that its action was part of a "conspiracy to wreck the World Federation of Labor." The TUC, he wrote, had shown great patience with "irresponsible critics" both at home and abroad who had heaped upon it abuse and vilification, but could no longer neglect its responsibility to take a lead in the situation. At the same time, James Carey and Michael Ross of the CIO arrived in Europe and held consultations with Saillant in Paris and with the Soviet trade union leaders in Moscow in the hope of winning over the Russians. The CIO still hoped that it could induce the majority of the Executive Board of the WFTU led by the Russians, to endorse the Marshall Plan, and thus lead the WFTU in a constructive international labor policy. However, soon after their visit, the Soviet leaders issued a long statement attacking the Marshall Plan as a "direct threat to the sovereignty of the nations of Europe."

On February 7, 1948, Saillant rejected the request of the TUC. He announced that the Soviet, French, Italian, and Mexican members of the Executive Bureau were opposed to holding the meeting in February. Saillant fixed the date of the meeting of the Executive Bureau for April 30, which, he said, was a compromise on his part as he had originally planned it for the first of May.

The British TUC then decided to act independently. At first, the AF of L wanted to take the lead in calling a conference, but relinquished the initiative to the British. Accordingly, after consulting with the trade unions of the Benelux countries,[2] the British TUC convened in London on March 9, 1948, an ERP Trade Union Conference. It was attended by the labor organizations of the ERP countries (except the French CGT and the Italian General Confederation of Labor), by the trade unions of the Western zone of Germany, and by representatives of the AF of L and the CIO. The conference endorsed the European Recovery Program, expressed its "earnest desire to see other countries brought within its scope," repudiated "any policy of aligning East against West," declared that it was satisfied that no unacceptable conditions were attached to the offer of American aid, and called upon the workers' organizations to give their whole-hearted support to make the program effective in the various countries. The conference set up an ERP Trade Union Advisory Committee to keep the trade unions of the participating countries informed on the progress of the program.

On April 3, 1948, the Foreign Assistance Act was signed by President Truman and became law. On April 16, the sixteen European countries participating in the ERP set up the Organization for European Economic Cooperation (OEEC). The Marshall Plan thus entered upon the stage of practical operations. It had many difficulties to overcome before it could become effective. One of the problems was the role of the trade unions in the program. Experience soon proved that it was necessary to win the cooperation of the

[2] Benelux is the name adopted by Belgium, the Netherlands, and Luxembourg.

workers if the recovery of Europe was to be advanced. The problem became especially serious in France and Italy, where the trade unions under Communist control actively opposed and sabotaged the work of the recovery agencies.

To counteract Communist activities, a second ERP trade union conference was convened in London in July, 1948. It too was attended by representatives of the CIO and the AF of L. The conference discussed ways and means of enlisting the support of labor in the different countries, and of persuading the governments to give organized labor a larger role in the ERP program. The conference decided to set up an ERP Trade Union Advisory Council with offices in Paris to maintain continuous relations with the OEEC as well as with officials of the Economic Cooperation Administration of the United States (ECA).

The ERP trade union conferences were denounced by the Communist elements in the WFTU. The British TUC and the CIO were accused of being "splitters of the labor movement." The trade union leaders of the ERP countries replied in kind, questioning the work of the WFTU and its capacity to represent a unified labor movement. Recriminations became bitter. It was soon evident that the breach between East and West over the Marshall Plan was causing a breach in the World Federation of Trade Unions as well.

### III. Break with the Communists

The divisions within the WFTU were sharpened by the struggle between reformist and Communist groups in the labor movements of the principal countries of Europe and in the United States. In France, Italy, and Western Germany the reformist elements broke away from the central labor organizations dominated by the Communists and formed independent organizations. The TUC in Great Britain and the CIO in the United States embarked upon a campaign to put the Communist minorities beyond the pale of the trade union movement. Beginning in 1947, this struggle reached its peak in 1949. Interwoven with the agitation over the Marshall Plan, it led to a realignment of forces in the national labor movements which had the effect of widening the breach in the WFTU.

*Reformists and Communists in France*

The earliest manifestations of this struggle appeared in France. After the liberation of Paris in August, 1944, and until the middle of 1947, French labor continued to be swayed by the spirit of unity aroused by the Resistance Movement. Reformists, socialists, syndicalists, and Communists worked together in the general Confederation of Labor (CGT), which gained a new height of over five million members, a new power in political life, and much prestige in the country. The Communists achieved a dominant position in the CGT in the course of 1946, but they generally used their power with moderation. The Communists continued to participate in the French coalition government in cooperation with the Catholic Popular Republicans (Mouvement Républicain Populaire) and the Socialist Party. During this period, the Communist leadership of the CGT moderated its wage demands, restrained the workers from striking, and carried on campaigns for increased output to speed recovery.

The situation was abruptly changed in the summer of 1947. As increasing economic hardships gave rise to strikes, the Communists decided to assume leadership of the labor discontent. At the same time, the Communist Party in the National Assembly broke with the government, was excluded from the government coalition, and went into opposition.

When Soviet Russia took its stand against the Marshall Plan, the French Communist Party and the CGT followed suit at once. In November, 1947, the CGT unleashed a series of strikes of miners, railwaymen, dockers, metal workers, and gas, electricity, and building trades workers which were among the bitterest in French history. The CGT demanded wage increases, attacked the Marshall Plan, and called for the readmission of the Communist Party into the government on its own terms. The country was aroused by what was regarded as a political general strike against the government and economic recovery.

The strikes were opposed by the reformists within the CGT, by the Catholic trade unions, and by some independent unions. After about two weeks, the government took strong measures to encourage those willing to work, and to repress sabotage. As the political character of the strike became clearer, the workers became impatient and resentful. The railwaymen were the first to begin to return to work, and that broke the strikes.

The strikes brought to a head the divisions within the CGT. The reformist groups, which centered around the weekly journal, *Force Ouvrière* (*Workers' Force*), and of which Leon Jouhaux was the chief spokesman, seceded from the CGT in December, 1947. Claiming to be the true heirs of the pre-1939 CGT, they took the name of *Confédération Générale du Travail-Force Ouvrière*. They received help from the American Federation of Labor, which sent them 100 typewriters, 25 mimeograph machines, office equipment, and food packages. The AF of L also gave them "an advance" of $25,000. By April, 1948, the Force Ouvrière (FO) was able to hold its first national convention.

The Force Ouvrière strongly defended the Marshall Plan. It took part in the ERP trade union conferences. It called on the French workers to support the work of the OEEC and the ECA.[3]

*Trade Unions and Politics in Italy*

Labor developments in Italy, while in some respects similar to those in France, had many distinctive features. When the Allies occupied Southern Italy and Rome, they helped to bring together the anti-Fascist labor leaders, who had fought against Mussolini in the Partisan Movement, and urged them to unite. In January, 1945, the *Confederazione Generale Italiana del Lavoro*—the Italian General Confederation of Labor (CGIL)—was formed as a united labor movement in which all shades of opinion were represented. Three general secretaries headed the organization, one from each of the three principal political groups—the Christian Democrats, the socialists, and the Communist Party. The Italian labor leaders were proud of this achievement of unity, which was in marked contrast to traditional divisions within European labor movements.

Owing to their compact organization, tireless energy, and the financial support of the Communist Party, the Communists in the CGIL soon gained the upper hand. The forceful Communist secre-

[3] After the formation of the FO, Jouhaux ceased to attend the meetings of the Executive Board of the WFTU.

tary, Giuseppe di Vittorio, became the actual leader of the organization, overshadowing his Catholic and socialist colleagues. When the CGIL held its first national convention in Florence in June, 1947, it claimed a membership of over five and a half million. It was estimated that some 80 per cent of the provincial and local labor unions were under Communist leadership and control.

The CGIL helped to found the World Federation of Trade Unions in October, 1945, and became one of its important affiliates. Di Vittorio was elected a member of the Executive Committee and the Executive Bureau of the WFTU.

The unity within the CGIL was based on the fact that the three principal political parties of Italy—the Christian Democrats, the socialists and the Communist Party—were cooperating during 1945-1946 in the de Gasperi government. This cooperation came to an end in 1947, when the Communists began attacking the Marshall Plan. De Gasperi forced the Communists out of the government, and they assumed the position of the major opposition party. From then on, the Communists not only opposed all de Gasperi's policies but acted as if their aim was to overthrow his government.

In view of this situation, the Christian Democrats would not remain in the CGIL. In 1948, they led their followers out of the CGIL and formed the *Libera Confederazione Generale Italiana dei lavoratori*— the Free Italian General Confederation of Workers (LCGIL). Giulio Pastore, who had been one of the three secretaries of the CGIL and who was known as a capable organizer, became the general secretary of the LCGIL. The main strength of the seceding Catholic unions was in the textile industry and among white-collar workers. It was estimated that the Catholic groups formed about 15 per cent of the membership of organized labor in Italy.

The LCGIL, though under Catholic leadership, was ready to admit all non-Communist elements. The two parties involved were the Republican Party and the right-wing Socialist Party (PSLI), which had broken away from the United Socialist Party of Italy under the control of Pietro Nenni because the latter favored cooperation with the Communists and was friendly to the Soviet Union. The Republican Party and the PSLI continued to form part of the de Gasperi government, but the labor leaders connected with these parties were anticlerical and reluctant to join the LCGIL. Neither would they remain in the CGIL, in view of increasing dissensions over the Marshall Plan and di Vittorio's antigovernmental activities. The Republican and right-wing Socialist labor leaders joined forces and early in 1949 left the CGIL to form a labor organization of their own, the Italian Labor Federation (FIL)—*Federazione Italiana del Lavoro*—which brought together the workers who were both anticlerical and anti-Communist. The FIL, like the FO in France, obtained assistance from the American Federation of Labor in funds, food, and publication facilities. Still, it remained relatively weak.

Several reorganizations took place in the Italian labor movement after 1949, which will be described in Chapter XXIV. For the period considered here, the fact to be noted is that the united labor movement of Italy broke up into opposing elements during 1947-1949. The CGIL lost members as a result. It also lost influence as a result of recurring political strikes which it called in support of policies of the Communist Party and which resulted in failure. Still, the CGIL remained the strongest labor organization of Italy, and continued to play an important part in the WFTU. But the LCGIL and the FIL formed a nucleus of anti-Communist labor forces in Italy which could be mustered against the WFTU.

### East-West Split in Germany

By mid-1947 trade union organizations had been reconstituted in the three Western zones of Germany. In the British zone, they were organized on a zonal basis and by the end of 1947 had a membership of over 2,500,000. In the United States zone, they were organized into three separate federations covering Bavaria, Hesse, and Wurttemberg-Baden, with a membership of some 1,500,000. In the French zone, which was the least industrialized, there were three regional federations with several hundred thousand members. In the Eastern Soviet zone, a central labor federation had been established, the *Freie Deutsche Gewerkschaftsbund* (FDGB)—Free German Trade Union Federation—claiming over three million members. The Berlin trade unions had a strong separate organization which formed part of the FDGB.

Most of the leaders of the trade unions in the Western zones had been trade union officials before 1933. They were agreed that the divisions within the German labor movement before 1933 had been responsible in large measure for the triumph of Hitler. They were determined to avoid divisions along political and religious lines. The West German trade unions thus came to include socialists, Communists, Catholics, and nonpartisans. The majority of the members and most of the leaders were socialists.

After the middle of 1947, when the American, British, and French occupation authorities proceeded with the political and economic integration of the Western zones, the trade unions of these zones began to amalgamate and set up a Trade Union Council to coordinate their activities. In April, 1948, this Council began formulating a program for combining all the trade unions of Western Germany into one organization.

While integrating their forces, the West German trade unions maintained relations with the FDGB of the Soviet Zone. During 1947-1948, representatives of the trade unions of all four zones met in a number of interzonal conferences to discuss the formation of an all-German labor federation. The trade union leaders of the Western zones hoped that by maintaining relations with the FDGB, they would help to hasten the unification of Germany and strengthen their own position in an all-German labor federation if and when it was formed.

However, before the end of 1948, these relations were broken off. The first East-West split took place in the trade unions of Berlin. The non-Communist elements in the West Berlin unions had gained strength in the course of 1947, owing to the more friendly attitude of the American occupation authorities, to the growing influence of the German socialists, to aid from the American Federation of Labor, and to their own efforts. Early in 1948, they were able to elect 280 delegates to a trade union conference which was to be held in Berlin. The Communists of the East sector of Berlin tried to revoke the credentials of a large number of these non-Communist delegates. The non-Communists then withdrew from the conference and formed the *Unabhängige Gewerkschafts Opposition* (UGO)—Independent Trade Union Opposition. The provisional council of the UGO declared that its affiliated unions would remain independent of all political parties, defend the right of free speech and of a free press, and concentrate on protecting the economic and social interests of their members.

The formation of the UGO led to the break of the West German trade unions with the FDGB. The break came at an interzonal conference which met near Linden in August, 1948. The delegates from the Western zones demanded that the delegation sent by the UGO be admitted to the conference. When the FDGB refused this request, the conference was adjourned. The FDGB subsequently made several attempts to resume four-zone meetings, but the Western trade union leaders ignored them. By this time, the growing division between West and East as a result of the Marshall Plan and of the Berlin blockade had put an end to expectations that an all-German labor federation could be formed.

Having broken with the FDGB, the Western trade unions proceeded to consolidate their own organization. The movement was accelerated by the founding of the Federal German Republic in the spring of 1949 and by the elections to the Bonn Parliament in August of the same year. In October, 1949, the trade unions of the three Western zones (now unified in the Federal German Republic) held a convention at Cologne and formed the *Deutsche Gewerkschaftsbund* (DGB)—German Federation of Trade Unions.

The Cologne convention was attended by 487 delegates representing over 5,000,000 members. It adopted a program which stressed the need to raise the worker's standard of living, to practice collective bargaining, to use strikes sparingly, to expand the social insurance system, and to promote protective legislation for women and young workers. It declared in favor of socializing basic industries such as coal, iron and steel, chemicals, power, and the banks. As one of its immediate policies, it put forth a demand for "co-determination," that is, the right of the workers to an equal voice with employers in all economic matters, including the right of labor to be represented on boards of directors of private and public corporations. The convention declared that the German Federation of Labor would be an "independent force," not committed to any political party. It repudiated both the Communist Party and neo-Fascist groups as destructive of the free labor movement.

The UGO gave its support to the German Federation of Labor

soon after the latter was founded, and merged with it the following year.

The trade union developments in Germany were a particular cause of friction in the WFTU. As related in a preceding chapter, the General Council of the WFTU at its meeting in Prague in June, 1947, had decided to set up a liaison bureau in Germany, but the British, American, and French members of the Allied Coordinating Committee had refused Saillant authorization to set it up. Saillant blamed the AF of L chiefly for this failure, but he also complained that the TUC and the CIO had not presented the case vigorously enough to their respective governments.

Saillant also failed in his efforts to promote an all-German labor organization. At his urging, the interzonal trade union conference held in Dresden in February, 1948, agreed to set up a "Central Council of German Trade Unions" and appointed a Working Committee to prepare a plan for its organization. Saillant's idea was that the Central Council would be recognized by the WFTU and would, with the aid of the latter, call a congress of trade unions of all four zones.

Saillant's plans did not materialize. The Working Committee was prevented from holding its meeting scheduled for March, 1948, by the refusal of the occupation authorities to permit delegates to attend. The Working Committee absented itself from the meeting of the Executive Bureau of the WFTU in April, 1948, to which it had been invited. In June, the UGO was recognized by the Western occupation authorities. In August, the UGO constituted itself as an independent trade union center and was recognized as such by the British Trades Union Congress. The same month occurred the break at the Linden interzonal conference, as described above. The movement for the unification of all German trade unions came to an end.

There were bitter recriminations in the WFTU over these developments. Saillant claimed that he had acted in accordance with the decisions of the Executive Bureau taken at its sessions at Prague in June, 1947, and at Rome in May, 1948. He blamed the British TUC for recognizing the UGO. He accused Elmer Cope of going to Linden "clandestinely" to break up the conference. The representatives of the TUC and the CIO in their turn accused Saillant of failing to apply the spirit and letter of WFTU decisions, and of giving support to the Communist elements in the German trade unions.

The question was the subject of prolonged debates at the session of the Executive Bureau in Paris in September, 1948. An ambiguous resolution was adopted which left the issues undecided.

### Anti-Communism in Great Britain and America

In contrast to conditions in France, Italy, and Germany, the Communists in Great Britain and the United States had during 1947-1949 little influence as political parties. They thus attached particular importance to the trade unions as a field of activity. While aware of their penetration into a number of unions, the British TUC and the CIO did not at first act vigorously against it. But as Communist activities assumed a concerted international character after the formation of the Cominform in the fall of 1947, the TUC and the CIO took the offensive.

The Communist issue in the British labor movement was of long standing. Toward the end of the 1930's, British Communists, following the Comintern directives of 1935, began to work in individual unions with a view to gaining positions of influence and control. They were helped after 1941 by Russia's entry into the war on the side of the Allies and by the friendly relations between the British and Soviet trade unions in the Anglo-Soviet Trade Union Committee. When Stalin dissolved the Comintern or Third International in 1943, the British Trades Union Congress rescinded a ruling passed in 1935, and again permitted its city trades councils to accept delegates from local unions who were members of Communist organizations. This enabled the Communists to gain influence not only in the trades councils but also in a number of national trade unions. By 1947, it was estimated that out of seventeen largest trade unions in England, with a membership of 100,000 each, the Communists had gained controlling positions in four, had some influence in six, but had no influence in the remaining seven.

Until 1947, the Communists presented few difficult problems for the British trade unions. The Communist Party supported the war effort between 1941 and 1945 and the policies of the Labour Government between 1945 and 1947. But after the break between the West and Soviet Russia over the Marshall Plan and the formation of the Cominform in September, 1947, Communist tactics in Great Britain as elsewhere underwent a change. The Communists began attacking the Labour Government and the Trades Union Congress, and embarked on campaigns to impede production. They accused the British labor leaders of becoming dependent on the "American Colossus of Big Business" and kept up a running fire in their journals against the Marshall Plan and the ERP.

Under its constitution, the British Trades Union Congress had only limited powers of control and discipline. It was in fact, a voluntary federation of nearly 200 large and small unions which varied in structure and function and which were autonomous in their internal affairs. Its industrial strength lay in its large unions, such as the Transport and General Workers' Union with over 1,000,000 members, the Union of General and Municipal Workers with over 800,000 members, the Amalgamated Engineering Union with some 700,000 members, the National Union of Mine Workers with over 600,-000 members, the National Union of Railway Men with over 400,000 members, and others. These large unions formed over half of the total membership of the TUC in 1948-1949, which was about 7,000,000. They had a predominant representation at the annual congresses of the TUC, but the smaller unions could make themselves felt by acting together. Similarly, in the General Council—the governing body of the TUC—policies were shaped by a process of give and take between the large and small unions.

In view of these conditions, the General Council of the TUC had to meet the Communist issue mainly by making clear the tactics of the Communists and by warning the unions against them. This the General Council did in several statements issued in March, October, and November of 1948. The two most important were entitled *The Tactics of Disruption* and *Defend Democracy—Communist Activities Examined*. In these statements, the General Council emphasized that the British trade union movement had a tradition of tolerance and respect for minority opinions. The point at issue, however, was not tolerance but whether decisions arrived at by democratic discussions and by a majority vote were to be respected and carried out. The trade union movement could not allow its policies and activities to be manipulated by persons who accepted the directives and dictates of outside bodies such as the Communist Party. The General Council called upon its national unions and local trades councils to be on guard against "crafty arrangements" by which the Communist Party managed to put its members into official trade union positions. The Council declared its determination to expose the Communist tactics continuously, "in order to combat infiltration and interference in trade union policy from a source outside the Movement and even outside these shores."

While the General Council took no specific action, its warnings and appeals had an effect. Only a few trade unions in England adopted rules to exclude Communists from office, but Communist influence in most of them began to decline during 1949.

In the United States, the drive against the Communists by the CIO took more drastic forms. In some of the CIO unions, officials known as Communists were removed from office. Unions which refused to change their officials had their charters taken away from them and were expelled. Most unions adopted rules making it impossible for Communists to hold office. Philip Murray, president of the CIO, directed the campaign, which reached dramatic heights after the CIO congress in Portland, Oregon, in November, 1948. After 1949, the Communists ceased to be a significant element in the organization.

## IV. The WFTU and the Trade Secretariats

The internal conflicts described above had one consequence which was crucial: they hampered the efforts of the WFTU to solve the problem of its relations with the International Trade Secretariats (ITS). The problem had twofold importance. In the first place, the Trade Secretariats, as explained in an earlier chapter, were a basic element in the structure of the international labor movement. As long as they stayed out of the WFTU, the latter was divorced from purely trade union activities and could not justify its claim to being a trade union organization. Second, the British Trades Union Congress, in joining the WFTU, had made its affiliation conditional on the achievement of a satisfactory agreement between the WFTU and the Trade Secretariats. Failure to reach such an agreement meant the withdrawal from the WFTU of its strongest and most influential affiliate.

At the time the WFTU was founded in Paris in October, 1945, most of the twenty-one International Trade Secretariats which had survived the war were only beginning to reestablish contacts with their prewar affiliated unions and to replenish their finances. The officials of these Secretariats thus viewed with interest the possibility of becoming part of a unified international labor organization. At the same time, these officials were apprehensive that the Secretariats would lose their independence of trade union action if they became mere trade departments of the WFTU, as was proposed under the latter's constitution. As related in a preceding chapter, the Paris Congress of 1945 postponed the issue by deciding that the trade departments should be governed by a "special regulation" which was to be worked out by the WFTU in consultation with the Secretariats.

The drafting of such a special regulation became one of the chief preoccupations of the WFTU. Saillant and his staff and the Executive Bureau of the WFTU took up the task immediately after the Paris Congress. Walter Schevenels, who had had much experience in dealing with the Secretariats before 1939, was put in charge of this work. In the course of the year, the WFTU prepared a draft which became the basis of discussion.

The "special regulation" prepared by the WFTU proposed to regroup the Trade Secretariats into thirteen trade departments of transport workers, miners, metal workers, factory workers, salaried employees, and so on. The offices of these departments were to be at the headquarters of the WFTU in Paris, with some exceptions when approved by the Executive Bureau of the WFTU. The budgets of the trade departments were to be obtained from the affiliation fees paid to the WFTU, after deducting the budget of the general office as fixed by the general secretary; the trade departments could, however, levy supplementary fees on their organizations if approved by the Executive Bureau. The trade departments could admit trade unions from national centers not affiliated with the WFTU, provided these unions did not interfere with the general policy of the WFTU. Each trade department was to elect a president, an executive committee, and a secretary, but the latter was to be subject to ratification by the executive organs of the WFTU. All staff appointments by the secretaries of the trade departments were to be subject to approval by the general secretary of the WFTU. After the trade departments were established, the International Trade Secretariats would cease to exist.

This special regulation, particularly its provisions with regard to finances, control of officers and staff, and location of headquarters, was not acceptable to the Trade Secretariats. As Saillant and the Executive Bureau were anxious to set up the trade departments as soon as possible, they accepted a number of amendments successively offered by the Trade Secretariats. Saillant then proposed to the Trade Secretariats to meet early in January, 1948, to discuss the amended draft and to take steps to put it into effect.

The proposed meeting did not take place. By this time, the officials of most of the Trade Secretariats were rapidly losing interest in joining the WFTU. In the first place, the larger Trade Secretariats were making progress in reestablishing themselves, and were becoming dubious of the wisdom of giving up their independent existence. The special regulation of the WFTU did not promise them the degree of autonomy to which they were used; under its provisions, they would become heads of trade departments subject to the authority of the general secretary of the WFTU. Second, most of the Trade Secretariats had their chief strength in Western Europe and were anxious to expand beyond Europe, particularly in the United States and Canada. They could expect to do so more easily by keeping on friendly terms with the American Federation of Labor, which was hostile to the WFTU. Third, most of the officials of the Trade Secretariats favored the Marshall Plan and wanted to have a share in the European Recovery Program, over which the WFTU was divided. Finally, most of the officials of the Secretariats had for years fought against Communist influence in their organizations; they had misgivings about joining the WFTU, which seemed to them to be falling under Communist control.

Negotiations between the WFTU and the Secretariats continued during the first half of 1948, but the Secretariats showed an increasing desire to break them off. The officials of the Secretariats were influenced in this respect by the events of these months—the founding of the UGO in Berlin, the split in the CGIL in Italy, the formation of the Force Ouvrière in France, the meeting of the ERP Trade Union Conference in London, and the general trend of Western labor to rally to the support of the Marshall Plan. They were also fortified in their stand by the American Federation of Labor, which made special appeals at this time to its affiliated unions to join their respective Trade Secretariats.

The lead in breaking off relations with the WFTU was taken by the International Transport Workers' Federation (ITF). This Trade Secretariat had carried on extensive trade union activities before 1939, had conducted an effective underground campaign against the Nazis during the war, and had regained much of its pre-war strength during 1946-1947. Its general secretary, J. H. Oldenbroek, of Dutch antecedents and a stanch defender of the West European type of trade unionism, was impatient with the activities of Saillant and eager to assert clearly the independence of the Trade Secretariats as a form of international trade unionism.

Oldenbroek induced the International Federation of Transport Workers to take a decisive step at its congress in Oslo in July, 1948. The congress adopted a resolution to set up a worldwide International of transport workers, including railwaymen, seamen, dockers, truck and autobus drivers, and workers in commercial aviation, which was to be independent in organization. The congress further declared that in view of developments in the international labor movement during the past two years, it was best for the Transport Workers' Federation to retain its independence "until such time as negotiations can be resumed with an all-embracing trade union International which offers sufficient prospects of an appropriate measure of autonomy for the International Trade Secretariats and guarantees the principle of free and democratic trade unionism."

The Oslo declaration was the signal for the other Secretariats to follow suit. On September 15, 1948, a conference of Trade Secretariats was held in Paris, at which a resolution was adopted that collaboration with the WFTU, as envisaged by the draft special regulation, was out of the question. Furthermore, the conference approved the declaration of the International Federation of Transport Workers adopted at Oslo. Oldenbroek presented the resolution of the conference to the Executive Bureau of the WFTU, which was meeting in Paris at the time.

With this declaration, the negotiations for bringing the Trade

Secretariats into the WFTU came to an end. The WFTU made an attempt to renew discussions early in 1949, but without results. By that time, events had begun to move rapidly toward a final split in the WFTU, which the Trade Secretariats did much to bring about.

The failure of the WFTU to win over the Trade Secretariats was due to the conditions described above. Saillant, however, laid the blame for this failure on the activities of the American Federation of Labor; on Irving Brown; on Schevenels, whom he accused of "double dealing" in his negotiations with the Trade Secretariats; and on Arthur Deakin, president of the WFTU. The latter took part in the Oslo Congress of the International Federation of Transport Workers as representative of the British General and Transport Workers' Union, of which he was secretary; he voted for the resolution directed against the WFTU. The important fact, however, was that the internal discords within the WFTU had reached a point which made the Trade Secretariats unwilling to affiliate with it.

## V. The Rift

As the discussions of the Marshall Plan grew more intense, the possibility that they might split the WFTU loomed up on the horizon. In view of increasing strains, the Executive Bureau and the Executive Committee of the WFTU devoted their sessions held in Rome in April and May, 1948, almost entirely to a discussion of the administration of the WFTU and its Secretariat. The representatives of the British TUC and the CIO stated their case against the management of the WFTU in strong terms. They accused Saillant of having proved himself biased in action and inadequate as an administrator; they berated the *Information Bulletin* of the WFTU as an inaccurate and misleading publication, abounding in criticisms of Great Britain and the United States while containing no critical comments of any kind on the Soviet Union and Eastern Europe; they denounced the attacks made by Saillant and the *Information Bulletin* on non-Communist trade union leaders; they expressed their dissatisfaction with the way the WFTU sent out missions to various countries, issued manifestoes, and particularly with its refusal to consider the Marshall Plan at an early date. Speaking for the CIO, Carey said that the "CIO was sufficiently dissatisfied with the administration of the WFTU to withdraw from the organization."

Despite mutual recriminations, an effort was made to avoid a split. A resolution was adopted reaffirming the declarations of the London and Paris conferences of 1945. It was agreed that "no one national center shall seek to dominate the affairs of the WFTU so as to exclude the point of view of any other national center or tendency." To secure this end, the Rome meetings adopted the following provisions: that any national center should have the right to submit any question on the agenda of the Executive Bureau; that the latter should hold regular quarterly meetings; that the general secretary should not engage in any other work,[4] except with the approval of the Executive Bureau; that the journals of the WFTU should not publish attacks on the policies or administration of national centers affiliated with the WFTU; and that an editorial board consisting of the general secretary and the three assistant secretaries be set up to direct the publications of the WFTU. These provisions were expected to re-establish a working balance between trade unionist and communist elements at all levels in the structure of the WFTU and to infuse new life into it.

The Rome agreement proved to be little more than an uneasy truce. Both sides soon accused each other of violating its provisions. As the OEEC and the ECA unfolded their operations in the summer of 1948, the Communist elements in the WFTU became more vociferous in their attacks on the ERP. On the other hand, the trade unions of the ERP countries accentuated their drive against the Communists. In September, 1948, the British Trades Union Congress refused to accept Saillant as a fraternal delegate to its annual congress at Margate, and requested that the WFTU send someone who could speak English and who was in favor of the Marshall Plan. The Margate Congress also refused to adopt a motion to support the WFTU unconditionally. Instead, it voted to leave the future relations of the TUC with the WFTU in the hands of the General Council.

Such was the background when the General Council of the British TUC met in October, 1948, and took a decisive step. Asserting that the WFTU could not reach agreement on "real trade union tasks,"

---

[4] As a result, Saillant had to resign from his post as national secretary of the French CGT.

the General Council proposed that the WFTU suspend its functions. Under this proposal, the five main contributing national centers were to appoint trustees to hold the accumulated funds of the WFTU, and these trustees were to meet in a year or earlier to discuss "the conditions in which an attempt to revive an international trade union body may be made." The General Council of the TUC further decided that if the WFTU refused to agree to its proposal, the British Trades Union Congress would withdraw.

Though milder in form, the action taken by the CIO soon afterward had the same general intent. At its convention in Portland in November, 1948, the CIO rejected a proposal to "endorse the WFTU and to make it effective in the United Nations." Instead, the convention voted to authorize the Executive Council of the CIO to take whatever action was required.

The climax came at the session of the Executive Bureau of the WFTU in Paris on January 17-21, 1949. Arthur Deakin, representing the British TUC, presented the latter's proposal for suspending the WFTU. In giving the reasons for the proposal, he stressed in particular the breakdown of negotiations between the WFTU and the Trade Secretariats. James Carey read a statement for the CIO in which, among other things, he said that the WFTU had reached a condition where it must accept the dictates of the Cominform or continue in a state of paralysis and inaction; that it was no use making meaningless compromises which merely concealed differences; that it was the Communists who had abandoned the fundamental principles on which the WFTU was founded and that by seeking to pervert the organization to serve their ends, they had irrevocably split it into two. "It is no use pretending," he declared, "that the WFTU is anything but a corpse. Let us bury it."

The representatives of the TUC and the CIO refused to accept the suggestion that the question be postponed until it could be discussed at the next congress of the WFTU. They demanded that the Executive Bureau make a unanimous decision in favor of the proposed suspension. When the Executive Bureau refused, they and Evert Kupers, representative of the Dutch unions, walked out of the meeting. The expected split had taken place.

Within the next few months, the split widened. The Executive Committee of the WFTU met in January and February, 1949, and condemned the action of Deakin, Carey, and Kupers. It authorized Saillant to proceed with the setting up of trade departments. As Schevenels had resigned, a new assistant secretary was appointed to take charge of this work. The WFTU sent out invitations to the Trade Secretariats to take part in the forming of trade departments. In March, 1949, the Trade Secretariats held a conference in Bournemouth, England, and declined the WFTU invitation. They warned that they would exclude from membership any trade union which joined a trade department of the WFTU. The WFTU then began convening "provisional organizing committees" of miners, metal, textile, and other workers. These activities of the WFTU were denounced by the Trade Secretariats as a hostile act similar to the disruptive tactics of the Red International of Labor Unions two decades earlier.

On June 29, 1949, the WFTU opened in Milan its second congress, which had been repeatedly postponed because of internal conflicts. The Milan Congress registered the split which had taken place in the WFTU. It brought together the Soviet trade unions, the CGT of France, the CGIL of Italy, the trade unions of Poland and other Communist-dominated countries of Eastern and Central Europe, the Latin American Confederation of Labor, and various radical labor groups of Asia and Africa. The national trade union centers of most countries of Western Europe, the British Trades Union Congress, and the CIO, which had played such an important part at the founding congress of Paris in October, 1945, had by now left the WFTU. They were mobilizing their forces for a new organization.

# International Confederation of Free Trade Unions
## 1949-1951

WITH the split in the World Federation of Trade Unions, the first stage in the realignment of organized labor, caused by the Marshall Plan and the East-West conflict, came to an end. The second stage was the unification of the forces opposed to the WFTU in a new labor International—the International Confederation of Free Trade Unions (ICFTU).

### I. Clearing the Ground

Before such unification could take place, a number of difficulties had to be overcome. The British TUC wanted to take the lead in launching the new organization. On the other hand, the American Federation of Labor had advocated since 1947 the calling of an international conference of free trade unions and had planned to take the initiative in arranging it. Another problem was the friction between the AF of L and the CIO, which had to be ironed out if both organizations were to have a part in the new International. The trade unions of the smaller countries of Western Europe wanted to assure for themselves a larger place in the new organization. There were also the questions of relations with the Trade Secretariats and the Christian trade unions.

It took several months after the split in the WFTU before the ground was cleared of these obstacles. Early in 1949, presidents Philip Murray of the CIO and William Green of the AF of L received letters from Sir Vincent Tewson of the British TUC and Leon Jouhaux of the French *Force Ouvrière,* suggesting that a new trade union International be formed and expressing the hope that both the AF of L and the CIO would take part in it.

Early in April, a British trade union delegation headed by Tewson arrived in Washington, in connection with ECA matters. It conferred separately with the leaders of the AF of L and the CIO. As a result of these consultations, a meeting was held later in the month by leaders of the AF of L and the CIO, at which an agreement was reached as to the conditions on which both organizations would take part in a new International. The main points of the agreement were that the British TUC should call a preliminary conference in Switzerland to which the Trade Secretariats were to be invited; that the AF of L and the CIO would affiliate with the new International and be represented at its congress in proportion to their recognized membership (about 7,500,000 for the AF of L and 6,000,000 for the CIO); that the AF of L and the CIO would each have one representative on the executive bodies of the new organization and vice-presidents if such posts were created; that the AF of L and the CIO would consult together on the appointment of a general secretary of the new organization. It was also agreed that the CIO would not use the argument of equality in the new International to support its claim for equality of status in the International Labor Organization. This point was of special interest to the AF of L, which claimed the exclusive right of being recognized in the ILO as the "most representative" American labor organization. The CIO had unsuccessfully disputed this claim for some years.

About the time this agreement was reached in Washington, the Belgian Federation of Trade Unions convened in Brussels a trade union conference of the smaller countries of Europe to consider their attitude toward the proposed new International. The conference was attended by trade union officials of Belgium, Luxembourg, Denmark, Sweden, Norway, and Switzerland. The conference endorsed the proposal for a new International, but specified that the latter should work out appropriate arrangements for cooperation with the Trade Secretariats and with the ERP Trade Union Council, and that it should treat the smaller countries on a basis of equality with the larger countries. It was the opinion of the conference that the general secretary of the new organization should be a trade unionist from a small country and that the headquarters should be located in one of the smaller countries of Western Europe. These conditions were in accord with the declaration made by the Executive Council of the American Federation of Labor in February, 1949, that "in the preparation for a new trade union international there must be a complete break with the methods of big power politics."

In accordance with the agreement between the AF of L and the CIO, the British Trades Union Congress took the initiative in calling the conference. It was to be held in Geneva, Switzerland, on June 25-26, 1949, toward the end of the annual session of the International Labor Organization. These arrangements assured a good attendance, since a large number of trade union leaders from many countries came to the session of the ILO at the expense of their respective governments.

## II. Geneva Preparatory Conference

When the preparatory conference met in Geneva, the Credentials Committee reported 127 delegates in attendance from 35 countries, representing 38 national trade union centers and 12 International Trade Secretariats, with an estimated membership of over 42,000,000. There were delegates and observers from the ERP countries of Europe, the United States and Canada, a number of Latin American countries, India, Iran, Southeast Asia, Japan, Australia, and New Zealand. For the first time since the end of the war, Japan was represented at a trade union conference. The Christian trade unions of France and Belgium sent representatives. The labor federation of Israel (The Histadrut) sent an observer, though it had not yet severed relations with the WFTU. There were observers also from the Organization of Free Trade Unions in Exile (composed of former labor leaders of Communist-dominated countries), which the AF of L had helped to form and finance. Paul Finet, secretary of the Belgian Federation of Trade Unions, and Sir Vincent Tewson, secretary of the British Trades Union Congress, were elected president and secretary respectively of the conference.

Two incidents occurred which illustrated some of the difficulties of the meeting. The conference had admitted delegates from the Peronist Argentine Federation of Labor who were attending the session of the ILO, but it also seated Jacinto Oddone, leader of the anti-Peronist Union Action Committee, living in exile. Oddone made a blistering attack on the Peron government for suppressing "in a most cruel way" civil liberties and trade union rights. He described the Peronist delegates as holders of jobs in government-controlled unions. The Peronist delegates demanded that Oddone be unseated. When the conference refused to do so, the Peronists walked out.

The other incident involved the Christian trade unions. Their presence was objected to by the delegates of the free unions of France, Belgium, and Holland. The representatives of the Christian trade unions stated that they were independent of employers and governments, that their denominational character did not prevent them from being defenders of the workers through collective bargaining and social legislation, and that they were anxious to do their part in unifying the forces of world labor against communism. The conference allowed them to remain.

In his speech of welcome, Robert Bratschi, president of the Swiss Trade Union Federation, struck the keynote of the conference when he said that the task before it was to construct a new International which would seek a solution for the problems confronting labor "in a spirit of true comradeship, democratic freedom and mutual respect." The American delegates expanded on this theme, but they also laid emphasis on the new world situation which made it necessary to pay increasing attention to the labor organizations of Latin America, Asia, and Africa so as to wean them away from Communist influence. George Meany, the then secretary-treasurer of the AF of L, assured the conference that the AF of L was aware that there were differences of doctrine and methods in the free labor movements of the different countries, and that it had no desire "to dictate or to tell the peoples or other unions what are the solutions of their problems." Carey spoke in similar vein. "We of the CIO," he said, "come here in the spirit of international solidarity and we are in this work heart and soul. But this does not mean that we think that we possess any monopoly of knowledge, of ideas or experience."

Other delegates emphasized issues closer to their own countries.

Tewson and Jouhaux warned that the new International must not become merely a negative body of self-defense against Communism, but must develop a large positive program around which the free trade unions of the world could rally in a "constructive and dynamic spirit."

After two days of general discussion, the conference agreed unanimously to establish a new International, and elected a Preparatory Committee to work out a constitution and to convene a constituent congress. The committee included Arthur Deakin of the British TUC, Leon Jouhaux, Irving Brown for the AF of L, Michael Ross of the CIO, Evert Kupers for the Benelux countries, G. Pastore for Italy, and one member each for West Germany, Scandinavia, the Middle East, Asia, Africa, Latin America, Australia, and New Zealand. J. H. Oldenbroek was included to represent the Trade Secretariats. Paul Finet and Vincent Tewson were to serve ex-officio.

### III. Founding of the ICFTU

The Preparatory Committee issued a call for an international trade union conference to be held in London from November 28 to December 9, 1949. Invitations were sent to 134 labor organizations and groups in all parts of the world. In extending invitations, the committee took account of organizations which could be regarded as free and democratic, and which, having been affiliated with the WFTU, had withdrawn from such affiliation.

In response to the call, there assembled in London 261 representatives from 59 national trade union centers and 28 other trade union organizations in 53 countries, claiming to speak for over 48,000,000 workers. Three fourths of the membership represented was in Europe and North America (44 per cent and over 30 per cent respectively). Large memberships were reported by the delegates from Brazil, Cuba, India, and Japan. Australia and New Zealand were not represented, though the latter sent greetings. There were delegates from about a dozen colonial and dependent areas of Latin America, Asia, and Africa. Of the eighteen International Trade Secretariats in existence, fourteen were represented. The AF of L had a delegation of ten, headed by William Green and including George Meany, Matthew Woll, George Harrison, and David Dubinsky. The CIO delegation, also of ten, included Walter Reuther, Allan Haywood, Michael Ross, and Michael Quill. The United Mine Workers of America were represented by a single delegate, Paul K. Reed.

For the first ten days, the London meeting sat as the World Free Labor Conference. It discussed and approved the draft constitution submitted by the Preparatory Committee, and agreed that the name of the new organization should be the International Confederation of Free Trade Unions (ICFTU). After the constitution was adopted, Paul Finet, chairman, declared that the new organization had been established. The conference reconstituted itself as the first congress of the International Confederation of Free Trade Unions.

*General Aims*

In the discussion of the constitution, the various groups at the conference gave voice to their particular ideas and demands. The delegates from the West Indies and other colonial areas described the "deplorable" conditions under which they lived and worked, and asked that the new organization help them to fight "against low wages and against insecurities" and for political freedom. "Wages should not be less in any part of the world," said the delegate from St. Lucia, "than that required by the average worker to eat a nutritious three meals a day and to provide the same for his wife and family." The delegates from Venezuela, Peru, and Uruguay called upon the new organization to "combat all forms of dictatorship," especially in those Latin American countries where anticommunism "has been made an excuse for many attacks on the working class." A delegate from India opposed the admission of trade unions organized on a religious basis. Various delegates urged the new International to keep out politics and "dogmas" and to combat communism not "negatively" but through constructive policies and methods.

The Preamble to the constitution laid emphasis on individual liberty, free labor, political democracy, and "the right of all peoples to full national freedom and sovereignty." It proclaimed the right of individuals to social justice, to work, to free choice of employment, to security of employment, to the security of their persons, to the protection of their industrial and economic interests through trade unions, and to change their government by peaceful and democratic means. The Preamble specified that trade unions must be free bargaining agencies deriving their authority from their members, and pledged the new organization to combat totalitarianism in any form.

The purposes of the ICFTU were stated in fifteen points, but the most important may be summarized as follows: to form a "powerful and effective" international organization of free and democratic trade unions; to help in the establishment and development of trade unions, particularly in economically and socially underdeveloped countries; to coordinate the defense of free trade unions against any campaign to restrict their rights and against attempts at infiltration by totalitarian or other antilabor forces; to promote mutual assistance among national trade union centers; to promote full employment and higher living standards; to assist in the rebuilding of the countries suffering from the ravages of the war and its aftereffects; to encourage the development of the resources of all countries, particularly the underdeveloped countries; to represent the free trade union movement in all international agencies which perform functions affecting the economic and social conditions of the working people; to promote educational work among the workers with the object of increasing their understanding of national and international problems; and to furnish information to its affiliated unions on labor conditions and the trade union movement in all countries.

### Economic and Social Demands

A long discussion took place on the statement of economic and social demands. The delegates from the countries of Europe were socialist-minded and generally allied with socialist parties, while the AF of L and the CIO were nonsocialist and nonpartisan. The delegates from Latin America and Asia held strong views on colonialism and "anti-imperialism." There were differences of opinion on international trade policy, cartels, migration, and other questions. Some observers expected that these differences would break up the new organization before it got started. However, only a few incidents occurred. Thus, the British were annoyed by the diatribes of some of the delegates from the West Indies and other colonies against "British imperialism," but their feelings were soothed by the delegates from India who paid tribute to the "enlightened policy" of the British

Labour government. In general, the discussion proceeded in a spirit of relative calm and desire for compromise and agreement.

The statement adopted by the London Congress was free from traditional socialist doctrines and in the spirit of postwar formulations of trade union demands. "We of the ICFTU," began the statement, "representing the productive forces of society, the workers by hand and brain, declare our deep and abiding confidence in the future of mankind." It then pointed out that science and technology made it possible to guarantee an adequate and expanding standard of living for all the peoples of the world, provided that free men and women would work together and achieve an enduring peace. The first task of the ICFTU, according to the statement, was to help complete the process of postwar reconstruction: to that end, it must give support to the European Recovery Program. But, the statement continued, there were important tasks beyond reconstruction, namely, to conquer poverty, to destroy tyranny and oppression, to defeat the forces of war and aggression, to establish the rights of free workers in all lands, and to give full reality to the watchwords: Bread, Peace, and Freedom.

Within the free and industrialized nations, according to the statement, the general goal of the ICFTU was to give a solid foundation to political democracy by achieving economic democracy. Even in advanced countries, millions of people remained in needless poverty and insecurity. This had to be changed by establishing an economy of "full employment, full production, and full distribution." With respect to basic industries which were vital to the successful functioning of the whole economy, democratic mechanisms had to be devised which would make them responsive to national necessities.

The statement enumerated a series of principles which it designated as the "charter of the rights and privileges of free workers in a free society." This "charter" restated the rights mentioned in the Preamble, but elaborated them in some detail. Thus, it affirmed that discrimination based on race, creed, color, or sex must be eliminated everywhere; that there must be equal payment for equal work; that labor must not be regarded or treated as "a commodity"; and that there must be universal recognition by governments and employers of the right of workers to form trade unions which would be "free bargaining agencies." The statement declared that the "so-called trade unions" in countries under Fascist, Communist, or other totalitarian regimes were not free and democratic organizations but "governmental instruments designed for the organized exploitation of workers for the benefit of a tyrannical state."

Among the specific aims which the ICFTU was to seek were international agreements relating to maximum working hours and minimum working conditions, a guaranteed annual wage; national systems of social security, including health services for every citizen; and free public education, including vocational training. In seeking these objectives, the ICFTU declared that it would rely as much as possible on collective bargaining and peaceful negotiations with employers, reserving the right to strike when necessary and calling for government intervention only in matters which were beyond the scope of free and voluntary arrangements between workers and employers.

In international relations, the ICFTU, according to the statement, would oppose high tariffs and try to create "ever-broadening areas of international economic cooperation." It declared as most urgent, immediate steps toward the economic integration and unification of Western Europe, including Germany. Austria, Germany, and Japan were to be brought into the United Nations as soon as possible to strengthen democracy in these countries. The industrially advanced countries, according to the statement, had a duty to help forward those great areas of the world which have not been materially affected by the industrial revolution and whose millions of inhabitants still languish under old-fashioned dictatorships or do not enjoy adequate political and economic independence. It was, therefore, necessary to give technical assistance to underdeveloped countries in "a spirit of mutual cooperation and not in a spirit of imperialism." As natural resources in some countries were inadequate for the needs of the population, the voluntary migration of workers was to be facilitated, with due regard for the protection of the standards of the workers in countries both of emigration and immigration.

That the above objectives be achieved, the ICFTU statement continued, the democratic world must live in peace. The threat of war, it said, now came from totalitarian systems of government, whether they were Communist, Fascist, Falangist, corporative, or militarist. These systems were "destructive of all moral and spiritual values."

The ICFTU promised to carry this message to the peoples "imprisoned in totalitarian slave states," and to support regional agreements for the defense of democracy which were in harmony with the Charter of the United Nations.

As the workers were "the first victims of war" and could mobilize the force of their organizations for peace, the ICFTU demanded the right of participation in all international bodies concerned with economic and social cooperation—the Economic and Social Council of the United Nations, the International Labor Organization, the Food and Agriculture Organization, the Organization for European Economic Cooperation, the World Bank, and so on.

## Form of Organization

The constitution of the ICFTU provided for a flexible and not too centralized form of organization. More than one national center from any one country could be admitted. Not only national centers but individual trade unions were made eligible for membership. The autonomy of affiliated organizations was guaranteed. Regional machinery was to be set up to give attention to special problems of the different areas. Arrangements were to be made for cooperation with the Trade Secretariats, which were to retain their independent existence.

The supreme authority of the ICFTU was to be a congress meeting once every two years. Representation at the congress was to be in proportion to membership on a regressive basis: one delegate for national centers with a membership up to 100,000, and a maximum of ten delegates for national centers with more than 5,000,000 members. Decisions of the congress were to be by majority vote, except in cases of proposals to amend the constitution or for the expulsion of members, when two thirds of the votes cast were required.

The congress was to elect a General Council, which was to meet between congresses to give effect to the decisions of the congress and to approve the budget. Each affiliated organization was entitled to representation on the Council: one member for an organization with a membership up to one million, and a maximum of four members for organizations with more than five million. The expenses of the members of the Council were to be paid by their respective organizations.

The congress was also to elect an Executive Board of nineteen members and a general secretary, who was to be a member of the Board ex-officio. The members of the Board were to be elected by the congress on a regional basis: five from Europe; two each from Great Britain, the United States, and Latin America; one from the West Indies; three from the Middle East and Asia; one from Africa; and one from Australia and New Zealand. The Executive Board was to meet twice a year and had the responsibility of directing the Confederation, convening the biennial congresses, and preparing an agenda for them. The Executive Board was to elect from its own members an Emergency Committee to deal with urgent problems arising between sessions of the board. Of the seven members of the committee, two were to be from Continental Europe, one from Great Britain, two from North America, one from Latin America, and one from Asia.

The officers of the ICFTU were to be a president, seven vice-presidents, and a general secretary. The president and vice-presidents were to be elected by the Executive Board from among its members. The general secretary was to be elected by the congress and be eligible for reelection at each biennial congress. He was to be responsible for the administration of the ICFTU and to have assistant secretaries, whose number was not specified. The affiliation fees were fixed at three pounds sterling per year per thousand members or part thereof for the first five million members, and two pounds sterling per thousand for additional members over five million.

### First Organizing Steps

The constitution was adopted by a roll-call vote, which showed 46,380,000 votes for it, none against, and 1,300,000 abstentions. There was evident satisfaction with the provisions which gave the countries outside Europe and North America considerable representation in the executive bodies of the organization. William Green, in his concluding address to the conference, called it a "wonderful constitution." J. H. Oldenbroek, *rapporteur* for the committee on the constitution, summed it up as a document which set up "a fighting international" to overcome "all over the globe the forces of aggression, of reaction, of oppression, of totalitarianism, which stand in the way of realization of universal human rights and the establishment of world peace."

The London Congress elected J. H. Oldenbroek of the Netherlands as general secretary. Oldenbroek had made his mark as secretary of the International Federation of Transport Workers. He had led the fight of the Trade Secretariats against the WFTU. He had a knowledge of languages, trade union experience, and good standing in international labor circles. He was acceptable not only to the Europeans but also to the AF of L and CIO, with whose leaders he had been in friendly contact for some years.

The congress approved the recommendation of the Preparatory Committee to locate the headquarters of the ICFTU in Brussels, Belgium. Thus, the selection of the general secretary and location of headquarters met the wishes of the smaller countries of Western Europe.

The congress then elected the General Council and an Executive Board. Among the nineteen members of the latter were Arthur Deakin and Vincent Tewson from Great Britain, Leon Jouhaux from France, Paul Finet from Belgium, Giulio Pastore from Italy, Eiler Jensen from Denmark, Hans Boeckler from West Germany, Bernardo Ibanez from Chile, Francisco Aguirre from Cuba, R. Bradshaw from the West Indies, Marcus Grant from Africa, E. Kato from Japan, and Deven Sen from India. William Green of the AF of L and Philip Murray of the CIO were both elected members of the Board.

The congress issued a manifesto with the slogan "Bread, Freedom and Peace," which appealed to the workers of "all countries, races and creeds to join in the mighty movement of free and democratic labor."

## IV. Establishment and Consolidation

Immediately after the London Congress, the officers of the ICFTU took steps to establish a working organization and to launch the activities called for by the constitution. Owing to housing shortages, it took several months before suitable headquarters were found in Brussels. The initial expenses involved were covered by special donations from a dozen or so trade union centers. The AF of L donated $25,000 for the purpose; the CIO, $20,000; the British TUC, £7,159; the West German Federation of Labor, £3,000; the United Mine Workers of America $1,000. Smaller sums were contributed by the trade unions of Canada, Denmark, Norway, Sweden, and New Zealand. The total donations were over $80,000.

By May, 1950, the offices of the ICFTU in Brussels were in working order, with a staff of twenty-eight economists, translators, clerical workers, and assistants. A year later the staff had increased to forty-eight persons. The work was organized into three departments—one dealing with organization, another with economic and social affairs, and the third with publications and publicity. In April, 1950, the publication of a fortnightly *Information Bulletin* was begun. In July, *the Free Labour World*, the official monthly magazine of the ICFTU, was started.

### Relations with the United Nations

One of the first acts of the ICFTU was to apply for consultative status, as a Category A nongovernmental organization, in the Economic and Social Council of the United Nations and in the International Labor Organization. The Economic and Social Council agreed to waive the requirement of a waiting period and granted the ICFTU categòry A status as of March 3, 1950. The AF of L relinquished its status in the Council in favor of the ICFTU. In July, 1950, the ICFTU opened a branch office in New York to deal with the work arising out of its status in the United Nations. The office was to be financed by special contributions of the AF of L and the CIO.

Representatives of the ICFTU took part in the proceedings of the eleventh session of the Economic and Social Council, held in Geneva in July and August, 1950. They submitted a well-reasoned statement on full employment, but their particular interest was in urging on the Council the need to consider questions of trade union rights and of forced labor which had been raised by the AF of L. The ICFTU submitted to the Council detailed documentation on the violation of trade union rights in a number of countries, particularly in the USSR and in Eastern Europe. They requested that study of forced labor in the Soviet Union be made. The ICFTU continued to press this problem on the attention of the Council at the latter's sessions in 1951.

In March, 1950, the ICFTU was also granted Category A status in the International Labor Organization, and took part in the thirty-third session of the International Labor Conference held in Geneva in June, 1950. The general secretary of the ICFTU was elected secretary of the Workers' Group. Thus, the ICFTU came into the role which the International Federation of Trade Unions (IFTU) had played in the ILO before 1939.

### Regional Problems

The London Congress at which the ICFTU was founded discussed at great length the need for developing regional activities and a regional organization. The delegates to the congress felt that the biggest problem before the ICFTU was to stimulate trade union organization in areas where they were weak, and to reconcile the interests of the labor organizations of the advanced with those of the less developed countries.

The ICFTU took the first step toward regional organization in Western Europe. In November, 1950, it set up a European Regional Secretariat with a small office in Brussels.[1]

In the course of 1950, the ICFTU sent missions to the Far East and Africa to survey economic and social conditions and to explore the possibilities of trade union action. The mission to Asia found evidence "of a decline in the power and influence of communist-dominated trade union movements" in the region, but warned that "the threat to the free trade union movement from such anti-democratic elements" remained great. The "crying need" of the labor movements of Asia, according to the ICFTU mission, was "for trade union leaders coming from the ranks of the workers." The mission also emphasized the need for a change in the antiunion attitude of employers, both indigenous and foreign, and of measures for raising "the terribly low level of wages and the starvation budgets of millions of workers."

In the fall of 1950, the ICFTU established a temporary Information and Advisory Center in Singapore to assist labor organizations in Southeast Asia. In May, 1951, an Asian Regional Conference was

[1] The work of the several regional organizations is described in Chapter XXIV.

held in Karachi, Pakistan, which set up an Asian Regional Secretariat with headquarters in Calcutta, India.

The several missions sent by the ICFTU to North, West, and East Africa found that labor conditions in most of these areas were extremely bad and that trade unionism was hampered by the traditions of colonial administration and by nationalist movements. They called upon colonial governments to eradicate illiteracy, abolish racial discrimination, and raise the very low levels of living. They found a strong Communist influence in the trade unions of several African regions, as a result of economic conditions and nationalist agitation. In March, 1951, the ICFTU convened an African Trade Union Conference at Duala, in the Cameroons, but no regional organization was set up.

Early in 1951, the ICFTU turned its attention to Latin America. The main problem here was to unify the labor organizations and groups which were opposed to the Confederation of Latin American Workers (CTAL) headed by Lombardo Toledano and affiliated with the WFTU. With the aid of the AF of L and the CIO, the ICFTU in January, 1951, sponsored an Inter-American Regional Conference in Mexico City which brought together some ninety delegates and observers from twenty-nine trade union organizations of the twenty-one countries of the Americas. The conference voted to establish an Inter-American Regional Organization (ORIT), which was to serve as the regional secretariat of the ICFTU for North, Central, and South America and for the Caribbean area.

A proposal to allow the Argentine Confederation of Labor to participate in the conference was overwhelmingly defeated. The headquarters of the ORIT were established in Havana, Cuba. The ORIT mapped out for itself a large program—to study methods of combating inflation, to support measures for the defense of democracy against the threat of dictatorship, to protect trade union leaders who were being persecuted in various countries, and to affirm the Good Neighbor Policy.

All these activities required funds beyond the capacity of the ICFTU regular budget. In February, 1951, the Emergency Committee of the ICFTU launched an appeal to its affiliated organizations to set up a Special Fund for Regional Activities of $700,000.

*Relations with the Trade Secretariats*

Like the IFTU before 1939 and the WFTU during 1945-1949, the ICFTU was confronted with the problem of establishing working relations with the International Trade Secretariats. The question was settled amicably, owing to the good will of both parties. Under the arrangements worked out early in 1950, the ICFTU and the Trade Secretariats agreed that they were "part of the same international trade union movement." This implied that the Trade Secretariats had to accept the general policy laid down by the ICFTU. On the other hand, the ICFTU recognized the autonomy of the Trade Secretariats and accepted their Coordinating Committee as their collective representative. The ICFTU and the Trade Secretariats agreed to give each other representation on their executive bodies as well as at their congresses and conferences.

*The Milan Congress, July, 1951*

That the ICFTU had made progress was shown by its second congress, held in Milan from July 4 to July 12, 1951. While not boasting of "great achievements," the general secretary, J. H. Oldenbroek, pointed out with some pride that, despite the Korean war and other unfavorable international conditions, the ICFTU had carried out a good part of the instructions of the London founding congress. It had laid, he said, the foundations of "the home of Free Trade Unionism."

A sign of progress was the growth of membership. On July 1, 1951, the general secretary reported, the ICFTU had the affiliation of 84 labor organizations in 66 countries with 52,500,000 members. About half of the trade unions affiliated with the ICFTU had belonged to the WFTU but had left it. From January, 1950, to March 31, 1951, the affiliated organizations had paid to the ICFTU about 20,000,000 Belgian francs (about $400,000) in dues, and had contributed many thousands of dollars more for initial expenses, regional activities, a film fund, and other purposes.

The Milan Congress was attended by over 200 delegates, advisers, and observers from 56 affiliated trade union organizations in 47 countries with a membership of over 47,000,000, from 12 Trade

Secretariats, and from several unaffiliated organizations. There were large delegations from the American Federation of Labor, the CIO, the British TUC, Western Germany, Italy, Sweden, Belgium, Brazil, Cuba, India, and Japan.

Paul Finet, president of the ICFTU, laid stress in his opening address on the problem of freedom and peace. "The trade union movement," he said, "is for democracy and against dictatorship, whether of the extreme Right or extreme Left." This theme was elaborated by many other delegates. Matthew Woll submitted to the congress a comprehensive statement prepared by George Meany on "The Aims of Free Trade Unionism and Its Struggle against the Totalitarian Menace."

While agreeing on this basic issue, the delegates gave vent to their particular ideas. Some European delegates wanted more international economic planning, international control of raw materials, and more freedom of international trade. The delegates from Italy urged that greater facilities be given Italian workers to emigrate to countries where there were more opportunities for work and jobs. The delegates from West Germany laid emphasis on "co-determination" in industry, that is, the right of workers to be represented on boards of directors of private and public corporations, and on the need for solving the refugee problem. The delegates from India called upon the "old imperialist powers" to adopt "new and progressive policies" in order to defeat "the alliance between Nationalism and Communism"; they asked the ICFTU to give priority to education and technical assistance in Asian countries. The delegate from Iran warned that "communist propaganda is unfortunately meeting with success as a result of the extreme poverty of the working class and the bad policy of our government," and expressed his appreciation of the support which the ICFTU missions gave to the democratic unions in Asia. The delegate from Brazil called for support to "all those trade union comrades living in countries which are unfortunate enough to suffer under totalitarian regimes such as Venezuela and Argentina." The delegate from Tunisia, Farhad Hachet, stated the sentiments of many other delegates when he said: "Colonial and dependent nations, whether Asian or African, suffer from a different kind of domination and oppression: Colonialism, which is even more nefarious than the others since it is the most ignominious method of domination over individuals and nations."

The congress adopted a number of resolutions which translated the ideas of the delegates into directives for action. The resolution on totalitarianism denounced in ringing terms the dictatorship and aggression of the Soviet Union, where "peace means war and democracy means tyranny." It also declared that there must be "no association with Franco, Peron or any other dictator" and that "dictators, however violent their anti-communism, are no asset in this struggle of the community of free nations." The resolution condemned as "cold-blooded aggression the assault upon South Korea" and expressed support for the action of the United Nations in Korea.

Other resolutions endorsed the "constructive and progressive activities" of the International Labor Organization; called on the United Nations to resume financial aid for the care and resettlement of refugees; reaffirmed the idea that the unification of Western Europe was urgent and that it should proceed on the basis of joint and coordinated planning designed to secure the most rational use of productive resources; asked that the principle of the European Coal and Steel Community (the Schuman Plan) be extended to other industries and that the trade unions be adequately represented in the executive bodies of this Community and of other European regional bodies; and appealed to all countries to accept immigrants on a large scale and to admit as many immigrants as could be absorbed without imperiling the working and living standards of the receiving countries.

In other resolutions, the congress expressed support for the efforts of the free nations to strengthen their military defenses in order to stave off aggression; requested the United Nations to investigate thoroughly the problems of dependent territories; endorsed the recommendations of the Economic and Social Council of the United Nations on full employment; and urged that greater efforts be made to fight the inflationary effects of rearmament by increased production, progressive taxation, effective price control, international commodity agreements and more equitable distribution of raw materials.

The congress reelected J. H. Oldenbroek as general secretary. Sir Vincent Tewson replaced Paul Finet as president. The seven vice-presidents, who with the president and general secretary were to constitute the Emergency Committee for 1951-1953, were Christian Fette of the Western German Federation of Labor, William Green, Eiler Jensen of Denmark, Leon Jouhaux of the French Force Ouvrière, Philip Murray of the CIO, H. Shastri of the Indian National Trades Union Congress, and Bernardo Ibanez of Chile. The congress also approved a budget estimated at 140,000 pounds sterling, or about $400,000.

## V. The ICFTU and the WFTU

One of the decisions of the Milan Congress was a resolution which rejected cooperation with the World Federation of Trade Unions. For about two years after the split in 1949, the WFTU continued to maintain its headquarters in Paris. But in January, 1951, the French government revoked the order of April 19, 1946, which permitted the WFTU to have offices in Paris as a "foreign association," and ordered it to leave the country within a month. The order was protested by the French CGT, by the trade unions of the "Peoples' democracies," and by a few scattered unions in Latin America and elsewhere. The WFTU also appealed to Trygve Lie for intervention by the United Nations on the ground that the order of the French government prevented the Federation from exercising its consultative functions in the Economic and Social Council. The protests were not numerous or weighty enough to have an effect on the French government. For a few months, the WFTU used the offices of the CGIL in Rome, and then moved to Vienna where it established itself with the help of the Soviet occupation authorities in the Coburg Palace in the Soviet zone.

After the ICFTU was founded, the WFTU attacked it and its leaders in most abusive language. In its official journal and in its public statements, the WFTU referred to the ICFTU as the "scab Brussels International," the "Yellow International," and as "United States weapon of war," and ridiculed the leaders of the ICFTU as the "troubadours of free trade unionism." In retaliation, the ICFTU denounced the WFTU as "the stooge of the Cominform" and a "spy agency of the Soviet Government."

Despite this verbal warfare, di Vittorio and Louis Saillant, president and secretary respectively of the WFTU, sent a telegram in July, 1951, to Paul Finet, then president of the ICFTU, proposing that the two organizations meet together to examine the "steps to be taken for the defense of the workers' vital interests." The proposal was based on a resolution of the Executive Bureau of the WFTU, which asserted that the "material condition of the workers in capitalistic, colonial and dependent countries" was "deteriorating from day to day" and that the workers could improve their condition only by "unity." Di Vittorio and Saillant asked Finet to name a date and place for a joint conference.

The proposal was rejected by the Executive Board of the ICFTU. The Milan Congress upheld the action of the board, and approved a strongly worded negative reply which was sent to the WFTU. In this reply, drafted with the aid of Irving Brown, Paul Finet, and J. H. Oldenbroek, the ICFTU ironically chided the leaders of the WFTU for being willing to enter "into conversations" with persons whom they called representatives of the "Yellow International" and other such names. The reply further stated that the ICFTU was aware of "the economic, social and political difficulties from which the world at large is suffering," but it was also aware that the WFTU had refused to cooperate in world economic recovery through the Marshall Plan and similar international programs, and had instead "chosen to support Communist military aggression against the Korean Republic and in other parts of the world," thus stopping further improvements in the people's living standards. "As long as you remain the faithful agents of the Cominform," the reply read, "carrying out the foreign policy of the Kremlin, there can be no unity of action where there is no unity of purpose."

Di Vittorio, in a long article in the official journal of the WFTU, denounced the reply of the ICFTU as "acrimonious," "insulting," and "shameful." Still, at its meeting in Vienna in November, 1951, the General Council of the WFTU again proposed to the ICFTU "to undertake common action in defense of the urgent economic and social demands of workers in capitalistic, colonial and dependent countries." The second proposal of the WFTU met with no response from the ICFTU.

## VI. THE ICFTU AND THE CHRISTIAN UNIONS

The Milan Congress also considered the relations of the ICFTU with the Christian trade unions. As already related, these unions re-emerged after the war in France, Belgium, and some other countries with increased memberships and influence. In 1946, they reconstituted the prewar International Federation of Christian Trade Unions, which had been weakened by Fascism and Nazism before 1939 and forced to suspend operations during the war. The new organization was christened the International Confederation of Christian Trade Unions (ICCTU).

As a result of their war experience, the Christian trade unions showed a desire to associate themselves with the general international labor movement. Delegates from the Christian unions of France, Belgium, and the Basque country were present at the Free World Labor Conference in London in November, 1949, at which the ICFTU was founded. After a long discussion, the ICFTU congress in London decided to invite all Christian trade unions to take part in its deliberations, on condition that within two years they "accept and give effect to the principle of affiliation to one trade union International." This was an invitation to the Christian trade unions to dissolve their International and to become affiliated with the ICFTU as independent federations from their respective countries.

In April, 1950, the Confederation of Christian Trade Unions met in Brussels and politely refused to commit hara-kiri. The General Council of the Christian Trade Union International expressed pleasure at the fact that various trade unions had decided to break with the WFTU, thus "refusing to serve as tools of communist policy," and in this spirit welcomed the foundation of the ICFTU. But instead of announcing its willingness to dissolve itself, the Christian International declared that it was ready to examine with the ICFTU "methods of collaboration in the international field," and instructed its Executive Bureau to make "the necessary approach for the purpose."

As a result of this action, no trade unions affiliated with the Christian International were admitted to the Milan Congress of the ICFTU. The door was left open to them, however, in case they became willing to accept the conditions of admission.

The Milan Congress thus clarified the aims and program of the ICFTU and consolidated its position. Its activities today as well as those of the other international labor organizations are described in Part Seven, which deals with current trends and outlook.

# PART SEVEN

## Current Trends and Outlook

# The Free Trade Union International in Action

AFTER more than a decade of war and postwar developments, the international labor movement has now assumed a form which is likely to continue for some time. It is carried on by three general organizations—the International Confederation of Free Trade Unions, the World Federation of Trade Unions, and the International Confederation of Christian Trade Unions—and by a number of International Trade Secretariats affiliated or allied with one or another of the general organizations.

To view the international labor movement as a factor in the world today, it is necessary to visualize the several organizations as they function from day to day and to understand the conditions which shape their activities. This chapter describes the activities of the International Confederation of Free Trade Unions. The other internationals are dealt with in the following three chapters. Their interrelations and outlook are considered in the final chapter.

## I. SCOPE AND CHARACTER OF THE ICFTU

The ICFTU is the most important labor international today. Its affiliated members include the British TUC, the strongest national trade union centers of Western Europe (excepting France and Italy) and of Canada, the AF of L and the CIO in the United States, the United Mine Workers of America, several substantial labor organizations in some countries of Latin America, two leading trade union federations in India, the Council of Trade Unions in Japan, the national labor federations of Australia and New Zealand, and smaller labor unions in the West Indies, the Middle East, Southeast Asia, and Africa. The ICFTU claims a membership of about 54,000,000 in 97 organizations in 73 countries. The total membership figure is subject to the qualification that some affiliated organizations may exaggerate their numbers. The figures reported by the ICFTU give, however, an idea of the worldwide extent of its affiliations and potential influence.

The ICFTU includes only trade unions which it regards as free, that is, those that are voluntary in origin and derive their authority from the consent of the members, that carry on collective bargaining and have the right to strike, that are democratic in structure and management, that are not controlled by political parties or governments, and that advocate constitutional and peaceful methods for improving economic and social conditions. The trade unions affiliated with the ICFTU differ in the degree to which they meet the above specifications. In some European countries, the trade unions are allied with the socialist parties. In Latin America and elsewhere, the dependence of the trade unions on the good will and support of the government is considerable. The important fact, however, is that the ICFTU refuses to admit Communist-controlled, Fascist, and government-sponsored labor organizations.

The emphasis on freedom and democracy marks not only the structure of the ICFTU but also its philosophy and general outlook. Briefly stated, its aim is to help build gradually and by legal methods a peaceful world based on political freedom, economic democracy, social justice, and cooperation between free and self-determining nations. These concepts are admittedly vague and allow for flexible interpretation. In some West European countries, the trade unions of the ICFTU regard socialism as their ultimate goal. Some trade unions in non-European countries which have had a rapid growth since 1945, e.g., in Japan and India, have programs which are clearly socialist. On the other hand, the AF of L and the CIO interpret the program of the ICFTU in the spirit of the New Deal and the Fair Deal. The ICFTU is not committed to any doctrinal system and allows for diversity of ideas, as long as they are in accord with its basic concept of a "free society based on free labor."

## II. Main Tasks

In the present historical situation, the ICFTU views the struggle for free labor in a free society as determined chiefly by the existence of totalitarian and dictatorial governments. Totalitarianism carries with it three evils: the destruction of individual liberty, the practice on a large scale of forced labor, and aggressive foreign policies which threaten the peace of the world. According to the ICFTU, Soviet Russia exemplifies these evils in the most extreme degree, and because of its vast territory and economic potential presents the greatest menace to free labor.

Besides totalitarianism, two other features in the present situation endanger the position of free labor, according to the ICFTU. One is the effort of some groups of employers in advanced industrial countries to undermine the gains made by labor in wage standards and social welfare, and to halt the movement toward industrial democracy. The other is the acquiescence of employers and some governments in the conditions of poverty under which workers in underdeveloped and dependent areas live, and their hostile attitude toward attempts to improve these conditions through trade union action. Because of such conditions and attitudes, the ICFTU maintains, the workers tend to lose faith in peaceful progress and become susceptible to Communist blandishments.

As the ICFTU sees it, its general aims impose on it six main tasks. It must, in the first place, combat Communist and Fascist ideas. Second, it must defend trade union rights wherever they are infringed upon. Third, it must help the workers in less developed countries to organize, to improve their living standards, and to achieve political freedom and self-government. Fourth, it must lend support to the labor movements of the advanced industrial countries to achieve economic democracy through greater participation in the management of industry and in shaping national economic policy. Fifth, it must help strengthen the United Nations as the chief instrument of collective security and world peace. Sixth, it must obtain adequate representation for organized labor in the United Nations and in other official international bodies so that the workers may have an active part in building a democratic and peaceful world.

### III. REARMAMENT AND AFTER

In view of threatening military aggression, the ICFTU recognizes that a defensive alliance of the free nations of North America and Europe is necessary. It supports, therefore, the North Atlantic Treaty Organization (NATO) and its program of rearmament. The ICFTU emphasizes, however, that NATO must have a defensive character. Should the Soviet bloc agree to disarmament and to effective international control of military weapons, the ICFTU would favor and "insist" on universal disarmament.

The ICFTU recognizes that the rearmament program requires sacrifices and that the workers must contribute their share, but urges that the sacrifices be shared equitably and be kept at a reasonable level. That can be done, it claims, by "intelligent planning" so as to strike a balance between military needs and economic capacities. Specifically, the ICFTU advocates that the economically stronger assist the weaker countries in financing military defense; that international measures be taken to increase exports from countries which must improve their balance of payments in order to reduce their dependence on foreign aid; that international commodity agreements be used to increase the production of needed raw materials and to secure their equitable distribution; and that the prices of such materials be stabilized with fairness to producers and workers. On the national level, the ICFTU calls for increased productivity, price and wage controls, and higher taxation to combat inflation. Where a shortage of manpower exists, the ICFTU proposes to extend normal working hours as an emergency measure. It calls attention, however, to the possibilities of meeting man-power needs by retraining of workers and by facilitating international migration.

While lending active support to the rearmament program, the ICFTU urges that plans be made now to meet the problems of frictional and cyclical unemployment which it expects will arise when the program begins to taper off or comes to an end. To ensure full employment during what it calls the "reconversion period," the ICFTU proposes that a high level of effective demand be maintained by appropriate wage and fiscal policies, encouraging private investment, public investment in housing, placing large private and public funds in underdeveloped countries to speed their economic growth, and reducing barriers to international trade and to the international mobility of labor. The ICFTU wants NATO to plan such measures now and to continue its economic and financial activities during the "reconversion period" so as to lay the ground for larger international economic cooperation on a permanent basis.

## IV. Activities and Methods

In pursuance of its tasks, the ICFTU carries on a wide range of activities. To combat communism, it publishes a monthly bulletin— *The Spotlight*—which presents material highly critical of economic and political conditions in the USSR and in the "People's democracies." It gives financial and organizing aid to its affiliated unions in their struggle against the Communists. It conducts and finances special campaigns to strengthen the anti-Communist unions, particularly in France and Italy, by training local trade union organizers and officials.

In furtherance of trade union rights, the ICFTU makes appeals to public opinion and protests to governments accused of curtailing such rights. When the government of Japan after the occupation adopted legislation which the Japanese trade unions regarded as restrictive, the ICFTU protested and requested an opportunity to discuss the question with a representative of the Japanese government, which was granted. In September, 1952, the ICFTU sent a telegram to the government of Uruguay protesting against the imprisonment of a number of trade unionists who gave their support to a general strike of tramwaymen for higher wages. It has protested to the French government against its repressive measures and arrests of trade unionists in Tunisia. It has repeatedly condemned in public statements the violation of trade union rights in Spain, Argentina, Venezuela, and other countries under dictatorial and military regimes. It has helped to improve labor legislation in Turkey, Greece, India, Brazil, and some other countries.

Largely as a result of the pressure by the ICFTU in the Economic and Social Council of the United Nations, a Committee on Trade Union Freedom was set up in 1951 jointly by the Council and the ILO.

The ICFTU has submitted and continues to submit complaints to this committee against the suppression of trade union freedom in the Soviet Union and the "People's democracies" as well as in other countries. The ICFTU feels that the procedures of the committee are too slow and has been making efforts to improve their effectiveness.

The ICFTU also extends financial aid for organizing and relief purposes to trade unionists deprived of the right to organize or carrying on activities in exile. In the course of 1952, the ICFTU voted £500 to the Spanish General Labor Union to conduct a trade union summer school for Spanish refugees working in France, made a grant of £1,000 to the Federation of Labor of Tunisia for the relief of its members and their families, loaned $1,000 to the Independent Trade Union Committee of Argentine operating in exile, and advanced smaller sums to trade union groups in several other countries.

To promote its economic and social program, the ICFTU takes advantage of its consultative status in the Economic and Social Council of the United Nations and in the specialized agencies. Representatives of the ICFTU attend regularly the biannual sessions of the Council and try to influence its deliberations and decisions by submitting written memoranda, by addressing the plenary sessions of the Council, and by maintaining informal contacts with members of friendly delegations. Matthew Woll and David Dubinsky of the AF of L and Jacob Potofsky and Michael Ross of the CIO are the official representatives of the ICFTU to the Council, but most of the work is carried on by a consultant, Miss Toni Sender. Important statements submitted to the Council, especially on economic questions, are usually prepared at headquarters in Brussels.[1]

In general, the ICFTU is in agreement with the social-economic policies of the United States and West European members of the Economic and Social Council, but its representatives aim to give these policies a larger content. The ICFTU, for instance, supports the recommendations of the Council with regard to full employment, but calls also for specific measures to implement them, such as higher wages, increased social security benefits, low-cost public housing programs, and public works. It advocates larger financial contributions for programs of technical assistance, international financing of economic development by means of low-cost and long-term intergovern-

---

[1] The economic department of the ICFTU is directed by Alfred Braunthal, who has had wide experience as an adviser to labor organizations in Western Europe and the United States.

mental loans, and especially that teams of experts sent by the United Nations to the underdeveloped countries include trade union advisers.

The spokesmen of the ICFTU have also had an active part in the Economic and Social Council in promoting the adoption of a Covenant on Human Rights, larger financial support for the United Nations Children's Emergency Fund, aid to refugees, and other social measures. In particular, the ICFTU has been active in the Council in the defense of trade union rights and in its campaign against forced labor.

Like other nongovernmental organizations, the ICFTU has no consultative status in the General Assembly of the United Nations, but it brings its views to the attention of the Assembly in other ways. It has addressed letters and documents to all the delegations in the Assembly on such questions as French policy in Tunisia, self-government in dependent areas, and racial segregation in South Africa. Representatives of the ICFTU interview members of the various delegations and keep in close contact in particular with the trade union members of the delegations. So far only a few countries—France, Belgium, and Holland—have included trade unionists in their delegations, and the ICFTU is now making efforts to have other countries follow the same practice.

Among the specialized agencies, the ICFTU has consultative status in the International Labor Organization and in UNESCO. The ILO has changed little in structure and functions since 1939, but has greatly expanded its operations. It has established a number of international industrial committees—for the textile, metallurgic, construction, chemical, and other industries—which meet periodically to discuss questions of wages, productivity, and labor-management relations. It conducts vocational courses in a number of countries in Asia. It carries on technical assistance programs, sending advisers to governments concerned with labor legislation and social security problems. The ICFTU exercises influence in the ILO because most of the worker-delegates to the Annual Conferences are members of affiliated trade unions. One of the assistant general secretaries of the ICFTU acts as secretary of the Workers' Group at the Conferences and in the Governing Body of the ILO.

The ICFTU has given particular attention in the past two years to the work of the ILO Committee on Trade Union Freedom. It has also made proposals to increase the number of industrial committees, to grant associate membership in the ILO to nonself-governing territories, and to give the trade unions a larger part in dealing with problems of migration. Like the International Federation of Trade Unions before 1939, the ICFTU feels that the main work for which the ILO was created, namely, the adoption of draft conventions for the establishment of international minimum labor standards, is too slow and often ineffective because governments do not ratify draft conventions or fail to enforce those ratified. However, owing to the demand of its Asian unions, the ICFTU is showing an increasing interest in this phase of the ILO.

The relations of the ICFTU with UNESCO are in the field of education considered below. Of the other specialized agencies, the ICFTU is interested in the work of the Food and Agriculture Organization (FAO) and of the World Health Organization (WHO). The ICFTU proposes to seek consultative status in the FAO and to establish closer relations with WHO for the exchange of information and for informal consultation.

In its work in the United Nations and the specialized agencies, the ICFTU is hampered by insufficiency of trained personnel and by dispersion of effort. At its meeting in December, 1952, the Executive Board of the ICFTU instructed the general secretary to coordinate these activities, but no specific measures for the purpose were indicated.

Outside the United Nations, the ICFTU devotes a great deal of time and energy to the economic and social problems of Western Europe. It maintains regular contacts with official European regional agencies such as the OEEC, the headquarters of NATO, the Council of Europe, the Economic Commission for Europe of the United Nations, and particularly with the European Coal and Steel Community set up under the Schuman Plan. Of the seventeen workers on the consultative committee of the community, twelve are workers from ICFTU affiliated trade unions of the six participating countries (France, Belgium, Holland, Luxembourg, Italy, and West Germany). Paul Finet, former president of the ICFTU, is one of the nine members of the High Authority of the Community. The ICFTU is demanding similar labor representation in the Council of NATO.

Both in the United Nations and outside, the ICFTU carries on campaigns of a political character. It has opposed the admission of Franco Spain to UNESCO and other United Nations agencies. It has repeatedly condemned the Peron regime in Argentina. In July, 1952, it issued a public statement requesting the British Government not to combine the three territories of Northern and Southern Rhodesia and Tanganyika into a Central African Federation without the consent of the native population. It conducted a campaign during 1952 on behalf of self-government in Tunisia and was influential through the AF of L and the CIO in bringing the issue before the General Assembly of the United Nations. In December, 1952, it published a statement condemning the proclamation of Colonel Perez Jimenez as provisional president of Venezuela and appealing to the United States government to deny him diplomatic recognition.

Most of the activities of the ICFTU have educational aspects since they involve discussion of ideas and programs. The ICFTU has, however, a specific program of workers' education—to train workers in the tasks of the trade union movement. The premise of this program is that workers' education is a phase of general education in the principles of democracy and international cooperation, and helps to prepare men and women for service in the interests of mankind. The program of the ICFTU provides for international summer schools, short-term courses in different localities, trade union colleges, trade union youth camps, publication of small books on the labor movements of different countries and guidebooks on methods of collective bargaining, and preparation of trade union films.

The educational activities of the ICFTU have been carried on largely in Europe. In 1951, two international summer schools were held: one in Paris, which was attended by some eighty trade unionists and which dealt with problems of European economic integration; a second in the Austrian Tyrol, at which forty-one workers from thirteen countries were present, which dealt with questions of national and international labor movements. In July 1952, a two-week course was arranged in Kiljara, Finland, which was attended by sixty-three workers, including ten from Asian, Latin American, and African countries. In November and December, 1952, special training courses lasting for a week or ten days were organized in France for teachers, salaried employees, and workers in various industries. Since then, the ICFTU has projected large international educational and organizing campaigns in France, Italy, and Greece, for which considerable sums of money have been assigned and in which British, French, and other trade unions as well as some of the Trade Secretariats are cooperating. The educational programs which the ICFTU has carried on outside Europe are considered in the next section.

In its educational activities, the ICFTU cooperates with UNESCO, especially with the latter's International Workers' Education Center, which arranges summer schools, and with its workers' exchange and scholarship programs. UNESCO has applied its programs in Europe, Latin America, and Asia, and the ICFTU now asks that they be extended to North Africa and the Middle East.

The ICFTU has held several international conferences on workers' education and is planning a World Conference on Education to be held in Stockholm in 1953. It has also approved plans for a Trade Union Education Foundation and for an International Film Institute to finance an expansion of its activities in these fields.

The ICFTU attaches greatest importance to the promotion of trade unionism in the underdeveloped countries. It regards such activities as a form of technical assistance—labor's Point Four Program—which can help to improve labor conditions and to promote ideas of freedom. It regards them also as a factor of peace since they foster a friendly attitude on the part of the workers of underdeveloped countries toward Western Europe and America. The activities of the ICFTU in underdeveloped countries take the form of sending missions to establish personal relations with local trade unionists, supplying financial aid and office materials, helping to arrange trade union conferences, and training organizers and leaders. These activities are described in the section which follows.

## V. CENTRAL AND REGIONAL ORGANIZATIONS

The activities of the ICFTU are directed by the general secretary, J. H. Oldenbroek, and an assistant secretary, Hans Gottfurcht, subject to the directives of, and review by, the Executive Board. The nineteen members of the board represent all parts of the world and thus serve to give the central organization its worldwide character.[2] The central headquarters in Brussels now have a staff of over sixty persons, the majority of whom are Europeans; a few are from the United States, Canada, Latin America, and Asia. Branch offices with small staffs of a few persons each are maintained in Paris, Geneva, and New York.

Distinct from the branch offices are the regional offices which serve the regional organizations of the ICFTU. The idea of separate regional bodies in the structure of the ICFTU stems from the desire to stimulate local initiative and responsibility, and to maintain harmonious relations with local labor leaders, without jeopardizing the unity and effectiveness of the international organization. The regional organizations have a large degree of autonomy but remain subject to the supervision and control of the central headquarters and the Executive Board of the Confederation.

## European Regional Organization (ERO)

The national trade union centers of Europe affiliated with the ICFTU form the European Regional Organization. They pay special dues to support it. The ERO holds periodic congresses, is directed by

[2] The four members of the board who represent North America are George Meany, president of the AF of L; Walter Reuther, president of the CIO; Claude Jodoin, vice-president of the Trades and Labor Congress of Canada; and Donald MacDonald, secretary-treasurer of the Canadian Congress of Labor. The two members representing Great Britain are Arthur Deakin, general secretary of the Transport and General Workers' Union of Great Britain, and Sir Vincent Tewson, secretary of the British Trades Union Congress. The five members representing Europe are Leon Jouhaux, president of the French Force Ouvrière; Louis Major, secretary-general of the Belgian Federation of Labor; Walter Freitag, president of the West German Federation of Trade Unions; Giulio Pastore, general secretary of the Italian Confederation of Workers' Unions; and Eiler Jensen, president of the Danish Trade Union Federation. The two members representing Latin America are Bernardo Ibanez, of the Workers' Confederation of Chile, and Francisco Aguirre, formerly general secretary of the ORIT. The member representing the West Indies is Grantley Adams, of the Barbados Workers' Union. The three members representing Asia and the Middle East are Toshio Nishimaki, of the All Japan Seamen's Union and general secretary of the Joint Council of Japanese Trade Unions; Harniharnath Shastri, of the Indian National Trades Union Congress; and Mahmoud Mochaver, of the Iranian Trades Union Congress. The member representing Africa is Marcus Grant of the Sierra Leone Council of Labor. The member representing Australasia is Jack Walsh, president of the New Zealand Federation of Labor.

a regional council, and has a small office in Brussels. Its secretary is Walter Schevenels. At its first congress in Lugano, Switzerland, in October, 1952, the ERO reported that its affiliated organizations had a membership of over 23,000,000.

The function of the ERO is to clarify and unify the position of the European affiliates of the ICFTU on questions of European policy. Thus, after the French government in March, 1952, called an intergovernmental conference to consider the formation of a European Agricultural Products Community, popularly referred to as the "Green Pool," to integrate and modernize agricultural production and marketing in Western Europe, the ERO set up a trade union advisory committee to support the plan and to study methods for its realization. The ERO has also arranged conferences of its affiliates to consider the problems of the European Coal and Steel Community, the economic effects of rearmament, and planning for post-rearmament employment.

The ERO maintains close relations with the Organization for European Economic Cooperation (OEEC). This is done through the ERP-Trade Union Advisory Committee (established in 1948), which is technically a separate organization but in practice is directed by the ERO through the Paris office of the ICFTU. Through the ERP committee, the ERO is kept informed on plans and draft reports of the OEEC and can make suggestions on them for consideration by the governments of Europe represented in the Council of the OEEC. The ERO has taken much interest recently in the proposals of the OEEC to expand the output of its member countries by 25 per cent in the next five years, and has stressed the importance of taking into account the human factor in plans for increasing productivity.

The ERO has acted also on questions of social policy and education. It has set up a Social Housing Committee to promote programs of public housing. It arranged a trade union summer school in June, 1952, for workers from European countries at the Château de la Brevière, near Compiègne, France. It has set up a Trade Union Youth Committee to cooperate with liberal, socialist, Catholic, and Protestant youth organizations in educational campaigns for European unification, in the Western sense of the term.

On all committees of the ICFTU which deal with major issues of European policy, the ERO is represented by its secretary or by members of its regional council. The ERO has sought, however, to establish direct relations with official European regional agencies and to widen the sphere of its activities. This has given rise to complaints of overlapping and to questions of jurisdictional powers between the ERO and the central secretariat of the ICFTU. The difficulty is most likely to be resolved by a stricter delimitation of the powers and functions of the ERO.

### Inter-American Regional Organization (ORIT)

The regional body of the ICFTU in Latin America is the Inter-American Regional Organization of Workers—*Organisaçion Regional Inter-Americana de Trabajadores* (ORIT). The membership of ORIT includes trade unions affiliated with the ICFTU in South and Central America, in Canada, the AF of L and the CIO in the United States, the United Mine Workers of America, and unions in the islands of the Caribbean. The offices of ORIT were in Havana, Cuba, during 1951-1952, but are now in Mexico City. The ORIT holds annual conferences, has executive bodies, and a general secretary, whose appointment is subject to approval by the ICFTU. The secretary during 1951-1952 was Francisco Aguirre. The present secretary is Luis Alberto Monge, formerly president of the Costa Rican Confederation of Labor. One of the assistant secretaries is Serafino Romualdi, formerly an organizer of the AF of L and for many years active in the labor movements of Latin America.

The ORIT is the successor to the Inter-American Confederation of Workers (CIT) formed in January, 1948, with the aid of the American Federation of Labor, to combat the Communist-orientated Latin American Confederation of Labor (CTAL) directed by Lombardo Toledano and affiliated with the World Federation of Trade Unions. The CIT was dissolved when the ORIT was organized by the ICFTU in 1951. Though the CTAL has lost greatly in membership and influence, it is still a factor in the Latin American labor movement. One of the main tasks of the ORIT is to consolidate the trade union forces opposed to the CTAL.

The ICFTU and the ORIT had some success in this respect during 1951-1952. They gained the affiliation of the principal labor organizations of Cuba, Mexico, Brazil, Uruguay, Colombia, and the West

Indies. They established a Caribbean Area Division of the ORIT with an office in Barbados. But they made little headway in Ecuador, Peru, Paraguay, or Central America, and were prevented from seeking affiliation in Argentina and Venezuela by the governments of these countries.

The difficulties of the ORIT are due to general conditions. Latin American workers have been slow to form stable trade unions and have for years been involved in doctrinal disputes between socialists, Communists, syndicalists, Catholics, and Fascists. Their efforts to organize are further complicated by the spread of dictatorial regimes which aim to repress or control free labor organizations. The nationalist temper of Latin American labor movements and their traditional "anti-imperialist" attitudes have been additional factors.

The tasks of the ICFTU and ORIT have recently been made more difficult by the efforts of the Argentine Confederation of Labor to build a Latin American trade union organization under its own auspices. In structure and functions, the Argentine labor unions are similar to the Fascist unions of pre-1939 Italy and to the falangist unions of Spain. They are part of the economic and political system set up by President Peron and the late Eva Peron under the banner of "justicialism." They are controlled by the government and financed by compulsory contributions and subsidies.

As is generally admitted, the government of Peron has aimed to use the labor movement to strengthen Argentina's influence abroad. The method at first was to place in Argentine embassies labor attachés whose mission was to make converts among organized workers and labor leaders. These efforts met with some response in Peru, Paraguay, Bolivia, and elsewhere. After several preliminary meetings, a conference was held in November, 1952, at Mexico City under Argentine auspices at which an "Association of Latin American Workers" was set up (ATLAS). Labor leaders from a number of Latin American countries took part in the formation of the new organization. Its watchwords are "anti-capitalism," "anti-imperialism," and "independence of Latin American workers."

The ICFTU and ORIT thus face in Latin America opposition from both Communists and Peronists, who are often said to work together. To strengthen the ORIT, the ICFTU relies on the support of the

AF of L, the CIO, and the United Mine Workers of America. With their aid, the ORIT can employ trained organizers and advisers and can assist friendly labor unions in their work.

At its second congress in Rio de Janeiro in December, 1952, the ORIT took several steps to make its organization more effective. The headquarters were transferred to Mexico City, partly to avoid interference from the new dictatorship in Cuba, partly to win the support of Mexican trade unions. A new secretary was installed. Provisions were made for a larger budget to intensify organizing and educational activities.[3]

The ICFTU does not minimize the difficulties it faces in Latin America. It looks forward, however, to greater returns for its efforts, particularly if economic and social developments should result in a weakening or break-up of existing dictatorial regimes.

*Asian Regional Organization (ARO)*

The trade unions of India, Japan, Pakistan, Ceylon, Malaya, the Philippines, and several other Asian countries, affiliated with the ICFTU, form the Asian Regional Organization. Its headquarters are in Calcutta, India. The secretary is Dhyan Mungat, a member of the Seamen's Union of India, who is assisted by a staff of about ten, mostly from India.

Trade unions have expanded greatly in the countries of Asia since the end of the war. Still, their membership is a small percentage of the working population. Wages are low, working and living conditions are bad, and industrial relations bear the imprint of feudal and caste traditions.

The extension of trade unionism in Asia has been connected with movements for national independence and revolutionary social changes. During 1945-1947, many labor federations and national unions joined the World Federation of Trade Unions. Some of them broke away after 1949 and affiliated with the ICFTU, but others continue to support the WFTU. The ICFTU thus sees its main task in Asia as that of supporting and building up stable trade unions free of Communist control and influence.

[3] In March 1953, the ORIT opened its third trade union training course at the University of San Juan, Puerto Rico, with students from Brazil, Nicaragua, Panama, Salvador and Uruguay.

The ICFTU has been particularly concerned about developments in Japan. Under the occupation, trade unions were encouraged and grew rapidly, reaching a membership of over six million by the middle of 1949. During 1946-1947, three central labor organizations came into being: the Japanese Federation of Labor (Sodomei), which was a revival of a prewar organization with a moderate program; the National Congress of Industrial Unions (NCIU), in which socialists, liberals, and Communists cooperated but in which the Communists soon became dominant; and the National Liaison Council of Labor Unions under Communist control. The struggle between these central organizations resulted in splits and reorganizations, but it also led to the unification of the anti-Communist unions, which in 1950 formed the General Council of Trade Unions (Sohyo). As the Japanese government, aroused by successive strike waves, dissolved the National Liaison Council in 1950 and as the NCIU disbanded the same year, Sohyo emerged as the only strong central labor organization, with about three million members.

Sohyo established friendly relations with the ICFTU. At its 1951 convention, it approved by 149 against 79 votes a motion to affiliate with the ICFTU. This was two votes short of the required two thirds' majority, but it was expected that affiliation would be approved the following year.

During 1951-1952, however, Sohyo was rent by internal divisions. The socialists who have a leading position in Sohyo split into a right and left wing over the Japanese Peace Treaty. The left wing gained influence in Sohyo and was reinforced by Communists who infiltrated into the organization. The result was criticism by leaders of Sohyo of the ICFTU as being a "tool of the Anglo-American bloc" and of "American monopoly capital." At the 1952 convention of Sohyo, a motion to affiliate with the ICFTU was defeated by 164 to 42 votes.[4]

The ICFTU regards the situation as serious since a number of left-wing and Communist unions may now join Sohyo in order to ac-

---

[4] Within recent months, a number of unions, including those of seamen and textile workers, have broken away from Sohyo to form the National Liaison Council of Democratic Labor Movements (Minroren) which is strongly anti-communist.

centuate its left-wing orientation. They find a fertile ground for their activities among Japanese workers who believe that their living standards are depressed by international policies which make it difficult for the Japanese economy to obtain raw materials at low prices and to find markets for its products, and that the government is unfriendly to organized labor.

Still, the ICFTU has the affiliation of a number of the strongest trade unions of Japan, such as those of seamen, railway workers, and miners, which form the Joint Council of Japanese Trade Unions. The ICFTU aims to help these unions to make Sohyo a trade union center independent of political parties and free of Communist influence. The ICFTU has opened an office in Tokyo for this purpose, to publish a trade union weekly in Japanese, and to promote trade union education and training courses.

In India, the problems of the ICFTU are somewhat different since the trade union movement there is divided between four central organizations. The All-India Trade Union Congress (AITUC), formed in the early 1920's, was for many years guided by a coalition of socialist, Communist, and Congress Party leaders, but came under Communist control during the Second World War. This was because the Congress Party leaders and the socialists opposed the war while the Communists supported it after June 22, 1941, and for that reason were favored by the British authorities. After the end of the war, the AITUC was split by the several political groups, which formed three new central bodies: the Indian National Trades Union Congress (INTUC) under Congress Party leadership, the Hind Mazdoor Sabha under socialist leadership, and the United Trade Union Federation under the influence of anti-Stalinist Communists. The two largest federations are the Indian National Trades Union Congress, with a claimed membership of 1,400,000, and the Hind Mazdoor Sabha, with some 600,000 members. Both of these federations have been affiliated with the ICFTU since its foundation in 1949.

The ICFTU has urged the two federations to unite in order to strengthen their forces against the Communist AITUC, which has several hundred thousand members. The strength of the ICFTU unions is among seamen, railway, and textile workers, and unification would help, according to the ICFTU, to increase their membership as well as to organize new groups of workers. The efforts of the ICFTU have so far not met with success owing to the political interests involved.

Because of linguistic difficulties, low levels of literacy, and social traditions, the unions in Asia are dependent for leadership largely on intellectuals and professional people. The ICFTU thus sees as one of its main tasks in Asia the training of workers for the functions of trade union management and leadership. With that in view, the ICFTU and the Asian Regional Organization opened in November, 1952, a resident trade union college in Calcutta, India. The first twelve-week course given in English opened with sixteen students from India, Japan, Hong Kong, Malaya, and Thailand. Such short-term courses are to be given continuously during the year for different groups of students. The Calcutta College is expected also to prepare study guides which will be translated into various Asian languages. The college has a director appointed by the ICFTU who works in cooperation with the regional organization.

The other duties of the Secretariat of the ARO is to distribute information on the ICFTU, to visit affiliated unions, and to assist them in their organizing activities. This work is proceeding slowly as the ARO has difficulty in finding personnel outside India.

*Other Regional Centers*

The other regional activities of the ICFTU are in the Middle East and in Africa. In the Middle East, the ICFTU has affiliated unions in Lebanon and Syria which are relatively weak. A representative of the ICFTU visited Turkey in 1952 to assist the local unions in forming a national federation. In the summer of 1952, a commission consisting of a Belgian, Swiss, German, and Lebanese trade unionist was sent by the ICFTU to make a survey of labor conditions in Lebanon, Syria, Iraq, Transjordan, and Iran. On the recommendation of this commission, the ICFTU has undertaken to conduct trade union training courses in the Middle East and to publish trade union literature in Arabic, French, English, and Persian. The work is to be directed by an information center in Beirut.

In Africa, the formation of a regional organization is hampered by the wide differences in economic and political conditions in the several subdivisions of the continent, by diversities of colonial administration, as well as by disagreements on trade union methods. In North Africa, the ICFTU has the affiliation of the well-established Tunisian Federation of Trade Unions and of a recently organized national labor union in Libya. The ICFTU has assisted these labor unions financially and with organizing advice. In French West Africa (Senegal, Dahomey, Ivory Coast, Cameroons), the local unions are organized as overseas branches of the trade unions of metropolitan France. They are thus divided between the three central labor organizations of France—the Force Ouvière affiliated with the ICFTU, the Communist-orientated General Confederation of Labor (CGT), and the French Confederation of Catholic Workers (CFTC). The ICFTU is opposed to this policy: it would like to organize independent local unions which could affiliate with it directly. This issue is still under discussion between the ICFTU and the Force Ouvrière.

In British Africa, there are independent labor unions in Sierra Leone and Nigeria on the west coast, and in Kenya and Northern and Southern Rhodesia on the east coast. Many of these unions are organized on color lines. The ICFTU has affiliations in Sierra Leone and Nigeria, and has also established contacts with some of the unions in the dependencies of the east coast, e.g., Kenya.

The unions in both French and British Africa are composed of different groups of workers—civil servants, railwaymen, miners, seamen, and unskilled workers. The French, but particularly British trade unionists during the period when the Labour government was in office, have trained some local leaders in methods of collective bargaining and trade union organization. In most of the dependencies, the unions are involved in nationalist movements. All these labor movements affect only a small part of the population, in the larger urban and trading centers, and are in an incipient stage.

Most of the program of the ICFTU is concerned with French West Africa and the British dependencies on the west coast. During 1953, the ICFTU is to conduct trade union courses in Dakar (Senegal) or Abidjan (Ivory Coast) in French. A four-week course in English will be given in Accra (Gold Coast), to be attended by twenty trade unionists from Sierra Leone, Nigeria, Gambia, and the Gold Coast. The ICFTU is more active in the British dependencies and maintains an office in Accra.

*The Regional Activities Committee*

The regional activities of the ICFTU are planned and reviewed by a special committee appointed by the Executive Board. Great Britain, France, Belgium, the USA, Canada, India, and Latin America are represented on the committee. Jay Krane, an American member of the staff of the ICFTU, is secretary of the committee.

## VI. Budgets and Point Four Fund

To finance its general activities, the ICFTU relies on affiliation dues, though its income is augmented by special donations, receipts from sale of publications, and other contributions. Its budget for 1952 was about $400,000. The New York office is financed in part by special contributions of the AF of L and the CIO. The European Regional Organization is self-supporting. The expenses of the Asian Regional Organization are paid by the ICFTU, while the Inter-American Regional Organization is supported in part by its North American members. Over half of the affiliated organizations of the ICFTU pay dues at reduced rates, and many of them are often in arrears. The ICFTU is thus supported largely by its affiliates in Europe, the United States, Canada, Australia, and New Zealand.

The regional activities of the ICFTU are financed by contributions to the Regional Activities Fund, which was originally fixed at $700,000. Between April 1, 1951, and March 31, 1953, payments to this fund amounted to about $470,000. Of this amount, the CIO contributed $100,000 and the British Trades Union Congress about $200,000; substantial amounts were paid by the trade unions of West Germany, Austria, Canada, Belgium, Norway, Denmark, Sweden, and Switzerland. The expenditures of the ICFTU for regional activities during 1951 and 1952, were about $153,000.

## VII. Problems of Growth

Whether the ICFTU can make further progress on the road which it has mapped out for itself will depend on its capacity to meet the problems of organization and internal cohesion which it faces. The most important of these problems are those which inhere in the character and distribution of its membership, in the diversity of interests and attitudes of the labor movements in different countries, and in the shifting balance of trade union power.

The ICFTU has a membership several times larger than that attained before 1939 by the International Federation of Trade Unions, with which it may be reasonably compared. Still, this membership is overwhelmingly in Europe and North America. There are large numbers of organized workers outside the ICFTU in Western Europe, and still larger numbers of unorganized workers in other parts of the world. The question of increased membership looms large in the eyes of international trade union officials. The general secretary of the ICFTU, J. H. Oldenbroek, sees a potential of 100,000,000 members which his organization may aim at.

The growth of the ICFTU in membership in the near future depends on two main conditions. The ICFTU must, in the first place, win over the workers of Communist-controlled unions, particularly in France and Italy. The other condition is the capacity of the ICFTU to help organize under its own auspices the unorganized or loosely organized workers in the countries of Asia, Africa, and Latin America. In these areas, the ICFTU faces difficulties due not only to economic and social conditions but also to its own methods of working. The ICFTU is dominated largely by habits and attitudes of the West European trade unionism which forms the heart of its organization. Trade union leaders and officials of Western Europe are given to rather slow and systematic procedures, to emphasis on regular dues paying and internal discipline, and to cautious dealing with wage and other industrial problems. They assume that trade unions in underdeveloped countries should be built on the same foundations, despite the fact that industrialization in these countries is new and that the workers are held down by conditions of poverty, illiteracy, and a sense of social inferiority and dependence.

The ICFTU is further hampered in its work in Asia, Africa, and Latin America by the appeal which anticolonial and nationalistic movements make to the workers. Some of the leading affiliates of the ICFTU, e.g., the British Trades Union Congress, the French Force Ouvrière, and the Belgian Federation of Trade Unions, are caught in a dilemma with regard to these movements. They decry colonialism and have shown a real interest in improving labor conditions in the dependencies of their respective countries. At the same time, they are concerned about possible economic dislocations which rapid de-colonialization might cause both in the home countries and in the dependent areas. The ICFTU takes a strong position in favor of economic advancement and self-government in nonself-governing territories and has the support in this respect of many of its affiliates in Europe and of American labor, but it is not always supported by some of its leading members. Thus, the representative of the Force Ouvrière on the Executive Board of the ICFTU did not vote for the action taken by the ICFTU in Tunisia. The activities of the ICFTU on behalf of economic and political reform in underdeveloped and dependent countries are thus often considered inadequate by trade union and labor leaders in those countries who are affiliated with the ICFTU.

The internal cohesion of the ICFTU is affected in large measure by the relations between its European members and American labor. There is no question that both the AF of L and the CIO have great influence on the policies and action of the ICFTU. The European trade union leaders accept this fact as part of the new world situation which has made the United States the leading world power. Still, the friction between European and American labor movements, which was marked before 1939, persists to some extent today. The AF of L is not so much concerned today as it was before 1939 about the fact that the West European trade unions are socialistic in outlook. Socialism in Europe has changed its character. It now stresses gradual social-economic reforms and condemns abrupt and total changes by violent methods. Also, while the socialists established in 1951 a new Socialist International, it has neither the influence or prestige of the pre-1939 Labor and Socialist International. The ICFTU maintains no relations with it. In view of this and as long as the ICFTU adheres to the policy of allowing its affiliated unions autonomy in their internal affairs, the American unions regard the socialist attitudes of European labor organizations as their strictly domestic concern.

Friction today is due chiefly to two reasons. One is the desire of European labor to maintain a position of leadership in the world trade union movement. The trade unions of Great Britain, France, and other West European countries feel that they created this movement and directed it for decades. They are still the greatest single compact labor force, with over 20,000,000 members. They play a leading role in the economic and political life of their respective countries. They have had years of experience in dealing with international problems and have been active participants in international diplomacy. While recognizing the new international power of American labor, they feel that they should hold the key position as guides of international labor relations.

These attitudes are reflected in the ICFTU, whose officers, officials, and staff are mainly from European countries. The European leaders of the ICFTU are sensitive to acts or statements by American labor which seem to put them in a secondary position or which carry suggestions of American financial and political power. They are troubled by the fact that the AF of L and the CIO maintain offices and special representatives in Europe and that the AF of L carries on a large international program of its own in Asia, instead of using its resources to strengthen the regional activities of the ICFTU.

The other cause of friction lies in the different world position of West Europe and America, and makes itself felt in particular in connection with the East-West conflict. The AF of L strongly opposes policies or action which may weaken in any degree the struggle of labor against the Soviet Union and other Communist countries. The trade unions of West Europe are inclined at times to be less uncompromising on this issue. The West German Federation of Labor, for instance, has been lukewarm, if not opposed, to the NATO program of rearmament as proposed for West Germany. The British trade unions have been receptive from time to time to proposals of expanding trade relations with the USSR in the hope of improving the British balance of payments and thus their employment situation. French non-Communist unions are susceptible to the influence of "neutralism" for fear that an accentuation of anti-Soviet attitudes may enhance the danger of war. These European attitudes have their counterpart in Asia, e.g., in India, where some of the labor organizations are influenced by the idea of building up a "third force" in world politics.

The leaders of the AF of L feel that, owing to such influences, the ICFTU is not always vigorous enough in combating communism. On the other hand, trade union leaders of Europe as well as of some

Asian countries warn that ICFTU must not become a "negative" anti-Communist organization but should pursue a "positive" program to eliminate the conditions on which communism thrives.

How these differences find expression in current issues may be illustrated in two ways. One issue arose out of trade union developments in Italy in 1951. As related in Chapter XXII, the anti-Communist unions broke away from the CGIL early in 1949 and organized two federations: the Free General Confederation of Labor (LCGIL), under Christian Democratic auspices and under the leadership of Giulio Pastore, and the Italian Federation of Labor (FIL), under Republican and socialist leadership. In April, 1950, the two organizations combined to form the Italian Confederation of Labor Unions (CISL), which brought together Christian Democrats, Republicans, and right-wing socialists and claimed a membership of about 1,500,-000. The CISL joined the ICFTU, and its secretary, Pastore, was elected to the Executive Board of the ICFTU.

A number of right-wing socialists, however, refused to join the CISL and formed a new central labor organization—the Italian Labor Union (UIL). It claimed an initial membership of about 300,000. The UIL declared that it was in the interest of the socialist workers of Italy to have an organization independent of both the Communists and the Christian Democrats. The UIL applied for admission to the ICFTU. The AF of L objected on the ground that the anti-Communist labor forces of Italy should be united. After a long delay due to these objections, the Executive Board of the ICFTU voted to admit the UIL. This decision reflected the desire of European members of the ICFTU to strengthen the socialist group in Italy. George Meany, representing the AF of L on the Executive Board of the ICFTU, cast a negative vote.

The other issue arose out of conditions in Yugoslavia. In October, 1951, the Yugoslav Federation of Labor held its second congress in Zagreb. It was attended by invited "fraternal" delegates from the British Trades Union Congress, the French Force Ouvrière, Scandinavian, Belgian, Dutch, and other trade unions. Their attendance was interpreted by some as an indication that the Yugoslav trade unions might be admitted to the ICFTU.

The AF of L expressed strong disapproval of the action of the

European trade unionists. The leaders of the AF of L declared that they favored generous aid to the Tito government as long as it was willing and able to resist Soviet military aggression, but that they drew the line between such aid and recognition of the Yugoslav trade unions. The latter are "state controlled organizations like those in Russia, Spain and other totalitarian countries" and "communist party auxiliaries," and for that reason are not fit for membership in the ICFTU. The European members and officials of the ICFTU denied any intention to sponsor the admission of the Yugoslav unions.

The friction due to these and several other incidents caused the AF of L to absent itself from the meeting of the General Council of the ICFTU in Berlin in June, 1952, and to withhold a contribution to the Regional Activities Fund. There were rumors of a break between the AF of L and the ICFTU. The president and secretary of the ICFTU, Sir Vincent Tewson and J. H. Oldenbroek, came to Washington to discuss the situation with leaders of the AF of L, and matters were adjusted. In December, 1952, the AF of L actively participated in the meeting of the Executive Board of the ICFTU held in New York. On June 1, 1953, the AF of L, the CIO and The United Mine Workers issued a joint statement endorsing the work of the ICFTU and outlining a program which they proposed to present to the third world congress of the ICFTU to be held in Stockholm from July 4 to July 11, 1953.

Despite the difficulties which beset its path, the International Confederation of Free Trade Unions has in the three years of its existence established itself as a worldwide organization and as the acknowledged spokesman of free labor. This record indicates the strength of the internal and external forces which have maintained it and determined the course of its development. The likely effects of these forces in the years immediately ahead are examined in the concluding chapter.

# The International Trade Secretariats

THE strength and importance of the ICFTU are enhanced by its cooperative relations with the International Trade Secretariats. After their reestablishment during 1946-1948, the Secretariats reasserted their claim to an independent place in the international labor movement. They rejected proposals of the World Federation of Trade Unions to transform them into subordinate trade departments. It was their opposition that prevented the WFTU from consolidating itself before it was torn apart by the East-West conflict.

In the course of their negotiations with the WFTU, the Trade Secretariats drew closer together. In March, 1949, they set up a Coordinating Committee to represent them collectively and to consider their common problems. This committee now meets regularly and maintains an office in London. Omer Becu, general secretary of the International Transport Workers' Federation, is chairman of the committee.

## I. Agreement with the ICFTU

After the London conference of 1949, the Executive Board of the ICFTU met with the Coordinating Committee of the International Trade Secretariats and worked out an agreement for mutual cooperation. In accordance with this agreement, the ICFTU recognizes the right of the Trade Secretariats to maintain their independence, to have autonomy in their internal affairs, and to have full jurisdiction in trade and industrial matters. The Secretariats, in turn, recognize the

ICFTU as the representative international organization of labor which formulates and executes general policies.

The relationships are cemented by means of a system of mutual representation. The Trade Secretariats send one delegate with consultative status to the Emergency Committee, two delegates to the Executive Board, and five to the General Council of the ICFTU. The Trade Secretariats may also be represented at the congresses of the ICFTU, in proportion to their membership. On the other hand, the ICFTU may take part in a consultative capacity in the conferences and meetings of the Trade Secretariats and of their Coordinating Committee. The cooperative relations are facilitated by a five-man liaison committee appointed by the Secretariats and financed by them.

## II. Composition and Membership

At the present time, eighteen International Trade Secretariats are members of the Coordinating Committee and allied with the ICFTU. The largest is the International Metal Workers Federation with nearly six million members in fourteen countries.[1] The second largest, with affiliations in over forty countries, is the International Transport Workers Federation with about five million members. The three smallest are the International Federation of Free Teachers Unions with 83,000 members in six countries, the International Federation of Tobacco Workers with 71,000 members in six countries, and the Universal Alliance of Diamond Workers with 12,500 members in seven countries.

Eight other Secretariats have over a million members each. They are the International Miners Federation with about 2,500,000 members in seventeen countries, the International Federation of Building and Wood Workers with about 2,000,000 members in nineteen countries, the International Federation of Unions of Employees in Public and Civil Service with about 1,770,000 members in twenty countries, the International Federation of Commercial, Clerical and Technical Employees with 1,314,000 members in twelve countries, the International Federation of Textile Workers Associations with 1,305,000 members in fourteen countries, the International Land

[1] The membership figures in this section are as of December, 1952.

Workers Federation with 1,073,000 members in fifteen countries, the International Federation of Industrial Organizations and General Workers Unions with 1,112,000 members in sixteen countries, and the Postal, Telegraph and Telephone International with 1,046,000 members in twenty-five countries.

The remaining five Secretariats, with less than a million members each, are the International Garment Workers Federation with 816,-000 members in fourteen countries, the International Graphical Federation with 584,000 members in eighteen countries, the International Union of Federations of Workers in the Food and Drink Trades with 591,000 members in sixteen countries, the International Shoe and Leather Workers Federation with 288,000 members in eleven countries, and the International Union of Hotel, Restaurant and Bar Workers with 165,000 members in eleven countries.

Most of the Secretariats are still essentially European organizations, though they have affiliations outside Europe. Twelve of the Secretariats have affiliated trade unions in the United States. A few of these Secretariats, e.g., the miners, textile workers, postal, and public service employees, have affiliated members also in India, Pakistan, Japan, and Canada. The International Transport Workers Federation is worldwide and maintains branch offices in New York, Latin America, and Asia.

There have been some changes since 1939 in the location and leadership of the Secretariats. The federations of transport workers, textile workers, garment workers, shoe and leather workers, and employees in the public service now maintain their headquarters in London or other cities of England. The federations of food and drink trades, tobacco workers, and hotel workers have their offices in Denmark or Sweden. The building workers, clerical employees, and general workers' unions are located in Amsterdam. The federations of metal workers, postal employees, and graphical workers have their offices in Berne, Switzerland. The offices of the diamond workers are in Antwerp, Belgium, and those of the land workers in Utrecht, Holland. Broadly speaking, the British play a larger part in the Secretariats than they did before 1939, but the Dutch, Belgians, and Swiss still exercise the greatest influence as officials and leaders of the Secretariats.

## III. Scope of Activities

The organization and activities of the International Trade Secretariats today are similar to those before 1939, as described in Chapter XIV. The Secretariats hold periodic conferences and congresses, at which they elect their executive committees and councils and appoint international secretaries. Between congresses, the executive bodies meet to discuss current problems. The Secretariats publish journals, make studies of wage and labor conditions in different countries, and extend aid to striking or unemployed workers.[2] They also carry on campaigns for international labor legislation and for the protection of trade union rights. These activities are financed from dues paid by the affiliated trade unions.

The Secretariats are concerned chiefly with problems of an industrial character, such as relative wages in different countries, hours of work, vocational guidance and training, night work, paid holidays, industrial hygiene and safety, and social security. Most of these problems involve not only national legislation but international agreements between governments. To promote the latter, the Secretariats maintain close relations with the International Labor Organization, as they did before 1939.

Since the end of the war, the Trade Secretariats have taken an active part in the international industrial committees established by the ILO. These committees are tripartite in character, that is, composed of representatives of governments, employers, and workers, and the Secretariats participate in them as representatives of the workers in their respective industries. The committees meet periodically to consider questions of productivity, wages and working conditions, management, and long-range planning to expand output and world demand. The Secretariats generally favor scientific management in industry to lower costs, provided it also leads to improved earnings for the workers, and advocate the forty-hour working week, paid

---

[2] For instance, the International Miners Federation and its affiliated unions contributed about $15,000 to Japanese coal miners who were on strike during 1952. Of this amount, about $450 came from the International itself, $10,000 from the United Mine Workers of America, over $3,000 from the miners' unions of Yugoslavia, and the remainder from miners' unions of Great Britain, Austria, Belgium, and the Gold Coast in West Africa.

annual holidays, and other measures for raising working and living standards.

The Trade Secretariats deal also with general international economic and social problems. Most of them lent support to the Marshall Plan. The International Transport Workers Federation had a particularly important role in the seaports of France and Italy in helping to prevent Communist sabotage in the loading and unloading of Marshall Plan supplies. The International Miners Federation and the International Federation of Metal Workers launched the idea of internationalizing the industries of the Ruhr in Germany even before the Schuman Plan was formulated. They have had a share in making the Plan popular among the workers and in obtaining representation for organized labor on the advisory committees of the European Coal and Steel Community set up under the Plan. The International Federation of Textile Workers has been advocating the integration of the textile industries of Western Europe. Most of the Secretariats have given aid to workers struggling to maintain trade union rights in various countries.

## IV. Nature and Forms of Cooperation

The Trade Secretariats are helped in their activities by cooperation with the .ICFTU. The latter can appeal to its national trade union centers to urge their affiliated unions to join the Trade Secretariats. The ICFTU assists the Trade Secretariats in their relations with the ILO and in their work in the international industrial committees of the ILO. Through joint committees and through its European Regional Organization, the ICFTU provides for the participation of the Secretariats in maintaining relations with official regional agencies in Europe. The International Federation of Metal Workers and the International Miners Federation, for instance, are members of a "committee of fifteen" established by the ICFTU to keep in contact with the work of the European Coal and Steel Community, and they finance jointly an office in Luxembourg for this purpose. Owing to its consultative status in the Economic and Social Council, the ICFTU can also bring the problems and demands of the Secretariats to the attention of the United Nations.

On the other hand, the Secretariats support the ICFTU in the industrial field and assist it financially and otherwise in its various activities, particularly in the underdeveloped countries. Ten Secretariats made financial contributions of about $20,000 to the Fund for Regional Activities of the ICFTU during 1951-1952. Several of them have taken part in missions sent by the ICFTU to Asia and Africa. Most of them cooperate with the ICFTU in educational and organizing campaigns. Thus, the International Federation of Metal Workers financed several trade union training courses which the ICFTU organized in France in the fall of 1952 and in which some 150 automobile, steel, and aviation workers took part. The Secretariats of land workers and of workers in the food and drink trades joined with the ICFTU to carry on an organizing campaign during 1953 among plantation workers in Asia and Latin America.

International trends indicate several lines along which the Trade Secretariats may develop. If and as industries in Western Europe become integrated, the Trade Secretariats may be drawn into a larger role in setting standards of employment. It is theoretically possible to envisage inter-European master collective agreements in integrated industries which would serve as a basis for national agreements in separate countries. Some of the larger and more active Trade Secretariats have discussed the possibility of such forms of international collective bargaining from time to time.

Another line of development is indicated in the primary producing industries, in connection with international commodity agreements to stabilize production, prices, and markets. It is but a step in the same direction to include in such agreements clauses setting minimum wage rates and standards of work. That the Trade Secretariats are turning their attention to such problems is shown by the first World Sugar Workers' Congress held in Havana, Cuba, in March, 1953. The congress was called jointly by the International Federation of Workers in the Food and Drink Trades, the International Federation of Land Workers, and the International Confederation of Free Trade Unions. It was attended by delegates from twenty countries and by officials of the international organizations. The congress formulated a program which among other things demanded the participation of sugar workers' unions in all future international sugar conferences and the fixing of basic minimum wages and fair working standards in international sugar agreements.

A third line of development is suggested by the work of the international industrial committees of the ILO. These committees are now under attack by employers of some countries and are of limited influence. The Trade Secretariats are now projecting as one of their main tasks not only the defense of existing committees, but their extension to more industries and a widening of their functions. These committees could in the opinion of the trade secretariats, become effective as agencies for promoting labor-management cooperation in matters of productivity, use of raw materials, and expansion of consumer demand if they had the support of employers' and management associations and of governments.

A fourth line of development lies in the enlargement of the role of the Trade Secretariats in the representation of organized labor in the United Nations and its agencies.

As the Trade Secretariats develop the activities projected above, they are likely to find the present scheme of their organizational relations with the ICFTU inadequate. The changes which may take place are considered briefly in the concluding chapter.

CHAPTER XXVI

# The World Federation of Trade Unions

THE World Federation of Trade Unions has suffered setbacks since its split in 1949. It had to leave Paris and move its offices to Vienna, where it has less scope for action. Its activities have been forbidden in a number of countries. Nevertheless, it is a factor creating special problems for the free international labor organizations.

## I. MEMBERSHIP

As a result of the split in 1949, the WFTU was abandoned by the national trade union centers of all West and North European countries except France and Italy, as well as by the CIO in the United States, the Canadian unions, and the larger labor organizations of Brazil, Cuba, India, Japan, Australia, New Zealand, and other countries. This meant a loss of tens of millions of members. Nevertheless, the WFTU claims to have a larger membership today than before the split. In February, 1951, it reported the affiliation of 64 trade union organizations in 56 countries with 78 million members. It now claims a membership of over 80 million.

It is impossible to check these figures on the basis of available data. Besides, membership has an uncertain meaning in many of the organizations connected with the WFTU, and their affiliation with it carries no specific obligations. The bulk of the membership of the WFTU is in the Soviet Union and the "People's democracies" of Eastern and Central Europe. The Soviet trade unions claim a membership of over 40 million, while the trade unions of Poland, Rumania, Bulgaria, Hungary, Czechoslovakia, and East Germany are estimated to have between 15 and 18 million members. In Western Europe, the WFTU has the affiliation of the large central labor organizations of France and Italy and of a small labor central in the Netherlands (EVC). The French General Confederation of Labor (CGT) and the General Confederation of Italian Labor (CGIL) have both lost greatly in membership since 1949 as a result of repeated splits, disastrous strikes, and disillusionment of the workers with their leadership. The CGT and the CGIL are now estimated to have between two and three million members each, though they claim much larger memberships.

In Latin America, the WFTU has the affiliation of the Confederation of Latin American Workers (CTAL), of which Vincente Lombardo Toledano is president. The CTAL too has declined in recent years, and its membership is of a fluctuating and uncertain character.

In Asia, the largest affiliates of the WFTU are the All-China Federation of Labor, which reports over eight million members, and the Indonesian Federation of Trade Unions, which claims over two million members. The trade unions in the Middle East, Ceylon, India, and the Philippines which belong to the WFTU probably have a total membership of less than a million. The WFTU also has groups of followers and trade union affiliates in Australia and New Zealand and in the dependent areas of Africa. In French Africa, the unions which are organized as branches of the CGT in metropolitan France are indirectly connected with the WFTU.

Thus, over three fourths of the claimed membership of the WFTU is in Soviet Russia and the "People's democracies" of Eastern and Central Europe, and another 10 per cent in China. In other words, about 85 per cent of the affiliations of the WFTU are in countries with Communist regimes.

## II. TYPES OF UNIONS

The WFTU claims to be "a free and voluntary association of trade unions which are non-party organizations having the objective of improving the worker's conditions." In reality, the trade unions of the WFTU are of two types, both of which have special features which distinguish them from the European and American trade unions affiliated with the ICFTU.

One type is that of the Soviet trade unions, which are governmental institutions and under the leadership and control of the Russian Communist Party. The Russian unions are part of the Soviet economic administrative structure, and perform functions assigned to them by the government with regard to increasing productivity, setting standards of work, fixing wage rates, and enforcing social security provisions. Membership in the Soviet trade unions is nominally voluntary, but in practice is made compulsory by the requirements of the government and the Communist Party. The Soviet unions carry on collective bargaining with the managements of state industrial enterprises, but under rules determined officially, with primary regard to the economic plans of the government. The workers do not have the right to strike. Elections of trade union officials are supervised and controlled by the government and the Communist Party. With minor modifications, the trade unions of the "People's democracies" in Europe and China follow the Soviet pattern.

The classical example of the other type is the trade unions of the

French CGT and the Italian CGIL. These unions are voluntary in structure, carry on collective bargaining independently of the government and of employers, and have the right to strike. They are, however, dominated by Communist leaders who owe their first allegiance to the political party. Communists today, as in the past, regard the trade unions chiefly as instruments of "class struggle" and as a means of mass support for their political ends now and for the "social revolution" eventually. Most of the trade unions of the WFTU in Latin America and Asia (outside China) are of this second type.

### III. CHARACTER OF THE WFTU

The WFTU was founded in Paris in 1945 as a nonparty organization. The constitution which it then adopted contained no reference to communism or any other social doctrine, and there were to be no alliances with any political party. Officials and spokesmen of the WFTU maintain that no change has taken place in this respect. The WFTU, they claim, is today a "trade union organization, not a party."

The real character of the WFTU becomes clearer when it is compared with the Red International of Labor Unions (RILU), whose activities between 1923 and 1935 were described in earlier chapters. The RILU was an outspokenly Communist organization, acting as the trade union arm of the Third International. It had its headquarters in Moscow, held its meetings immediately after the congresses or plenums of the Third International, and was openly guided by the decisions and directives of the latter. The two internationals were interlocked through mutual representation in their executive committees. Whatever tactics the RILU followed—whether organizing dual unions or "boring from within" or advocating "unity"—it did so in accordance with the policies of the Third International.

The WFTU does not follow such pattern. It is not connected formally with the International Communist Information Bureau, or Cominform, established in 1947. It is, however, controlled and directed by Communists whose political affiliations make them subject to the directives of the Cominform. The president of the WFTU is Giuseppe di Vittorio, a leader of the Italian Communist Party. The majority of the Executive Committee consists of Communists— Russian, French, Czechoslovak, Chinese, and others. Other members of the committee and the general secretary, Louis Saillant, have consistently acted in accord with the Communist majority. The dominating figures of the WFTU are Communist leaders from the USSR, France, and Italy. Furthermore, the WFTU depends for its support on the Soviet trade unions. The WFTU does not publish financial statements, but it is clear that its activities can be financed primarily by contributions from the USSR and the "People's democracies" in Europe. French and Italian workers are not known as good dues payers, and the same may be said of the trade unions of Latin America and Asia. Without the Soviet trade unions, the WFTU would have no basis for existence.

Under present-day world conditions, Soviet Communists would have no interest in an organization like the former RILU. The latter was allowed to lapse in 1935 because the Russians found that it was doing them more harm than good among the workers. The interests of Soviet communism can best be served now by an international organization which appears to be of a nonparty character, which maintains its headquarters outside Russia, and which can espouse Communist views and objectives under the guise of legitimate economic and social demands of the labor movement. The WFTU is organized and conducted so as to meet these specifications.

The character of the WFTU is revealed in its formulations of general ideas, its persistent praise of the Soviet Union, its hostile attitude toward the Western powers and especially the United States, and its specific policies and slogans. In the past few years, the official journal of the WFTU—*World Trade Union Movement*, published in eight languages—has carried numerous articles and editorials by Soviet writers and by Louis Saillant expounding approvingly "Leninist-Stalinist" doctrines on "monopoly capitalism," on the role of the state, on proletarian dictatorship, and on the revolutionary role of the "anti-imperialist" movements in colonial and nonindustrialized countries. The proclamations, declarations, and May Day manifestoes of the WFTU bristle with denunciations of "American imperialists striving for war domination" and of the "bloc of imperialist states . . . speeding up preparations for another world war." The United States and the Western powers in the publications of the WFTU are named as the "aggressors in Korea."

But the publications of the WFTU extol the Soviet Union as the protagonist of world peace and the defender of oppressed nations and colonial peoples. All criticism of the Soviet Union is denounced as the "slander of warmongers." The Iron Curtain is said to exist only in the imagination of such "slanderers." On the occasion of the thirty-fifth anniversary of the Bolshevik Revolution, in November, 1952, the official journal of the WFTU featured a page of greetings headlined: "World Workers Enthusiastically Greet the Builders of Communism." The telegram sent by the WFTU to the General Council of the Soviet trade unions congratulated them on the "tremendous successes achieved by the peoples of the Soviet Union in the peaceful construction of an enthusiastic and happy life," and referred to "comrade Stalin" as the "friend and guide of the workers of the whole world." Louis Saillant led a delegation of the WFTU to Moscow to take part in the celebration of the anniversary.

In accordance with these attitudes, the WFTU has denounced the Marshall Plan, NATO, the Schuman Plan, and other Western policies. It has attacked the defense programs of the Atlantic Pact Powers, contrasting them with the "small war expenditures" of the USSR. It has called for the withdrawal of all foreign troops from Korea and for admitting the Chinese People's Republic to the United Nations.

In economic matters, the WFTU has shown a similar discrimination between the Soviet Union and the West. It has found fault with the nationalization of industry in Great Britain and France, describing them as "injurious to the workers" and as steps toward "State monopoly capitalism." It has criticized the international economic policies, especially the export control measures, of the United States. But it describes in glowing terms the industrial growth of the USSR and the "People's democracies" and their programs of land collectivization, and finds nothing to criticize in these countries.

The WFTU is extremely critical of the trade unions of the Western countries, denouncing them for alleged limitations of vision, collaborating with employers, and "obstructing the class struggle." But for the trade unions of the Soviet Union and of the "People's democracies" it has only praise. These trade unions are, in its view, of a "higher type" than those of "capitalist countries" for the very reason that they are part of the social-economic administration of those countries. By implication, the WFTU regards the Soviet trade unions as the model of the status which Western trade unions should aim to achieve.

The WFTU is now trying to popularize the slogan of "united front from below" launched by Stalin at the congress of the Russian Communist Party in October, 1952, and taken up by the Cominform. This slogan differs from the pre-1939 "united front" in that it is addressed to the rank and file. The WFTU urges the workers in "capitalist" countries to unite, without regard to political affiliations or religious beliefs or whether organized or not, and to fight under its leadership for full employment, sliding scales of wages, equal pay for equal work, a minimum living wage, abolition of racial discrimination, and also for the "supression of all forms of forced labor." It calls upon its affiliated unions to fight for "democracy in the unions" and to form "united action committees" in the factories in order to "step up the struggle for economic and social demands." In Latin America, Asia, and Africa it calls on the workers to "link up all the time" their economic demands with "the fight for national independence and peace."

## IV. Trade Departments

The new feature in the organization of the WFTU since 1949 is the establishment of twelve trade departments. These are composed of national and individual unions of miners; metal workers; chemical, textile, and building trades workers; seamen and dockers; land and air transport workers; postal and communication employees; agricultural, food, and educational workers. They bear such names as the Mine Workers' Trade Unions International, the Metal Workers' Unions International, and so on. These names are intended to suggest that they are autonomous organizations, though they are subordinate to the secretariat of the WFTU.

The bulk of the membership of the trade departments is in the USSR, the "People's democracies," Eastern Germany, France, Italy, and China. Only a very few trade unions from other countries are affiliated. The trade departments tried at first to set up headquarters in Western Europe, but were forced by the action of the governments to move to Eastern Europe.

The trade departments hold periodic meetings and congresses at which they formulate industrial and economic programs that usually go beyond the demands of the non-Communist unions. They call, for instance, for noncontributory social insurance systems, for unemployment insurance benefits equal to three fourths of wages, for three-week holidays with pay, and so on. At the same time, the trade departments urge the workers to form peace committees in the factories and in the shops, on the docks and on board ships, to organize exchange delegations for visits to the Soviet Union, and to support other Communist-sponsored policies.

The trade departments are the means by which the WFTU tries to gain a foothold in national and local unions and to maintain contacts with groups of workers and with workers' shop and factory committees in the democratic countries. Only a few of the trade departments are of industrial importance, particularly those of seamen and dockers and of metal workers. The former, for instance, exercise influence in France, where the trade unions affiliated with the Communist-controlled General Confederation of Labor (CGT) have a dominant position in the hiring halls on the docks and in the ports.[1]

## V. General Activities

In its general activities, the WFTU cooperates closely with organizations known to be Communist-inspired and Soviet-sponsored. During the past few years, the WFTU has arranged "workers' rallies" and conferences against the defense programs in France and Italy, against rearmament in Germany and Japan, and against the Schuman Plan. It has sponsored conferences on youth problems, in "defense of children," and on social security. It collected signatures for the Stockholm Peace Petition. It took an active part in organizing trade union delegations to the World Peace Congress in Vienna in December, 1952, held under the auspices of the World Peace Council.

Other activities of the WFTU are for the purpose of influencing

[1] The data of this section have been obtained largely from an article entitled "The WFTU and Its Trade Departments" in the August, 1952, issue of *The World Today*, published by the Royal Institute of International Relations in London. According to this article, some of the trade departments maintain also "an elaborate network of couriers" who carry on underground activities.

labor and social movements in different parts of the world. Its officials attend meetings and congresses of affiliated or friendly national trade union centers, especially in Asia and Africa. Close relations are maintained with the Confederation of Latin American Workers (CTAL). The WFTU has given aid in particular to labor and nationalist movements in the Middle East and Southeast Asia.

The WFTU continues to have consultative status in the Economic and Social Council of the United Nations and in the International Labor Organization. Invariably, its representatives in these bodies criticize, often in abusive language, the proposals of the delegations of the United States, Great Britain, and other Western powers, and support the position of the Soviet delegation. In most discussions in the Economic and Social Council in which they have a right to take part, namely, on such questions as full employment, trade union rights, forced labor, financing of economic development, the representatives of the WFTU submit long statements and voluminous statistics of a questionable character to bolster up extreme proposals of little immediate practical relevancy. Neither in the Economic and Social Council nor in the International Labor Organization have the proposals of the WFTU had effect except to arouse the irritation and impatience of most delegations. At its session in Vienna in June, 1952, the Executive Committee of the WFTU complained that a "coalition of reactionary trade union leaders, imperialist governments and employers" enabled the ILO "to bury" nineteen complaints presented by the WFTU with regard to violations of trade union rights. The WFTU does not regard it as odd that it never complains about trade union conditions in the USSR or the "People's democracies." The WFTU uses its position in the United Nations also to attack the ICFTU, and representatives of the two organizations are often engaged in stormy word battles. The WFTU maintains its consultative status in the United Nations owing to the support not only of the Soviet bloc but also of governments which have to deal with radical labor movements at home.

The WFTU has been in retreat for some time not only in Western Europe but in other parts of the world as well. Its participation in the work of the Economic and Social Council has been steadily reduced.

Still, owing to the special conditions described in earlier chapters, it remains a force in some countries, particularly in the underdeveloped and dependent regions of the world.[2]

# The Christian Trade Unions

TRADE unions organized on a denominational Christian basis now exist not only in Western Europe but also in Canada, Latin America, and a few other countries. They are combined in two internationals. The smaller—*L'Internationale Ouvrière Protestante*—includes only labor organizations of Protestant denominations. Its affiliated membership is in Germany, Denmark, and Switzerland. It has recently established an office in Canada to spread its ideas.

The other and far more important organization is the International Confederation of Christian Trade Unions (ICCTU), which is predominantly Catholic. The origin and development of this International were traced in earlier parts of this book. Its current activities form the subject matter of this chapter.

[2] The WFTU is now making another effort to appear as a bona-fide trade union organization. At its meeting in Vienna in April, the Executive Board of the WFTU decided to call a Third World Trade Union Congress to be held in Vienna in October, 1953. It is characteristic of the methods of the WFTU that the Executive Board did not address or call upon its claimed affiliates, but issued an "appeal" to "all trade unions of the whole world" to attend the congress. The obvious purpose is to sow confusion in the labor organizations which are opposed to it and which regard it as a thinly-disguised Communist-front organization, and to try to counteract the effect of the Stockholm Congress of the ICFTU.

### I. MEMBERSHIP AND ORGANIZATION

Before the advent of Nazism and Fascism, the mainstay of the Christian Trade Union International was in Central and South Europe. Today, the International has no affiliations there. Since 1946, the German and Austrian trade unions have been organized on a unified basis, including workers without regard to political affiliation or religious beliefs. The once strong Christian trade unions in these countries have thus ceased to have a separate existence. In Italy, the Italian Federation of Free Trade Unions includes Catholic, Republican, and socialist workers, and is affiliated with the ICFTU. The Christian trade unions of Hungary, Czechoslovakia, and Yugoslavia were destroyed by the Fascist regimes before 1939 and by the war. They cannot exist today under Communist regimes. In Spain, Christian trade unionists are said to carry on underground activities, as they are not permitted by the falangist regime of General Franco to function openly.

The main strength of Christian trade unionism is now in France, Belgium, and Holland. The French Confederation of Christian Workers claims over 750,000 members and has considerable influence in the French labor movement. The same is true of the Belgian Federation of Christian Trade Unions, whose membership in 1951 was over 550,000. In the Netherlands, there are two Christian labor organizations—the Catholic Labor Movement, with about 325,000 members, and the Christian National Federation of Trade Unions (Calvinist), with about 150,000 members. The membership of these unions is largely in coal mining and among textile, metal, and office workers. There are smaller unions of Christian workers in Luxembourg and Switzerland.

Outside Europe, the largest Catholic labor organization is in Canada, where the *Confédération des Travailleurs Catholiques du Canada* reported 93,000 members in 1952. In recent years, Christian trade unions have come into being in several Latin American countries —Costa Rica, Ecuador, Chile, Uruguay, and Brazil. There are now small trade unions of Christian workers also in French colonies and dependencies—Tunisia, Morocco, Dahomey, Madagascar, the Cameroons, Martinique, Viet-Nam, and a few others. These unions have been organized with the aid of the Catholic trade unions of France. There is a Catholic trade union federation in the Belgian Congo.

Compared with the ICFTU and the WFTU, the International Confederation of Christian Trade Unions is a small organization. At its eleventh congress held at The Hague in July, 1952, the ICCT reported that it had affiliated organizations in fourteen countries—France, Belgium, Holland, Luxembourg, the Saar, Switzerland, Canada, Ecuador, Chile, Brazil, Argentina, Uruguay, Dutch Guiana, and Viet-Nam. Its total membership is about two million, concentrated in Western Europe.

As before 1939, the headquarters of the ICCTU are in Utrecht, Holland. J. P. Serrarens, who had served as general secretary since 1920, resigned in July, 1952, to become a member of the Court of the European Coal and Steel Community under the Schuman Plan. He was replaced by his assistant, A. Vanistendael. The president of the organization since 1949 has been Gaston Tessier, leader of the Catholic trade unions of France. The ICCTU holds biennial congresses, is directed by a General Council and Executive Committee, and maintains a small secretariat. As before 1939, there are also in existence Christian international trade secretariats of miners, metal workers, textile workers, agricultural workers, public service employees, and several other groups of workers. These secretariats are affiliated with the ICCTU. The budget of the latter, which is financed from dues of affiliated organizations, is small.

## II. Policies and Activities

The International Confederation of Christian Trade Unions is guided today, as before 1939, by Catholic ideas of social justice and labor welfare, as outlined in Chapter XV. Some changes have taken place since the war in the application of these ideas to current policy. The French Catholic trade unions, in particular, which played a large part in the Resistance Movement, came out of the war and the struggle for national liberation with a large economic and social program. They supported the legislation for nationalization of the coal mines, banks, and several other industries which the French government enacted in 1945-1946. They are advocates of economic and social planning as applied, for instance, in the Monnet Plan for the modernization and expansion of French industry.

The Christian trade unions lay stress on what they call industrial democracy. They want the workers to have a larger share in the management of plants so that they may have greater interest in the success and welfare of the enterprises in which they work. They also favor national industrial councils in which workers and employers can cooperate in considering the larger problems of the national economy, e.g., fiscal and trade policies. The leaders of the Christian trade unions regard such councils as a means of combatting both communism and "liberal capitalism" and of giving concrete expression to the Christian ideal.

On many issues of international policy, the Christian Trade Union International takes a position similar to that of the International Confederation of Free Trade Unions. It supported the Marshall Plan and the ERP not only as measures of immediate recovery but also as applications of international planning for the solution of Europe's long-range problems. It has been an ardent supporter of the Schuman Plan and of European economic integration. It supports the work of the United Nations and the specialized agencies. It has differed with the ICFTU, however, on questions of rearmament and peace. In 1951, the General Council of the Christian International adopted a resolution requesting that the four great powers (the United States, Great Britain, France, and the USSR) "examine objectively the material and moral conditions necessary for peaceful coexistence between rival ideologies." The resolution was justified by the ICCTU as motivated by a desire to avoid war. It was criticized by the ICFTU as an expression of "neutralism."

Like the ICFTU, the Christian Trade Union International has consultative status as a Category A organization in the Economic and Social Council of the United Nations and in the International Labor Organization. The representatives of the ICCTU take a modest part in the proceedings of the Council, limiting themselves to brief statements on labor and social questions. In general, they have been in accord with the policies of the Western powers in the United Nations. In the ILO, the Christian International is represented in the Workers' Group and takes an active interest in its deliberations. The Christian trade union leaders have criticized the ILO, for the slowness of its procedures and have recommended changes in its methods of work in order to speed the adoption and ratification of draft conventions. The ICCTU is also represented on the Advisory Committee of the European Coal and Steel Community, on which it has five members.

Besides those described, the activities of the ICCTU are largely of an educational character. It arranges conferences for the discussion of current problems. It publishes a monthly journal in French, entitled *Labor*, and occasional papers and pamphlets.

### III. Relations with Other Unions

The Christian trade unions justify their separate existence on the theory that freedom of association includes freedom to form denominational unions. Such unions are desirable, in their view, for moral reasons—to promote religious and ethical ideas among the workers and to combat communism and other doctrines which they regard as inimical to religion and the Church.

The Christian trade unions deprecated at one time not only the more violent forms of labor action in Europe but also peaceful strikes. At present, they support strike movements as a means of last resort, practice the usual methods of collective bargaining, and aim to promote labor and social legislation by parliamentary means. For the latter purpose, they maintain friendly relations with political parties which share their general views, especially in Belgium and Holland.

The Christian trade unions maintain that it is not necessary to have only one central labor organization in a country, that it is desirable to allow for pluralism and diversity in organization, and that it is better to achieve unity of action through cooperation of independent labor organizations with differing philosophies and general points of view. In France, they have cooperated with the *Force Ouvrière*, and at times with the communist-controlled CGT, to raise wages. In other countries, relations between the Christian and other trade unions have been and remain generally strained. In Belgium, for instance, the free trade unions claim that the Christian trade unions have not proved dependable in strikes or in collective bargaining with employers. Relations are further complicated by recurring political issues. Thus, in 1950, the Belgian free trade unions, which are allied with the socialist parties, opposed the return of King Leopold III to Belgium, while the Catholic trade unions supported the Catholic Party, which favored his restoration to the throne.

## IV. Relations with the ICFTU

The leaders of the International Confederation of Free Trade Unions see no good reason for the existence of the Christian Trade Union International. In accordance with the ruling adopted in 1949, the ICFTU does not admit any Christian trade union which is affiliated with the ICCTU. Some Christian trade unions, e.g., those of the Basque country in Spain, have affiliated with the ICFTU. In Italy, the CISL, which is predominantly Catholic, is affiliated with the ICFTU. In the Catholic unions of France there is a group which has advocated affiliation with the ICFTU.

The majority of the Christian trade unions, however, maintain that they need their own international organization to defend their ideas and to protect the moral interests of their members. They look forward to the growth of the ICCTU in the future. The ICCTU has expressed the opinion that the unified trade unionism of Western Germany and Austria is unstable and that the organized Christian workers in these countries may break away and form independent denominational trade unions. The ICCTU also sees a field for its activities in the undeveloped countries not only among the Christian but also among the non-Christian population. In Northern Africa it has appealed to Moslems and in Viet-Nam to Buddhists to join the Christian trade unions. It is not clear what effect the ICCTU expects such developments to have on its doctrines and program.

Relations between the ICCTU and the ICFTU are not always friendly. The leaders of the ICFTU have sneeringly described the Christian Trade Union International as the "midget international" and have upbraided it for its alleged "neutralism." The leaders of the ICCTU have in reply expressed "pride in their poverty" and have made insinuations about the "mysterious flow of gold" into the coffers of the ICFTU, which is a hint at the large financial contributions from American trade unions.

Despite these occasional outbursts, the ICCTU and the ICFTU cooperate for many practical purposes. Where international labor representation is concerned, as in the Workers' Group in the International Labor Organization or on the Advisory Committee of the European Coal and Steel Community, they make arrangements for a division of places and for cooperation in voting. The Christian trade unions of France and Belgium cooperate with the European Regional Organization of the ICFTU and in the work of the Advisory ERP Committee.

At its Hague Congress in July, 1952, the Christian Trade Union International proposed to the ICFTU that the two Internationals form a liaison committee for systematic consultation and cooperation. From the point of view of the ICFTU, such a joint committee would enhance the importance of the Christian International without adding anything to its own strength or influence. The Belgian and Swiss members of the ICFTU are particularly opposed to such formal cooperation. On the other hand, some American members on the Executive Board of the ICFTU, especially Victor Reuther (brother of Walter Reuther) of the CIO, have urged such cooperation. By way of compromise, the ICFTU has decided to maintain informal relations with the Christian International, but to cooperate with it only on specific issues. With regard to the World Federation of Trade Unions, the Christian International maintains an attitude of opposition and has rejected offers of cooperation with it.

In practice, the Christian Trade Union International thus tends to reinforce the action of the ICFTU in the United Nations and in other international governmental organizations. This was the role which it played before 1939 in relation to the International Federation of Trade Unions. Insofar as conditions are similar, the history of international labor relations thus tends to repeat itself.

# Interpretation and Outlook

WHAT lies ahead in the international labor movement is indicated by the record of its past and present. The record is that the free international labor organizations, which alone are considered in this chapter, have in the long run expanded in scope and functions. They reemerged on a larger scale after two wars which seemed to spell their doom. Assuming that general international conditions remain essentially unchanged, they will continue in their present course.

This means that the International Confederation of Free Trade Unions, the International Trade Secretariats allied with it, and the International Confederation of Christian Trade Unions will try to expand their present activities. For practical purposes, the rivalry between the Free Trade Union International and the Christian Trade Union International is of minor importance, and is giving way to cooperation. But the hostility of these internationals to the World Federation of Trade Unions is bound to remain. The struggle of the ICFTU and the Trade Secretariats against both communism and the WFTU will thus continue to be a feature of the international labor situation.

In the context of present international relations, the ICFTU and the International Trade Secretariats can play an increasingly important part by cementing the labor movements of the world, outside the Soviet orbit, in defense of Western democratic ideals and institutions. How they will play this role, and to what extent, will be determined by the concrete forms which internal and external factors shaping their activities may take in the years immediately ahead. Before scanning the immediate horizons, however, it may be helpful to outline a general analysis of the dynamics of the international labor organizations, based on the historical survey.

## I. Factors of Development

In general terms, international labor developments have been and are determined by the interaction of national interests and international aims and ideals with changing economic and social conditions. The purposes which brought the international labor movement into being —the desire to reduce economic competition between workers of different countries, to practice mutual aid across national frontiers in industrial disputes, to advance labor standards and trade union rights by international agreement, to give international support to movements for national independence, to promote international programs for greater economic equality and social justice, to prevent wars and establish lasting peace among nations, and to cultivate a sense of a common workers' destiny—have continued to be and are operative today. But these purposes have come and continue to come into conflict with ideas of national interest and with nationalist attitudes in the different countries. This conflict is the process through which changing conditions in various countries and in the international environment modify the programs of international labor organizations and their methods of action.

Only the main forms of this conflict need be considered here. To begin with, the growth of a world economy and the internationalization of capitalist enterprise have proceeded irregularly and at a much slower pace than was expected by the early advocates of international labor action. International combinations and cartels have been formed in a few industries only, and private foreign investments have had a decreasing role in international economic life. The spread of industrialization to new countries is accompanied by the formation of national capital and by efforts to expand domestic industry through protectionist and nationalist policies. Wars and revolutions, the rise of new national states, the power conflicts of great nations, and the emergence of militant nationalism in formerly dependent and colonial countries have repeatedly caused dislocations in world markets and the breakdown of financial and other international institutions. In general, national economies have grown much more rapidly than the international economy, and often at the expense of the latter.

The international aims of labor have been and are limited by these general conditions. In advanced industrial countries, the workers find that they may serve their immediate interests more effectively by promoting foreign economic policies which give their countries a competitive advantage in world markets. Workers in underdeveloped countries in their turn, are reluctant to press for higher standards if the latter appear to threaten the position of their industries in world trade. Furthermore, the inner logic of trade unions is to concern themselves more and more with questions of national policy, since these impinge directly or indirectly on the basic trade union function of improving working and living conditions. Trade unions in all countries thus tend to give increasing attention to national economic policies, in disregard of the possibilities of international economic cooperation, which, even under favorable circumstances, is beset with difficulties.

Nationalist attitudes, due to economic conditions, are reinforced by political and cultural factors. With the growth of political democracy and free public education, contacts between social-economic groups and classes become greater, national traditions and ideals become the heritage of all the. people, and national modes of thinking permeate labor organizations and movements.

International labor cooperation has been and is further impeded by the fact that, owing to the unequal economic development of different countries and to the influence of national traditions, labor movements tend to form national and regional patterns. The forms and methods of the labor organizations of a country during any given period are shaped largely by the general social-economic structure—the degree of industrialization, relative importance of different industries, dependence on foreign trade, character of management, and relative economic strength of different groups of workers; it makes a great deal of difference whether miners or building trades workers or semiskilled and unskilled workers in mass industries play a predominant role in trade union organization. On the other hand, the spirit and outlook of a labor movement are influenced by the dynamics of the economy. In an industrially advancing country, with a forward-looking management, organized labor is moved by opportunities and hopes of economic advancement through peaceful collective bargaining and orderly industrial relations. In industrially static countries or where industries are declining, workers become imbued with a sense of insecurity and frustration, which inclines them toward radical social ideas and militant methods of action. A similar situation develops in newly industrializing countries, in which incipient labor unions seek to enhance their strength by appeals to emotion-laden ideas and ideals.

National labor patterns find expression not only in forms of organization and methods of action but also, and in particular, in long-run programs of social change. Such programs involve ideology—that is, interpretations of historical processes and concepts of social and ethical values—and are especially conditioned by national backgrounds. American "pure and simple" trade unionism, British gradualism and Fabianism, German socialism, French syndicalism, Asian and Latin American nationalism, have been and continue to be the manifestations of national and regional tendencies in labor movements. As the social-economic configuration of a country changes, the character and philosophy of its labor movement also change. Thus, syndicalism began to lose ground in France after 1919 and has declined steadily since. But as economic and social changes do not proceed uniformly in all countries, the tendency toward national labor patterns persists.

National attitudes also create problems of power relations in international labor organizations. The labor movement of each country places value on its own forms and ideas, and claims sovereign rights which it is reluctant to delegate to an international body. The stronger labor organizations of the larger countries tend to play a dominating role internationally, thus reproducing in the labor movement a condition similar to that of "big power" politics in general international relations.

Labor cooperation between different countries is further complicated by internal divisions within each country, which are due to a variety of reasons. Some are the result of historic accident or personal rivalries between labor leaders. Some reflect divergencies of short-run interests of different groups of workers. Still others spring from religious differences, as shown by the formation of Catholic trade unions. Owing to these various causes, there have generally been and continue to be in most countries two or more rival, if not hostile, national trade union centers which cannot easily be combined internationally, if at all.

Strong as the divisive nationalist forces are, the forces of internationalism in the labor movement persist because they too are generated by the conditions of modern life. The international economy is reestablished after every breakdown; though slowly and irregularly, it continues to grow: that cannot be otherwise in view of the world distribution of natural resources, population, capital equipment, and human skills. Political upheavals continue to have repercussions across national frontiers; the threat of war stimulates efforts to settle national differences by international adjustments; there is a steady effort to cement more closely the scientific and cultural relations between nations. Wars themselves arouse the desire for international cooperation and give rise to international institutions of increasing scope and functions. Under these influences, the international aims of organized labor reassert themselves, and in the long run gain in strength.

As already pointed out, the forces of internationalism, like those of nationalism, take on different concrete form under the impact of changing conditions. The new feature of the present international situation, which is the result of the war and of the emergence of underdeveloped countries as political powers, is the increasing role of permanent intergovernmental agencies for international cooperation. One has only to list the numerous international agencies which have been set up or projected since 1945 for the development of natural resources, the regulation of international trade, the promotion of foreign investments, the achievement of full employment, and so on, to realize that a new system of international relations is being built, based on continuous international consultation and action.

Insofar as governments play a larger role in international economic and social relations, conflicts between ideas of national interest and international goals may have an even wider field of operation. The process of building an international economy and a system of international political cooperation may thus not be more rapid or less arduous in the future than it has been in the past. A realization of this by the free international labor organizations gives rise to efforts to achieve a workable balance between national and international action. The readjustments, now in process, involve general ideas, policies, and organization. In ideology, more emphasis is being placed on immediate economic and social objectives and less on ultimate goals. To eliminate friction due to doctrinal differences, social theories are eliminated from programs and broad aims are formulated in general terms on which agreement can be more easily reached. To meet the challenge of the militant nationalism of Asian and Latin American labor groups, constructive proposals are advanced to accelerate economic development and political freedom and self-government.

On questions of policy, the readjustment is toward a larger participation in intergovernmental agencies, such as the United Nations and the International Labor Organization. This implies an abandonment of extreme ideas of "class struggle" and acceptance of methods of cooperation with employers, management, and other social groups and with governments.

In organization, the readjustments aim at greater flexibility and inclusiveness. To gratify the sense of national labor sovereignty, the free international labor organizations grant their national affiliates autonomy in domestic affairs and doctrinal matters. To meet the divisions in the free labor movements of different countries, the international organizations now admit more than one national trade union center from a single country, and even individual unions not affiliated with their national centers. To allow for national and regional conditions, they are developing regional secretariats and giving regional labor organizations and their leaders a larger voice in international administrative bodies.

In the nature of the case, adjustments between national and international aims and methods of action, are never final but change with changing conditions. The course of the free international labor organizations will thus continue to be determined by the interplay of national and international forces. The section which follows considers what concrete forms this process may take and what problems it may create in the years immediately ahead.

## II.  HORIZONS AHEAD

Current trends indicate that economic and political pressures will in the years immediately ahead stimulate organized labor in countries outside the Soviet orbit toward greater international cooperation through the ICFTU and the Trade Secretariats. The main pressures today are created by the trend toward economic integration in Western Europe, by efforts to reorganize world markets so as to solve problems of dollar shortages and employment, by population dislocations in many countries, by expanding plans for the economic development of underdeveloped countries, by the work of the United Nations, and by concern for political freedom and world peace. The operations of the European Coal and Steel Community, for instance, make it necessary for the workers of the six countries concerned (France, Belgium, the Netherlands, Italy, Luxembourg, and West Germany) to deal with wages and working conditions in these two basic industries on a supranational basis. The reemergence of Germany and Japan as competitors in world markets is a stimulus to organized labor in England, France, Belgium, and other countries to consider the possibilities of international arrangements for the orderly development of some of their industries, such as textiles. Population pressures and dislocations in Italy, Germany, and elsewhere are giving rise to projects of mass resettlement, in which organized labor in various countries wants to have a voice in order to adjust the interests of workers in countries of emigration and immigration.

American labor has an interest in these economic problems, since their solution will affect the trends and character of world trade and thus indirectly work and wages in the United States. To an even greater extent, American labor organizations are impelled to cultivate ties with the labor movements of other countries by their concern to root out Communist influence in trade unions, to stem the growth of extreme nationalist and Fascist labor movements, and to protect trade union rights against the encroachments of dictatorial regimes.

The trend toward closer international labor relations is further stimulated by the growth of labor organizations in Asia, Latin America, and Africa which are opposed to Communism and dictatorship. These labor organizations look to the International Confederation of

Free Trade Unions and to the International Trade Secretariats for assistance in organizing the workers, in combatting the Communists, in extending trade union rights, and in promoting political freedom and selfgovernment in their respective countries.

A large factor in maintaining the interest of organized labor in international cooperation is the work of the United Nations and the specialized agencies. This work impinges on all aspects of the life of the workers. The Economic and Social Council of the United Nations deals with questions of full employment, world trade, foreign investment, financing economic development, technical assistance to underdeveloped countries, fiscal policy, and so forth. The International Labor Organization considers problems of trade union rights, vocational training, social security, and international minimum labor standards. The Food and Agriculture Organization is developing plans for improving food production, modernizing land tenure systems, and raising levels of nutrition. The World Health Organization is engaged in activities for the improvement of public health services and the prevention of disease, which have a bearing on personal efficiency and capacity to work. The International Bank for Reconstruction and Development is an important source of funds and a planning agency for economic development. The United Nations Educational, Scientific and Cultural Organization carries on programs for reducing illiteracy and for assisting workers' education. The national labor organizations of separate countries can express their views on these programs and activities, and take part in shaping and promoting them, only through international organizations which represent them collectively, such as the International Confederation of Free Trade Unions and the International Trade Secretariats.

While the above factors favor greater international labor cooperation, they will be counteracted by specific nationalist policies and attitudes. On questions of migration, for instance, the labor organizations of Australia are accentuating their demand for restrictive policies, and the limitation of immigration has long been a policy of the majority of labor organizations in the United States. On issues of commercial policy, large groups of workers in different countries favor higher tariffs instead of freer trade. Workers in underdeveloped countries are supporting measures of a restrictive and nationalist character in the belief that they can speed economic development. International labor action will also be hampered by the continuing divisions within the labor movements of different countries.

Several problems in particular are likely to challenge the capacity of the ICFTU and the Trade Secretariats. In France and Italy, effective ways must be found to weaken the hold of the Communists on the trade union movement, to build up more solid organizations of the free type, and in general to strengthen the prestige and influence of free international unionism. In Western Europe, generally, new problems may come to the fore owing to the fact that economic recovery is reaching a point where further advance will depend on increasing labor productivity and on readjustments in production methods and costs to meet competition in world markets. National labor organizations may cooperate in making such readjustments, but they have to do so with due regard for maintaining existing working and living standards. The results may be disputes over wages, hours, and other working conditions and a straining of industrial relations, which may be aggravated by unemployment. While these problems have to be settled by the workers of different countries on a national basis, they raise the question of the help which international labor organizations may render. Similar issues faced the International Federation of Trade Unions between 1924 and 1928, when Europe was making its post-First World War readjustments, as described in Chapter XIII. The question is whether pending industrial and economic readjustments in Western Europe may create similar problems for the ICFTU and the Trade Secretariats.

An increasingly serious problem outside Western Europe and North America is the spread of dictatorial regimes, which restrict or destroy free trade unionism; this has taken place in Latin America, the Middle East, and elsewhere. The ICFTU and the Trade Secretariats have to meet this issue; otherwise, they can hardly hope to win the workers of these countries and to expand their organization. This issue confronted the International Federation of Trade Unions between 1930 and 1934. The attempt was then made to defend trade union rights by international boycotts and embargoes. Their small success at that time is a warning against their easy use now. Furthermore, under present conditions, they might create industrial disturbances which would play into the hands of the Communists and Fascists. The ICFTU and the Trade Secretariats have relied in the past two or three years on the ILO to help in the solution of this problem, but they find the results unsatisfactory. The question is, what other methods they may use which can be effective.

The problems raised by the labor movements of Asia and Africa, referred to in earlier chapters, are likely to become more pressing. In Japan, India, and several other countries, the national labor organizations expect more effective assistance from European and American labor in meeting problems of employment and wages through readjustments in world trade and international financing of economic development. In the dependent and colonial areas of Africa, the chief issue is greater help from the ICFTU and the Trade Secretariats in promoting self-government and in raising the very low levels of living.

An analysis of their current statements and discussions indicates that the ICFTU and the Trade Secretariats believe that they have made progress since 1949, but that they must take more decisive measures if they are to meet the most pressing problems stated above. It is clear that some of these measures might be merely an extension and improvement of present activities. Thus, the ICFTU and the Trade Secretariats might enlarge their budgets and facilities for regional activities; they might initiate more vigorous organizing campaigns in France and Italy as well as in Asian and Latin American countries; they might strengthen their representation in the agencies of the United Nations and improve the research facilities for servicing their representatives; they might put more vigor and imagination into their publications and into their appeals to the workers as well as to international public opinion.

The question also arises of some changes in structure and organization. The ICFTU Executive Board might be made more representative of the expanding trade unions outside Western Europe and North America. In particular, greater organic unity between the ICFTU and the trade secretariats might be achieved. This problem, which has been debated for years, looms up with more urgency in view of current international trends. The ICFTU and the Trade Secretariats, working in unity, could orientate their regional activities toward practical industrial problems. They could, for instance, stimulate a greater understanding, and possibly acceptance, in some developed and in most underdeveloped countries of modern methods of management and labor-management cooperation. With their combined resources, they might play a more effective part in their consultative work in the Economic and Social Council of the United Nations and in other intergovernmental agencies. In general, they might be able to coordinate their industrial and political activities more fully than is possible under their present cooperative arrangements.

The course of the several international labor organizations will depend in large measure on the attitudes of their leaders. In international labor organizations leadership plays an even greater role than in national labor movements. During the past decade or so, there has grown up an "international labor élite" who give direction to the movement for international labor cooperation. The members of this élite change from time to time, but its core consists of groups of labor leaders and officials from a number of countries who have long tenure of office and who in the course of their work have acquired considerable knowledge of, and a special interest in, international problems and relations.

In considering international labor problems, the national labor leaders are influenced by their position in their respective countries. Many of them have held and hold high positions in the councils of their governments and in political parties. They often act in an advisory capacity to their governments and serve as members of national delegations to international conferences and to the United Nations. Though they are usually designated for such positions as representatives of organized labor, they tend to view international problems from general national points of view.

A counterbalancing influence is exercised by the emergence of a group of international officials and leaders whose primary interest is to develop the international organizations. The influence of this group is limited, however, in several ways. The international officials are elected or appointed by national labor leaders; as a rule, they are less known and have less power and prestige; they have relatively small funds for staff, research, and general activities. They often find it difficult to steer an independent course amidst the currents of conflicting national labor movements and rivalries of national labor leaders.

The ICFTU and the Trade Secretariats have taken measures to strengthen their international leadership. International secretaries and other high officials are chosen from smaller countries to counterbalance the influence of the big countries. The Executive Board of the ICFTU has members from Canada, Latin America, India, Japan, Australia, New Zealand, and Africa to offset in some measure the predominance of Europe and the United States. The principal officials of the international organizations are given opportunities to visit and address conferences and meetings of national affiliates so that they may establish personal contacts and become better known. The secretaries and officials of the several international organizations maintain personal relations to enhance their *esprit de corps*.

Still, in the years immediately ahead, the course of the ICFTU and the Trade Secretariats will be shaped mainly by the national labor leaders of the larger and more important countries of Western Europe and the United States. Younger men are coming to the fore in the labor movements of these countries who have shown faith in the value of international cooperation in general and of international labor cooperation in particular. They may be more inclined to strengthen the international leadership by giving the latter greater powers and resources for action.

It is clear from the history of the past hundred years that the idea which originally inspired the international labor movement, namely, that it can be the main directive force in international relations, has not been borne out by experience. The free international labor organizations have been and remain a subsidiary factor in international life. But the International Confederation of Free Trade Unions and the International Trade Secretariats can play an important historic role as a constructive opposition within the framework of changing international relations. They can help to improve working and living conditions and promote peaceful economic and political reforms. They stand guard for freedom and democracy, warning those who are unaware and reminding those who would forget that failure to meet the problems of economic and social welfare on a world scale can only strengthen the forces of violence and dictatorship. Furthermore, as long as international relations remain tense, they are a force in helping to prevent war not only by strengthening the United Nations but also by supporting measures of defense against aggression. It is in this respect that the greatest change has taken place in the free international labor organizations, as compared with their absolute pacifist attitude in the past. They take this new position because experience has shown that aggression leads to war and obstructs the workers' progress toward bread, freedom, and peace. Experience also is the basis of their faith that their activities help to build more firmly the foundations of a free international society.

# Glossary of Abbreviations

AF of L, American Federation of Labor. Largest national labor organization in the United States.

ARO, Asian Regional Organization, Asian part of the International Confederation of Free Trade Unions.

CFTC, Confédération Française des Travailleurs Chrétiens. The Catholic workers' organization in France.

CGIL, Confederazione generale italiana del lavoro (Italian General Confederation of Labor). Largest labor organization in Italy under Communist control.

CGT, Confédération Générale du Travail. The largest labor organization in France under Communist control.

CGTU, Confédération Générale du Travail Unitaire. Communist-controlled labor organization in France from 1922 to 1936.

CIO, Congress of Industrial Organizations. National labor organization in the United States, formed between 1935 and 1937.

CISL, Confederazione italiana sindicati lavoratori (Italian Confederation of Workers' Unions). Formed in April, 1950, as a result of merger of the LCGIL and the FIL.

CIT, Confederacion Inter-Americana de Trabajadores (Inter-American Confederation of Workers). Anti-communist organization formed with aid of AF of L in 1948; succeeded by ORIT.

CROM, Confederacion Regional Obrera Mexicana (Mexican Regional Confederation of Labor). Formed in 1918.

CTAL, Confederacion de Trabajadores Latina Americana (Confederation of Workers of Latin America). Formed in 1938.

CTM, Confederacion Mexicana de Trabajadores (Mexican Confederation of Workers).

DGB, Deutscher Gewerkschaftsbund (German Federation of Labor). Formed in 1949 by labor unions of the German Federal Republic.

ECA, Economic Cooperation Administration. Administrative organization for the European Recovery Program.

ECOSOC, Economic and Social Council. One of the five principal organs of the United Nations.

ERO, European Regional Organization. European part of the International Confederation of Free Trade Unions, formed in 1950.

345

ERP, European Recovery Program. American program for economic aid to Europe, also known as the Marshall Plan.

FAO, Food and Agricultural Organization. A specialized agency of the United Nations.

FDGB, Freie Deutscher Gewerkschaftsbund (Free German Federation of Labor). Labor organization in East Germany under Communist control.

FIL, Federazione italiana del lavoro (Italian Federation of Labor). Formed in 1949; joined with LCGIL in 1950 to form CISL.

FO, Force Ouvrière (Workers' Force). Formed in France in 1947 in opposition to Communist-controlled CGT.

ICCTU, International Confederation of Christian Trade Unions.

ICFTU, International Confederation of Free Trade Unions. Formed in 1949.

IFTU, International Federation of Trade Unions. Formed in 1919 and dissolved in 1945.

ILO, International Labor Organization. Autonomous inter-governmental organization under the League of Nations from 1919 to 1939; since 1946 a specialized agency of the United Nations.

ILO, International Labor Office. Administrative office of the International Labor Organization, formed in 1919.

ITF, International Transport Workers' Federation.

ITS, International Trade Secretariats.

IMWA, International Working Men's Association. International syndicalist organization formed in Berlin in 1923.

IWW, Industrial Workers of the World. Revolutionary labor organization in the United States, formed in 1904.

LCGIL, Libera confederazione generale italiana dei lavoratori (Free General Confederation of Italian Workers). Formed by Catholic and other anti-Communist labor unions in 1948; merged into CSIL in 1950.

NATO, North Atlantic Treaty Organization.

OEEC, Organization for European Economic Cooperation. Formed by the sixteen countries cooperating in the European Recovery Program.

ORIT, Organisacion regional Inter-Americana de Trabajadores. Inter-American regional organization of the ICFTU, formed in 1951.

RILU, Red International of Labor Unions (also known as the Profintern). Trade union organization connected with the Third International from 1921 to 1935.

TUC, Trades Union Congress. Central labor organization of Great Britain.

UGO, Unabhängige Gewerkschafts-Organization. Independent Labor Organization formed by anti-Communist labor unions of West Berlin, Germany, in 1948; merged with DGB in 1949.

UIL, Unione italiana dei lavoratori (Italian Workers' Union). Socialist labor union formed in 1951.

UNESCO, United Nations Educational Scientific and Cultural Organization. One of the specialized agencies of the United Nations.

WFTU, World Federation of Trade Unions.

WHO, World Health Organization. A specialized agency of the United Nations, formed in 1946.

| Region and Country | Name of Affiliated Organization | Membership as of | |
|---|---|---|---|
| | | January, 1953 | January, 1951 |
| *Europe* | | | |
| Austria | Oesterreichischer Gewerkschafts-bund | 1,318,327 | 1,279,520 |
| Basque Country | Solidaridad de Trabajadores Vascos (in exile) | 5,000 | 5,000 |
| Belgium | Fédération Générale du Travail de Belgique | 660,340 | 631,075 |
| Cyprus | Cyprus Workers' Confederation | 5,000 | 4,000 |
| Denmark | De Samvirkende Fagforbund i Danmark | 662,383 | 630,748 |
| France | Confédération Générale du Travail-Force Ouvrière | 1,000,000 | 1,000,000 |
| Germany | Deutscher Gewerkschaftsbund | 6,047,387 | 5,500,000 |
| Great Britain | Trades Union Congress | 8,020,079 | 7,883,355 |
| Greece | Confédération Générale du Travail de Grèce | 318,618 | 277,000 |
| Iceland | Aethydusamband Islands | 24,866 | 24,000 |
| Italy | Confederazione Italiana Sindacati Lavoratori | 1,812,051 | 1,702,000 |
| | Unione Italiana del Lavoro | 466,846 | * |
| Luxembourg | Confédération Générale du Travail du Luxembourg | 20,000 | 20,000 |
| Malta | General Workers' Union | 13,713 | 10,653 |
| Netherlands | Nederlands Verbond van Vakveren-igingen | 433,198 | 402,000 |
| Norway | Arbeidernes Faglige Landsorganis-jon i Norge | 514,592 | 487,000 |
| Saar | Einheitsgewerkschaft des Saarlandes | 58,363 | 80,000 |
| Spain | Unión General de Trabajadores de España (in exile) | 20,000 | 20,000 |
| Sweden | Landsorganisationen i Sverige | 1,338,000 | 1,256,690 |
| | Tjännstemännens Centralorganisa-tion | 310,000 | 272,002 |
| Switzerland | Schweizerischer Gewerkschaftsbund | 382,819 | 380,904 |
| Trieste | Camera Confederale de Lavoro di Trieste | [2] | 55,203 |
| Europe, Total | | 23,431,582 | 21,921,150 |

| Region and Country | Name of Affiliated Organization | Membership as of | |
|---|---|---|---|
| | | January, 1953 | January, 1951 |
| *North and Central America* | | | |
| British Honduras | General Workers' Union | 8,240 | 2,500 |
| Canada | Trades and Labor Congress of Canada | 522,369 | 400,000 |
| | Canadian Congress of Labour | 350,000 | 350,000 |
| Costa Rica | Confederación Costarricense de Trabajadores (Rerum Novarum) | 16,000 | 20,000 |
| Mexico | Confederación Nacional de Trabajadores | 3 | 135,000 |
| | Confederación Proletaria Nacional | 3 | 256,000 |
| | Confederación de Trabajadores de Mexico | 1,000,000 | * |
| Panama | Confederación Obrera Campesina de la República de Panama | 10,500 | 10,000 |
| United States | American Federation of Labor | 8,379,245 | 7,142,603 |
| | Congress of Industrial Organizations | 6,200,000 | 6,300,000 |
| | United Mine Workers of America | 600,000 | 600,000 |
| North and Central America, Total | | 17,086,354 | 15,216,103 |
| *Caribbean Area* | | | |
| Barbados | Barbados Workers' Union | 8,184 | 14,000 |
| Cuba | Confederación de Trabajadores de Cuba | 1,200,000 | 800,000 |
| Dominica | Dominica Trade Union | 5,877 | 5,400 |
| Grenada | Grenada Workers' Union | 750 | 3,000 |
| Haiti | Union Nationale des Ouvriers de Haitii | 3,500 | * |
| Jamaica | National Workers' Union of Jamaica | 5,000 | * |
| Mauritius | Mauritius Trade Union Council | 2 | 10,000 |
| Puerto Rico | Confederación General de Trabajadores de Puerto Rico—CIO | 2 | 100,000 |
| | Federación Libre de los Trabajadores de Puerto Rico | 100,000 | 125,000 |
| | Federación del Trabajo de Puerto Rico | 25,000 | * |
| St. Kitts-Nevis | St. Kitts-Nevis Trades and Labor Union | 6,131 | 7,056 |
| St. Lucia | St. Lucia Workers' Cooperative Union | 1,500 | 1,500 |
| | St Lucia Seamen and Waterfront Workers' Trade Union | 850 | * |
| | St Lucia Civil Service Association | 2 | * |

| Region and Country | Name of Affiliated Organization | Membership as of January, 1953 | Membership as of January, 1951 |
|---|---|---|---|
| Surinam | Surinaamse Werknemers Organisatie | 20,150 | 20,000 |
| | Surinaamse Mijnwerkers Unie | 2 | 3,150 |
| | Paranam Mijnwerkers Bond | 900 | * |
| Trinidad | Trinidad and Tobago Federation of Trade Unions | 10,156[4] | * |
| | Trinidad and Tobago Teachers' Union | 1,879 | * |
| Turks Islands | Turks Islands Workers' Union | 376 | * |
| Virgin Islands | Federal Labor Union N 23853 | 2,000[2] | * |
| Caribbean Area, Total | | 1,392,253 | 1,089,106 |
| *South America* | | | |
| Argentina | Comité Obrero de Acción Sindical Independiente (in exile) | 40,000 | 40,000 |
| Bolivia | Confederación Boliviana de Trabajadores | 2 | 12,500 |
| Brazil[5] | Confedereçâo Nacional dos Trabalhadores no Comercio | 2 | 1,200,000 |
| | Confedereçâo Nacional dos Trabalhadores na Industria | 2 | 1,500,000 |
| | Federeçâo Nacional dos Trabalhadores em Transportes Maritimos e Fluviais | 136,044 | 100,000 |
| | Federeçâo Nacional dos Trabalhadores em Emprezas de Carris Urbanos | 50,000 | 75,000 |
| | Federeçâo Nacional dos Condutores de Veiculos Rodoviarios | 2 | 200,000 |
| | Federeçâo Nacional dos Empregados de Turismo e Hospitalidade | 6 | 200,000 |
| | Federeçâo Nacional dos Trabalhadores Ferroviarios | 75,000 | * |
| | Federeçâo Nacional dos Estivadores | 35,687 | * |
| British Guiana | Man-Power Citizens' Association | 6,000 | * |
| | British Guiana Labour Union | 2,629 | 2,000 |
| Chile | Confederación de Trabajadores de Chile | 2 | 115,000 |
| | Federación Nacional de los Trabajadores del Petróleo de Chile | 2 | 1,500 |
| Colombia | Confederación de Trabajadores de Colombia | 2 | 200,000 |
| | Unión de Trabajadores de Colombia | 2 | 200,000 |
| Ecuador | Confederación Obrera del Guayas | 1,300 | * |
| Falkland Islands | Falkland Islands Labour Federation | 575 | 600 |

| Region and Country | Name of Affiliated Organization | Membership as of | |
|---|---|---|---|
| | | January, 1953 | January, 1951 |
| Peru | Confederación de Trabajadores del Perú | 2 | 350,000 |
| Uruguay | Comité de Coordinación de Sindicatos Autónomous | 7 | 20,000 |
| | Confederación Sindical del Uruguay | 40,000[7] | — |
| Venezuela | Confederación de Trabajadores de Venezuela (in exile) | 2 | 200,000 |
| South America, Total | | Figures inadequate for summation | 4,416,600 |
| *Asia* | | | |
| Ceylon | All-Ceylon Trade Union Congress | 48,000 | 43,000 |
| China | Chinese Federation of Labor | 169,528 | 107,605 |
| Hong Kong | Hong Kong and Kowloon Trades Union Council | 115,000 | 121,000 |
| India | Hind Mazdoor Sabha | 829,752 | 833,154 |
| | Indian National Trades Union Congress | 1,333,184 | 1,538,156 |
| Japan | Joint Council of Japanese Trade Unions | 1,854,860 | 3,050,000 |
| Korea | Federation of Korean Trade Unions | 2 | 800,000 |
| Lebanon | Ligue des Syndicats des Employés et des Ouvriers dans la République Libanaise | 14,000 | 14,000 |
| Malaya | Malayan Trade Union Council | 65,375 | 75,000 |
| Pakistan | All-Pakistan Confederation of Labour | 324,000 | 276,000 |
| Persia | Iranian Trades Union Congress | 2 | 120,000 |
| Philippines | National Labour Union | 20,000 | * |
| Singapore | Singapore Trades Union Congress | 21,305 | * |
| Thailand | Thai Labour Union | 8 | 50,000 |
| | Thai National Trade Union Congress | 69,530[8] | * |
| Asia, Total | | 4,864,534 | 7,027,915 |
| *Africa* | | | |
| British Cameroons | Cameroons Development Corporation Workers' Union | 16,000 | * |
| | The Likomba Plantations Workers' Union | 3,000 | * |
| Gambia | Gambia Labour Union | 2 | 2,000 |
| Gold Coast | Gold Coast Trades Union Congress | 74,000 | * |

| Region and Country | Name of Affiliated Organization | Membership as of | |
|---|---|---|---|
| | | January, 1953 | January, 1951 |
| Kenya | Kenya Federation of Registered Trade Unions | 45,000 | * |
| Libya | Libyan General Workers' Union | 18,000 | * |
| Madagascar | Syndicat Fédéral des Fonctionnaires, Agents, Employés Malgaches et Assimilés des Services Publics de Madagascar et Dépendances | 8,000 | * |
| Sierra Leone | Sierra Leone Council of Labour | 2 | 14,000 |
| Tunisia | Union Générale Tunisienne du Travail | 48,000 | * |
| **Africa, Total** | | 212,000 | 16,000 |
| *Australasia* | | | |
| Australia | Australian Council of Trade Unions | 856,332 | * |
| New Zealand | New Zealand Federation of Labour | 180,000 | 200,000 |
| **Australasia, Total** | | 1,036,332 | 200,000 |

* Admitted after January 1, 1951.

1 Figures of membership from Report of Secretary-General of ICFTU to the Third World Congress of ICFTU held in Stockholm, July 4-11, 1953. The author is responsible for rearranging figures by regions and for regional summaries of membership.

2 Despite reminders, these organizations did not reply in time to questionnaire.

3 The CNT and the CPN amalgamated with two other organizations in July, 1952 to form the *Confederación Revolucionaria de Obreros y Campesinos* (CROC). This new organization has not yet made a decision about international affiliation.

4 The Seamen and Waterfront Workers' Trade Union and the Railway Workers' Trade Union (Trinidad) formed the Trinidad and Tobago Transport Workers' Council, which informed the ICFTU on August 7, 1952 that it had changed its name to Trinidad and Tobago Federation of Trade Unions. Three other organizations, which had been accepted into affiliation by the ICFTU as individual organizations, have since joined this national center.

5 Brazilian trade unions were forbidden by law to affiliate with an international organization. It was not until 1952 that a law was passed enabling the Brazilian trade unions to affiliate officially with the ICFTU.

6 The Federação Nacional dos Empregados de Turismo e Hospitalidade is affiliated with the Confederação Nacional dos Trabalhadores na Industria.

7 The Confederación Sindical del Uruguay has superseded the Comité de Coordinación de Sindicatos Autonomous.

8 The Thai Labour Union has changed its name to Thai National Trade Union Congress.

# Bibliography

## PART ONE

BEER, M., *History of British Socialism*, 2 vols., London, 1919-20.

GUILLAUME, J., *L'Internationale: Documents et Souvenirs: (1864-78)*, Pàris, 1905-10.

HOBSON, J. A., *Richard Cobden—The International Man*, London, 1919.

MARX, KARL, and ENGELS, FRIEDRICH, *The Communist Manifesto*, 1848.

MUIR, RAMSAY, *Nationalism and Internationalism* (2nd ed.), London, 1919.

POSTGATE, R. W., *Revolution from 1789 to 1906*, London, 1920.

———, *The Workers' International*, London, 1920.

SCHLUETER, HERMANN, *Die Internationale in Amerika*, Chicago, 1918.

TAWNEY, R. H., *The British Labor Movement*, Yale University Press, 1925.

VILLETARD, EDMOND, *History of the International*, London, 1874.

WEBB, SIDNEY and BEATRICE, *The History of Trade Unionism*, New York, 1920.

WEST, JULIUS, *A History of the Chartist Movement*, London, 1920.

## PART TWO

AMERICAN FEDERATION OF LABOR, proceedings of conventions, 1881-1914.

*American Federationist, The*, 1895-1914.

BERNSTEIN, E., *Evolutionary Socialism*, New York, 1909.

BRISSENDEN, P. F., *The I.W.W., A Study in American Syndicalism,* New York, 1919.

HILLQUIT, MORRIS, *History of Socialism in the United States*, New York, 1910.

INTERNATIONAL SECRETARIAT OF NATIONAL TRADE UNION CENTERS, *International Reports of the Trade Union Movement, 1903-13*, Berlin.

KAUTSKY, KARL, *The Economic Doctrines of Karl Marx*, London, 1925.

———, *The Social Revolution*, Chicago, 1902.

LAIDLER, HARRY W., *Socialism in Thought and Action*, New York, 1921.

LEVINE, LOUIS, *Syndicalism in France*, New York, 1914.

ORTH, S. P., *Socialism and Democracy in Europe*, New York, 1913.

SASSENBACH, J., *Twenty-Five Years of International Trade Unionism*, Amsterdam, 1926.

SECOND INTERNATIONAL, proceedings of the congresses, 1889-1910.

TROTSKY, LEON, *War and the International*, 1914.

WALLING, WILLIAM E., *The Socialists and the War*, New York, 1915.

## PART THREE

AMERICAN FEDERATION OF LABOR, proceedings of conventions, 1900-25.

BEVAN, EDWYN, *German Social Democracy during the War*, London, 1918.

COLE, G. D. H., *A Short History of the British Working Class Movement* (Vol. III), London, 1927.

CONFERENCE DES TROIS INTERNATIONALES, held in Berlin in April, 1922, report of proceedings, Brussels, 1922.

DUTTE, R. PALME, *The Two Internationals*, London, 1920.

EXECUTIF ELARGI DE L'INTERNATIONALE COMMUNISTE, held in Moscow in February-March, 1922, Report, Paris, 1922.

FARBMAN, M., *Bolshevism in Retreat*, London, 1923.

FIMMEN, EDO, *The International Federation of Trade Unions*, Amsterdam, 1922.

HILLQUIT, M., *Present Day Socialism*, New York, 1920.

INTERNATIONAL FEDERATION OF TRADE UNIONS, Reports of Activities, 1922-24, Amsterdam.

———, Report of Congress at Rome, Amsterdam, 1923.

INTERNATIONAL LABOUR OFFICE, Report presented to the Peace Conference of 1919, Geneva, 1920.

KELLOGG, PAUL, and GLEASON, ARTHUR, *British Labor and the War*, New York, 1919.

LENIN, N., *Sur la Route de l'Insurrection*, Paris, 1924.

LENSCH, PAUL, *Three Years of World Revolution*, London, 1918.

LOSOVSKY, A., *Aims and Tactics of the Trade Unions*, Moscow, 1921.

*Manifeste et Resolutions de l'Internationale Communiste*, introduction by Boris Souvarine, Paris, 1919.

MERRHEIM, A., *Amsterdam ou Moscou*, Paris, 1924.

MERTENS, CORNEILLE, *Le Mouvement Syndical International*, Bruxelles, 1923.

O'NEAL, JAMES, *American Communism*, New York, 1927.

RED INTERNATIONAL OF LABOR UNIONS, *Die Organizationsfrage auf dem Zweiten Kongress*, Berlin, 1923.

RETINGER, J. H., *Morones of Mexico*.

ROSMER, A., *Le Mouvement Ouvrier pendant la Guerre*, Paris, 1936.

SAPOSS, DAVID, *Left Wing Unionism*, New York, 1926.

SCHNEIDER, D. M., *The Workers' Party and American Trade Unions*, Baltimore, 1928.

STROEBEL, HEINRICH, *The German Revolution and After*, New York, 1923.

TANNENBAUM, FRANK, *The Mexican Agrarian Revolution*, Washington, 1929.

TOYNBEE, A., *Europe after the Peace Conference*, London, 1925.

TROTSKY, LEON, *Nouvelle Etape*, Paris, 1922.

WALLING, WILLIAM E., *The Mexican Question*, New York, 1927.

ZINOVIEV, G., *World Revolution and the Communist International*, 1920.

### PART FOUR

AMERICAN FEDERATION OF LABOR, *proceedings of conventions*, 1925-30.

ARENDT, JOSEPH, *La Nature, l'organization et le Programme des Syndicats Ouvriers Chrétiens*, Paris, 1926.

BARNES, G. N., *History of the International Labour Office*, London, 1926.

BRAILSFORD, H. N., *Socialism for To-day*, London, 1925.

BUKHARIN, N., *Historical Materialism*, New York, 1925.

CHURCH, A. G., *The Christian Trade Union Movement in Germany* (no date).

COMMUNIST INTERNATIONAL, reports of congresses, 1919-28.

CONFÉDÉRATION INTERNATIONALE DES SYNDICATS CHRÉTIENS, reports of congresses, 1922-28.

DOBB, MAURICE, *Russian Economic Development since the Revolution*, London, 1928.

EASTMAN, MAX, *Since Lenin Died*, London, 1925.

FIMMEN, EDO, *Labour's Alternatives*, London, 1924.

INTERNATIONAL FEDERATION OF TRADE UNIONS, Reports to and proceedings of congresses, 1921-28; also yearbooks, 1925-27.

INTERNATIONAL LABOUR OFFICE, reports of the director, 1921-28, Geneva.

INTERNATIONAL WORKING MEN'S ASSOCIATION, reports of congresses, 1920-28.

*Internationale Syndicale Chrétienne pendant les Années 1922-25*, Utrecht, 1925.

KROPOTKIN, P., *The Conquest of Bread*, New York, 1906.

LABOR AND SOCIALIST INTERNATIONAL, report and proceedings of Third Congress, Zurich, 1928.

LAIDLER, H. W., *A History of Socialist Thought*, New York, 1927.

LASKI, H. J., *Communism*, London, 1927.

LENIN, N., *State and Revolution*, London, 1919.

LOSOVSKY, A., *Le Mouvement Syndical International*, Paris, 1926.

———, *La Conférence Syndicale Anglo-Sovietique*, Paris, 1925.

LUBIN, ISADOR, and EVERETT, HELEN, *The British Coal Dilemma*, Washington, 1927.

MARX, KARL, *Critique du Programme de Gotha*, with preface by Amedée Dunois, Paris, 1922.

MONATTE, PIERRE, and others, *Left Wing Trade Unionism in France,* London, 1927.

PAN-AMERICAN FEDERATION OF LABOR, proceedings of Fifth Congress, Washington, 1927.

PERIGORD, PAUL, *The International Labor Organization,* New York, 1926.

ROKKER, RUDOLF, *Die Prinzipienerklarung des Syndikalismus,* Berlin.

RYAN, J. H., *Industrial Democracy from a Catholic Viewpoint,* Washington, 1925.

STALIN, J., *Le Léninisme Théorique et Pratique,* Paris, 1925.

TRACEY, HERBERT, *The Book of the Labour Party,* London, 1925.

TROTSKY, LEON, *Whither Russia,* New York, 1926.

### PARTS FIVE, SIX, AND SEVEN

ALEXANDER, ROBERT J., *World Labor To-day,* League for Industrial Democracy, New York, 1952.

AMERICAN FEDERATION OF LABOR, proceedings of conventions, 1930-52.

AMERICAN FEDERATION OF LABOR, *American Labor Looks at the World,* 1952.

CONFÉDÉRATION INTERNATIONALE DES SYNDICATS CHRÉTIENS, *De Montreux à Paris,* 1934-37.

CONFÉRENCE SYNDICALE MONDIALE, February, 1945, Report, London, 1945.

CONGRESS OF INDUSTRIAL ORGANIZATIONS, proceedings of conventions, 1940-52.

DEPARTMENT OF STATE, U. S., *Development of the Reconstruction Policy of the United States,* July, 1947.

———, *Peace and War, U. S. Foreign Policy, 1931-41.*

———, *In Quest of Peace and Security, Selected Documents on American Foreign Policy, 1941-51.*

———, *The United States and the United Nations, Reports of the President to the Congress.*

DUBINSKY, DAVID, "Rift and Realignment in World Labor," *Foreign Affairs,* January, 1949.

———, "World Labor's New Weapon," *Foreign Affairs,* April, 1950.

EARLE, EDWARD MEAD (editor), *Modern France,* Princeton, 1951.

EHRMAN, HENRY W. *French Labor: From Popular Front to Liberation,* New York, 1947.

EINAUDI, MARIO, and others, *Communism in Western Europe,* 1952.

ERP THIRD INTERNATIONAL TRADE UNION CONFERENCE, 1950, Paris.

GALENSON, WALTER (editor), *Comparative Labor Movements,* New York, 1952.

INTERNATIONAL CONFEDERATION OF FREE TRADE UNIONS, report of First Congress, 1949, London.

———, *Bread, Peace, Freedom* (pamphlet), 1949.

———, report of Second Congress, Milan, 1951.

———, General Secretary's Report to Third World Congress, 1953.

INTERNATIONAL FEDERATION OF TRADE UNIONS, press reports, 1929-39.

———, yearbooks, 1930-38.

JOSEPHSON, MATTHEW, *Sidney Hillman: Statesman of American Labor*, 1952.

L'INTERNATIONALE SYNDICALE CHRÉTIENNE (journal), 1929-40 and 1946-51.

L'INTERNATIONALE SYNDICALE ROUGE (journal), 1931-33.

LORWIN, LEWIS, L., *Labor and Internationalism*, New York, 1929.

LORWIN, VAL, "French Trade Unions Since Liberation," reprint from *Industrial and Labor Relations Review*, July, 1952.

——— "Communist strategy and tactics in Western European Labor Movements," reprint from *Industrial and Labor Relations Review*, April 1953.

MEANY, GEORGE, *The Last Five Years* (pamphlet), Washington, 1951.

*New Leader, The,* weekly journal, published in New York.

PRICE, JOHN, *The International Labour Movement*, London, 1945.

ROSS, MICHAEL, "American Labor's World Responsibilities," *Foreign Affairs,* October, 1951.

STURMTHAL, ADOLF, *The Tragedy of European Labor, 1918-39*; New York, 1943.

———, "The International Confederation of Free Trade Unions," *Industrial and Labor Relations Review*, April, 1950.

UNITED NATIONS, reports of the Secretary-General, 1946-52.

———, Economic and Social Council, proceedings of sessions, 1946-52.

WORLD FEDERATION OF TRADE UNIONS, *Report of Activity*, presented to the Second Congress of the WFTU in Milan (for period 1947-49).

———, Report of the proceedings of the Second World Trade Union Congress, Paris, 1947.

*World Today, The,* review published monthly by the Royal Institute of International Affairs in London.

(A large part of the material for Parts Six and Seven was obtained from current journals, news sheets, and mimeographed reports published by the several organizations referred to in the text and from the publications of the Bureau of Labor Statistics of the U.S. Department of Labor such as the *Monthly Labor Review* and *Notes on Labor Abroad.*)

# Index of Names

Adler, Friedrich, 46, 132
Aguirre, Francisco, 273, 295, 297
Albert I, King of the Belgians, 29
Adams, Grantley, 295
Appleton, William A., 54, 60
Atlee, Clement R., 208, 218

Baboeuf, Francois Noel, 4
Bakunin, Michael, 13, 14, 21, 25, 150
Balabanov, Angelica, 53
Bauer, Otto, 133
Bebel, Ferdinand August, 23
Becu, Omer, 310
Bernstein, Eduard, 23, 46
Bevin, Ernest, 105, 208, 240
Bidault, Georges, 207, 240
Blanqui, Louis Auguste, 3, 4, 6
Blum, Leon, 177
Böckler, Hans, 273
Bourderon, A., 54
Bradshaw, Robert, 273
Branting, Karl Hjalmar, 20, 48
Bratschi, Robert, 265
Braunthal, Alfred, 290
Bright, John, 5
Brown, Irving, 236, 242, 258, 266, 281
Brown, J. W., 98, 108
Bukharin, Nikolai I., 111, 113, 114
Burns, John, 20
Butler, Harold B., 130

Caballero, Francisco Largo, 179, 189
Cachin, Marcel, 49, 66
Calles, Plutarco E., 93, 94, 116
Carey, James B., 207, 240, 241, 242, 258-261, 265
Carranza, Venustiano, 87, 88, 89, 92
Chiu, H. Fan, 217, 222
Chiang-Kai-Shek, Generalissimo, 113, 209
Churchill, Winston Spencer, Sir, 197, 200, 208, 209.
Citrine, Walter, Lord, 108, 109, 167, 171, 174, 192, 193, 198, 199, 201, 203, 205, 208, 210, 211, 213, 217, 219, 221, 222, 223, 225
Clemenceau, Georges, 51
Cobden, Richard, 5
Colins, J. G. C. H., 5
Cook, A. J., 105
Cope, Elmer, 220, 228, 233, 251
Coullery, Dr, 11
Cremer, William R., 8, 9
Curran, Joseph Edwin, 207

Daladier, Edouard, 194

Deakin, Arthur, 208, 222, 227, 240, 258, 260, 261, 266, 273, 295.
Debs, Eugene Victor, 24
De Brouckère, Louis, 184, 185
De Gasperi, Alcide, 247
De Gaulle, Charles André Joseph Marie, 207, 212
De la Huerta, Adolpho, 87, 88, 94
De la Rocque, Col., 177
De Leon, Daniel, 24
Denikin, Anton, 66
Di Vittorio, Giuseppe, 217, 222, 240, 247, 280, 281, 319
Diaz, Porfirio, 86
Dollfuss, Engelbert, 173, 174, 176
Dubinsky, David, 180, 242, 266, 290
Duncan, James, 40
Dunne, William F., 77

Ebert, Friedrich, 46, 77
Edwards, Ebenezer, 223
Engels, Friedrich, 6, 14, 111
Erban, Evan, 222

Fette, Christian, 280
Fimmen, Edo, 60, 75, 104, 105, 123, 127
Finet, Paul, 242, 264, 266, 267, 273, 278, 279, 280, 281, 292
Foster, William Z., 40, 71, 84
Fourier, Charles F. M., 3
Frachon, Benoêt, 179
Franco, Francisco, 189, 190, 326
Freitag, Walter, 295
Frossard, Ludovico-Oscar, 49, 66, 74

Gompers, Samuel, 33, 37-41, 54, 56-60, 78-83, 86, 88, 89, 90, 91, 93, 94, 117
Gottfurcht, Hans, 294
Grant, Marcus C., 273, 295
Green, William, 180, 193, 198, 199, 201, 262, 266, 272, 273, 280
Grimm, Robert, 46
Guesde, Jules B., 19, 23

Haase, Hugo, 29
Hachet, Farhad, 278
Hardie, J. Keir, 20, 27
Harding, Warren G., 83
Harrison, George McGregor, 266
Haywood, Allan, 207
Haywood, William D., 71, 149, 267
Henderson, Arthur, 30, 49, 57
Hicks, George, 98, 108, 193
Hillman, Sidney, 207, 209, 210, 211, 213, 217, 221, 222, 226

Hillquit, Morris, 24
Hindenburg, Paul von, 101
Hitler, Adolf, 170, 172, 173, 175, 180, 188, 190, 193, 194, 197, 198, 199, 201, 223, 249
Hodges, Frank, 105
Hughes, Charles Evans, 83, 94
Hyndman, Henry Mayers, 19, 46
Hynes, John P., 59

Iglesias, Santiago, 86
Isaacs, George Alfred, Sir, 208
Ibanez, Bernardo I., 273, 280, 295

Jacobsen, Hans, 167
Jaurès, Jean Leon, 23, 27, 29
Jensen, Eiler, 179, 273, 280, 295
Jodoin, Claude, 295
Jouhaux, Leon, 40, 54, 55, 57, 60, 107, 167, 177, 182, 183, 184, 191, 192, 212, 214, 217, 218, 222, 246, 262, 266, 273, 280, 295

Kamenev, Leo, 49, 109
Kato, E., 273
Kautsky, Karl, 22, 23, 29, 46, 133
Kolchak, Vladimir, 51, 66
Kollontai, Alexandra, 74
Krane, Jay, 304
Kropotkin, Peter, 21
Kupers, Evert, 179, 213, 217, 222, 242, 260, 261, 266
Kuznetsov, Vladimir, 207, 217, 222

Ladd, William, 5
Legien, Carl, 32, 33, 54, 55, 59
Le Grand, Daniel, 5
Leipart, Theodore, 107, 108, 167, 172
Lenin, Nicholas, 28, 46, 47, 49, 70, 99, 109, 111, 141, 146
Leo XIII, Pope, 36, 154
Lewis, John L., 83
Lie, Trygve H., 227, 280
Liebknecht, Karl, 29, 46
Lloyd George, David, 28
Longuet, Jean, 46, 47, 50
Losovsky, Arnold, 71, 148
Lovett, William, 3, 4
Luxembourg, Rosa, 28, 29, 46.

MacArthur, Douglas, 232
MacDonald, Donald, 295
MacDonald, James Ramsay, 30, 46.
Madero, Francisco I., 86, 87.
Major, Louis, 295
Mann, Tom, 19, 71, 149.
Marshall, George C., 239.
Marx, Wilhelm, 101
Marx, Heinrich Karl, 5-7, 9-14, 19, 21, 22, 53, 99, 111, 132, 133, 141, 142, 146, 149.
Mazzini, Giuseppe, 9
Meany, George, 265, 266, 278, 295, 308.
Merrheim, A., 46, 54
Mertens, Corneille, 54, 59, 60, 107, 167, 179
Millerand, Alexander, 23

Mochaver, Mahmoud, 295
Molotov, Vyacheslav M., 211, 240
Monatte, Pierre, 55, 71
Monge, Louis Alberto, 297
Monmousseau, Gaston, 149
Morones, Luis N., 89, 90, 91
Morris, William, 19
Mudaliar, Arcot Ramaswami, Sir, 226
Mueller, Herman, 29
Mungat, Dhyan, 299
Murray, John, 86, 91
Murray, Philip, 206, 254, 262, 273, 280
Mussolini, Benito, 46, 172, 174, 202, 246

Nenni, Pietro, 247
Nishimaki, Toshio, 295
Noske, Gustav, 46

Oddone, Jacinto, 265
Obregon, Alvaro, 92, 93, 94
Odger, George, 8, 9
Oldenbroek, J. H., 214, 257, 266, 272, 273, 277, 279, 281, 294, 305, 309
Oudegeest, Jean, 54, 55, 56, 58, 60, 75, 81, 82, 83, 98, 99, 107, 108
Owen, Robert, 3, 5

Pastore, Giulio, 247, 266, 273, 295, 308
Perkins, George W., 41
Pétain, Henri Philippe, 198
Potofsky, Jacob, 290
Proudhon, Pierre J., 11, 21, 25, 150
Purcell, Albert, 98, 108

Quill, Michael, J., 267

Radek, Karl, 76, 77, 109
Reed, Paul K., 267
Reuther, Victor, 331
Reuther, Walter Philip, 267, 295
Romualdi, Serafino, 297
Roosevelt, Franklin D., 170, 192, 194, 200, 209, 218
Roosevelt, Theodore, 28
Rosenblum, Frank, 221, 240
Rosmer, Alfred, 149
Ross, Michael, 207, 242, 266, 267, 290
Rutz, Henry, 236
Rykov, Aleksei, 114

Saillant, Louis, 207, 210-213, 217, 220-225, 227, 228, 231, 232, 233, 237, 240-243, 251, 255-259, 261, 280, 281, 320, 321
Saint-Simon, Claude H., 3
Sassenbach, Johann, 59, 83, 98, 107, 109, 166, 167
Scheidemann, Philipp, 46
Schevenels, Walter, 167, 182, 198, 199, 205, 207, 211, 217, 219, 220, 255, 258, 261, 296
Schorch, Johann, 167
Sen, Deven, 273
Sender, Toni, Miss, 290
Serrarens, J. P., 160, 327

Serrati, Giacinto M., 77
Shastri, Harniharnath, 280, 295
Shaw, George Bernard, 20
Shvernik, Nicolai, M., 182
Sorel, Georges, 25
Spaak, Paul-Henri, 225, 227
Stalin, Joseph V., 49, 109-114, 171, 193, 218, 252, 321, 322
Stamboliski, A., 76
Stegerwald, A., 37
Stolz, Giri, 167, 182, 186
Stresemann, Gustav, 75
Sylvis, William H., 12

Tarasov, M., 207, 211, 213, 222
Tayerle, Rudolf, 167, 184
Tessier, Gaston, 214, 327
Tewson, Vincent, Sir, 242, 262, 266, 273, 279, 295, 309
Thomas, Albert, 46, 130, 168
Thomas, Rolland, J., 207
Thorez, Maurice, 184, 185
Tillet, Benjamin, 20
Tobin, Daniel J., 58, 237
Tolain, Henri, 9
Toledano, Vincente Lombardo, 210, 211, 213, 217, 222, 276, 293, 317
Tomski, Michael, 71, 99, 102, 109

Trevino, Ricardo, 90
Tristan, Flora, 5
Trotsky, Leon, 46, 49, 109, 112, 113, 114
Truman, Harry S., 218, 243

Vaillant, Edouard, 23, 27
Vandervelde, Emile, 29, 46, 73
Vanistendael, A., 327
Vargas, Canuto, 91
Villa, Francisco, 88

Waldeck-Rousseau, René, 23
Walsh, Jack, 295
Watt, Robert Joseph, 193
Webb, Beatrice, 19
Webb, Sidney James, 19
Wilson, Woodrow, 28, 48, 51, 58, 61, 79, 89, 90, 93
Woll, Matthew, 80, 181, 183, 266, 278, 290

Yudenich, Nicolai, 66
Yvetot, Georges, 40

Zankov, Alexander, 76
Zapata, Emiliano, 88
Zetkin, Clara, 46
Zinoviev, Gregory, 49, 53, 76, 77, 101, 102, 109, 112, 113, 144

# Index of Subjects

Africa, labor missions to, 275, 276; trade unions in, 302, 303, 315
African Trade Union Conference, 232, 276
All-China Federation of Labor, 317
All-India Trades Union Congress, 280, 301
All-Union Council of Soviet Trade Unions, 77, 99, 106, 108, 182, 201. *See also* Soviet trade unions
Allied Control Commission of Germany, 218, 223, 224
Amalgamated Clothing Workers of America, 221
American Federation of Labor, and Second International, 21, 24, 25; and Labor Secretariats, 33, 36-41; and First World War, 56, 58, 60, 63, 77-82; and IFTU, 80-85, 93, 98, 115, 121, 168, 170, 172-174, 180, 181, 187, 188, 190, 191, 193, 197-199, 205, 218, 219; and Latin America, 85-94, 116, 117, 297, 299; and Trade Secretariats, 127, 256, 258, 262-268, 312; and Germany, 173, 174, 224, 236, 248, 249, 251; and Soviet trade unions, 183, 184, 235; and British TUC, 38, 201-206, 210, 212; and WFTU, 221, 224-226, 231-237; and Marshall Plan, 239, 242-248; and ICFTU, 262-268, 273-278, 285, 286, 304, 306-309
American Peace Society, 5
Amsterdam International, 63-69, 72, 74, 75, 77, 80-85, 94, 99-103, 105-109, 114, 116-122, 128-131, 137, 144, 148, 153, 161, 162. *See also* International Federation of Trade Unions
Anglo-American Trade Union Committee, 201
Anglo-Russian Advisory Committee, 100, 102, 106, 108, 114
Anglo-Soviet Trade Union Committee, 199-202, 204, 252
Annual Wage, 270. *See also* Wages
Anti-imperialism, 66, 101, 137, 139, 268, 298
Argentine Confederation of Labor (before 1939), 117, (Peronist), 265, 276, 298
Argentine Regional Workers' Federation, 87
Argentine Trade Union Committee (in exile), 290
Asia, labor missions to, 275, 278, 315
Asian Regional Organization, 275, 276, 299-302, 304
Asiatic Labor Conference, 171
Association of Latin American Workers (Atlas), 298
Atlantic Charter, 200, 229
Australian Trade Unions, 121, 339
Australian Labour Party, 28
Austrian Socialist Party, 38, 133, 173

Autonomy, national labor, 78, 80, 82, 120, 214, 271, 306, 337

Bakery and Confectionery Workers of America, 127
Belgian Federation of Christian Trade Unions, 159, 326
Belgian Federation of Trade Unions, 57, 121, 242, 262, 264, 305
Belgian Labor Party, 20, 51
Bern Conference of 1917, 50, 51
Bern International, 63, 64, 65, 66, 72, 75. *See also* Labor and Socialist International
Bern Trade Union Conference, 55, 56, 57
Black International, 21
Blanquists, 9, 19, 23
Bolsheviks, xiv, xv, 30, 49-53, 65-68, 134. *See also* Russian Communist Party.
Boot and Shoe Workers' Union of America, 127
Boycotts, international, 64, 125, 152, 161, 173, 180, 340
British coal miners strike, 103-107
British general strike, 104-106
British Communist Party, 139, 252, 254
British Labour Party, 24, 30, 49, 50, 65, 77, 103, 132, 197, 221
British Miners' Federation, 105
British Trades Union Congress, 33, 38, 57, 65, 81, 98, 100, 103-109, 170, 174, 179, 189, 191, 198, 200-207, 219, 222, 232, 241-244, 251-254, 258-264, 274, 278, 285, 304, 305, 309

Cairo Declaration, 209
Calcutta trade union college, 302
Canadian Catholic Confederation of Labor, 326
Canadian Congress of Labor, 295
Canadian Trades and Labor Congress, 295
Capitalism, general crisis of, 142, 143, 144
Cartels, international, xi, 150, 152, 218, 229, 268, 333
Casa del Obrero Mundial, 87-90
Catholic trade unions, *See* Christian trade unions.
Chartists, 4, 6, 7
Chinese Communist Party, 113
Chinese Revolution, 112, 113
Christian trade unions, 103, 129, 153-162, 203, 206, 212, 214, 215, 245, 247, 262, 264, 265, 281, 282, 326-331
CIO, *See* Congress of Industrial Organizations
Class struggle, xiv, 6, 23, 112, 119, 132, 133, 135, 142, 147, 149, 155, 156, 215, 319, 321, 337

Co-determination, 250, 278
"Cold War," viii, 238
Collective bargaining, xvii, 32, 33, 62, 69, 80, 93, 124, 125, 157, 158, 177, 178, 232, 250, 265, 270, 286, 293, 303, 315, 329
Colonialism, vii, xvi, 27, 66, 67, 100, 141, 143, 267, 268, 276, 278, 305
Combinations, international, 123, 124, 127, 315, 333. *See also* Cartels
Cominform (Communist Information Bureau), 238, 240, 252, 253, 260, 280, 281, 319, 322
Comintern, *see* Third International
Committee on Trade Union Freedom, 289, 291
Communist International, *see* Third International.
Communist Manifesto, 6, 53
Communist parties, *see* Third International
Communists, *see* Third International
Confederacion Regional Obrera Mexicana (CROM), 89-94, 116, 117
Congress of Industrial Organizations (CIO), 180, 181, 190, 201-207, 210, 213, 219, 220, 222, 239, 240-244, 251, 252, 254, 258, 260-268, 273, 274, 276, 278, 285, 286, 293, 297, 299, 304, 306-309, 317
Coordinating Committee of Trade Secretariats, 310, 311
Costa Rican Confederation of Labor, 297
Council of Europe, 292
Currency stabilization, 64, 119, 167, 179, 186

Dawes Plan, 97, 100, 101
Democracy, political, 50, 51, 62, 65, 119, 168, 169, 174, 189, 197, 200, 234, 267, 269, 270, 276, 278, 286, 293, 334; economic, 269, 286, 287. *See also* Industrial democracy.
Denazification, 223, 224, 229
Depression, industrial, 68, 82, 84, 168. *See also* Economic depression
Diamond Workers' Universal Alliance, 125, 311
Dictatorship, 51, 68, 166, 180, 231, 267, 270, 276, 278, 279, 298, 338
Dictatorship of the proletariat, 6, 49, 50, 52, 65, 84, 112, 134, 141, 142, 152
Direct Action, 25, 87, 152
Disarmament, 120, 121, 136, 168, 169, 192, 288
Disarmament Conference, 169, 170, 175, 190
Draft conventions of ILO, *see* International Labor Organization

Economic and Social Council of the United Nations, 209, 211, 218, 225-228, 230, 235, 271, 274, 279, 280, 289, 290, 291, 314, 324, 328, 339, 342
Economic Commission for Europe, 292
Economic Cooperation Administration (ECA), 244, 246, 259, 263
Economic councils, 119. *See also* Industrial Councils

Economic depression, 165, 167, 168
Economic development, xvii, xviii, 209, 290, 324, 337, 338, 339, 341
Economic planning, 168, 179, 186, 194, 202, 278, 279, 288, 296, 327
Education, free public, 22, 57, 93, 209, 270, 334
Eight-hour day, 12, 15, 21, 38, 57, 63, 131, 157, 166
Embargo, international, 64, 103-105, 119, 161, 188, 340
Emergency international trade union council, 199, 205
European Agricultural Products Community, *see* "Green Pool"
European Bureau of the AF of L, 236, 237
European Coal and Steel Community, xviii, 279, 292, 296, 314, 327, 329, 331, 338
European Recovery Program, 240, 242-244, 253, 259, 269, 328. *See also* Marshall Plan
European Regional Organization, 275, 295, 296, 297, 314, 331
ERP Trade Union Committee, 243-244, 263, 296
ERP Trade Union Conference, 242, 243, 244, 256

Fabian Society, 19, 65
Fair Deal, 286
Finance-capitalism, 135, 143
Fascism, 74, 102, 160, 165, 166, 168, 169, 170, 172-179, 182-184, 187, 189, 191, 192, 215, 218, 270, 282, 326
Fascist trade unions, 129, 286, 298, 338. *See also* Fascism.
First International, 7-15, 26, 53, 150
First World War, xiii, xiv, 22, 30, 36, 37, 41, 61, 88, 89, 143, 154, 194, 340
Five-Year Plan, 112, 171
Food and Agriculture Organization, viii, 271, 292, 339
Force Ouvrière, 246, 248, 256, 262, 303, 305, 306, 309, 329
Forced labor, 274, 287, 324
Forty-four hour week, 166, 167
Forty-Hour week, 167, 168, 177, 179, 180, 187, 209, 313
Fourteen points, 48, 51
Franco-British Trade Union Committee, 206
Franco-Soviet Trade Union Committee, 206, 217
Free German Trade Union Federation, 248, 249, 250
Free speech, 22, 86, 134, 208, 231
Free trade, 5, 10, 119, 160, 339
Free Trade Union Committee, 236
Free trade unions, 121, 159, 168, 173-175, 187, 205, 234-237, 242, 257, 262, 265-268, 275, 277, 286, 287, 309, 333-337, 340
Freedom, political, 93, 132, 135, 200, 265, 267, 278, 286, 287, 337

French Communist Party, 73, 74, 101, 177, 221, 245
French Confederation of Catholic Workers, 158, 206, 303, 326
French General Confederation of Labor (CGT), 25, 33, 40, 54, 57, 60, 176-178, 191, 198, 205-207, 212, 217, 219, 232, 241, 243, 245, 246, 261, 280, 303, 317, 319, 329
French Revolution, 3, 4, 20
French Socialist Party, 28, 47, 48, 49, 50, 66, 100, 177, 245
Full employment, 202, 215, 230, 268, 269, 274, 279, 288, 290, 324, 336, 339
Fund for Regional activities, 276, 304

General Assembly of United Nations, 225-227, 231, 291, 293
General strike, 25-27, 33, 40, 67, 75, 76, 87, 92, 103, 104, 135, 152, 173, 206, 245
Genoa Conference, 72, 73
German Communist Party, 70, 75, 76, 101. *See also* Third International
German Federation of Christian Workers, 158. *See also* Christian trade unions
German Federation of Labor, 98, 108, 121, 170, 172
German Federation of Trade Unions, 250, 274, 280, 307
"Green Pool," 296
Guedists, 20

Hind Mazdoor Sabha, 301
Hitler-Stalin Pact, 193, 194, 198
Hours of labor, *see* Eight-hour day, Forty-hour week.
Housing programs, 290, 296

Imperialism, 52, 141, 143, 144, 197, 208, 234, 241, 270
Independent Labour Party of Great Britain, 20, 24, 30, 46, 48, 66, 69, 102, 134, 197
Independent Socialist Party of Germany, 48, 66, 69, 74
Independent Socialists of France, 19, 23
Independent Trade Union Opposition in West Germany, 249, 250, 251, 256
Indian National Trades Union Congress, 301
Indonesian Federation of Trade Unions, 317
Industrial councils, 156, 157, 159, 194, 328
Industrial democracy, 79, 119, 123, 287, 328
Industrial Workers of the World, 24, 25, 40, 66, 71, 87, 91, 92, 149
Inflation, 61, 209, 239, 276, 279, 288
Inter-American Confederation of Workers (ICT), 297
Inter-American Regional Organization (ORIT), 276, 297-299, 304
International Association of Machinists, 94, 127, 236
International Bank for Reconstruction and Development, viii, 271, 339
International Cartel Office, 119
International Chamber of Commerce, 226

International commodity agreements, *see* Raw materials
International competition, 123, 124, 127
International Confederation of Christian Trade Unions, viii, xiii, 282, 285, 326-332
International Confederation of Free Trade Unions (ICFTU), vii, viii, x, xiii, 262-282, 285-309, 310, 311, 318, 325, 327, 328, 330-332, 338-341, 343, 344
International Conference on Trade and Employment, 230
International Cooperative Alliance, 226
International Federation of Boot and Shoe Operatives, 312
International Federation of Building Trades and Woodworkers, 122, 311
International Federation of Christian Trade Unions, 311
International Federation of Commercial, Clerical and Technical Employees, 311
International Federation of Free Teachers' Unions, 130, 138, 153-162
International Federations of Garment Workers, 312
International Federation of Metal Workers, 122, 311, 314, 315
International Federation of Textile Workers, 122, 311, 314
International Federation of Tobacco Workers, 311
International Federation of Trade Unions, 33, 34, 36, 40, 41, 53-60, 63, 64, 78, 98, 104, 106, 127, 165-176, 180-194, 197-199, 203-205, 207, 210, 212, 213, 217, 218, 221, 275, 277, 292, 304, 331, 340. *See also* Amsterdam International
International industrial committees, 291, 313, 314, 315, 316
International Labor Charter, 57, 58
International Labor Office, 64, 128, 130, 168. *See also* International Labor Organization
International Labor Organization, viii, xvii, 58, 63, 67, 78-81, 91, 115, 118, 126, 128-131, 152, 154, 161, 162, 165, 166, 168, 180, 199, 263-265, 271, 274, 275, 279, 289, 291, 292, 313, 314, 316, 324, 328, 331, 337, 339
International Ladies Garment Workers Union, 127, 180, 189
International Land Workers Federation, 311, 312, 315
International Left Communist Federation, 113
International Longshoremen's Association, 127
International Miners Federation, 31, 103-106, 122, 311, 313, 314
International Monetary Fund, viii
International Reconstruction Office, 72
International Secretariat of Christian Trade Unions, 19, 36, 37
International Secretariat of National Trade Union Centers, 19, 30-36, 39-41
International Socialist Bureau, 26, 28, 29, 45-48

International Solidarity Fund, 174, 187, 189
International Trade Secretariats, xiii, **xiv**, 19, 30-32, 36, 39, 41, 105, 114, 118, 122-128, 130, 138, 147, 148, 173, 179, 181, **183**, 187, 191, 199, 203, 205, 210, 212-214, 220, 230, 237, 239, 254-258, 260-264, 266, 271, 277, 285, 294, 310-317, 332, 338-341, 343, 344
International trade unionism, 35, 39, 123-126
International Transport Workers Federation, 103-105, 122, 123, 125, 126, 173, 214, 257, 258, 273, 310-312, 314
International Union of Workers in Food and Drink Trades, 125, 312, 315
International Workingmen's Association, *see* First International
International Working Men's Association (syndicalist), 74, 92, 94, 138, 149-153
International Working People's Association, 21
International Working Union of Socialist Parties, *see* Vienna Union
Israel, Labor Federation of, 264
Italian Communist Party, 221, 246, 247, 248, 319
Italian Confederation of Labor Unions (CISL), 308, 330
Italian Free General Confederation of Workers (LCGIL), 247, 248, 308
Italian General Confederation of Labor (CGIL), 243, 246-248, 256, 261, 280, 308, 317, 319
Italian Labor Federation (FIL), 248, 308
Italian Labor Union (UIL), 308
Italian Socialist Party, 28, 45, 46, 49, 50, 77, 133, 246, 247

Japanese Federation of Labor, 300
Japanese Council of Trade Unions, 285, 300, 301
Japanese trade unions, 232, 300, 301
Justicialism, 298. *See* Argentine Confederation of Labor

Labor and Socialist International, 75, 77, 84, 100, 102, 103, 105, 118, 132-138, 167, 169, 184, 185, 188-190, 192, 306. *See also* Second International
Labor Convention, *see* Versailles Peace Treaty
Labor legislation, international, 5, 15, 20, 21, 35, 56, 125, 126, 136, 161, 313
Labor Monroe Doctrine, 93, 94
Latin American Confederation of Labor, 203, 210, 261, 276, 297, 317, 323
League of Nations, xi, xvii, 51, 52, 59, 60, 64, 72, 75, 79, 81, 91, 97, 115, 119-121, 128, 131, 136-138, 143, 144, 152, 161, 165, 168, 169, 175, 185, 188, 190, 191
Leeds conference (of 1916), 55-57
"Left" socialists, *see* Socialists
Leninism, 99, 102. *See also* Third International
Locarno treaties, 97, 100
London Trades Council, 8, 9

London Workingmen's Association, 3, 4
Loyalists (of Spain), 183, 189, 190

"Majority" socialists, *see* Socialists
Marshall Plan, xv, xvii, 238-245, 247, 250, 253, 256-258, 262, 281, 314, 321, 328
Marxism-Leninism, 99, 141
Marxists, 20, 22-25. *See also* Socialists, Third International
Mensheviks, 133. *See also* Russian Social-Democratic Party
Mexican Confederation of Workers, 178
Middle East, labor mission to, 302
Migration, xiv, 27, 35, 36, 39, 41, 79, 86, 91, 92, 115-117, 119, 121, 124, 126, 128, 270, 278, 279, 288, 292, 338, 339
"Minority" socialists, *see* Socialists
Monnet Plan, 328.
Monopoly, 10, 119, 123, 143, 150
Mutualists, 11

National Labor Union, 12, 37, 38
National Minority Movement, 148
National Resistance Council, 206, 207
Nationalist movements, *see* Colonialism, Imperialism
Nationalization, 13, 50, 62, 66, 79, 82, 133-135, 141, 168, 178, 321, 327
NATO (North Atlantic Treaty Organization), xvii, 239, 292, 307, 321
Nazis, 172-175, 187, 197, 198, 204, 218, 223, 257, 282, 326
New Economic Policy (NEP), 70, 71, 74, 109-111
New Deal, 286
New Freedom, 28
New Zealand Federation of Labor, 266, 295
New Zealand Labour Party, 28
Non-governmental international organizations, 226, 227
North Atlantic Treaty Organization, *see* NATO
Norwegian Federation of Trade Unions, 178, 180, 184
Norwegian Labor Party, 135

Opposition groups, *see* Third International
Organization for European Economic Cooperation (OEEC), 239, 243, 244, 246, 259, 271, 292, 296
ORIT, *see* Inter-American Regional Organization

Paid annual vacations, 62, 167, 177, 313
Pan-African Trade Union conference, 232, 276
Pan-American Federation of Labor, 85-94, 115-117
Paris Commune (of 1871), 13, 14
Paris Peace Conference (of 1946), 229, 230
Parliament of the proletariat, *see* Second International
Peace, *see* World Peace
People's democracies, 280, 289, 317, 318, 321, 324

Peronists, 265, 276, 298
Plumb Plan, 79, 80, 82
Point-Four program, xvii, xviii, 294, 304
Polish insurrection, 8, 9
Polish trade unions, 103
Polish Independent Socialist Party, 133
Popular front, 177, 189
Post Office Clerks, National Federation of, 127
Postal, Telegraph and Telephone International, 312
Postwar reconstruction, 202, 203, 209, 219, 225, 229-231, 240, 269
Productivity, 291, 296, 313, 316, 340
Profintern, *see* Red International of Labor Unions
Public works, 167, 168, 186, 229, 290

Railroad Brotherhoods, 79, 80, 201-203
Rationalization, *see* scientific management
Raw materials, international control of, 64, 119, 136, 137, 179, 186, 278
Rearmament, 279, 288, 289, 296, 328
Red International of Labor Unions, 67, 70-72, 77, 83, 92, 94, 99, 101, 102, 106, 114, 117, 121, 138, 145, 147-149, 153, 171, 172, 176, 178, 234, 261, 319, 320
Refugees, 279, 291.
Regional organization, 275, 276, 294-304
Reparations, 61, 68, 72, 75, 97, 120, 121, 135, 229
Resistance movement, 206, 245, 327
Revisionists, 22-25
Right socialists, *see* socialists
Ruhr, the, 66, 75, 120, 230, 314
Russian Communist Party, 66-69, 72, 74, 99, 109, 111-113, 135, 146, 147, 171, 201, 318, 322. *See also* Third International
Russian Revolution, 48, 53, 143
Russian Social-Democratic Party, 133

Sanctions, 169, 183, 188, 189
Schuman Plan, *see* European Coal and Steel Community
Scientific management, 119, 313
Second International, 19-33, 38, 41, 45, 51, 53, 66, 69, 79, 87, 132. *See also* Labor and Socialist International
Second World War, xv, 165, 194, 229, 301
Security Council (of the United Nations), 209, 231, 232
Shop stewards committees, 66, 82
Social Democratic Federation of England, 19, 20
Social Democratic Party of Germany, 19, 22, 23, 28, 29, 48
Social insurance, 22, 55, 57, 58, 62, 208, 209, 215, 250, 270
Social-Reformists, xiv, xv, xvii, 15, 28, 33. *See also* Second International, International Confederation of Free Trade Unions
Social revolution, xiv, 20-23, 25, 52, 66, 87, 133, 319. *See also* Second International, Third International

Social security, *see* social insurance
Socialism, xiv, 3, 10, 15, 23, 26, 50, 57, 59, 64, 65, 87, 118, 132, 133, 141, 145, 155, 168, 286, 316. *See also* Socialists
Socialist International, *see* Labor and Socialist International, Bern International
Socialist Labor Party of America, 20, 24, 38
Socialist Party of the United States, 24, 28, 45, 49, 57, 79, 84
Socialist parties, xiv, 19, 21-23. *See also* socialists, Second International
Socialists, "Center", 45, 46, 52, 67, 69, 133-135; "Left", 45, 46, 47, 48, 50, 69, 77, 134-136; "Right", 45-50, 51, 52, 55, 65, 67, 74, 132, 133, 135
Socialist Trade and Labor Alliance, 24
Socialization, 14, 25, 60, 62, 64, 65, 81, 123, 132, 133, 250
Sodomei, *see* Japanese trade unions
Sohyo, *see* Japanese trade unions
Soviet trade unions, 72, 77, 98, 100, 107, 114, 148, 165, 172, 175-185, 192, 193, 200, 201, 204, 205, 207, 210, 219, 220, 261, 317, 318, 320-322
Spanish civil war, 189, 190
Spanish General Labor Union, 290
Spartacus Bund, 48
Specialized agencies, viii, xviii, 127, 228, 233, 292, 328, 339
State, theories of the, 14, 141, 142, 150-152, 156-158
Stockholm conference (of 1917), 47-49
Strike aid, international, xiv, 31-35, 41, 103, 119, 125
Sudanese Federation of Labor, vii.
Swedish Social-Democratic Party, 20, 48
Swedish trade unions, 153. *See also* Amsterdam International
Swiss Socialist Party, 20
Swiss Federation of Trade Unions, 55, 218, 265
Syndicalism, 25, 33, 87, 150-152, 155, 335
Syndicalists, 33, 36, 46, 48, 66, 71, 74, 87, 92, 117, 121, 148, 170, 221, 245

Tariffs, 64, 167, 186, 270, 339
Technical assistance, 270, 278, 290, 291, 294, 339
Technological unemployment, *see* Unemployment
Third International, 45-53, 63, 65-74, 76, 77, 79, 83, 98, 99, 101, 102, 106, 109, 112-114, 138-147, 149, 153, 171, 172, 176, 177, 184, 185, 192, 252, 319
Totalitarianism, 172, 234, 268, 270, 273, 278, 279, 287
Trade Secretariats, *see* international trade secretariats
Trade Departments, 213, 214, 216, 255, 261, 322, 323. *See also* World Federation of Trade Unions
Trade Union Educational League, 84, 85, 148
Trade union rights, 274, 287, 289, 313, 314, 324, 338

Trade unionism, relation to socialism, 24, 25, 34; types of, 24, 25, 32, 33. *See also* International trade unionism
Tunisian Federation of Labor, 290, 303
Two-and-a-half International, *see* Vienna Union

Underdeveloped countries, xii, xvi, xviii, 294-304, 306, 315, 330, 336, 338, 339
Unemployment, 63, 68, 75, 82, 100, 115, 130, 166-171, 239, 288, 340
Unitary Confederation of Labor (in France), 148, 177
United action, 72, 136, 166, 176, 177, 178, 183
United Brotherhood of Carpenters and Joiners, 127
United Brotherhood of Painters, 127
United front, 73, 74, 84, 98, 99, 101, 114, 148, 177, 322
United Mine Workers of America, 79, 83, 127, 203, 267, 274, 285, 297, 299, 309, 313
United Nations, viii, ix, xviii, 200, 208, 209, 211, 215, 218, 224-229, 231, 233, 235, 260, 270, 273, 279, 280, 287, 291, 292, 314, 316, 321, 328, 331, 337-339, 341, 342
United Nations Charter, 209, 218, 225, 271
United Nations Children's Emergency Fund, 291
United Nations Educational Scientific and Cultural Organization (UNESCO), viii, 291-294, 339
United States of Europe, 119
Unity, international labor, xiii, xiv, 60, 77, 97, 99, 106, 114, 148, 178, 179, 184, 200, 204, 219, 222, 322
Universal suffrage, 3, 4, 22, 65

Versailles Labor Charter, 58, 59
Versailles Peace Treaty, xvii, 58, 59, 61, 63, 79, 81, 91, 128
Vienna Union, 69, 70, 72, 75. *See also* Bern International
Vocational training, *see* International Labor Organization

Wages, 9, 24, 62, 69, 82, 103, 110, 123, 125, 157, 167, 291, 299, 313, 338, 340
War and peace, *see* World peace
War debts, 64, 72, 120, 167
Washington Conference on limitation of armaments, 83
Workers' control, *see* Industrial democracy
Workers' education, 115, 186, 215, 293, 294, 296, 303
Workers' Group, *see* International Labor Organization
World Federation of Trade Unions, vii, viii, xiii, 214-242, 251, 262, 264, 266, 273, 276, 277, 280, 281, 285, 297, 299, 310, 317-325, 327, 331, 332
World Health Organization, viii, 292, 339
World Free Labor Conference, 267
World Labor Conference, in London, 202-212, 240, 259; in Paris, 212-214, 240, 259
World Peace, xii, 27-30, 39, 119, 123, 169, 170, 190-194, 197, 201, 203, 206, 208, 211, 213, 215, 219, 225, 229-231, 234, 235, 269-271, 273, 278, 287, 328
World revolution, xiv, 65, 67, 111, 141, 144, 145. *See also* Third International
World Sugar Workers' Congress, 315

Yugoslav Federation of Labor, 308, 309

Zimmerwald Commission, 47, 49, 52, 54